Between two stools

Manchester University Press

Dear Greg

Between two stools

Scatology and its representations in English literature, Chaucer to Swift

At long last I squeezed it out!

Peter J. Smith

This for you with much love. All the best for independence (he he he ...)

Manchester University Press

Manchester and New York

Distributed in the United States exclusively
by Palgrave Macmillan

Published by Manchester University Press
Oxford Road, Manchester M13 9NR, UK
and Room 400, 175 Fifth Avenue, New York, NY 10010, USA
www.manchesteruniversitypress.co.uk

Distributed in the United States exclusively by
Palgrave Macmillan, 175 Fifth Avenue, New York,
NY 10010, USA

Distributed in Canada exclusively by
UBC Press, University of British Columbia, 2029 West Mall,
Vancouver, BC, Canada V6T 1Z2

British Library Cataloguing-in-Publication Data
A catalogue record for this book is available from the British Library

Library of Congress Cataloging-in-Publication Data applied for

ISBN   978 0 7190 8794 3 hardback

First published 2012

Typeset
by Action Publishing Technology Ltd, Gloucester
Printed in Great Britain
by TJ International Ltd, Padstow

For Nessie, 'Arel and Skipper

'Fundamentally, there's something religious about the fact that we're made of shit. We consist of the stuff.' (Gilbert and George, www.tate.org.uk/modern/exhibitions/gilbertandgeorge/rooms/room13.shtm)

'Having a crap is one of the most relaxing and intimate moments one has.' (Antony Gormley, *The Guardian*, 28 August 2010, p. 11)

'We are here on Earth to fart around. Don't let anybody tell you any different.' (Kurt Vonnegut, *A Man Without a Country* (Bloomsbury: London, 2006), p. 62)

'Interestingly, while human sweat is a more or less socially accept-able "dirty" substance, and even human urine apparently seems to have been historically more acceptable than it is today, human faeces are certainly not. We have a very low threshold of tolerance to turds – or even mention of them.' (Virginia Smith, 'Evacuation, Repair and Beautification: Dirt and the Body', in Rosie Cox *et al.*, *Dirt: The Filthy Reality of Everyday Life* (Profile Books: London, 2011), 7–36, p. 13)

'Farts are not all equal. Most are ho-hum, run-of-the-mill farts that are just a question of necessity. Some, however, are great and noble farts. They have resonance, volume, stink, they bring relief, express one's mood, extend the self outward; they are one's very soul expressed, squeezed, enfleured, captured, and displayed as an offering of the self, available just for a moment, then gone on the wind. In erupting from the body, the fart splits the body open, rendering it no longer single and hermetically sealed. Its orifice apert, the body has become double within itself; difference and otherness are within. This is the Fart Absolute, the distillate of distillate of one's being.' (Valerie Allen, *On Farting: Language and Laughter in the Middle Ages* (Palgrave: Houndmills, 2007), p. 102)

Contents

List of Illustrations

Preface

Fifteen or twenty members of a department of English Literature seated around a table justifying to the Head of Research – a particularly humourless Professor of Chemistry – their areas of academic expertise. The professor has little interest in the Humanities and barely conceals his boredom when one enthusiastic lecturer details her study of nineteenth-century female autobiography. Mention of the more canonical authors causes him to ask a desultory question or two but in general he is, like a parodic version of himself from a *Times Higher Education* sketch by Laurie Taylor, only really interested in the production of income, 'grant capture' or the commercial exploitation of research – a tall order given the department's unmitigated dedication to literary and thus non-income-generating subjects. The discussion rotates until it arrives at a member of the department who outlines his interest in the representation of flatulence and the historical shifts in the literary accounts of excrement. The professor turns a dark purple and, outraged, enquires how this is to be kept off the front pages of the newspapers: 'Tommy Taxpayer's Education Funding Flushed Down the Pan'; 'Scholars Talk Shite' or 'Crappy Academic in So-called Research Fiasco'. He is adamant: the university will be pilloried in the media and brought into disrepute. The inquisitee is non-plussed and crumbles, muttering something about the university having an external relations department or press officer to deal with precisely such crises. A more senior member of the department wades in to his rescue with the golden words 'academic freedom', and the discussion moves on around the table.

While such hostility typifies one response to the professional
study of scatology, the other more common reaction is bemuse-
ment. Introduced at conferences as 'the man who works on poo',
I have long been accustomed to entertaining other delegates with
obscure fart stories, some of which appear in the following pages.
In fact the intellectual justification of one's research, it seems to
me, comes only after the event, that is, once one's interest in a
topic is aroused and one has dedicated at least some thought and
time to the area. Any justification is thus bound to be post-hoc.

In his foreword to David Inglis's sociological account of defecatory manners, Mike Hepworth avers that 'a historical sociology of
excretion ... no longer requires a coy subtitle or indeed any
further academic justification'.[1] But isn't this protesting too
much? After all, Mary Douglas's *Purity and Danger* appeared in
1966 while Norbert Elias's *The Civilising Process* dates back to
1939. John G. Bourke's *Scatologic Rites of All Nations* (1891) is
well over a century old. However, the abiding irritation of the
Chemistry Professor and the laughter of the conference delegates
seem to suggest that scatology as an academic subject remains
novel enough to arouse responses, negative or positive, which
place it, if not outside, then at least at the margins of traditional
scholarly discussion. Whether this monograph will facilitate its
integration within the acceptable boundaries of academic
discourse remains to be seen. In one way, I hope it doesn't.

NOTE

1 David Inglis, *A Sociological History of Excretory Experience: Defecatory
  Manners and Toiletry Technologies* (Edwin Mellen Press: Lampeter, 2000),
  p. xv.

Acknowledgements

Frankly, like a costive misfit from a poem by Swift, I have laboured for a long time to void this excrementitious matter. The assistance and patience of those along the way has been both generous and astounding. The Arts and Humanities Research Council and Nottingham Trent University funded various periods of leave. Individuals who have read draft chapters, offered advice, specific references or just intellectual and moral support are legion. Among their number are Neil Allan, Valerie Allen, Diana Barnes, Alan Brissenden, Paddy Bullard, Gordon Campbell, Roger Craik, Kevin Crawford, Sarah Cummins, Michael Davies, Steve Earnshaw, Paul Edmondson, Steve Ellis, Russ Ganim, Bob Godfrey, John Goodridge, Beth Gregory, Michael Hattaway, Lynne Hapgood, Peter Holbrook, Peter Holland, Lisa Hopkins, John Jowett, Kate Loveman, Jean-Marie Maguin, David Matthews, Andrew McRae, Susan Signe Morrison, William Nelles, Harry Newman, Michelle O'Callaghan, Jeff Persels, Ken Phillips, Paul Prescott, Chris Ringrose, Valerie Rumbold, David Salter, Héloïse Sénéchal, Will Sharpe, Karen Shook, Priscilla Smith, Stan Smith, Mahendra Solanki, Fiona J. Stafford, James Stredder, Erin Sullivan, Jay Thomson, Susie Tombs, Janice Valls-Russell, Greg Walker, Marcus Walsh, Stanley Wells, Charles Whitworth and Greg Woods. Richard J. Larschan read more of the book in its various manifestations than he would care to remember. His expertise saved me from several clumsy errors. Any things of darkness that remain, I must acknowledge mine.

Matthew Frost at MUP has been nagging me for years to get him a manuscript and his good humour is almost enough to compensate for the paucity of his advance. Staff at the British Library, the Wellcome Collection and the Shakespeare Institute have been especially and continually helpful.

My three siblings have treated this project (and my entire professional career, come to that) with a healthy scepticism and I dedicate this volume to them with the most profound affection.

Introduction

My father has a theory about the link between mind and bowel being both crucial and very direct. It's another of his ideas which he keeps trying to interest people in; he has a manuscript on the subject ('The State of the Fart') which he also sends away to London to publishers now and again and which they of course send back by return.[1]

Thy worst. I fart at thee.[2]

I

Illustration 1 shows the surgery of Dr Panurgus. A young well-dressed aristocrat, in slashed doublet, earring, sword and spurs, lies on a low table, his head entering a furnace in order 'to purg the Gallants Braine.' Floating up from the chimney above him are a catalogue of contemporary iniquities, 'these ayrie Castles': tennis, drinking, smoking, bear-baiting, fencing, playing backgammon and cards (presumably for money), gambling at dice, hunting with dogs and so on. A bare-breasted courtesan and the comic and tragic masks represent the evils of the flesh and the theatre, while an acrobatic descent on a rope from the tower of (the pre-Fire) St Paul's symbolises the perils of treating religion as a plaything. The many objects indicate the level of the young rake's Epicurean indulgence.

Upstage of him stand a beautifully turned-out couple, the lady holding in one hand an elaborate fan of feathers. Her other hand holds a lead with a squirrel attached to the end of it. The word 'squirrel' was in this period (1620s) a cant term for a 'prostitute'

1 Martin Droeshout, *Doctor Panurgus* (1621).

or 'vagina' and the keeping of such pets taken to be a demonstration of vanity and decadence. In John Lyly's *Endymion*, Sir Tophas asks Epiton 'What is that the gentlewoman carrieth in a chain? EPITON: Why, it is a squirrel. TOPHAS: A squirrel? O gods, what things are made for money!'³ The contemptuous attitude suggests that the keeping of pet squirrels anticipates the contemporary penchant of female celebrities to carry toy dogs in handbags. The lady awaits her turn to enter the purging MRI-like oven: 'But now youre manly humors boile so highe / That you must in the Gallants Fornace lye.'

In the picture, the lady's partner stands in an arrogant pose, his cloak swathed around him and accoutred with ruff, hat and garter, the latest fashion accessories. The inscription next to him reads:

> Stay good Sir Briske, spruce master Cittyzsinne
> I haue a potion for your worth within
> A Dosis [dose] Sir where the Ingredients be
> Religion Truth plaine dealing Honestie
> It will expell proud Humors Sly deceits
> Knaues Peacocks foxes Jayes & couzening weights.

The spelling of 'Cittyzsinne' is a none-too-subtle dig at contemporary urban vices (city sin), while the name of the knight is glossed by *OED* as 'To smarten up, to dress finely, to trim', citing several contemporary instances.[4]

The engraving's top right-hand corner offers an explanation of the image as a whole:

> To this grave Doctor Millions doe resorte,
> Both from the Cvntry, Citty, & the Covrt,
> Whence thovgh they com as thick as raine can fall,
> Svch is his skill as he can Cvre them all,
> For by his waters, drvggs, Conserves and potions
> He pvrgeth fancies, follies, Idle motions.

Note that *OED* offers a definition of 'motion', citing Shakespeare's *Merry Wives of Windsor* (III.i.105): 'The involuntary action of the intestines, leading to discharge of their contents; an evacuation of the bowels. Also, chiefly in *plural* [as in this instance], that which is evacuated; the fæces.' The significance of this somatic term is to suggest that social and political purges are at least as reliant upon physical as mental therapies. When Macbeth discusses his ruined realm with the Doctor he insists on the connection between political and intestinal and urinary well-being: 'If thou couldst, doctor, cast / The water of my land, find her disease, / And purge it to a sound and pristine health' (V.iii.52–4). Three lines later he talks of voiding the English invaders as though Scotland were excreting them: 'What rhubarb, cyme, or what purgative drug / Would scour these English hence?' (57–8).

The picture offers further details of the doctor's clientele and insists on their social diversity:

> The wittles Peasant; Farmer Hoording corne
> The Gentry racking rents for Hound & Horne
> The Iustice bribd & the voluptuous knight
> That takes no pleasure but in vaine delight.

Further customers include 'The smooth tongu'd Shop man'; 'the luxurious roaring Rioter'; 'The two tongu'd Lawyer & base Flatterer'; 'The periurd Lover'; 'The lauish Gamester' as well as 'many frantick Feminines' who need to be purged of 'Steelettoes [the fine lady in the picture is wearing a dagger at her waist] girdles patches painted brests / Points powders feathers [note her fan] washes & the rest / When witching lust baits & damned plots of hell / The red hot furnace only must expell.' Satires of the period such as John Earle's *Microcosmography or A Piece of the World Discovered in Essays and Characters* (published only seven years after this engraving), pilloried contemporary vices in the manner of a list of social types, each prone to their peculiar stereotypical flaw. Earle too includes caustic accounts of a flatterer, an attorney, a shopkeeper and so on.

The engraving insists on the purgation of vice from country, court and city, across all social classes. But it also insists that purification is not merely mental or psychological. In fact, the most striking section of the picture demonstrates that purgation is ineluctably physical. Stage right is dominated by a character who could have stepped straight out of Ben Jonson's *The Alchemist*. Dressed in imposing robes, the doctor administers to the mouth of a 'rude Rusticall' a laxative made up of 'wisdoms force and understanding', a dose of such potency that the patient is already perched on a close stool, his hose round his knees and in the process of excreting a curious diversity of fecal matter: 'The Goose, foole, woodcock, Buzzard, Calfe, & Asse'. The quack's name, 'DOCT PANVRGVS', is engraved on the dresser upstage (on either side of his hat).

The print is complicated not least by the plenitude of annotation, thought bubbles, names of ingredients ('Continency', 'Discretion', 'Civility', 'Piety', 'Vertue' and so on) and what appears to be a satire on the burdensome debates of religious difference – hence the two clerics in the square frame downstage centre, each stooping under the weight of the churches they are supporting. But the naming of the doctor offers a clue as to how to read the image as a whole. *Dr Panurgus* is clearly inspired by Rabelais's *Gargantua and Pantagruel*, not 'Englished' by Sir Thomas Urquhart until 1653 but already well known enough to figure in *As You Like It* (see Chapters 2 and 4). By the 1620s (this engraving is usually dated to 1621), as Huntington Brown and Anne Lake Prescott have shown, Rabelais was well known in England and personified ideas of scatological comedy in the same way that Machiavelli was a watchword for political cunning.[5]

This comedic discourse was invigorated by another to do with bodily health. Essentially Galenic in origin, the Renaissance body was kept in order by the correct balance of the four humours. Phlebotomy and purging were the order of the day, designed to keep the bodily fluids in kilter. Laxatives, purges, clysters, enemas, carminatives and emetics were designed to cleanse the body of unwelcome influences. Similarly, bodily effluent could be taken to the wise woman or the doctor to aid diagnosis (as we have just seen in the case of Macbeth's request to his doctor regarding Scotland's political health). The pages that follow aim to demonstrate the medical, psychological and humoral significance of fecal matter. But, for now, the image of *Doctor Panurgus* is important to an explanation of this book's title.

Stage left, sandwiched between the curve of the brick furnace and the writing beneath, is the engraver's signature: 'MD *sculpsit.*' The monogram is the abbreviated form of 'Martin Droeshout: sculpsit. London.' which appears at the bottom of the most iconographic engraving in English, perhaps world, literature. That is, Martin Droeshout is the engraver of a defecating rustic, his hose pulled down and weird effluent pouring from his bowels, but Martin Droeshout is also the engraver of the head of Shakespeare that appears as the frontispiece of the First Folio (1623). The engraver of this bizarre scatological satire is the same as that of the most canonical image of our greatest dramatist (a fact that, as far as I am aware, has never been remarked upon before now).[6]

For my purposes, the fact that Droeshout is the engraver of

both images is enormously significant. When Heminges and Condell commissioned the engraving would they not have been worried that the portrait of their beloved and 'gentle' playwright might be tainted by the scatological comedy of the artist's fecal engraving which had appeared just two years earlier? Were they ignorant of the existence of *Doctor Panurgus*? Or might it be that the squeamishness we feel nowadays towards matters scatological is a relatively recent historical phenomenon?

In the course of the following chapters, I will contend that the 'two stools' of my title stand for two broadly distinctive attitudes towards scatological writing. The first is a carnivalesque, merry, even hearty disposition typified by the writings of Chaucer and Shakespeare. The second is self-disgust, an attitude characterised by a withering misanthropy and hypochondria. Will Stockton sums up this seismic shift in sensibility: 'feces loses its carniva-lesque association with renewal and rebirth throughout the sixteenth and seventeenth centuries'.[7] As evidence of this, Keith Thomas notes how conduct books of the earlier period included advice about passing wind but that this disappears following the Restoration: '[By the last quarter of the seventeenth century] the fart had begun its journey from the realm of the comic and embar-rassing to the new category of the sordid and unmentionable.'[8] The key figure in this transition, I argue, is John Wilmot, Earl of Rochester: Chapter 4 will detail the reasons for this, as it were, fundamental movement of attitude. Of course, I am not proposing that the 'merry poo versus miserable poo' model is adequate for the understanding of something as complex as a humour that derives from a sense of physical imperfection or decay. Rather I contend that this is a convenient, albeit oversimplified, dichotomy with which to begin to explore the variety of responses to scatology in the English literary tradition.

More central here is to acknowledge that, in the 1620s at least, the same artist could engrave the portrait of the man who has become the world's most influential playwright at almost the same time that he was engraving the image of a cerebral and graphically intestinal purge. In the work of Droeshout we find that combination of high and low culture that figures forth the capacity to run canonical and carnivalesque together. Sanctioned and civilised artefacts (the First Folio portrait) and scatological humour *co-exist in the oeuvre of the same artist*, evidence of the culture's aptitude (now lost) to occupy a position between two stools.

II

The chapters which follow are ordered, for the most part, chronologically: after all 'even physical processes have an historical dimension.'[9] While recent publications such as Jeff Persels and Russell Ganim's *Fecal Matters* (2004), Valerie Allen's *On Farting* (2007), Susan Signe Morrison's *Excrement in the Late Middle Ages* (2008), Sophie Gee's *Making Waste: Leftovers and the Eighteenth-Century Imagination* (2010) and Will Stockton's *Playing Dirty: Sexuality and Waste in Early Modern Comedy* (2011) constitute a contemporary critical project to describe the representation of scatology in literature, culture or the arts, they remain, to date, rare examples of a preparedness to discuss such material. Chapter 1 will consider the history of bowdlerisation of Chaucer's fabliaux and reflect upon the current state of scatological commentary. While such studies may appear to testify to the arrival of scatology as an academic subject, Chapter 1 will assert that it remains if not outside, then at least at the margins of conventional scholarship.

The first of two chapters on Shakespeare, Chapter 2, examines theatrical naming in the early modern period. It considers the importance of Plato's *Cratylus* alongside traditions of character naming from medieval morality plays and *commedia dell'arte* and notes the propensity of Shakespeare to give characters 'meaningful' names. The chapter proposes that, in the comedies, such names are often associated with forms of sexuality and, even more commonly, with aspects of anality and flatulence. It places this anality in the context of the social conditions of the early modern period and identifies a post-Victorian reluctance to dwell on such issues, given the canonical status of the Bard. The chapter demonstrates the key influence of the debate surrounding the publication of Sir John Harington's *A New Discourse of a Stale Subject, Called The Metamorphosis of Aiax* and the various replies it prompted. It argues that the text is a source for works by John Marston, Ben Jonson and Robert Burton, among others, and shows how *The Metamorphosis* significantly influenced *As You Like It* and *Hamlet*. The chapter concludes that, while unfortunately the passage of time now requires allegorical names to be decoded by scholars, we nevertheless ought to be aware of these names' early modern scatological connotations.

Chapter 3 offers an answer to the riddle set up by Malvolio's cryptic question – MOAI – 'What should that alphabetical position portend?' – which occurs in the box-tree scene (II.v) of *Twelfth Night*. The chapter surveys a number of solutions to this puzzle as proposed by critics, editors and actors from the eighteenth century to the present day. All are found, in their own ways, to be wanting. Some are exposed as literal-minded, too arcane, reliant upon language games that are unavailable to a theatre audience or flawed by chronology. The chapter builds on the semantic discussion of Chapter 2 and demonstrates that according to some rhetoricians of the day, language signifies inherently rather than conventionally. This linguistic veracity is shown to condemn Malvolio as he repeats a scatological acrostic (which he does not register) even while he utters it. Yet at the same time, and in spite of its apparent reliability, the subtle metamorphosis of language, and the slipperiness of its allegorical nature, ensure that critics and scholars, in their attempts to answer the riddle, have themselves been reduced to the level of the bewildered steward. The chapter concludes with a discussion of the work of the pacifist and Quaker Reginald Reynolds, who responds creatively to the scatology of the early modern period and offers a rare post-Victorian enthusiasm for it – while, at the same time, pioneering ecological modes of waste disposal and husbandry with which we have lately become urgently familiar.

Chapter 4 contrasts what it identifies as 'innocent scatology', characteristic of English literature of the mid-1650s (and earlier), with the caustic and malevolent obscenity in that composed following the Restoration. The chapter argues that, between the earlier and later periods, there occurs an irrevocable shift in sensibility due to the experience of defeat suffered by the Royalist faction. Using Sir Thomas Urquhart's 1653 translation of François Rabelais's *Gargantua and Pantagruel* and 'Upon a Journey to Epsom Well' by Sir John Mennes and James Smith, the chapter constructs a version of scatological obscenity along Bakhtinian lines, where it is understood as celebratory, amusing and parodic, but never threatening. As a counter to this, the chapter juxtaposes the writings of John Wilmot, Earl of Rochester, and notes their savage, misanthropic tone as well as the way these texts overlay anal and vaginal references so that sources of waste and fecundity are indiscriminately and disturbingly mingled together. Citing work on Rochester by Graham Greene, among others, and on Tudor and Stuart slang by Gordon Williams, the discussion seeks to demonstrate a relation between this darkening of tone and the demise of the political potency of the Royalist/Cavalier cause. The mordant poetry of the post-Restoration era signals the extinction of the kinds of jubilant scatology of earlier periods and looks forward, in its corrosiveness, to some of the writings of the eighteenth century.

Chapter 5 begins with a discussion of the Rochesterian inheritance on the work of Jonathan Swift in terms of human and equine rationalities. It then moves on to rehearse the strongly divided critical responses to Swift's use of scatological imagery, from the excoriation of Thackeray and Aldous Huxley, to the enthusiasm of Dickens and the exculpation of Norman O. Brown. The discussion proposes that the antipathy of the former group arises from mistaking Swift's various narrators (with their anality and mysophobia) for Swift himself. In fact, consideration of several of the scatological poems, as well as extracts from *Gulliver's Travels*, demonstrates that Swift is working in an anti-Petrarchan and anti-Platonic literary tradition. In 'The Lady's Dressing Room', for instance, the object of the satire is Strephon's precious sensitivities towards natural bodily functions. Celia's soiled laundry is the evidence of her humanity and her natural appetites, both sexual and dietary. In 'Cassinus and Peter', the focus shifts as the poem interrogates not the fastidiousness of an inexperienced lover but the well-established conventions of Petrarchan love and Renaissance modes of masculine homosociality. Such scatological moments do not merely dramatise profound masculine anxieties in relation to female bodily actuality. They also enact the powerful conflicts between the reality of physical functions and all idealising poetic traditions. According to this analysis, then, anality in Swift is not a form of contamination, but rather a mode of genuineness, sincerity and even of love.

Chapter 6 is again focused on the eighteenth century but considers other writers in the wake of the discussion of Swift in Chapter 5. Scatological texts by James Boswell, Tobias Smollett, Daniel Defoe, John Oldham and John Gay are contextualised against the real physical conditions of urbanisation, especially in the cases of London and Edinburgh. The capital is shown to occupy a paradoxical position: at once the seat of government, the court, banking and commerce and yet replete with poverty, sewage and disease. The mid-1660s provide a key moment in this narrative, one of plague and fire. In 1665 Marchamont Needham published his theory of miasma, and this aerial pollution is shown to underpin the pejorative attitudes of many of the above writers. The chapter goes on to compare Swift's 'A Description of a City Shower' with Jonson's excremental epic, 'Upon a Famous Voyage.' I argue that, while Jonson's epic is profoundly negative in its portrayal of disease and civic corruption, Swift offers his shower as a type of cleansing deluge. The river, flowing water, the stream – all symbolic of something coming into being – suggest new beginnings and the purging of decay. 'Upon a Famous Voyage', on the other hand, festers on the stagnant Fleet. The chapter develops this notion of the excremental landscape and the spirituality of a coprophilic paradise ('A Panegyric on the Dean, In the Person of a Lady in the North') which is now a paradise lost. The argument proceeds to examine the spirituality of defecation (with reference to Cloacina's altars) and to consider the episode of Gulliver shitting in the Temple. This analysis leads into a discussion of the religious sect, the Æolists, who belch and fart as their mode of preaching. Finally I discuss *The Benefit of Farting Explain'd* (1722) and compare it to *The London Spy* (1698–1700). The latter, which focuses on instances of social and political corruption, brings us back to those writers at the opening of this chapter. A clear contrast is accordingly made between the inventive and Rabelaisian anality of Swift, on the one hand, and the functional scatology of his contemporaries on the other – one more instance of the bifurcation in attitudes towards 'shiterature', encapsulated in the 'two stools' of this volume's title.

NOTES

1 Iain Banks, *The Wasp Factory* (Abacus: London, 1990), p. 67.
2 Ben Jonson, *The Alchemist*, edited by F. H. Mares (Methuen: London, 1971), I.i.1, p. 12.
3 John Lyly, *Endymion*, edited by David Bevington (Manchester University Press: Manchester, 1996), II.iii.147–50, p. 110. For 'squirrel' as a sexual term see Gordon Williams (ed.), *A Dictionary of Sexual Language and Imagery in Shakespearean and Stuart Literature*, 3 vols (Athlone: London, 1994), III, 1299.
4 The furious Hotspur, in the heat of battle, is brought a message by a perfumed courtier: 'he made me mad / To see him shine so brisk' (*I Henry IV*, I.iii.52–3).
5 Huntington Brown, *Rabelais in English Literature* (Harvard University Press: Cambridge, MA, 1933) and Anne Lake Prescott, *Imagining Rabelais in Renaissance England* (Yale University Press: New York and London, 1998).
6 Although there has been some difference of opinion as to whether Martin Droeshout senior or junior engraved the folio portrait, the fact that it comes only two years after *Doctor Panurgus* makes it likely that the same artist executed both. See J. L. Nevinson, 'Shakespeare's Dress in his Portraits', *Shakespeare Quarterly*, 18 (1967), 101–6; Mary Edmond, 'It was for Gentle Shakespeare Cut', *Shakespeare Quarterly*, 42 (1991), 339–44; Christiaan Schuckman, 'The Engraver of the First Folio Portrait of William Shakespeare', *Print Quarterly*, 8 (1991), 40–3; June Schlueter, 'Martin Droeshout *Redivivus*: Reassessing the Folio Engraving of Shakespeare', *Shakespeare Survey*, 60 (2007), 237–51. See also Tarnya Cooper (ed.), *Searching for Shakespeare* (National Portrait Gallery: London, 2006), p. 48.
7 Will Stockton, *Playing Dirty: Sexuality and Waste in Early Modern Culture* (University of Minnesota Press: Minneapolis and London, 2011), p. 90.
8 Keith Thomas, 'Bodily Control and Social Unease: The Fart in Seventeenth-Century England', in Angela McShane and Garthine Walker (eds), *The Extraordinary and the Everyday in Early Modern England: Essays in Celebration of the Work of Bernard Capp* (Palgrave: Houndmills, 2010), 9–30, pp. 21–2.
9 Thomas, 'Bodily Control', p. 9.

1

Turning the other cheek: scatology and its discontents in *The Miller's Tale* and *The Summoner's Tale*

I

And those especially who have a dislike to some particular kind of food, sometimes take it under compulsion, and then promptly bring it up; or, if they force themselves to keep it down, they are nauseated and feel their stomach turned up, and endeavouring to relieve itself of its discomfort.[1]

[T]he crucial element in the collapse of feudalism is peasant resistance to the seigneurial extraction of surplus profit from the agrarian economy. [Evident is the expression of] a powerful, self-confident peasant economy – a self-confidence visible throughout the latter medieval period and nowhere more dramatically than in the rising of 1381.[2]

[The fart may be read politically.] But then again, it may not. The safest position, as long as you are not in the direct line of fire, is to hear the noise for what it most materially and literally is: nothing more nor less than a very loud fart.[3]

These quotations typify the three (e)states of critical opinion on Chaucer's fart. The first: Galen (writing not of course specifically about Chaucer, nor even literature) offers a lively account of the retching response of an intolerant body. If forced to digest something inimical to it, the stomach will be queasy, eager to excrete that which induces revulsion – for 'body', we might also read social body, political ideology or religious system. In literary terms, read school or university syllabus, critical reputation or prevailing arbiter of wider cultural tastes (the sensory metaphor is, as we will see, unavoidable) such as the media, the church (see below) or other ideological state apparatuses. The ingested emetic thus stands for those works deemed by the body politic to be offensive and requiring to be purged one way or the other, most usually by the mechanisms of expurgation or censorship.

The second: for the Marxist literary historian, Lee Patterson, the ebullient low-life of Chaucer's literary world represents the rebellious agrarian peasantry whose revolutionary ardour precipitates the decline of feudalism. Scatology and obscenity function to destabilise the prevailing feudal norms and problematise class relations or, if that is too anachronistic, the hierarchy of seigneur and peasant.

The third: for Peter W. Travis, if we light the blue touch-paper, we should be prepared to retire very quickly. The fart may be 'an extremely complex political sign'; the splitting, in *The Summoner's Tale*, of Thomas's fart into twelve equal pieces *may* symbolise the redistribution of earthly pelf demanded by the increasingly vociferous peasantry (cf. Patterson); but equally, it may be . . . a fart.[4]

In summary then, the three positions are as follows: the depiction of medieval flatulence may be offensive – something to be expelled or, at any rate, eschewed; it may symbolise, in the manner of Bakhtinian carnival, a democratising impulse, a radical politic; or it may do nothing more than express the concrete materiality of a digesting body, the physical realities of eating and defecating. As Travis insists so eloquently, 'the fart is a fart is a fart'.[5]

Why such a fuss? It should be clear at the beginning of the twenty-first century that what Greg Walker calls the 'bowdlerisation of human experience' is something that no longer pertains.[6] Surely, while the second of these three positions may strike us as symbolically over-ingenious not to mention historically imprecise, and the third over-obvious, the squeamishness of the first position is no longer tenable – look what happened to Absolon! Yet the very paucity of scatologically explicit studies of Chaucer, the continued omission of a number of the fabliaux from modern editions, the frequent condemnation of the poet's scatological jokes are indicative of a sensibility which remains under the thumb of a censorial Victorianism, as a recent example will demonstrate.

In June 2006 *The Guardian* newspaper reported the difficulties faced by an adaptation of *The Canterbury Tales*.[7] That conspicuous envoy of cultural values, The Royal Shakespeare Company, had taken its dramatic version of Chaucer's poem on international tour. Unfortunately its spirited adaptation, by Mike Poulton, and its unabashed direction, by Greg Doran, Rebecca Gatward and Jonathan Munby, were to come face to face with the full disapproval of the Spanish Catholic Church.[8] In spite of the fact that the Dominican monastery of Almagro contained only two friars, the RSC's performance, scheduled to take place there, was forbidden. *The Washington Post*'s description of the production offers some sense of the emphasis it placed on scatological humour: 'It is nothing short of astonishing how much flatulence a major classical theatre company has to muster in the noble cause of bringing six hours of Chaucer to the stage.'[9] The production was thought to be 'inappropriate' to its holy environs and, as the RSC's Jeremy Adams explained, 'We were aware that the church had some concern about the content of the tales. Obviously we did not want to cause offence but, at the same time, we did not want to present a production that was overly compromised.' The farts must stand, that is, in the name of freedom of expression and artistic integrity. While this rumble of discontent was eventually assuaged by having the unedited production relocate to a theatre which, ironically, happened to be situated inside a former church, the recentness and intensity of its articulation make the controversy worth noting here. For it is not the case that the values of the Catholic authorities enact a stilted and repressive conservatism over which our progressive and permissive mores have triumphed, nor, contrariwise, that they embody an antiquated standard of decency from which our degenerative times have fallen off; indeed, if Chaucer's poetry is indicative of the acceptability of flatulent humour, the medieval period may have been a good deal less nervous about calling a fart a fart than we are at the present time. While the ways 'in which we excrete today are enswathed in feelings of secrecy, disgust, guilt and complex ploys of euphemism', this, argues David Inglis, is 'a relatively recent historical development'.[10] With the kind of delicious irony that Chaucer himself would have loved, the Catholic Church is acting here with a modern sensibility, for as Inglis carefully shows, and as *The Canterbury Tales* explicitly illustrates, 'The society of medieval Europe was generally more lax about defecatory matters than our own age.'[11] To employ Michel Foucault's damning verdict, it is we who are the 'Other Victorians'.[12]

The first significant censor of Chaucerian scatology was his translator John Dryden, for whom the poet was 'a rough diamond [who] must be polished, ere he shines'.[13] For all his enthusiastic approval of the variety of social classes and professions represented by Chaucer's pilgrims – 'Here is God's plenty!' – Dryden omitted *The Miller's Tale* and the *The Summoner's Tale*, among others: 'I have confined my choice to such tales of Chaucer as savour nothing of immodesty.'[14] As David Matthews has shown, this tendency for translators either to expurgate the fabliaux or bowdlerise them beyond recognition is firmly entrenched during the nineteenth and twentieth centuries.[15] He instances Mary Haweis's 1887 prose version of *The Miller's Tale* in which the misplaced kiss is so diluted that Absolon is met by a broom 'of no great purity, which he received on his face with considerable force'. The subsequent burning of Nicholas results in the rather vague loss of 'whole patches of skin'.[16]

Dorothy Wordsworth's exceptional approval of one of Chaucer's most flatulent stories may be inspired by seasonal goodwill. On Boxing Day 1801 she records, 'After tea we sate by the fire comfortably. I read aloud *The Miller's Tale*.'[17] This enthusiasm was clearly shared by her ostensibly sombre brother who recorded, in typically arch detail, his response to Chaucer: 'Beside the pleasant Mill of Trompington / I laughed with Chaucer, in the hawthorn shade / Heard him, while birds were warbling, tell his tales / Of amorous passion.'[18] (He is probably reading *The Reeve's Tale* which is set in Trumpington but perhaps the place name itself suggests to Wordsworth a pun on 'trumping' or 'trumpeting' and flatulence.[19])

But the critical reputation of Chaucer's fabliaux has fared consistently less well from the nineteenth century. In a metaphor which, like Galen's with which we began, calls to mind the very

bodily processes of digestion and evacuation which he is so eager
to euphemise, Charles Cowden Clarke, in 1833, condemns what
he considered to be the perverse obscenity of the fabliaux: 'as a
distaste for vice will assuredly keep pace with love of virtue, so a
well regulated and delicately instructed mind will no more crave
after and feed upon impure writings, than a healthy and natural
stomach will desire and select carrion or dirt'.[20] For Thomas R.
Lounsbury, writing in 1892, the fabliaux were, similarly, a source
of pollution, 'great stains upon the poet's writings'.[21] In 1906
Robert Kilburn Root averred that the scatology of The Miller's Tale
made it an anomaly amid an otherwise perfectly respectable
canon: 'It is certainly a pity that such excellent skill was expended
on a story which many of Chaucer's readers will prefer to skip.'[22]
In 1928 John Matthews Manley implicitly admonished Dorothy
Wordsworth for her unladylike audacity, pronouncing that The
Miller's Tale should remain in the boys' locker room: it is 'not fit to
be read in mixed company' and Mary Haweis's description of her
target audience is explicit in its exclusion of women: her translation is directed to 'grooms, valets, coachmen, and cabmen'.[23]

Alisoun's own thrilled laughter at Absolon's humiliation –
'"Tehee!" quod she, and clapte the wyndow to' (I, 3740) – might
be seen as a feminist rebuttal of this patriarchal disapproval.[24]
However, even in the year of Les Evénements, when the feminist
movement was finding its feet as part of a larger student rebellion
in continental Europe, Edward Wagenknecht also judged female
sensitivities too delicate to cope with Chaucer's scatological
fabliaux, censoriously berating the 'perversions that are now
spoken of openly in college classrooms and in mixed company'.[25]
The following year Haldeen Braddy sought to palliate our
outraged sensibilities by assuring us that 'this discreditable sort of
filth [which is] Chaucer at his worst, figures small in the total'.[26]
In 1971 James Winny, writing of the detail paid to Alisoun's
rough pubic hair, proposed that this is 'Another remark for which
Chaucer might well apologise.'[27] So by 1977, Peter G. Beidler can
reasonably assert that 'very few [commentators on Chaucer's
fabliaux] make any direct comment on the kiss and the fart. Most
scholars have not yet faced up [to them].'[28] For John Cook, writing
in 1986, the texts do not appear to deserve serious critical

treatment; they are little more than a giggle. He associates them with a genre of comic films renowned for their ribaldry rather than any claim to the status of cinematic art:

> Teachers of sixth-form students will know the 'problem' of teaching Chaucer if the 'A' level set text is the *Miller's Tale*. The story is about illicit sex, about farting and pissing, about an arse branded with a hot iron. The atmosphere seems closer to a *Carry On* film than to the high seriousness we expect of great literature.[29]

The *Carry On* films with their cheap *double entendres*, their rib-nudging knowingness, their winking, *risqué* reliance on a panoply of smutty jokes and heaving low-cut cleavages, belong to a species of late twentieth-century English comedies distinguished by a heavy dependence on camp (one thinks also of *The Benny Hill Show*, *Are You Being Served?* and, *primus inter pares*, *Up Pompeii*). They are part of a cultural moment and they have their place but, as Cook suggests, it would be absurd to attribute to them 'the high seriousness we expect of great literature'.

In an essay published as recently as 2006, Tiffany Beechy reiterates the critical quandary raised by Chaucer's scatology: 'The bawdiest of *The Canterbury Tales* have always been problematic for the critics.'[30] However, she then tantalisingly claims that 'the door to this aspect of Chaucerian satire has begun to open'. Her evidence for this includes the existence of Beidler's article (cited above) and the publication, in 2004, of *Fecal Matters in Early Modern Literature and Art: Studies in Scatology*. In their introduction to this collection of essays, the volume's editors, Jeff Persels and Russell Ganim, identify what they call 'the last taboo':

> This collection of essays was provoked by what its editors considered to be a curious lacuna: the relative academic neglect of the copious and ubiquitous scatological rhetoric of Early Modern Europe, here broadly defined as the representation of the process and product of elimination of the body's waste products (feces, urine, flatus, phlegm, vomitus). [Scatology] still retains the power to make us blush, to provoke shame and embarrassment. Discussion of excrement is generally relegated to one of two extremes: the objective, clinical discourse of medical and social sciences (e.g., gastroenterology, psychology, anthropology) or the subjective, gross indecency of infantile insult or juvenile jest (e.g., *South Park*).[31]

Between Two Stools is itself part of the same project identified by Beechy in the work of Persels and Ganim; indeed it is no accident that Chapter 4 of the present book started life as an essay in *Fecal Matters*. More recently still, Valerie Allen bravely extends 'the business of butthole-scholarship' in her assertion of a parallel between a period that exists as 'the age median between classicism and Renaissance', that is, the middle ages, and the fart 'which does not exist *qua* fart until it passes the anal threshold'.[32] For Allen the fart's gossamer delicacy, its ethereal dimension, casts it as anything but oafish: 'the medieval fart shape-shifts continuously between smell and sound, air and vapour, always on the move between earthly elements, bodily senses, people, and buttocks'.[33]

In spite of Susan Signe Morrison's pioneering 'fecopoetics' – an approach that aims to rematerialise the body which, she argues, has become theoretically rarefied by feminist and especially psychoanalytic criticism – she concedes as recently as 2008 that 'the recent critical debate about the history of the body has tended to avoid the topic of excrement'.[34] 'The stench of material flesh,' she continues forcefully, 'can be hidden by theoretical musings.' In too many historical and literary accounts of the middle ages, corporeal experience is deodorised and its representation euphemised. Morrison's approach is thus hands-on or, more precisely, pants-down. She seeks to rub our noses in the midden of medieval poetry, philosophy and theology. Like 'ecopoetics', the term from which it is mischievously derived, 'fecopoetics' is a morally or at least politically engaged criticism. Rather than flush away what modernity condemns as disgusting of the middle ages, we need to acknowledge, affirm even, our relationship with the past:

> Excrement is not a sign of otherness, but a sign of similarity between periods; the medieval is connected to us in the twenty-first century. The 'civilizing process' is just that – a process – never a finished state. Part of our civilizing process is to recognize the value of that which we deem uncivilized and to see ourselves in that threatening, filthy alterity.[35]

While these publications constitute a contemporary movement, as it were, to describe the representation of scatology in literature, culture or the arts, they remain, to date, rare examples of a preparedness to discuss such material. Although *The Miller's Tale* has received some, albeit reluctant or limited, critical attention (principally, as we will see, by virtue of its status as an 'answer' of sorts to *The Knight's Tale*), *The Summoner's Tale* seems to elicit even more stately condemnation. In correspondence with Thomas R. Lounsbury (28 April 1892), the future president of the United States, Theodore Roosevelt, picked out the tales of the Summoner and the Friar as being, 'on the score of cleanliness ... very nearly indefensible ... as literature I don't think they have a redeeming feature'.[36] A week later (3 May 1892) in a letter to Cecil Arthur Spring Rice, who was to become British Ambassador to the United States, Roosevelt pulled no punches: 'I think [Chaucer] is altogether needlessly filthy – such a tale as the "Sompnour's" for instance is unpardonable, and indeed unreadable.'[37] In 1923 J. S. Kennard judged it to contain 'the humour of stable boys and swineherds' and H. D. Sedgwick, eleven years later, seconded its suitability as a story for agricultural labourers, summarising it as 'another of those stable-boy stories'.[38] Marchette Chute is rather more blunt, describing *The Summoner's Tale* as 'worthless'.[39] Beechy is unequivocal about the ostrich-tendencies of scholars faced with the violent obscenity of *The Summoner's Tale*: '[the tale's] fierce scatology has not, to my knowledge, been approached in close study'.[40] Even when it is, as in an essay by Penn R. Szittya (which seems to have gone unnoticed by Beechy), it is characterised as an exercise in bathetic triviality rather than anything serious or important. Just as Cook treats Chaucer's scatology with all the seriousness one would accord to the *Carry On* series, so Szittya concludes his essay by musing that the significance of the *Tale* is in its leading literary scholars on a flatulent goose-chase:

> Scholarly work on the *Summoner's Tale* is somewhat disconcerting, for the busy researcher often suspects that at his back he hears the Summoner, roaring with laughter as the *magistri* of a later age set about studiously analyzing the unwholesome vapors he left above the cartwheel for a bemused posterity.[41]

Thus, as recently as 2006 (and as Cook maintains), 'Confronted with this kind of language, modern criticism often looks the other way.'[42]

II

And to him that striketh thee on the one cheek, offer also the other.
(Luke 6: 29)[43]

Looking the other way, turning, as it were, the other cheek, is an action that appears three times in *The Miller's Tale*. As 'hende Nicholas' (l. 3199) attempts to grab Alisoun, she jumps beyond his grasp 'And with her heed she wryed faste awey' (l. 3283). Later, John the carpenter is described as snoring because 'his head myslay' (l. 3647) and following the misplaced kiss, Absolon laments that he was not quicker at turning his head away, 'allas, I ne hadde ybleynt!' (l. 3753). It is as though the motif indicates the squeamishness (an important word in the *Tale*), with which characters within the story, and critics beyond it, as we have seen, respond to the scatology it contains.

This weird symbiosis of figures within and without the fiction is something of which students of Chaucer's work have long been aware. He exists, after all, both as the author of *The Canterbury Tales* and as a character within it. In this instance, Chaucer the pilgrim is able to blame the Miller for his drunken obscenity whilst the Miller blames his drunkenness for his obscenity – 'Wyte it the ale of Southwerk, I you preye' (l. 3140). While Chaucer the pilgrim is begging his reader to 'Turne over the leef and chese another tale' (l. 3177), Chaucer the poet is keen to place *The Miller's Tale* in a position of prominence – so keen in fact that he overrules the Host, who would have the Monk follow the Knight in the order of their recitations (l. 3118). Of course, this kaleidoscopic shifting of authorship and authority, the elision and evasion of points of narrative stability, are essential to Chaucer's art but also, as the motifs of the turning heads and turning pages symbolise, constitute an attempt to exculpate the poet from the reader's disapproval: 'Blameth nat me' (l. 3181), Chaucer the pilgrim but *also* Chaucer the poet insists. As Cook puts it,

'Narrative authority is in constant circulation and this undermines the bids for power made by particular stories or by
particular narrators.'[44] While the full force of Nicholas's fart is
going to knock Absolon and the squeamish reader sideways, there
is the sense that the poet is able to hide behind firstly his persona
as the reporter of *The Miller's Tale*; secondly, the fictional character
of Robyn; and, thirdly, the beer of Southwark. In addition, the
furious reaction of the Reeve (himself a carpenter and so not
about to welcome a tale in which a member of his trade is so
viciously savaged), offers further corroboration that this tale will
be little more than 'lewed dronken harlotrye' (l. 3145). In his final
nervous retraction, Chaucer the poet admits that several of 'the
tales of Caunterbury ... sownen into synne' (l. 1085). There is
something belt-and-braces about the insistence with which
Chaucer side-steps any accusation of poetic impropriety. Surely
this guilty conscience is, in part, responsible for the timidity of
modern critical discourse which we have witnessed.

   Chaucer the pilgrim's insistent and embarrassed apology for
the scurrility of Robyn's story allows Chaucer the poet to place it
immediately after *The Knight's Tale*. As has long been recognised,
the story of the two Oxford clerks competing for the sexual favours
of fair Alisoun is a parodic retelling of the story of the two
Athenian warriors competing for the love of fair Emelye. In spite
of the generic distance between the two tales, Karma Lochrie
suggests that the women in each are similarly configured as
objects of male attention: 'It is true that Alison is more vividly
delineated a character than is Emelye, but she is every bit as much
an abstraction produced by male desire for the twin purposes of
sexual and poetic exchange as Emelye.'[45] In its shift from the
distant, romantic landscape of the mythical ancient world to the
urban setting of contemporary Oxford, the values of courtly
romance are brought cheek by jowl with those of the fabliau. The
Miller's response to the Knight, much to the abashment of
Chaucer the pilgrim, represents a carnivalesque turning upside
down of the ideological hierarchy of the three estates, scatologically inverting medieval social orthodoxy.

   Given that the reward for the best tale is itself a Bakhtinian
repast – 'a soper at oure aller cost' (l. 799) – the carnivalesque

mode is especially appropriate. Indeed, Cook identifies unwelcome
flatulence at the dinner table as being, as it were, the quintessence
of the *Tale*'s narrator: 'The Miller ruffles feathers, causes embarrassment, like a fart at a polite dinner-party. After the elaborate,
idealised and violent fore-play [*sic*] of the Knight's Tale we are
rapidly brought into a carnal world where desire is to be gratified
rather than restrained [not quite true, Absolon's desire for Alisoun
is never gratified].'[46] Robyn is quite explicit that his story will
engage that of the Knight and 'quit' it: 'I kan a noble tale for the
nones, / With which I wol now quite the Knyghtes tale' (ll.
3126–7). Lest we accuse the capernoited Robyn in this aim of
being an aggressive braggart, we should note that the idea has
already been placed in his head by the proposal for a storytelling
contest and, moreover, that this has recently been reiterated by
Harry Bailly, who has just asked the Monk to tell a story 'Somwhat
to quite with the Knyghtes tale' (l. 3119). This tit-for-tat rivalry
will be considerably simplified when we get to the Friar and the
Summoner in the third fragment of *The Canterbury Tales*. When
the Friar shows that all summoners are corrupt and self-interested, the Summoner responds with the disarmingly obscene
retort that all friars are so wicked, the only suitable dwelling place
to be found for them is Satan's anus (III, 1690–1). As Allen
explains: 'At the worse possible place in the universe, Satan's
butthole, reason is inverted, strained to snapping point, turned
inside out and upside down.'[47] But the conversation between the
stories of Knight and Miller is a good deal more sophisticated than
the adversarial dispute between Friar and Summoner. Indeed it is
the similarities between the tales which bring their uneasy friction
to the point of combustion.

Following Palamon's martial and therefore, as he hopes,
marital, triumph over Arcite, the latter, in spite of the administering of emetics and carminatives begins to fade fast: 'Hym gayneth
neither, for to gete his lif, / Vomyt upward, ne dounward laxatif' (I,
2755–6). As he takes his leave of Emelye, Arcite laments the
solitary condition of the grave which awaits him: 'now in his colde
grave / Allone, withouten any compaignye' (ll. 2778–9). This
isolated condition, a forlorn eternity of separation from the love
object, is a desolate prospect – one that will crop up, in later works,

SCATOLOGY AND ITS DISCONTENTS

in Juliet's terrified anticipation of the Capulet tomb, Claudio's horrified vision of rotting after death, John of Gaunt's dying words and Andrew Marvell's account of his mistress's decaying virginity – a vivid formulation of the medieval *contemptus mundi* motif.[48] It is thus with conspicuous and mischievous relish that the Miller picks up the line at the outset of his tale. As he introduces his first rival lover, 'hende Nicholas', he notes that his lodgings, within the house of John the carpenter, are a place of privacy (a key word to which we shall return) and meditation: 'A chambre hadde he in that hostelrye / Allone, withouten any compaignye' (ll. 3203–4). Nicholas's chamber, the place in which he will hatch his scheme to copulate with the Miller's wife, the place to which he retires in fraudulently abject contemplation of the flood to come, thus functions as a parody of the isolated grave of the courtly lover who has forfeited his life in chivalric quest for his lady. Given that the domestic setting, rather than the open graveyard, will function as the place from whence a mighty thunderclap fart will issue (l. 3806), we might think of romance isolation as being interred while that of the fabliau is more likely to be in turd.

As well as Robyn's plagiarising the particular line describing the unaccompanied darkness of Arcite's tomb, there are other even more flagrant examples of sardonic intertextuality. Arcite's love melancholy impels him to be 'solitarie . . . and ever allone' (l. 1365), just as Nicholas will later prompt John's officious enquiry by taking to his bedroom in solitary confinement (l. 3420). Nicholas, says Alisoun, suffers 'a maladye' (l. 3416), just as Arcite is genuinely afflicted with 'the loveris maladye' (l. 1373). The seriousness of this term is reinforced when the word reappears to describe the injury sustained by Arcite who has fallen from horseback: the spectators suggest that he should pull through: 'Men seyde eek that Arcite shal nat dye; / He shal be heeled of his maladye' (ll. 2705–6), but, as the rhyme hints, Arcite will not make it. Through the offices of the misdirected kiss, however, Absolon does make a full recovery: 'he was heeled of his maladie' (l. 3757). It is as though the terms and poetics of courtly love are being impersonated and evacuated of high seriousness by their association with the quotidian coarseness of the Miller's mucky story.

Elsewhere the verbal echoes are even more resonant. As she kneels in prayer in the temple of Diana, imploring the goddess to preserve her chastity, Emelye is struck by an unprecedented sight:

> The fires brenne upon the auter cleere,
> Whil Emelye was thus in hir preyere.
> But sodeynly she saugh a sighte *queynte*,
> For right anon oon of the fyres *queynte*
> And quyked agayn, and after that anon
> That oother fyr was *queynt* and al agon;
> And as it *queynte* it made a whistelynge,
> As doon thise wete brondes in hir brennynge,
> And at the brondes ende out ran anon
> As it were blody dropes many oon.
>
> (ll. 2331–40, my emphases)

The insistent repetition here of *queynte*, meaning variously 'contrived' or 'curious' as well as 'quenched' or 'extinguished', accents the word. Indeed its use at the end of two consecutive lines (ll. 2333–4) provides a clunking rhyme which points up the term and its disparate meanings. Robyn uses exactly this word and exactly this device when he describes Nicholas's frantic clutching of Alisoun. Nicholas, having waited for the carpenter to be away on business, approaches Alisoun and makes his intentions perfectly clear in a way that only the most canny of students are able: 'As clerkes ben ful subtile and ful queynte; / And priviley he caughte hire by the queynte' (ll. 3275–6). Here, there is a brilliant mismatch between his apparent guileful sophistication and the crudity of the term for that organ by which he grabs her. While the flickering flames and mysterious drops of hymenal blood signify the loss of Emelye's virginity in the heavily symbolic courtly language of *The Knight's Tale*, *The Miller's Tale* takes exactly the same terms, uses identical poetic devices and describes, in obscene detail, the groping of Alisoun's vagina.[49]

But Robyn is not done with the term, for just as his tale is an attempt to 'quite the Knyghtes tale' (l. 3127), as we have seen, so the misplaced kiss has the effect of quitting and quenching the love-sickness from which Absolon has been suffering: 'His hoote love was coold and al yqueynt; / For fro that tyme that he hadde kist hir ers, / Of paramours he sette nat a kers' (ll. 3754–6). The cure which the misplaced kiss supplies Absolon is graphically physical as is the 'maladye' from which he suffers since he is, in modern parlance, not so much love-struck as cunt-struck. This, as we have seen, is a parody of the romanticised idealism with which Palamon and Arcite regard Emyele. The quitting thus occurs at two levels, both within the story – Absolon is quit of his romanticised fantasies – and at the level of the framing device of the pilgrims, since the Miller is able to appropriate the Knight's vocabulary and poetic techniques and overturn them. This is an essential device of Chaucerian comic writing, argues David Aers: 'The comedy often works by invoking courtly language and then foregrounding the physical areas of human experience that its high idiom seeks to sublimate.'[50]

This quitting can be read in two ways. For Lee Patterson, as we have seen at the outset, the Miller is triumphant and his refutation of the values inscribed in *The Knight's Tale* represents a politically subversive conquest: 'Compared to the moral anarchy over which the Knight has (however unwittingly) presided, the *Miller's Tale* seems to articulate a world of perfect moral sense.'[51] For David Williams, however, *The Miller's Tale* is a diseased counterpart of the Knight's heroic story: 'With the purpose of requiting the Knight, whose tale ends in a reassertion of an ordered and orthodox cosmos, the Miller presents a sickly and inverted world in which a number of aberrations are countenanced by its inhabitants as normalcy.'[52] The critical embarrassment, documented at the beginning of this chapter, may be responsible for Williams's patrician tone, but whether we agree with him or with Patterson, the concept of one tale being in conversation with the other is fundamental to an understanding of both. They mirror each other, as mutually defining as the two halves of a diptych.

A further instance will illustrate this conversation between the tales in specifically scatological terms. As befits the noble Theseus, 'That gretter was ther noon under the sonne' (l. 863), his closing homily is an extended and eloquent defence of the apparent randomness of Providence. He gives a Boethian account of the hidden purposes of 'The Firste Moevere of the cause above' (l. 2987), which urges patient endurance rather than too much

enquiring or struggling: 'And heer-agayns no creature on lyve, /
Of no degree, availleth for to stryve' (ll. 3039–40). The kind of
passivity personified by patient Griselda in *The Clerk's Tale* is what
is required. Moreover this uncuriousness is not merely theological
or philosophical, it is also axiomatic in medical terms. In John
Arderne's contemporary tract on the treatment of anal fistulae
and haemorrhoids, it is vitally important not to enquire into the
motivations of the Creator: 'ffor god, that is deler or rewarder of
wisdom, hath hid many thingis fro wise men and sli₃e whiche he
vouchesaf aftirward for to shewe to symple men.'⁵³

In *The Miller's Tale* John the carpenter gives his own version of
this 'ignorance-is-bliss' theology: 'Men sholde nat knowe of
Goddes pryvetee' (l. 3454). Even before he begins his tale, Robyn
himself appears to espouse this pacific philosophy. He tells the
Reeve that 'An housbonde shal nat been inquisityf / Of Goddes
pryvetee, nor of his wyf' (ll. 3163–4). Although the lines sound
similar, there are two crucial differences. Firstly, 'Men' has become
'housbonde' and, secondly, the 'pryvetee' is shared by God (whose
ways are proverbially mysterious) and the wife whose deceit
enables her to cuckold her husband: 'Who hath no wyf, he is no
cokewold' (l. 3152). The re-framing of the theological debate in
domestic terms transforms the Boethian claims of *The Knight's Tale*
about the enigmatic workings of the *Primum Mobile* into the
household wrangles, in *The Miller's Tale*, of wife and over-curious
husband. As *The Merchant's Tale* so brilliantly demonstrates, the
wife will always be able to exculpate herself from a damning
situation. Blessed by Proserpine, May readily convinces her
husband that, even though he sees her copulating in a tree, she is
in fact acting for his own benefit (to restore his eyesight); as
Proserpine puts it, 'alle wommen [even though] they be in any gilt
ytake, / With face boold they shulle hemself excuse' (IV, 2267–9).
The specifically sexual sense of 'pryvetee' in Robyn's advice to the
Reeve is brought sharply into focus: '"Pryvetee" has two chief
meanings in Middle English, "private affairs" and "private
parts".'⁵⁴ Thus what sounds like a self-effacing maxim on the
importance of passivity before God in fact turns out to be little
more than a smutty joke about allowing the wife to distribute her
own genitals as she sees fit: 'The *Miller's Tale* thus blasphemously

– and deliciously – elevates Alison's private parts and their unknowability to the level of God's.'[55] But, as Thomas J. Farrell points out, this is not a *double entendre* but a multiple *entendre*: 'The nouns "pryvete" or "privates" could be used in reference to the anus, the vagina, the uterus, and the penis (in either its sexual or excretory function), either singly or in various combinations; Chaucer exploits that range of meaning fully.'[56] Citing *The Pardoner's Tale*, Farrell insists that Chaucer 'also uses the common homonym "pryvee," meaning "privy" (*CT*, VI.527)'. *The Miller's Tale* is built upon a quibble between these various senses of 'pryvee'. Nicholas will warn John of the imminence of the flood 'in pryvetee' (l. 3493) though he is unable to discourse more widely on the motivations of God: 'I wol nat tellen Goddes pryvetee' (l. 3558). John is not allowed to alert his servants but only Alisoun, 'And to his wyf he tolde his pryvetee' (l. 3603), and preparations are made to suspend themselves from the rafters 'in pryvetee' (l. 3623). Prompted by John's absence and his feckless desire for John's wife, Absolon intends surreptitiously to visit his home and 'Ful pryvely knokken at his wyndowe' (l. 3676). The frequent use of the term to mean 'secretly' or 'cunningly' demonstrates the multiple deceptions upon which the plot of the fabliau is based, but there are also uses which rely on the further punning senses as outlined by Farrell. As we have already seen, 'hende Nicholas' catches Alisoun between the legs 'prively' (l. 3276), so that the vaginal connotations of the term are evoked. Little suspecting that his rectum will become a ring of fire, Nicholas opens the window 'And out his ers he putteth pryvely' (l. 3802). Not only does the word suggest the secrecy with which Nicholas prepares to humiliate Absolon, but it also implicitly suggests the 'privy' orifice, the anus itself, with which the 'squaymous' (l. 3337) parish clerk is to be greeted. The anal connotations of the term are those aroused by its use in *The Summoner's Tale* (see below). As Thomas encourages the Friar to explore his rectal cavity in order to find his hidden treasure, he instructs him to 'grope wel bihynde. / Bynethe my buttok there shaltow fynde / A thyng that I have hyd in pryvetee' (III, 2141–3) where the final word is both an adverb meaning 'secretly' and a noun meaning 'anus'.

The multivalent term 'pryvetee' works like a refrain throughout *The Miller's Tale* to suggest the enigma firstly of God's purpose and secondly, and sacrilegiously, of Alisoun's 'hole' (l. 3732). Absolon, it turns out, worships both, 'Sensynge the wyves of the parisshe faste' (l. 3341) – that is, in his capacity as thurifer, he censers them but uses their proximity to inspect them at closer quarters, sensing them, and selecting the most attractive to whom he pays particular attention: 'And many a lovely look on hem he caste, / And namely on this carpenteris wyf' (ll. 3341–2). This voyeurism is thus calculated and premeditated, while its execution, under the pretence of conducting an ecclesiastical responsibility, is intensely hypocritical. Indeed in likening Absolon to a cat laying in wait for a mouse (ll. 3346–7), his desire for her is seen to be not only studied, but predatory. This contrasts with the fickleness of female desire likened, as we have seen, to the riddle of the ways of the Creator. The similarity between the mysteries of God's providential purpose and Alisoun's pudendum is outrageously fitting. Absolon's confusion is worth citing in full:

> This Absolon gan wype his mouth ful drie.
> Derk was the nyght as pich, or as the cole,
> And at the wyndow out she putte hir hole,
> And Absolon, him fil no bet ne wers,
> But with his mouth he kiste hir naked ers
> Ful savourly, er he were war of this.
> Abak he stirte, and thought it was amys,
> For wel he wiste a womman hath no beard.
> He felte a thyng al rough and long yherd,
> And seyde, 'Fy! Allas! What have I do?'
> 'Tehee!' quod she, and clapte the wyndow to.
>
> (ll. 3730–40)

Absolon's bewilderment – 'Fy! Allas! What have I do?' – is shared by a number of the tale's commentators. Louise M. Bishop opines: 'the greatest confusion in the *Miller's Tale* does not just come from flesh, it comes more specifically from holes'.[57] Wolfgang E. H. Rudat suggests that 'the word *ers* refers to the female pudendum, and Absolom [*sic*] has performed an involuntary act of (almost-) cunnilingus'.[58] H. Marshall Leicester agrees, albeit in somewhat blunter terms: 'It does not in fact sound like he has kissed an ass, but a cunt.'[59] On the other hand, Chaucer uses the word 'ers' twice of Nicholas specifically to mean 'anus' (ll. 3802 and 3810), and Hanks wittily associates the 'privy' kiss with the foul air of the fart: 'As it happens [Absolon] gains a kiss that savors more of the privy than he had bargained for.'[60] As Walker sums up, 'there remains considerable scholarly disagreement about exactly where and upon what Absolon plants his lips'.[61] For Morrison, this confusion is deliberate and explained in relation to the association of autonomous female sexuality and excrement: 'Women carry the burden of sexual filth.'[62]

This confusion, of a piece with the mystery of the female 'pryvetee', as we have seen, remains unresolvable, for while it is clear that Nicholas, during Absolon's second visit puts 'out his ers ... / Over the buttok, to the haunche-bon' (ll. 3802–3), the Miller describes Alisoun's mysterious aperture as an unspecified 'hole' (l. 3732). Following her clapping to of the window, we hear how Absolon, almost Howard Hughes-like, attempts to clean his mouth: he 'froteth now his lippes / With dust, with sond, with straw, with clooth, with chippes' (ll. 3747–8). Reminiscent of Gargantua's catalogue of abstergents, this fetishistic wiping transforms Absolon's mouth into an anus.[63] Of course, if it is Alisoun's vagina he has kissed 'Ful savourly' (l. 3735), his obsessive rubbing of his lips is unsurprising given that she has been until recently engaged 'In bisynesse of myrthe' (l. 3654) with Nicholas. In this case, Rudat's 'act of (almost-) cunnilingus' becomes rather an act of fully fledged felching.

The confused sexuality of the misplaced kiss and the uncertainty over the destination of Absolon's lips are intensified by a homosexual subtext which occurs during his second visit.[64] Instead of Alisoun offering her 'hole', Nicholas intends to turn the other cheek and to proffer his own arse to the eager lover outside the window. Of course, Nicholas has no idea that Absolon is armed with a flaming coulter but, were his plan to run smoothly, Absolon would place his mouth against another man's anus.[65] This prospective homosexual reading is given credence by a couplet which juxtaposes the phallic and the oral so blatantly as to suggest fellatio: Absolon promises various gifts to Alisoun 'if thou me kisse' (l. 3797). The following line describes how 'This Nicholas was risen for to pisse' (l. 3798) so that the labial 'kisse' and penile 'pisse' are run together. (Earlier Absolon himself rhymed 'mysse' and 'kisse' (ll. 3679–80) in an ironic adumbration of the misplaced kiss.) In the light of this prospective homosexual anilingus, the actual burning with the hot coulter is highly suggestive of the *lex talionis* assassination of King Edward II which took place fewer than sixty years before the composition of *The Canterbury Tales*. Dolores Warwick Frese, noting the parallel, goes as far as to suggest that, 'The rather fearful symmetry of fact and fiction here invites us to revise that commonplace criticism that suggests that the poetry of Chaucer is peculiarly free of specific historical referents.'[66]

In Christopher Marlowe's dramatic version of the story (first performed around 1592), the executioner is called, ominously, Lightborne (which is the literal translation of Lucifer). In *The Miller's Tale*, the outraged and humiliated Absolon offers his 'soule . . . unto Sathanas' (l. 3750). This darker side of Absolon's return visit is underlined by Raymond P. Tripp, who points out that, 'Few students of the tale, caught up in the rough and ready comedy of its conclusion, have paid sufficient attention to the ugliness of Absolon's intentions. The hot coulter, for all its appropriate sexual symbolism, is a murderous weapon.'[67] Tracey Jordan is also insistent on the petulance and brutality of the attack, especially in gender terms: 'When Absolon's romantic ideal of love is applied to a real woman and turns out to be something physical and degrading, he is ready to retaliate against her with the greatest cruelty.'[68] While these sombre reminders correctly alert us to the viciousness of Absolon's intentions, Tripp is also right that 'the rough and ready comedy' of the tale distracts us. For it is at this point that Chaucer offers us perhaps the most famous and distinctive fart in the whole of English literature:

> And out [of the window] his ers he putteth pryvely
> Over the buttok, to the haunche-bon;
> And therewith spak this clerk, this Absolon,
> 'Spek, sweete bryd, I noot nat were thou art.'
> This Nicholas anon leet fle a fart
> As greet as it had been a thonder-dent,
> That with the strook he was almoost yblent.

(ll. 3802–8)

The passage is dense with ingenious poetic echoes. We have already seen the ambiguity of the term 'pryvely' which suggests both the devious nature of the practical joke and anticipates its toiletry content (as in 'privy'). The mention of the buttock also prepares us for what is to follow, while the detail of the 'haunchebon' reminds us that Nicholas is naked and that earlier, in his seduction of Alisoun, he 'heeld hir harde by the haunchebones' (l. 3279).[69] Absolon is then said to speak and, brilliantly, his invocation to Alisoun (as he thinks) is to 'Spek'. There is thus a conversation set up between the dapper wooer and the poised anus. The delicacy of Absolon's description of his lover as a 'sweete bryd' is immediately and outrageously trounced by the power of the flatulent thunderclap. The word 'bryd' translates as 'bride' or 'sweetheart' as when, earlier, Absolon calls, 'sweete Alisoun, / My faire bryd' (ll. 3698–9), but it also translates as 'bird' and so ironically accords with the phrasal verb, 'to let fly', which suggests both the quivering emancipation of the fledgling and, at the other extreme, the emphatic boldness of the clamorous fart. Only at this point does that tantalising detail in the earlier description of Absolon suddenly make sense: despite his debonair and jaunty disposition, Absolon 'was somdeel squaymous / Of fartyng' (ll. 3337–8). This apparently offhand remark, hardly worth noting, has been planted with devious and premeditated wiliness, only to be, here, quite literally detonated.

In fact, throughout the tale we have had instances of the ways in which Absolon's sensual prissiness makes him a fastidious figure. We hear of his burning of incense in the church, his employment of 'greyn and lycorys, / To smellen sweete' (ll. 3690–1) before visiting his love. He is musical and 'syngeth in his voys gentil and smal' (l. 3360) – perfectly suited to the kind of delicate aubade he intends to perform for Alisoun (l. 3698). He combs his soft, blonde hair (ll. 3314, 3374, 3691). He anticipates the delicious taste of Alisoun, comparing her to 'sweete cynamome' (l. 3699) and, in a peculiarly sexually inappropriate image, himself to the lamb desirous 'after the tete' (l. 3704). Absolon is careful to prepare his complexion and his wardrobe (ll. 3316–24). His shoes are the height of fashion (l. 3318). Smell, hearing, touch, taste and sight are all carefully documented. The misplaced

kiss has already offended his sense of touch – 'He felte a thyng al
rough and long yherd' (l. 3738) – while contact with Alisoun's
unkempt pubic hair contrasts with his own fetishistically well
groomed 'joly shode [handsome parting]' (l. 3316). His sense of
taste is outraged by the kiss and we have seen him rubbing his lips.
Nicholas's fart not only offends Absolon's hearing and sense of
smell, but the final detail specifies that it almost strikes him blind.
Maybe this is merely poetic licence, a way of exaggerating the
intensity of Nicholas's flatulence, but perhaps it is also an indication of the flames produced, as every schoolboy knows, by the
contact of such a volume of flammable gas with the burning
coulter. In meteorological terms, this is the flash of lightning
which accompanies the 'thonder-dent' (l. 3807) and the sudden
and wholly unexpected blaze, remembering that 'Derk was the
nyght as pich, or as the cole' (l. 3731), would be enough
temporarily to deprive Absolon of his sight.[70]
    The sheer force of Nicholas's fart is not unrelated, in classical
medicine, to the strength of his sexual libido. Indeed the two are
directly proportional to each other. According to Constantinus
Africanus' De Coitu which was certainly known to Chaucer, there
is a direct correspondence between sexual appetite and flatulence:

> When a man has a tremor, it comes from the evil effects of super-
> fluity. When he has a bad smell, it comes from the putrid mixture
> which is dissolved by the warmth of intercourse. When his belly is
> distended, this happens because his natural warmth is weak (a
> sickness of this kind is caused by the melancholy humor); such
> men desire intercourse all the time, because of the great windiness
> it generates.[71]

Constantinus is insistent on the correlation between foodstuffs
that produce both wind and seed. Indeed both seem symptomatic
of a nourishing diet: 'things which nourish and generate
windiness or are assimilated into its essence produce semen ...
Foods only generate semen if they are very nourishing. We say
also that semen consists of humor and spirit; it is made from the
moisture of food, which must be one that generates semen, i.e.,
very nutritious and wind-producing, since these qualities
harmonize with the essence of semen.'[72] In the light of this reci-

procity, the vigour of Nicholas's fart, as powerful as a clap of thunder, is testament to his commanding virility. It is this virility which makes him attractive in Alisoun's eye. Indeed, it is at this point that we should note the synonymous relationship between the anus and the organ of sight itself. In summary, the Miller reminds us how the carpenter's wife has been 'swyved ... And Absolon hath kist hir nether ye' (ll. 3850–2). Not only does this recall the virtually blinding intensity of Nicholas's fart, but it links the swyving with the sense of sight. With the kind of sophistication we expect of the tale, we are reminded that Alisoun was earlier described as possessing 'a likerous ye' (l. 3244). She it is who embodies and drives forward the fabliau itself. In the words of Bakhtin, 'The popular tradition is in no way hostile to woman and does not approach her negatively ... Womanhood is shown in contrast to the limitations of her partner (husband, lover, or suitor [in *The Miller's Tale*, all three]); she is a foil to his avarice, jealousy, stupidity, hypocrisy, bigotry, sterile senility, false heroism, and abstract idealism.'[73]

It has long been noted of *The Miller's Tale* that everyone is punished – everyone, that is, except Alisoun. It is Alisoun's flirtatiousness, her 'likerous ye', which has provoked Nicholas to swyve her, which has caught the attention of Absolon in church and brought the two rivals together. While the Miller treats her as an object of a male gaze – 'There nys no man so wys that koude thenche / So gay a popelote or swich a wenche' (ll. 3252–4) – it is Alisoun's eyes, both upper and lower, that precipitate the story and lead so ineluctably to its, and her, climax.

III

And he shall send his angels with a trumpet, and a great voice: and they shall gather his elect from the four winds, from the farthest parts of the heavens to the utmost bounds of them ... And as in the days of Noe, so shall also the coming of the Son of man be. For as in the days that were before the flood, they were eating and drinking, marrying and giving in marriage, even till that day in which Noe entered into the ark ... But know this ye, that if the goodman of the house knew at what hour the thief would come, he would certainly watch, and would not suffer his house to be broken open. (Matthew 24: 31–43)

The prophecy of the apocalyptic Second Coming runs as a subtextual current throughout *The Miller's Tale*. While one story-line dwells on the swyving of Alisoun, the misplaced kiss and the burning of Nicholas's arse, the parallel plot deals with the foolish carpenter who has been instructed to suspend, for each of them, 'knedyng tubbes thre' (l. 3564) or else 'a kymelyn' (l. 3548) that is, a large tub for brewing beer, from the eaves of the house and wait for the rising waters of a second Noah's flood.[74] When the water reaches the correct level, the three will cut their cords and float to safety. While John snores in his trough, Nicholas and Alisoun quietly descend to indulge sexually in 'the revel and the melodye' (l. 3652). It is testament to the prowess of Robyn's story-telling, that the reader almost forgets about the sleeping carpenter until the climax of the tale.[75] At the moment that Nicholas receives the hot iron, his agonised screaming awakens the carpenter who assumes the deluge has arrived:

> Of gooth the skyn an hande-brede aboute,
> The hoote kultour brende so his toute,
> And for the smert he wende for to dye.
> As he were wood, for wo he gan to crye,
> 'Help! Water! Water! Help, for Goddes herte!'
> This carpenter out of his slomber starte,
> And herde oon crien 'water!' as he were wood,
> And thoughte, 'Allas, now comth Nowelis flood!'
> He sit hym up withouten wordes mo,
> And with his ax he smoot the corde atwo,
> And doun gooth al; he foond neither to selle,
> Ne breed ne ale, til he cam to the celle
> Upon the floor, and ther aswowne he lay.
>
> (ll. 3811–23)

Nicholas's cry for water to cool his burning arse from which the Miller, with loving detail, has informed us that a whole span of skin has been seared, is misinterpreted by John who, cutting his cord, falls onto the floor below, breaking his arm (l. 3829).[76]

The passage cited above from Matthew resonates in accord with this comic episode within the tale. The appetites, both dietary and sexual, lack moderation. In particular, Alisoun is described in terms of a dish to be consumed. Her apron is 'as whit as morne milk' (l. 3236), her eyebrows are black as sloes (l. 3246), she is as pretty as a pear tree (l. 3248), her mouth is sweet as mead or a new fallen apple (ll. 3261–2). Absolon longs to taste her and waits for her like a cat for a mouse (l. 3346). He is unable to eat any more than is a young girl: 'I may nat ete na moore than a mayde' (l. 3707) though, of course, the line can also be translated to mean that his appetite is solely dedicated to the consumption of a girl (which figuratively occurs during the misplaced kiss). Lechery and greed are at their height and, as in the case of Sodom and Gomorrah, will bring down the wrath of God. Biblical echoes abound: the flood is a repeat of that found in Genesis, also mentioned in the extract from Matthew, and Noah's name resonates throughout *The Miller's Tale* (ll. 3518, 3534, 3539, 3560, 3582, 3616, 3818, 3834). Noah, in his capacity as a ship-wright, prefigures John the carpenter while the vociferous Mrs Noah, mentioned as being troublesome by Nicholas (l. 3540), anticipates the marital tensions between John and Alisoun.[77] In addition, Joseph's trouble about Mary links the jealous old carpenter, father of Jesus, to Robyn's artisan who 'demed hymself been lik a cokewold' (l. 3226). In *The Pageant of the Shearmen and Taylors*, Josoff similarly remarks, 'All olde men, insampull takc by me, – / How I am be-gylid here may you see! – / To wed soo yong a chyld.'[78] The carpenter of *The Miller's Tale*, that is, has typological equivalents in both Old and New Testament. The Annunciation is also blasphemously parodied in Nicholas's choice of song: '*Angelus ad virginem*' (l. 3216) while his 'a-nyghtes melodie' (l. 3214) comically anticipates the euphemistic 'revel and the melodye' (l. 3652) of his and Alisoun's sexual symphony.

The biblical passages are also pointedly blustery: Matthew 24: 31 talks of 'a trumpet, and a great voice: and [the angels] shall gather together his elect from the four winds' while Genesis 8: 1 describes the ebbing of the flood waters: 'and [God] brought a wind upon the earth, and the waters were abated', so that Nicholas's stormy flatulence is of a piece with this scriptural context. Even the carefully noted detail of the window is biblically motivated; Robyn mentions it with obsessive frequency (ll. 3695, 3708, 3727, 3732, 3740, 3789, 3801). Genesis is specific about the portal from which the height of the flood waters is monitored by sending out birds: 'And after that forty days were passed, Noe, opening the window of the ark which he had made, sent forth a raven' (8: 6). The passage from Matthew also suggests the importance of observation in anticipation of the arrival of the Son who will come like a thief in the night. On the return visit of Absolon, Alisoun hears him knock on the window and asks, 'Who is ther / That knokketh so? I warrante it a theef' (l. 3790–1). To ensure the biblical echo is not lost on us, the response underlines the divine presence, 'Why nay … God woot, my sweete leef, / I am thyn Absolon' (ll. 3792–3, my emphasis).

Other biblical references intensify the bathetic comedy of *The Miller's Tale*: Absolon has played Herod on the platform of the medieval stage (l. 3384), while his name derives from the treacherous son of King David whose beauty is legendary and whose hair is so lustrous that it weighs 'two hundred sicles, according to the common weight' (II Kings 14: 25–6).[79] The weapon he uses is the shoe of a plough which inverts Isaiah's prophecy of demilitarisation: during 'the last days' the Lord shall 'rebuke many people: and they shall turn their swords into ploughshares' (2: 1–4). The function of this detailed biblical reference is, on one level, to reinforce the ignorance of John, whom the Miller has already described as a 'gnof' (l. 3188). Probably the most significant thing about Noah's flood is that, following the decline of the waters, God promises never to repeat the scourge: 'and there shall no more be waters of a flood to destroy all flesh' (Genesis 9: 15). In the Chester pageant of *Noah's Flood* much is made of the serene symbolism of the rainbow: 'My bowe betwene you and mee / in the fyrmamente shalbe, / by verey tokeninge that you may see / that such vengeance shall cease. / That man ne woman shall never more / be wasted by water as hath before.'[80] Reference is also made to Noah's flood in the *Second Shepherds' Play* in such a way as to underline the severity of the storm and its unusual character: 'Was neuer syn Noe floode / Sich floodys seyn, / Wyndys and ranys so rude, / And stormes so keyn / Som stamerd, som stod / In dowte, as I weyn.'[81] In one sense then, it is obvious to everyone except John that the inundation which Nicholas so fearfully anticipates is a ruse. Public humiliation is part of the poetic justice of this tale: 'The folk gan laughen at his fantasye' (l. 3840); 'And every wight gan laughen at this stryf' (l. 3849). Clearly the authority of the scriptures, and John's ignorance of them, intensifies not only his position as a churl, but this very public laughter.

While the weight of biblical reference is profoundly ironic given the scatological content of the tale, it also undermines John's protestations about the importance of knowing the Creed. He tells Nicholas that 'blessed be alwey a lewed man / That noght but oonly his bileve kan!' (ll. 3455–6). The line also suggests that they are blessed who rely on faith without supporting evidence and so echoes the words of Christ who pronounces that 'blessed are they that have not seen, and have believed' (John 20: 29). The approval of those who rely only on their faith comes about as a response to Thomas who doubted the word of the disciples who claimed to have met the resurrected Christ: 'Except I shall see in his hands the print of the nails, and put my finger into the place of the nails, and put my hand into his side, I will not believe' (John 20: 25). In order to underline the allusion, the Miller has John swear twice by 'Seint Thomas' (ll. 3425 and 3461), who is likely to be the disciple rather than the saint Thomas Becket (whose shrine, boasting a pair of lice-ridden underpants, is the destination of Chaucer's pilgrims), described earlier as 'Seint Thomas of Kent' (l. 3291).[82] The insertion of the finger into a bodily cavity looks forwards neatly to the digital penetration of an old man, in *The Summoner's Tale*, who is called, with considered mischief, Thomas.[83]

IV

[B]ut if one strike thee on thy right cheek, turn to him also the other. (Matthew 5: 39)

The evangelists' insistence on turning the other cheek is, as we have seen, parodied by the buttock turning of *The Miller's Tale*. In *The Summoner's Tale*, Friar John gropes Thomas's anus in an attempt to accrue the invalid's deathbed bequest. Instead of acquiring the fabulous wealth he anticipates, he is rewarded with a fart. But rather than turn the other cheek, arguably the manoeuvre just performed by the fart's donor, Thom-*arse*, John is outraged and determined to be revenged: 'But I on oother wyse may be wreke [avenged], / I shal disclaundre [slander] hym over al ther I speke' (III, 2211–12). The reaction of the lady of the manor is to let the matter drop: 'Is ther oght elles? Telle me feithfully ... I seye a cherl hath doon a cherles dede. / What shold I seye? God lat hym nevere thee!' (ll. 2203–7). Her suggestion, that this is a deed not worthy of a reaction, is an affront to the indignant Friar; this, she says, is nothing more than a boorish action performed by a boor. Note how the Friar's reply implicitly seems to proffer the sense of passive rejoinder: 'But I on oother wyse ...' negates the pacific reaction of turning the other cheek even as it intimates it as a possible response. Christian humility, suffering in the face of personal affront, is something of which the corrupt and self-interested Friar John is not capable. The inability of several of the clerics in *The Canterbury Tales* to act in accordance with Christ's submissive teachings is found both within the fictional characters of the particular stories as well as within the group of pilgrims themselves. Just as the Miller answers the Knight, so the Summoner's story is a direct response to the calumny of summoners contained in *The Friar's Tale*. But whereas the 'quitting' of the Knight was accompanied, as we have seen, by linguistic allusion and the sophisticated inversion of the language of courtly love, the Friar and the Summoner attempt bluntly to outdo one another in scurrility and obscenity. In the case of *The Summoner's Tale*, this depravity is reliant upon one of the finest scatological jokes in medieval literature.

Just as in *The Miller's Tale*, the fart, in 'the bum-centred comedy' of *The Summoner's Tale*, is a long time coming.[84] There is a good deal of anecdotal gestation, of narrative rumbling, before its spectacular release. But also, just as with *The Miller's Tale*, the letting-fly is preceded by careful, relevant but almost nonchalant particularity. Robyn, we noted above, slipped in the detail of Absolon's squeamishness towards farting which was brought sharply into focus with Nicholas's flatulent insult. In the case of the Friar, the outrage of the fart is intensified by the Summoner describing the verbose sanctimony of John who discourses on various subjects so that, by the time the fart comes, its gusty discharge seems entirely appropriate repayment for his smug long-windedness (ll. 2011–12). Moreover, in his attentions to the physicality of Thomas's wife and his own greed, John is behaving with stereotypical anticlerical self-interest. On greeting the woman, he clasps her a little too tightly for propriety's sake: 'The frere ariseth up full curteisly, / And hire embraceth in his armes *narwe*' (ll. 1802–3, my emphasis). We are reminded of the way in which John the carpenter confined Alisoun: 'Jalous he was, and heeld hire *narwe* in cage' (I, 3224, my emphasis). While the friar's phallic excitement is hinted at in the action 'ariseth up', an indication of the inappropriateness of John's lewd behaviour is provided by Arderne's advice against fondling the female relatives of patients under treatment. Medical etiquette dictates that the examining doctor observe some decorum – if only to avoid the jealous wrath of powerful men:

> Considere he no 3t ou*er* openly the lady or the dou 3ters or oþer fair
> wy*m*men in gret me*n*nes [houses] ne pro*f*re tham no 3t to kisse, ne
> touche not pr*i*uely ne ap*er*tely thair pappes, ne thair handes, ne
> thair share [that is, their pubic region], that he renne no 3t into the
> indignacion of the lord ne of noon of his.[85]

That this is the advice of a secular professional makcs Friar John's ecclesiastical harassment all the more flagrant.

But worse is to come: he 'kiste hire sweete, and chirketh as a sparwe / With his lyppes' (ll. 1804–5). Not only is John's tweeting at Thomas's wife oddly inappropriate for a supposedly holy man, but the fact that he chirps like a sparrow is significant. The sparrow is associated, right down to the time of Shakespeare and beyond, with sexual indulgence. Describing the passionless and inhibited Angelo to the disguised Duke, Lucio remarks that, 'Sparrows must not build in his house-eves, because they are lecherous.'[86] Indeed since classical times, the sparrow could be consumed as an avian Viagra:

> Another medicine which is taken before intercourse because it is
> amazingly stimulating: take the brains of thirty male sparrows and
> steep them for a very long time in a glass pot; take an equal amount

of the grease surrounding the kidneys of a freshly-killed billy-goat, dissolve it on the fire, add the brains and as much honey as needed, mix it in the dish and cook until it becomes hard; make it into pills like filberts and give one before intercourse.[87]

Chaucer is aware of the sparrow's wanton associations, calling the bird the son of Venus (*The Parlement of Foules*, l. 351). Indeed it is fitting that the Summoner himself in the *General Prologue* is described as being 'hoot ... and lecherous as a sparwe' (I, 626). Just as Absolon uses his church office as a voyeurist's vantage point, so Friar John tells Thomas's wife, 'Yet saugh I nat this day so fair a wyf / In all the chirche, God so save me!' (ll. 1808–9) where the concluding exclamation is nicely inapt and inept.

Whereas Alisoun's dietary blazon, discussed above, anatomised her in terms of victuals, here lechery and greed are treated separately rather than superimposed. While Nicholas was motivated solely by sexual interest in Alisoun, the Friar in *The Summoner's Tale* is both lecherous and greedy. In St Luke's Gospel, Christ instructs his disciples in the ways of a mendicant way of life: 'Carry neither purse, nor scrip, nor shoes ... And in the same house remain, eating and drinking such things as they have ... Remove not from house to house' (10: 4–7). It is specifically this last instruction that is contravened by John and his fellows, as the Summoner points out: 'In every hous he gan to poure and prye' (l. 1738); 'So longe he wente, hous by hous' (l. 1765). In his efforts to accumulate more and more money and food, John directly defies the instructions of Christ.[88] The Summoner describes how John inscribes his tablets with the names of those who gift him 'a busshel whete, malt, or reye, / A Goddes kechyl [cake], or a trype [bit] of chese, / ... Bacon or beef' (ll. 1746–53) in order that he might demonstrate that he is going to pray for them. In a damning detail, the Summoner notes that these names are subsequently erased to make room for more (ll. 1757–9). John's insistence to the wife that she cook him just the tiniest morsel smacks of bogus humility:

> Have I nat of a capon but the lyvere,
> And of youre softe breed nat but a shyvere,
> And after that a rosted pigges heed –

> But that I nolde no beest for me were deed –
> Thanne hadde I with yow hoomly suffisaunce.
> I am a man of litel sustenaunce;
> My spirit hath his fostrying in the Bible.
> The body is ay so redy and penyble
> To wake, that my stomak is destroyed.
>
> (ll. 1839–47)

Even as he suggests things she may feed him on, John insists that 'My spirit hath his fostrying in the Bible', and that his body, racked by penance, is hardly able to ingest anything. Yet as Ian Lancashire has pointed out, this is all the more hypocritical, given that the visit to Thomas's house takes place during Lent.[89] Thomas remarks that he has not seen John since the beginning of March, some two weeks previously (ll. 1782–3). John's wish-list of food is therefore ironically announced around the middle of the month, during what should be the liturgical year's most abstemious period.

The tone darkens when we hear that, also within the last fortnight, Thomas and his wife have suffered the loss of their son (l. 1852). There is no way that John could know this, since, as the wife remarks, it occurred 'Soone after that ye wente out of this toun' (l. 1853). But John, without missing a beat, improvises his way round this unforeseen incident, sanctimoniously protesting that 'His deeth saugh I by revelacioun' (l. 1854). The brethren of his order know considerably more, John claims, 'of Cristes secree thynges, / Than burel [secular] folk' (ll. 1871–2). We are reminded of the injunction of the Knight, the Miller and Nicholas not to pry overly into 'Goddes pryvetee', while John's suggestion that he is privy to the ways of God, because he is constantly fasting and denying himself the culinary and other luxuries of this earthly life, is all the more contemptible: 'We han this worldes lust al in despit' (l. 1876). T. W. Craik is damning, suggesting that the pseudo-vision cynically manipulates the vulnerability of the bereaved mother: John's 'pretended vision of her dead baby borne to bliss is a masterpice [sic] of imaginative lying and fulsome sentiment'.[90] John's clumsy inattention to their grief is confirmed when he goes on to illustrate his homily on the evils of anger by citing the story of Cambises who, defying accusations of drunkenness, demonstrated his steady hand by shooting an arrow into a small child (ll. 2061–73). The exemplum seems particularly ill-chosen.

Once unleashed, John's hobby horse takes off at full gallop. His constant reference to biblical figures is the nominal equivalent of the scriptural allusions we witnessed in *The Miller's Tale*. He mentions Lazar and Dives (l. 1877), Moses (l. 1885), Elijah (ll. 1890 and 2116), Elisha (l. 2116), Aaron (l. 1894) and 'Oure Lord Jhesu' (l. 1904) as though to endorse his own apparently temperate behaviour and, following therefrom, the more efficacious nature of his devotions: 'oure preyeres ... Been to the hye God moore acceptable / Than youres, with youre feestes at the table' (ll. 1911–14). The Fall of Adam and Eve resulted from 'glotonye' (l. 1916), John insists.[91] He goes on to compare those who over-indulge to Jovinianus, a heretical monk of the fourth century against whom St Jerome directed his *Adversus Jovinianum*. So stuffed are they with food, that when they attempt to recite the opening of Psalm 44 (*'Eructavit cor meum ...'*, 'My heart hath uttered [a good word ...]'), they are interrupted by involuntary burping: 'Whan they for soules seye the psalm of David: / Lo, "buf!" they seye, *"cor meum eructavit!"*' (ll. 1933–4). The choice of that particular psalm is illustrative of the manner in which the narrative voice, the Summoner's but ultimately Chaucer's of course, is undermining the Friar since *eructo* also translates as 'I belch forth' or 'I vomit'. There is a blustery imperative, as it were, behind the selection of this psalm, while the eructive grunt itself is symptomatic of irritable vowel syndrome.

The eructation signifies John's own greedy appetite, matched only by the fervour of his acquisitiveness. Under the guise of collecting money for the construction of 'hooly houses' (l. 1718), the Friar is constantly obliging his congregations to part with their cash. Indeed, he tells the ailing Thomas, his suffering is the direct result of his being too penurious in his alms-giving: 'Youre maladye is for we han to lyte' (l. 1962). Rather than diversify his portfolio, Thomas would be much better advised, says John, to invest the whole lot with his own order: 'Lo, ech thyng that is oned in himselve / Is moore strong than whan it is toscatered' (ll. 1968–9). In an adumbration of the divided fart, John insists that a coin, cut into a dozen fragments, is worthless: 'What is a ferthyng worth parted in twelve?' (l. 1967). In the light of what is to come, it is no accident that the coin chosen is a fart(h)ing which both contains and therefore suggests its near homonym. Of course, adds John rapidly, not a penny of this bequest will come his way – 'noght of youre tresor I desire / As for myself' (l. 1974–5) – but rather it will be used 'to buylden Cristes owene chirche' (l. 1977). The cloister, John goes on, has not even a finished foundation: 'unnethe [hardly] the fundement / Parfouned [completed] is' (ll. 2103–4) yet, as with the farthing, the choice of the word 'fundement' is loaded. The *OED* cites Robert of Gloucester's *Metrical chronicle* of 1297 as the first usage of 'fundament' meaning 'foundations'. Intriguingly, it cites the very same source as the first usage of the term to mean 'the buttocks ... the anus'. Clearly both senses are implicit in Chaucer's pun.

Without rehearsing the intricacies of Freudian theory, it is not irrelevant to point out the connection between financial and visceral costiveness so central to *The Summoner's Tale*. For Freud, explains Beechy, the equation of money and filth

> invokes the foundational role of feces as the first object of exchange. It is the first thing of value to itself (because it is perceived as part and product of itself) that the infant is asked to give up in exchange for approval or some other reward. Every subsequent object of exchange – money especially, since the only value it has is exchange value – retains the fecal association in the unconscious.[92]

Put more baldly, 'Shit and gold stand as repressed metaphors for each other.'[93] In the light of this association it is entirely fitting that the miserly Thomas, who in psychoanalytic terms is the very archetype of the anally retentive personality, should keep his brass up his arse. In spite of the Friar's laborious preaching on the importance of divesting himself of his earthly wealth, Thomas is unimpressed; indeed, John's wearisome exhortation further infuriates him (ll. 1948–53). Thomas's short temper is described in micturient terms. As his wife puts it, 'He is as angry as a pissemyre [ant]' (l. 1825). The *OED* explains the derivation of the term from 'piss + mire ... from the urinous smell of an anthill'.[94] Again the scatological humiliation is being carefully prepared for.

John's eager groping under the sheets is peculiar given that,
during his outburst, Thomas makes perfectly clear that there is
nothing left of his fortune:

> As help me Crist, as I in fewe yeres,
> Have spent upon diverse manere freres
> Ful many a pound; yet fare I never the bet.
> Certeyn, my good have I almoost biset.
> Fawel, my gold, for it is al ago!
>
> (ll. 1949–53)

Thomas it seems, has already been absolved by the curate: 'I have
been shryven this day at my curat. / I have hym toold hoolly al
myn estat' (ll. 2095–6). Clearly 'estat' means his spiritual state or
condition, his sins and his faults which require absolution, but
there is also a material connotation to the word which is in play
here. Thomas has confessed his sins, but he also seems to have
divested himself of his estate. The word 'hoolly' suggests both
'wholly' or 'entirely', but also 'holy'. There is a sustained ambiva-
lence between the spiritual and the material which runs
throughout *The Summoner's Tale*, undermining the Friar's claims
to be uninterested in personal gain. Repeatedly prayers, masses
and religious ritual are priced up, reified into exchangeable
commodities, while those who do the praying, John and his fellow
friars, are labourers. He repeatedly refers to them as 'Werkeris of
Goddes word' (l. 1937); John describes himself as a 'werkman
worthy [of] his hyre' (l. 1973) and he asks Thomas rhetorically,
'who kan teche and werchen as we konne?' (l. 2114). The rapidity
and efficiency of his order's capacity to recite 'trentals' (l. 1717)
make the friars a better investment than the priest who is only able
to sing a single mass each day (l. 1728). Earl Birney describes
John's singing of trentals as taking place 'in a peculiarly stream-
lined manner which his own friary was ingenious and cynical
enough to provide. [John] is a confident and successful master-
salesman.'[95] There is thus an edge of commercial competition
which is wholly inappropriate to the religious calling. As Linda
Georgianna puts it, 'From the very beginning of the tale the friar
establishes his mode of free enterprise, with its strong emphasis on
accounting procedures and competitive market forces,' and, she

adds wittily, 'the friar's hawking of his order's version of trentals lends a whole new meaning to the term "mass production".'[96]

The financial self-interest of churchmen is something John Wyclif condemns in specifically scatological language; simoniacs are condemned for the selling of true preaching: 'Also generaly prelatis regnen in symonye, as bischopis, munkis, chanons, & freris, & lesse curatis; for bischopis, munkis & chanons sillen þe perfeccion of cristis pouert & his apostlis, & also trewe prechynge for a litil stynkyng muk or drit.'[97] Not only is the seeking of earthly wealth a refutation of the poverty of Christ and the apostles but it is, in itself, nothing more than filth. Spiritual truth is degraded, mired, by its reification into an exchange object.

Philosophically and theologically fitting, the reward for Friar John's obsession with money is the cupped hand full of fart. Mary Hayes suggests that Christ's command to receive His flesh and blood in the bread and wine of the Last Supper is being parodied in 'Thomas's pseudo-eucharistic offering to Friar John'.[98] John's outstretched hand certainly recalls the receipt of the Communion. While Absolon receives Nicholas's fart in the face in order, as we have seen, to offend as many of his senses as possible, John's receipt of Thomas's fart in the hand symbolically dirties that part of the body most readily associated in opposite ways with suppliant prayer and grasping avarice. While seeking for Thomas's fortune under the blankets, the Friar is presented with a very unusual kind of 'back-hander'. The physicality of the search is powerfully realised:

> 'Now thanne, put in thyn hand doun by my bak,'
> Seyde this man, 'and grope wel bihynde.
> Bynethe my buttok there shaltow fynde
> A thyng that I have hyd in pryvetee.'
> 'A!' thoghte this frere, 'That shal go with me!'
> And doun his hand he launcheth to the clifte
> In hope for to fynde there a yifte.
> And whan this sike man felte this frere
> Aboute his tuwel grope there and heere,
> Amydde his hand he leet the frere a fart;
> Ther nys no capul, drawynge in a cart,
> That myghte have lete a fart of swich a soun.

> The frere up stirte as dooth a wood leoun –
> 'A, false cherl,' quod he, 'for Goddes bones!
> This hastow for despit doon for the nones.
> Thou shalt abye this fart, if that I may!'

(ll. 2140–55)

The graphic description of the search intensifies the insult when it comes just as, in *The Miller's Tale*, the detail of Absolon's squeamishness magnified the effects of his encounter with the flatulent Nicholas.[99] Note especially the sense of excited eagerness conveyed by the repetition of the verb 'grope'. Thomas instructs the Friar to 'grope well bihynde' and he then feels John 'Aboute his tuwel grope there and heere'. Previously the verb had been used by John to refer to the ways in which a confession should be conducted: he criticises the curates who, in his opinion, are negligent and slow 'To grope tendrely a conscience/In shrift' (ll. 1817–18) and *OED* does cite this line to illustrate its definition: 'To make examination or trial of; to examine, sound, probe (a person, the conscience, etc.)' but it also cites an instance from the late fourteenth century in which the verb is used of a physical action 'in [an] indecent sense'. The reification of the spiritual, so characteristic of John's rapacity, is signified by the ambiguous application of a verb which usually connotes physical manipulation (clutching, grabbing or fingering) to a state of spiritual piety. The verb reappears here in such a way as to question its previous use and Allen insists on its secular/spiritual ambiguity: 'Middle English *grope* ranges in meaning from fondling someone amorously, to a physician's searching of a wound, to a priest's examination of a penitent's conscience.'[100]

The Summoner is specific and explicit about the destination of John's hands, mentioning both the cleft between Thomas's buttocks and his 'tuwel' or arsehole. The uncertainty about the destination of Absolon's kiss is here replaced by a particularity which is graphically realised. In a development of the confusion between the spiritual and the material and in anticipation of the problem of the division of the fart, it is spoken of as though it has an economic value. John tells Thomas that 'Thou shalt abye [that is, pay for] this fart' (l. 2149). The comparison of the fart to that of a straining carthorse both captures the exertion of Thomas who is so eager to offend the Friar, and neatly foreshadows the mathematical solution of its division into equal parts by placing it at the hub of a cartwheel. The groping and the farting are exactly suited to the degraded nature of Friar John's declaratory religiosity for while the fingering of the cleft is a parody of the disciple's determination to feel the wound in Christ's side, the creative breath of the Holy Ghost is scatologically figured in the flatus under the sheets. According to the Scriptures, God 'formed man of the slime of the earth: and breathed into his face the breath of life, and man became a living soul' (Genesis 2: 7). In the Towneley *Creation*, God describes the process of breathing in his animating spirit: 'Spreyte of life I in the[e] blaw, / Good and ill both shall thou knaw.'[101] The Latin *spiritus* meaning 'a breath of air', 'an exhalation', gives us both 'Holy Spirit' and 'suspiration' and the Bible repeatedly associates the presence of God with gusts of air. In the book of Job, for example, we hear that: 'The spirit of God made me, and the breath of the Almighty gave me life' (33: 4). John's handful of fart is a parodic reworking of this idea, the soul of mankind travestied by the vaporous outburst of Thomas's bowels. In John 20, the very chapter in which Doubting Thomas expresses his scepticism over the resurrection of Christ which only touching his wounds will allay, Jesus literally inspires his followers: 'When he had said this, he breathed on them: and he said to them, Receive ye the Holy Ghost' (20: 22). The word repeatedly used for divine *inspiration* and occasionally the Holy Spirit itself (as in Acts of the Apostles 2: 2) is 'flatus'.[102]

As was first recognised by Alan Levitan, the division of the fart into a dozen equal pieces, in accordance with Thomas's bequest (ll. 2131–6) is a scatological parody of the descent of the Holy Ghost at Pentecost.[103]

And when the days of the Pentecost were accomplished, they were all together in one place. And suddenly there came a sound from heaven, as of a mighty wind coming, and it filled the whole house where they were sitting. And there appeared to them parted tongues, as it were of fire, and it sat upon every one of them. And they were all filled with the Holy Ghost, and they began to speak with diverse tongues, according as the Holy Ghost gave to them to speak. (Acts 2: 1–4)

The mighty wind and fiery tongues become parodically debased in *The Summoner's Tale* into the foetid flatulence of the sick old man. While the Acts describes the gift of tongues which will allow the apostles to preach the good news world-wide, Thomas's abdominal gas is appropriate reward for John's hot air. The satirical treatment of the Holy Spirit is of a piece with the association of evil with scatology. St Paul allies rebellious behaviour with the malign influence of 'the prince of the power of this air, of the spirit that now worketh on the children of unbelief' (Ephesians 2: 2) so that the life-giving breath of the Holy Spirit is here a Satanic flatulence which inspires doubt. This motif is wide-spread in the literature of the medieval period: 'Late medieval art lovingly and copiously embroiders the demonic with shit.'[104] A stage direction to *The Castle of Perseverance* demands that the actor playing Belial risk life and limb (or anus, at least) in representing the devil's explosive flatulence: 'and he Þat schal pley belyal loke Þat he haue gunnepowdyr brennynge In pypys in hys handys and in hys erys and in hys ars whanne he gothe to batayl'.[105] Indeed, James J. Paxson speculates that the performance of such roles necessitated the fire-proofing of the actor's anus with clay.[106] In the *Ludus Coventriae*, following his expulsion from Heaven, Satan expresses his horror of fire: 'Ffor fere of fyre a fart I crake / In helle donjoon' (ll. 81–2) though, as in the case of Nicholas's flaming fart, this is likely to augment the combustion rather than blow it out.[107] Later in the same sequence, Satan lets fly for sorrow: 'with a ffart my brech I breke / my sorwe comyth ful sone' (ll. 355–6). Having failed to tempt Christ, the Devil is so confused and upset that he farts: 'What Þat he is I kan not se / Whethyr god or man what Þat he be / I kan not telle in no degre / Ffor sorwe I lete a crakke' (ll. 192–5). Chaucer is aware of this infernal anality and we have already noted the angry exchange between Summoner and Friar in which the former places the latter's kind up Satan's rectum: '"Hold up thy tayle, thou Sathanas!" quod he [an angel]; / "Shewe forth thyn ers, and lat the frere se / Where is the nest of freres in this place!"' (III, 1689–91). Cutting short *The Tale of Sir Thopas*, the Host interrupts Chaucer the pilgrim with an outburst that draws on this proverbial hellish scatology: '"Myne eres aken of thy drasty speche. / Now swich a rym the devel I biteche! / This may well be rym dogerel," quod he. / ... "By God," quod he, "for pleynly, at a word, / Thy drasty rymyng is nat worth a toord!"' (VII, 923–30). As well as this devilish rhyming being not worth a turd, it is repeatedly characterised as 'drasty'. Larry D. Benson glosses the term as 'crappy'.[108]

The association of Satan with scatology is initially uppermost in the minds of the characters within the fiction of the *Tale* who ponder the division of the fart. In order to rub John's nose in it, as it were, Thomas has insisted that his gift be divided equally between the friars 'Withouten fraude or cavillacioun' (l. 2136). The Lord of the Manor, whom John immediately visits, opines that such a riddle must originate with Satan himself: 'I trowe the devel putte it in his mynde' (l. 2221). Thomas is surely possessed by a demon (l. 2240) and the Lord concludes, 'Lat hym go honge hymself a devel weye!' (l. 2242). Yet, as the Lord becomes increasingly intrigued by the ingenious nature of the riddle, he concludes that Thomas 'nys no fool, ne no demonyak' (l. 2292).

The mathematical poser is fascinating – how to divide 'the soun or savour of a fart' (l. 2226) in such a way as to render each of the friars an equal portion. In a brilliant pun the Lord refers to this as a problem of 'ars-metrike' (l. 2222). The word is used in *The Knight's Tale* (I, 1898) to mean the 'art of measurement' or 'arithmetic' and it has that meaning here, but its compound form clearly also suggests the word 'arse'. Thomas's insistence on the avoidance of 'cavillacioun' makes clear that he (and therefore Chaucer) is sceptical of the casuistic methods of contemporary scholarly debate, theological and philosophical; as Travis rightly insists, 'part of the fart-and-cartwheel's satiric thrust is obviously directed against *any* form of elevated discourse'. He goes on, 'posterior analytics is clearly a send-up of scholastic choplogic' and a further satire on the friars who were the greatest exponents of the scholastic method.[109] The force of the satirical attack is in its insistent recapitulation of the equating of the spiritual and the material.

As we have seen, the divine or demonic connotations of God's breath or Satan's fart respectively make the contents of John's cupped hands all the more intangible. Yet he is obliged to divide it into equal pieces and, in order to do this, the fart must undergo a process of reification which will, in turn, require that it be measured. But, as the Lord points out, the fart is characterised by insubstantiality and entropy: 'The rumblynge of a fart, and every soun, / Nis but of eir reverberacioun, / And evere it wasteth litel and litel awey' (ll. 2233–5). The application of technical vocabulary to the fart in order to quantify its sound and smell demonstrates the absurdly prosaic thinking of Friar John who, as we have already seen, is perfectly able to quantify, both in terms of effort and remuneration, his prayers for the souls of the dead (ll. 1724–32). His struggle to apportion the fart equitably among the members of his order thus parodically undermines the computation of prayer and godly observance which he crudely and publicly enumerates in order to attract material reward. Such avaricious accountancy is revealed to be, at best, unchristian and, at worst, because of the Satanic connotations of flatulence, infernal. On the other hand, while the hypocritical Friar is increasingly characterised in a negative light, the riddler himself, Thomas, is treated with an escalating admiration. The Lord twice refers to him as 'nyce' (ll. 2227 and 2232) which carries the apparent sense of 'foolish' but also of 'discerning' or 'scrupulous'. The Lord readily concedes that such a puzzle has never been formulated 'Biforn this day' (l. 2223) and he describes Thomas as treating John 'shrewedly' which translates as 'shrewishly' or 'insultingly' but also as 'shrewdly' or 'intelligently'. Indeed, by the time Jankyn has formulated his solution, 'the cherl, they seyde, subtiltee / And heigh wit made hym speken as he spak' (ll. 2290–1), while Jankyn himself is compared for his insight to Ptolemy or Euclid (l. 2289). Everyone, with the exception of John, comes out of the *Tale* smelling of roses.

The solution to this infernal riddle is provided by Jankyn, attendant to the Lord of the Manor and, surely not coincidentally, the servant charged with apportioning the meat, the 'kervere' (l. 2242). The squire will, in exchange for 'a newe gowne' (l. 2293), explain how to carve the fart into equal portions. The process demands a still day 'Withouten wynd or perturbynge of air' (l. 2254), to ensure that the fart is not dissipated. A cartwheel with twelve spokes should be brought into the hall and each friar is to sit with his nose at the end of a different spoke. Friar John, worthy of 'the firste fruyt' (l. 2277), may place his own nose under the hub. Thomas, 'with bely stif and toght / As any tabour' (ll. 2276–8), should be brought in and sat on top of the wheel's axis. As he farts both 'the soun of it [and] the stynk' (ll. 2273–4) will work their way equally out towards the waiting friars, except John who will receive the most immediate portion.

Not only is the solution enchantingly inventive in its own terms, but it recapitulates several of the satirical thrusts of the *Tale*. To begin with, medieval iconography often pictured the apostles receiving the Pentecostal gift of tongues while sitting round a circular table so that the arrangement of the seated friars visually reinforces the earlier allusions to the descent of the Holy Ghost considered above.[110] Moreover, the seating plan is also familiar from the images of King Arthur and the Knights of the Round Table. The circle is obviously an image of geometrical and therefore philosophical (or theological) perfection – Jankyn's aptitude is compared to that of Euclid. Circularity signifies eternity as well as harmony. The Ptolemaic cosmology imaged the planets spinning about the Earth while, beyond the outer sphere, the First Mover imparted the energy which span the whole edifice – Jankyn, as noted above, is also compared to the astronomer (l. 2289).

In addition, there are a couple of further, specifically Christian, allusions which render the solution especially appropriate. To begin with Thomas is encouraged to fart three times; John, his nose under the hub of the wheel, is to have 'the firste smel of fartes thre' (l. 2284). That the number of farts matches that of the persons of the Holy Trinity reinforces the parodic treatment of John's religious hypocrisy. Furthermore, the reward for the explanation – 'a gowne-clooth' (l. 2247) – is also biblically significant. According to St John's Gospel (19: 23–4), the soldiers who attended the Crucifixion divided Christ's garments equally among them. However, his coat, which was seamless, was too valuable to tear and they agreed to cast lots for it. The instructions as to the fart's equal apportionment suggest the division of Christ's raiment while Jankyn's reward of the new gown reminds us of the value placed on Christ's vestment. The association, in both cases, of the divided fart with Christ's self-sacrifice, demonstrates the outrageous sanctimony and religious corruption of John whose protestations continually refer to the invisible glories of prayer and spirituality but whose belly and purse are firmly focused on the things of this world. As Robert Hasenfratz neatly puts it, 'The coda cleverly reveals the secret life of the body which the friar would deny, though its brilliance is to connect the friars to the opposite end of the alimentary canal.'[111]

These implicit references to the story of the Crucifixion are typical of the subtlety by which Chaucer intensifies the scatological complications of The Miller's Tale and The Summoner's Tale. While Nicholas's fart almost blinds Absolon and while John fingers Thomas's cleft in glorious detail, both tales demonstrate their capacity to sustain, at the same time as a rough and ungainly comedy, a degree of delicate intimation which relies on intertextual reference (between The Knight's Tale and The Miller's Tale, for instance), biblical allusion, parody of Petrarchan and chivalric styles and the appropriation and subversion of erudite expectations. On one level the outrageous obscenity, sexual and scatological, stems from the generic conventions of the fabliau. But in the brilliance of their sustained craftiness, both tales illustrate the complexity and refinement of Chaucer's scatological rhetoric – a rhetoric that, as we have seen, for all its ingenuity and refinement, appears superficially coarse and therefore remains capable of alienating those readers who, like Absolon, are 'somdeel squaymous / Of fartyng' (I, 3337–8).

NOTES

1 Galen, On the Natural Faculties (Encyclopædia Britannica: Chicago, 1990), p. 423.
2 Lee Patterson, '"No Man his Reson Herde": Peasant Consciousness, Chaucer's Miller, and the Structure of the Canterbury Tales', in Lee Patterson (ed.), Literary Practice and Social Change in Britain, 1380–1530 (University of California Press: Berkeley, 1990), 113–55, p. 121.
3 Peter W. Travis, 'Thirteen Ways of Listening to a Fart: Noise in Chaucer's The Summoner's Tale', Exemplaria, 16 (2004), 323–48, p. 348.
4 Travis, 'Thirteen Ways', p. 325.
5 Travis, 'Thirteen Ways', p. 345.
6 Greg Walker, 'Rough Girls and Squeamish Boys: The Trouble with

Absolon in *The Miller's Tale'*, in Elaine Treharne (ed.), *Essays and Studies 2002* (D. S. Brewer: Cambridge, 2002), 61–91, p. 64.

7 *G2* supplement of *The Guardian*, 20 June 2006, p. 2. My review of the production (co-written with Greg Walker) is in *Cahiers Elisabéthains*, 69 (2006), 53–7.

8 Poulton's translation is available as *Chaucer's The Canterbury Tales, Adapted for the Stage* (Nick Hern Books: London, 2005). Part One was first performed in The Swan Theatre, Stratford-upon-Avon, on 16 November 2005 and Part Two on 23 November 2005.

9 Cited in *The Guardian*.

10 David Inglis, *A Sociological History of Excretory Experience: Defecatory Manners and Toiletry Technologies* (Edwin Mellen Press: Lampeter, 2000), pp. 1 and 4.

11 Inglis, *Sociological History of Excretory Experience*, p. 66.

12 Michel Foucault, *The History of Sexuality*, translated by Robert Hurley (Penguin: Harmondsworth, 1981), pp. 1–13.

13 John Dryden, *Essays of John Dryden*, edited by W. P. Ker, 2 vols (Clarendon: Oxford, 1900), II, 265. It is profoundly ironic that while, on the one hand, Dryden was censuring and censoring Chaucer, on the other, he attempted to cultivate a rakish persona. This seems to have resulted in the boorish and maladroit employment of obscenity. Rochester writes, 'Dryden in vain tryd this nice way of Witt, / For he to be a tearing Blade thought fitt. / But when he would be sharp he still was blunt: / To frisk his frolick fancy hee'd cry Cunt.' Nor can we attribute this account to Rochester's personal animosity; Thomas Shadwell describes a similarly gawky outbreak of Tourette's: 'The Mirth by foolish Bawdry is exprest; / And so debauch'd, so fulsome, and so odd, / As ... / *Let's Bugger one another now by G-d* / (When ask'd how they should spend the Afternoon) / This was the smart reply of the Heroick Clown.' Indeed, Dryden seems gloomily aware that he will never be as aristocratically outrageous as those whom he envied: 'My Conversation is slow and dull, my humour Saturnine and reserv'd: In short, I am none of those who endeavour to break Jests in Company, or make reparties' (John Wilmot, *The Works of John Wilmot, Earl of Rochester*, edited by Harold Love (Oxford University Press: Oxford, 1999), p. 73 and Brean S. Hammond, '"An Allusion to Horace", Jonson's Ghost and the Second Poets' War', in Edward Burns (ed.), *Reading Rochester* (Liverpool University Press: Liverpool, 1995), 166–86, pp. 185 and 181).

14 Dryden, *Essays*, II, 262–3. Other tales omitted include the Reeve's, the Shipman's, the Merchant's and 'above all' the Wife of Bath's, the latter of which 'would have procured me as many friends and readers, as there are *beaux* and ladies of pleasure in the town'.

15 David Matthews, 'Infantilizing the Father: Chaucer Translations and

Moral Regulation', in *Studies in the Age of Chaucer*, 22 (2000), 93–114, p. 95.

16 Matthews, 'Infantilizing the Father', p. 95.

17 Dorothy Wordsworth, *Journals of Dorothy Wordsworth*, edited by E. de Selincourt, 2 vols (Macmillan: London, 1952), I, 96.

18 William Wordsworth, *Prelude*, III, 278–81, in *The Fourteen-Book Prelude*, edited by W. J. B. Owen (Cornell University Press: Ithaca and London, 1985), p. 68.

19 *OED* cites a mid-nineteenth century usage: 'There are many degrees of broken wind, which receive appellations according to the noise emitted by the horse, and on this account he is called a ... trumpeter.'

20 Charles Cowden Clarke, *Tales from Chaucer in Prose* (Effingham Wilson: London, 1833), p. iii.

21 Cited by Dolores Warwick Frese, 'The Homoerotic Underside in Chaucer's *The Miller's Tale* and *The Reeve's Tale*', *Michigan Academician*, 10 (1977), 143–50, p. 143.

22 Robert Kilburn Root, *The Poetry of Chaucer: A Guide to its Study and Appreciation* (Peter Smith: Gloucester, MA, 1957), second edition, p. 179.

23 Geoffrey Chaucer, *The Canterbury Tales*, edited by John Matthews Manly (Holt: New York, 1929), p. 559. Haweis is cited in Matthews, 'Infantilizing the Father', p. 94.

24 Geoffrey Chaucer, *The Riverside Chaucer*, edited by Larry D. Benson (Oxford University Press: Oxford, 1988). This and all subsequent references to Chaucer's work are from this text.

25 Edward Wagenknecht, *The Personality of Chaucer* (Norman: University of Oklahoma Press, 1968), p. 117.

26 Haldeen Braddy, 'Chaucer: Realism or Obscenity?', *Arlington Quarterly*, 2 (1969), 121–38, p. 137.

27 Geoffrey Chaucer, *The Miller's Tale*, edited by James Winny (Cambridge University Press: Cambridge, 1971), p. 80.

28 Peter G. Beidler, 'Art and Scatology in The *Miller's Tale*', *The Chaucer Review*, 12 (1977), 90–102, p. 91.

29 John Cook, 'Carnival and *The Canterbury Tales*: "Only equals may laugh" (Herzen)', in David Aers (ed.), *Medieval Literature: Criticism, Ideology and History* (St Martin's Press: New York, 1986), 169–91, p. 170.

30 Tiffany Beechy, 'Devil Take the Hindmost: Chaucer, John Gay, and the Pecuniary Anus', *The Chaucer Review*, 41 (2006), 71–85, p. 71.

31 Jeff Persels and Russell Ganim (eds), *Fecal Matters in Early Modern Literature and Art: Studies in Scatology* (Ashgate: Aldershot, 2004), p. xiii.

32 Valerie Allen, *On Farting: Language and Laughter in the Middle Ages* (Palgrave: Houndmills, 2007), pp. 5 and 2. My review of Allen's book appeared in *The Times Higher Educational Supplement*, 1812, 21 September 2007, p. 22.

33 Allen, *On Farting*, p. 64.

34 Susan Signe Morrison, *Excrement in the Late Middle Ages: Sacred Filth and Chaucer's Fecopoetics* (Palgrave: Houndmills, 2008), p. 4. My review of Morrison's book appeared in *The Times Higher Educational Supplement*, 1879, 15 January 2009, p. 53.

35 Morrison, *Excrement*, p. 158.

36 Thomas A. Kirby, 'Theodore Roosevelt on Chaucer and a Chaucerian', *Modern Language Notes*, 68 (1953), 34–7, p. 34.

37 Kirby, 'Theodore Roosevelt', p. 36.

38 Both cited by Earl Birney, 'Structural Irony within the *Summoner's Tale*', *Anglia*, 78 (1960), 204–18, p. 204.

39 Birney, 'Structural Irony', p. 1.

40 Beechy, 'Devil Take the Hindmost', p. 71.

41 Penn R. Szittya, 'The Friar as False Apostle: Antifraternal Exegesis and the *Summoner's Tale*', *Studies in Philology*, 71 (1974), 19–46, p. 46.

42 Cook, 'Carnival and *The Canterbury Tales*', p. 170.

43 All Biblical quotations are from the Douay-Rheims Bible available online at www.drbo.org.

44 Cook, 'Carnival and *The Canterbury Tales*', p. 171.

45 Karma Lochrie, 'Women's "Pryvetees" and Fabliau Politics in the *Miller's Tale*', *Exemplaria*, 6 (1994), 287–304, p. 297.

46 Cook, 'Carnival and *The Canterbury Tales*', p. 182.

47 Allen, *On Farting*, p. 82.

48 *Romeo and Juliet*, IV.iii.29–56; *Measure for Measure*, III.i.118–32; *Richard II*, II.i.74–83; Andrew Marvell, 'To his Coy Mistress', ll. 27–8, in *The Poems*, edited by Hugh MacDonald (Routledge and Kegan Paul: London, 1952).

49 Marvell also uses the 'quaint'/'queynte'/'cunt' word play in 'To his Coy Mistress': 'And your quaint Honour turn to dust; / And into ashes all my Lust' (ll. 29–30).

50 David Aers, *Chaucer* (Harvester: Brighton, 1986), p. 82.

51 Patterson, '"No Man his Reson Herde": Peasant Consciousness, Chaucer's Miller, and the Structure of the *Canterbury Tales*', p. 130.

52 David Williams, 'Radical Therapy in *The Miller's Tale*', *The Chaucer Review*, 15 (1981), 227–35, p. 228.

53 John Arderne, *Treatises of Fistula in Ano, Hæmorrhoids, and Clysters*, edited by D'Arcy Power, EETS, o.s. 139 (Kegan Paul, Trench, Trübner and Co.: London, 1910), p. 2.

54 D. Thomas Hanks Jr, '"Goddes Pryvetee" and Chaucer's Miller's Tale', *Christianity and Literature*, 33 (1984), 7–12, p. 7. Lochrie concurs: 'Mystery, secret, a secret sin or desire, and sex organ are all meanings attached to the word "pryvetee"' ('Women's "Pryvetees" and Fabliau Politics', p. 292).

55 Louise M. Bishop, '"Of Goddes pryvetee nor of his wyf'": Confusion of Orifices in Chaucer's *Miller's Tale*', *Texas Studies in Language and Literature*, 44 (2002), 231–46, p. 246.

56 Thomas J. Farrell, 'Privacy and the Boundaries of the Fabliau in The *Miller's Tale*', *English Literary History*, 56 (1989), 773–95, p. 783.

57 Bishop, '"Of Goddes pryvetee nor of his wyf'": Confusion of Orifices in Chaucer's *Miller's Tale*', p. 239.

58 Wolfgang E. H. Rudat, 'The Misdirected Kiss in *The Miller's Tale*', *Journal of Evolutionary Psychology*, 3 (1982), 103–7, p. 104.

59 H. Marshall Leicester, Jr, 'Newer Currents in Psychoanalytic Criticism, and the Difference "It" Makes: Gender and Desire in The *Miller's Tale*', *English Literary History*, 61 (1994), 473–99, p. 487.

60 Hanks Jr, '"Goddes Pryvetee" and Chaucer's Miller's Tale', p. 9.

61 Walker, 'Rough Girls and Squeamish Boys', p. 71.

62 Morrison, *Excrement*, p. 48.

63 See Book I, Chapter 13 of François Rabelais, *Gargantua and Pantagruel*, translated by Sir Thomas Urquhart and Pierre Le Motteux, introduced by Terence Cave (Everyman: London, 1994).

64 As Lochrie puts it, 'A riddle is set into motion with the confusion of orifices and genders, and the homosocial network of cuckoldry suddenly becomes sexualised in the process' ('Women's "Pryvetees" and Fabliau Politics', p. 300).

65 Lochrie describes, apparently without irony, how 'Nicholas's attempt to improve on Alisoun's joke *backfires*' ('Women's "Pryvetees" and Fabliau Politics', p. 301, my emphasis).

66 Frese, 'The Homoerotic Underside', p. 147.

67 Raymond P. Tripp Jr, 'The Darker Side to Absolon's Dawn Visit', *The Chaucer Review*, 20 (1986), 207–12, p. 211.

68 Tracey Jordan, 'Fairy Tale and Fabliau: Chaucer's *The Miller's Tale*', *Studies in Short Fiction*, 21 (1984), 87–93, p. 92. James Winny agrees, accounting for the crudity of the description of Alisoun's pubis in the following terms: 'Its courseness is justified by the need to bring the amorous fop Absolon to terms with the reality which his romantic posturings have hitherto avoided' (*The Miller's Tale*, p. 80).

69 Paula Neuss finds the gross punishment of Nicholas suited to his unsubtlety: 'Nicholas's action in heaving the whole of his private parts over the window-sill is hardly worth the stealth and secrecy we have come to expect of him, and he deserves what he gets' ('*Double-Entendre* in The *Miller's Tale*', *Essays in Criticism*, 24 (1974), 325–40, p. 337).

70 Robyn is insistent on the darkness of the night. See: ll. 3352, 3422, 3445, 3633 and 3684–6.

71 Paul Delany, 'Constantinus Africanus' *De Coitu*: A Translation', *Chaucer Review*, 4 (1970), 55–65, p. 61. On Chaucer's reference to this tract, see p. 55.

72 Delany, 'Constantinus Africanus' *De Coitu*: A Translation', p. 62.

73 Mikhail Bakhtin, *Rabelais and His World*, translated by Hélène Iswolsky (Indiana University Press: Bloomington, 1984), p. 240.

74 The kymelyn, similar to a barrel, may itself have a scatological relevance given that medieval latrines were fashioned from such vessels. In his examination of the contents of a fifteenth-century barrel-latrine, James Greig notes the presence of umbelliferous seeds which 'seem to have been appreciated in the past for their powers of preventing flatulence'. ('The Investigation of a Medieval Barrel-latrine from Worcester', *Journal of Archaeological Science*, 8 (1981), 265–82, p. 273.) On the sanitation of the Middle Ages see also Ernest L. Sabine, 'Latrines and Cesspools of Mediaeval London', *Speculum*, 9 (1934), 303–21.

75 Peggy Knapp argues that the two plots are joined by the word 'water': 'The water that Nicholas needs later to cool his burning behind is a comic economy in that it suddenly links the two plots just when the audience had nearly forgotten the first.' 'Robyn the Miller's Thrifty Work', in Steve Ellis (ed.), *Chaucer: The Canterbury Tales* (Longman: London, 1998), 62–77, p. 75.

76 The computation of the hand's breadth is coincidentally used of anal measurements elsewhere. John Arderne details the case of Thomas Broune 'that had holes [that is, anal fistulas] by whiche went out wynde with egestious odour; that is to sey, 8 hole$_3$ of the to[ne] party of the ersse, and 7 on tothir side; Of whiche some hole$_3$ was distant fro the towell by *the space of a handbrede of a man*, so that bothe his buttok*is* was so vlcerat and putrefied with-in that the quitour and filthe went out ich day als mych as an egg-shcl mi$_3$t take' (*Treatises of Fistula in Ano*, p. 2, my emphasis).

77 Mrs Noah's crabbiness was clearly proverbial and often featured in the drama of the time. See *Noyes Fludd*, ll. 197–208, 246 and following, in R. M. Lumiansky and David Mills (eds), *The Chester Mystery Cycle*, EETS, s.s. 3 (Oxford University Press: London, 1974).

78 *Pageant of Shearmen and Taylors*, ll. 133–5, in Hardin Craig (ed.), *The Coventry Corpus Christi Plays* (Oxford University Press: London, 1957).

79 II Kings 18: 9–15 recounts how the biblical Absolom is killed following his hair being tangled in 'a thick and large oak'.

80 *Noyes Fludd*, ll. 309–14, in Lumiansky and Mills (eds), *The Chester Mystery Cycle*.

81 *Second Shepherds' Play*, ll. 183–8, in Martin Stevens and A. C. Cawley (eds), *The Townley Plays*, EETS, s.s. 13 (Oxford University Press: Oxford, 1994).

82 'Sant Thomas of Kent' also appears thus in the Third Shepherd's speech. See *Second Shepherds' Play*, l. 661, in Stevens and Cawley (eds), *The*

Townley Plays. On Becket's underwear see Morrison, *Excrement*, pp. 79 and 190.

83 Given the profusion of Johns (Alisoun's husband, the Friar in *The Summoner's Tale*, the Evangelist) and Thomases (the old man in *The Summoner's Tale*, Doubting Thomas, 'Thomas of Kent'), one wonders whether the names' frequent coincidence is a mischievous allusion to 'John Thomas', glossed by Gordon Williams as a 'penis. Commonest of names since medieval times' (*A Dictionary of Sexual Language and Imagery in Shakespearean and Stuart Literature*, 3 vols (Athlone: London, 1994), II, 744).

84 Aers, *Chaucer*, p. 43.

85 Arderne, *Treatises of Fistula in Ano*, p. 5.

86 *Measure for Measure*, III.i.433.

87 Delany, 'Constantinus Africanus' *De Coitu*: A Translation', pp. 64–5.

88 Although not strictly relevant to my argument here, there is a magnificent fart brought on by greed in the fifth passus of *Piers Plowman*. The banquet guests 'seten so til evensong, and songen umwhile, / Til Gloton hadde yglubbed a galon and a gille. / His guttes bigonne to gothelen as two gredy sowes; / He pissed a potel in a Paternoster-while, / And blew his rounde ruwet at his ruggebones ende, / That alle that herde that horn helde hir nose after / And wisshed it hadde ben wexed with a wispe of firses!' (William Langland, *The Vision of Piers Plowman*, edited by A. V. C. Schmidt (J. M. Dent: London, 1978), p. 54).

89 Ian Lancashire, 'Moses, Elijah and the Back Parts of God: Satiric Scatology in Chaucer's *Summoner's Tale*', *Mosaic*, 14 (1981), 17–30, p. 20.

90 T. W. Craik, *The Comic Tales of Chaucer* (Methuen: London, 1964), p. 123.

91 Chaucer's Pardoner agrees – see VI, 505–12. The Pardoner goes on to compare excessive consumption to the process of voiding in the privy: 'Whan man so drynketh of the white and rede / That of his throte he maketh his pryvee / Thurgh thilke cursed superfluitee' (526–8).

92 Beechy, 'Devil Take the Hindmost', p. 73.

93 Allen, *On Farting*, p. 93.

94 Allen cites a medieval practical joker's handbook wherein ants' eggs are used to brew a fart potion: 'Likewise if any man taketh the eggs of Pismires [ants] and breaketh them, and casteth them into water, and give them to any man in a drink, he ceaseth not anon to fart' (*On Farting*, p. 35).

95 Birney, 'Structural Irony', p. 206.

96 Linda Georgianna, 'Lords, Churls, and Friars: The Return to Social Order in *The Summoner's Tale*', in Susanna Greer Fein, David Raybin and Peter C. Braeger (eds), *Rebels and Rivals: The Contestive Spirit in The Canterbury Tales* (Western Michigan University Press: Kalamazoo, 1991), 149–72,

p. 156. She acknowledges the joke to be the coinage of John Crafton.

97 John Wyclif, *The English Works of Wyclif Hitherto Unprinted*, edited by F. D. Matthew, EETS, o.s. 74 (Trübner & Co.: London, 1880), p. 68.

98 Mary Hayes, 'Privy Speech: Sacred Silence, Dirty Secrets in the *Summoner's Tale*', *The Chaucer Review*, 40 (2006), 263–88, p. 265. Perhaps understandably, Arderne is graphically detailed about digital insertion: 'at first putte the leche Þe schewyng fynger of his left hande enoynted with oile, or som oyntment, in-to Þe lure of Þe pacient'; 'Aftirward be it enoynted wiÞ Þe fynger atuix Þe buttoke₃'; 'And putte in Þi fynger, anoynted first with some of Þe forseid Þings, into Þe lure' (*Treatises of Fistula in Ano*, pp. 22, 30 and 77).

100 Allen, *On Farting*, p. 178.

101 *Creation*, ll. 168–9, in Stevens and Cawley (eds), *The Townley Plays*.

102 Szittya, 'The Friar as False Apostle', p. 23.

103 See Bernard S. Levy, 'Biblical Parody in the *Summoner's Tale*', *Tennessee Studies in Literature*, 11 (1966), 45–60. In footnote 15, he acknowledges Levitan's idea as 'a significant original contribution to Chaucer studies'. Levitan's findings subsequently appear as 'The Parody of Pentecost in Chaucer's *Summoner's Tale*', *University of Toronto Quarterly*, 40 (1971), 236–46. See also Szittya, 'The Friar as False Apostle' and Lancashire, 'Moses, Elijah and the Back Parts of God'.

104 Allen, *On Farting*, p. 79.

105 *The Castle of Perseverance*, in Mark Eccles (ed.), *The Macro Plays*, EETS, 262 (Oxford University Press: London, 1969), p. 1.

106 James J. Paxson, 'Theorizing the Mysteries' End in England, the Artificial Demonic, and the Sixteenth-Century Witch-Craze', *Criticism*, 39 (1997), 481–502. On the technicalities of on-stage pyrotechnics, see Philip Butterworth, *Theatre of Fire: Special Effects in Early English and Scottish Theatre* (Society for Theatre Research: London, 1998).

107 K. S. Block (ed.), *Ludus Coventriae or The Plaie called Corpus Christi*, EETS, e.s. 120 (Oxford University Press: London, 1922).

108 Chaucer, *The Riverside Chaucer*, p. 216.

109 Travis, 'Thirteen Ways', p. 341. Allen ventures that the humour 'emerges from the demystification of an elevated concept, from the exposure of its base origins: arithmetic, the art of number, one of the seven liberal arts is all about dividing farts' (*On Farting*, p. 143).

110 Levitan includes eight relevant illustrations of this configuration. Most famous is the inside of the cupola of St Mark's in Venice ('The Parody of Pentecost in Chaucer's *Summoner's Tale*').

111 Robert Hasenfratz, 'The Science of Flatulence: Possible Sources for the *Summoner's Tale*', *The Chaucer Review*, 30 (1996), 241–61, p. 257.

2

Ajax by any other name would smell as sweet: Shakespeare, Harington and onomastic scatology

I

William Camden's encyclopaedic *tour de force*, *Britannia*, was published in Latin in 1586. In his scrapbook supplement to the volume, *Remaines of a Greater Worke, Concerning Britaine* (1605), he devotes no fewer than five separate chapters to naming and nomenclature. In his explanation of naming, which precedes dictionary definitions of 'Usuall Christian names', he emphasises the importance of recovering the lost meanings that such familiar names once generated: 'So that it were grosse ignorance and to no small reproach of our Progenitours, to thinke their names onely nothing significative, because that in the daily alteration of our tong, the signification of them is lost, or not commonly knowne.'[1]

The Saussurean vocabulary is especially apposite. Camden is attempting to recover the lost signifieds of the, by now, all-too-commonplace signifiers. His mission is not merely to reinvigorate the connotative force of such apparently neutral labels, nor simply to restore linguistic richness to language itself. Like all good sociolinguists, Camden is concerned with the interplay between the sign of which he writes and the discourses of class and power in which it constructs social meanings. Names, as he points out right at the beginning, 'were first imposed for the distinction of persons ... and have beene especially respected as whereon the glorie and credite of men is grounded, and by which the same is convayed to the knowledge of posteritie'.[2]

As in so many other subjects, Michel de Montaigne occupied a sceptical and oppositional position. In his essay 'Of Names', translated by John Florio in 1603, Montaigne argued that names were little more than arbitrary signs: 'Is it Peter or William. And what is that but a word for al mouths? or three or foure dashes of a pen, first, so easie to be varied'.[3] For the pragmatic French philosopher, there was nothing significant about signification: 'There is both name, and the thing: the name is a voice which noteth and signifieth the thing: the name is neither part of thing nor of substance.'[4]

But despite typifying the opposite view of designation, Montaigne is in agreement with Camden on the social importance of names, 'it is a common saying, "That it is good to have a good name:" As much to say, good credit or good reputation.'[5] The use of the term 'credite' in Camden cited above – 'glorie and credite' – as well as here has an obvious economic connotation and Stephen Greenblatt has explained the importance of naming to the capitalist enterprise:

> it is in the market place and in the state apparatus linked to the circulation and accumulation of capital that names themselves are forged. Proper names ... are bound up not only with the property one has in oneself, that is, with the theory of possessive individualism, but quite literally with the property one possesses, for proper names are insisted upon in the early modern period precisely in order to register them in the official documents that enable the state to calculate and tax personal property.[6]

This materialist rationale of designation is perfectly illustrated in Thomas Hobbes's insistence on the propriety of naming in order to facilitate accountancy: '*Subject to Names*, is whatsoever can enter into, or be considered in an account; and be added one to another to make a summe ... The Latins called Accounts of mony *Rationes*, and accounting, *Ratiocinatio*: and that which we in bills or books of account call *Items*, they called *Nomina*; that is *Names*.'[7] This economic function of naming sharpens the central dichotomy of the Renaissance debate: is language a convenient and conventionally shared approximation for meaning or does it possess 'positive terms' (a concept which Saussure devised and rejected as a possibility)? Is the name for something a token of its quintessence?

The debate is grounded in Plato's dialogue *Cratylus*, which records the argument between the eponymous speaker, who is convinced 'that there is a kind of inherent correctness in names', and the sceptical Hermogenes, who insists that 'no name belongs to any particular thing by nature but only by the habit and custom of those who employ it and who established the usage'.[8] In his insistance on Hermogenean arbitrariness, Montaigne follows François Rabelais whose Pantagruel pronounces: 'it is a mere abusing of our Understandings to give credit to the words of those, who say that there is any such thing as a Natural Language. All speeches have had their primary Origin from the Arbitrary Insitutions, Accords and Agreements of Nations in their respective Condescendments to what should be noted and betokened by them.'[9] Cratylic naming may thus be seen as the model for Camden, while in anticipation of the French post-structuralists, Rabelais and Montaigne advocate the Hermogenean position.

In spite of the objections of Rabelais and Montaigne, there are good reasons for supposing a widespread belief in the causal link between name and referent in the early modern period. Foucault's *The Order of Things* has characterised the era as one of analogy, as a period of history hankering after a world-view in which the universe was seen to be 'folded in upon itself'.[10] Language, writes Foucault, 'was an absolutely certain and transparent sign for things'. Yet, at the same time, Foucault recognises the sixteenth century as the period 'when resemblance was about to relinquish its relation with knowledge and disappear ... from the sphere of cognition'.[11] For the early moderns, this linguistic opacity could be traced back to man's first disobedience, as Roger Fenton explains:

> When *Adam* in Paradise did first giue names vnto things, they were so significant and expressiue, as if nature her selfe had spoken. But since the fall, a libertie remaining in the sons of *Adam* to terme things as it pleased them to conceiue, God likewise and his Angels vouchsafing to speake with the tongues of men, to the end that men might conceiue them: euer since, I say, names haue been no definitions.[12]

While Fenton's explanation of linguistic arbitrariness is sited firmly in theological certainty, Montaigne's playful scepticism may be taken as dramatising a characteristic modernity in relation to this ontological debate. Although they illustrate the common currency of the idea of an Adamic or pre-Babel language, one that was (to use Foucault's adjective) 'transparent', Montaigne's misgivings were not necessarily enough to persuade the Renaissance that such a transparent language was no longer a possibility. As C. L. Whitby wryly points out, 'The emphasis that Montaigne lays upon the separateness of name and thing argues the existence of a common belief in the opposite.'[13] Such common belief was frequently rooted in religious conviction, as well as the philosophical and epistemological assumptions of the period. In his section on 'Anagrammes', Camden demonstrates this semantic faith: 'names are divine notes, and divine notes do notifie future events; so that events consequently must lurke in names', and he goes on emphatically, 'each man's fortune is written in his name ... all things are written in heaven, if a man could read them'.[14] Camden's fanatical insistence on Cratylic naming, however, may well reveal his own doubts and even an underlying nostalgia for the certainties of the past, which informs his entire endeavour to document an idealised *Britannia*.[15] This paradox has been noted by Thomas Healy who points out that the Cratylic debate is symptomatic of an illogicality at the heart of the Humanist aspiration to transcend man's fallenness:

> Within a humanist perception of language ... was the ability to extend and supplement existing reality and to indicate a higher reality in a perfection phenomenally lost ... But by asserting the ability of language to create true fictions, this celebration of the power of language is also helping to de-centre language's supposed referential relation with the world of epistemological things.[16]

Given this fundamental paradox at the heart of meaning and its contiguity with issues of faith and transcendental signification, it is no surprise to find that the problem of naming was not simply the preserve of the philosopher or philologist.

II

As Anne Barton has demonstrated, in Renaissance theatre the naming of parts was influenced by dramatic practice from the allegorical traditions of medieval literature and morality plays. She suggests that the formulation of stock characters (as in New Comedy and *commedia dell'arte*) constrained the dramatists towards being user-friendly in the naming of their characters: the 'stock names of New Comedy ... constituted a code, helping the audience to find its way quickly into the situation and circumstances of the play'.[17] Barton goes on to ally Jonson with the Cratylic school of naming while she associates Shakespeare primarily with the Hermogenean position. In promoting such a dichotomy, however, there is a danger of being overschematic for, as I will show, Shakespearean naming is far from arbitrary.

Barton does acknowledge that some Shakespearean naming is Cratylic. In *Othello* for example, the names are carefully ascribed and connotatively rich.[18] Tragedy, it seems, is serious enough to warrant careful naming; as Barton notes, 'the names of tragic characters are almost always inseparable from their stories'.[19] She identifies several other plays such as *The Tempest*, *II Henry IV*, *Cymbeline*, *Pericles* and *Romeo and Juliet* which include significant names. To these we might add further plays in which naming is of particular importance, e.g. *Coriolanus* or *The Winter's Tale*.[20] Given the Shakespearean propensity to highlight names in the Roman plays, the histories, the tragedies and the romances, it would seem strange if the comedies did not display this appellative interest. However, Barton asserts that compared with the Cratylic tendencies of other dramatists, for Shakespeare the naming of characters 'is secondary'.[21] In this she follows in the tradition of G. Wilson Knight who argued that in comparison with the names of Marlovian and Miltonic characters, 'Shakespeare might at first appear rather dull. His exotic names ... do not stick out.'[22]

For Barton, Shakespeare's comedies are 'generically unlikely to favour Cratylic names' as the playwright was 'by temperament ... not only inclined to be careless when it came to naming parts, but wary of onomastic determinism'.[23] Indeed her reading of Shakespearean comedy leads her to the conclusion that 'by comparison with a nomenclature such as the one developed in the Italian improvised theatre of the mid-sixteenth century, Shakespeare's naming is fairly random'.[24]

Given that the debate around the significance of naming (as illustrated by Camden versus Rabelais and Montaigne cited above) was very much alive in the early modern period and that, as Barton herself admits, both tragedies and histories show an awareness of the issues at stake, it would be nothing less than anomalous if the same concerns were not found in the comedies. In fact, reconsideration of the *dramatis personae* in the light both of the Renaissance interest in naming and Shakespeare's other plays, yields a rich vein of names that *are* significant, even if their meaning is not immediately apparent. Although Shakespeare avoids labelling his characters in the allegorical manner of medieval dramatists, many of their names are connotatively redolent, especially in sexual or fecal ways. Harry Levin is less averse to recognising the dramatic device of 'speaking names' or, as he calls them, 'charactonyms'.[25] For Levin, 'the power of naming is intimately allied to the gift of characterization'.[26]

Bawdy names in Shakespearean drama have been noted by Helge Kökeritz, but he suggests that 'the group is very small' and deals only with *Pistol, Dr Caius, Quickly* and *Doll Tearsheet*.[27] Phallic names also include *Lance* and *Snout* (the captain of *commedia* often sported a long and penile nose).[28] *Falstaff* may itself be an inversion of such names – 'false staff' or 'fall staff' – implying the impotence contingent on excessive corpulence and Sir John's waning virility, the latter of which is dramatised for us in *II Henry IV* in which Falstaff's first lines foreground his physical decline, 'what says the doctor to my water?' (I.ii.1).

Female characters may also possess suggestive names: *Mistress Overdone, Doll Tearsheet, Mistress Quickly, Goneril, Jane Nightwork* and *Kate Keepdown*. Given the sexual connotations of the verb 'to do' in the early modern period, Overdone's nine husbands have plainly taken their toll on her.[29] *Tearsheet* suggests the rumbustious nature of its bearer's profession. *Quickly* is decoded by Kökeritz as 'quick lye' though this probably refers to the hostess in her youth since now, as Falstaff tells us, she is a kind of otter, neither fish not flesh since 'a man knows not where to have her' (*I*

Henry IV, III.iii.127). Wilson Knight uneasily draws attention to the gonorrhoeal connotations of the name of Lear's eldest-born: *Goneril* 'contains undertones of an unpleasant disease'.[30] Jane Nightwork's name has an obvious relevance to her hours of employ while the name of the prostitute, Kate Keepdown, is highly suggestive.[31]

Master Froth, who appears (with Kate) in *Measure for Measure* and is a frequent visitor to the stews, might suggest semen, though his name is also close to the contemporary word 'frote' which, in the dictionary published by Milton's nephew Edward Phillips, is defined as 'to rub'.[32] This is the early definition noted by the *OED*, though usually applied to animals (compare modern 'frottage' defined as the fetishistic rubbing of clothed bodies). The *OED* defines 'froth' as 'foaming saliva issuing from the mouth'. After the boar has gored Adonis it is described 'With frothy mouth, bepainted all with red, / Like milk and blood being mingled both together' (*Venus and Adonis*, ll. 901–2). The *OED* also notes that the term could be applied contemptuously to persons, as is the case when Pistol insults Slender, 'froth and scum, thou liest' (*The Merry Wives*, I.i.150). Other instances of the use of connotatively rich names might include the executioner in *Measure for Measure*, Abhorson, who is both abhorrent and a whoreson (if not simply an abortion), while in *Much Ado About Nothing*, Beatrice mischievously enquires after Benedick in a way which plainly sends up his pretensions as a lady's man by refering to him as 'Signor Montanto' (I.i.29).

Gobbo is most commonly decoded in connection with the Italian word for 'hunchback' although there is no indication whatever that the play requires either father or son to be played thus. Rather, I would suggest, the character is named in accordance with a Rabelaisian, gastral interest. The *OED* notes the OF *gobber*, 'to swallow' and Shylock refers to his servant as 'a huge feeder' (II.v.45). The word 'gob' as a slang for 'mouth' was current from the mid-sixteenth century and the character's preoccupation with dinner and cooking as well as his rapacious appetite would make this name coarsely appropriate. But *Gobbo* may warrant further examination in the light of the fecal possibilities that the term generates. The name appears in early editions variously as *Iobbe*, *Iobbo*, *Job*, and *Gobbo*. As the [dʒ] sound was represented graphically by the letter 'i', *Iobbo* may well have been pronounced ['dʒɔbo].[33] The slang expression for a stool, 'job', is of course widespread and may well lie behind Shakespeare's naming of Lancelot and his father.[34]

Another group of names refers to biliousness, to passing wind, either anally or orally. *Peto* implies 'fart' (compare modern French *péter*). Phillips defines *petard* as 'a kinde of Engine like a Mortar, wherewith strong gates are burst open in war'. In his poem 'An Execration upon Vulcan', Jonson links this explosive weaponry to 'the Divels-Arse' (ll. 201–7).[35] Phillip's following entry in the dictionary is a definition of the word *petarrade* which is particularly flatulent, 'a gun-shot of farting, a jerking out of a horse behind, commonly accompanied with farting'. In his *Remaines*, Camden cites an example of the extraordinary literalness of the name:

> *Baldwin le Pettour*, who had his name, and held his land in Suffolke, *Per saltum, sufflum & pettum, sive bumbulum*, for dauncing, pout-puffing, and dooing that before the King of England in Christmasse holy dayes, which the worde *Pet* signifieth in French. Inquire if you understand it not of *Cloacinas* chaplaines, or such as are well read in *Ajax*.[36]

John Florio's *Queen Anna's New World of Words* (1611) gets quite carried away with the Italian expressions for anal eruption:

> Pettare, *to fart, to crackle, to rattle.*
> Pettaro, *a farter, a cracker, a ratler.*
> Pettaruolo, *as* Petardo. *Also a farter.*
> Petteggiare, *to fart or blurt at.*
> ...
> Petti, *all manner of fartes.*[37]

In the light of this obsessive definition, the connotations of Shakespeare's *Peto* are unmistakable.

Dogberry is a similarly windy name and may have suggested 'dog fart'. The *OED* notes the meaning of 'berry' as 'a gust or blast of wind'. This rare use is found uniquely at the turn of the sixteenth century. (The *OED* cites only three examples: one from 1598, significantly the year of the first performance of *Much Ado*, and two from 1611.)[38] *Belch* is another eructive name as illustrated by Toby's characteristically vulgar performance. As he swaggers on drunkenly to inform Olivia of the arrival of the young Cesario, he attempts to disguise his excessive drinking by blaming his wind on indigestion: "'Tis a gentleman here. (*He belches*) A plague o'these pickle herring!' (I.v.116–17)[39]

Nick (also known as Bully) Bottom (*A Midsummer Night's Dream*) and Pompey Bum (*Measure for Measure*) have surnames that foreground unashamedly Shakespeare's ribald sense of humour. Yet in the case of these names, their apparent unsubtlety ought to alert us to their potential complexity. In fact, 'bottom' is defined by Phillips as 'a blossom or bud'. Thus this apparently vulgar name paradoxically makes explicit the affinity between Nick the weaver and the fairy band that includes the fragile Peaseblossom and Mustardseed. The name is, in this sense, a secret talisman which allows its bearer to enter the supernatural world.[40] It is worth noting that this magical overtone is lost on a modern reader and thus the irony of the name (which is simultaneously delicate and gross) is lost as well. Wilson Knight, for example, misses this subtlety when he remarks that Bottom's name is appropriate because 'He is a stupid, earthy man'.[41] Bottom, whilst being the most coarse of the rude mechanicals, is also the only human being in the play to converse and indeed couple with a faerie queene and yet his appearance and his name imply that he is both an ass and an arse.

Pompey's surname is double-edged in the same kind of way. Escalus relishes the ironic distance between the lofty status of the classical name and the sordidness of the pimp in the dock in front of him:

ESCALUS	What's your name, Master Tapster?
POMPEY	Pompey.
ESCALUS	What else?
POMPEY	Bum, sir.
ESCALUS	Troth, and your bum is the greatest thing about you; so that, in the beastliest sense, you are Pompey the Great.

(II.i.203–9)

The comic effect of Pompey's bald response ('Bum, sir') and the healthy disrespect for authority that it implies, is enough to evoke audience sympathy on his behalf, while the arrogant superiority of Escalus's classical joke often serves, in production, to alienate him from the audience. In this way, Shakespeare demonstrates the remoteness of the ruling classes from the world of the ordinary Viennese with whom we sympathise throughout the play and with whom we find ourselves allied in this instance. We are plainly on Pompey's side during this trial, and his acquittal, which is the combined result of Elbow's incompetence and Escalus's rather patronising indulgence, comes as an obvious relief. In his essay 'Of Names', Montaigne foregrounds the arbitrariness of naming by focusing on the unsuitability of this very name for a member of the lower classes, 'Who letteth my horse boy to call himselfe Pompey the great?'[42] The answer is obviously 'no-one' despite the fact that Escalus implies that such a name will inevitably be soiled as a direct result of its association with a brothel-keeper. Shakespeare repeatedly illustrates a fondness for juxtaposing grandiloquent names with daft low-life characters – Costard intro- duces himself near the end of *Love's Labour's Lost* thus, 'I Pompey am, Pompey surnamed the Big' (V.ii.544) – and it is tempting though inaccurate, to suggest that Shakespeare's tendency to associate names of low-born characters with sexual and fecal puns is symptomatic of his disdain for them.

Shakespeare's reactionary politics are commonly deduced from the attitudes to the mob expressed in such plays as *Julius Caesar* and *Coriolanus*. However, such an argument is in danger of over- simplification. To begin with, the contempt for the plebians, expressed by Casca and Coriolanus, is not necessarily that of the playwright and indeed both of these characters, though noble, are shown to be arrogant and cynical in various places. Of greater relevance to the issue of apparently significant naming, though, is the change in sensibility or social attitude which makes Renaissance views of physicality and their linguistic expression seem strangely casual to a modern audience. Writing of late Middle English, Percy Hide Reaney notes the correlation between linguistic register and social existence:

> The language of the time was much less inhibited than that of today and much that we regard as indecent or obscene was to them

normal and natural. In an age when sanitation was non-existent the normal functions of the body and its various parts were referred to openly and without shame by their ordinary everyday terms, no watering down from water-closet to W.C. and then to lavatory, and finally to toilet ... The actual day-to-day talk of the populace was undoubtedly less restrained than that of the poets as is clearly proved by the nicknames bestowed on friends and enemies alike.[43]

Among the nicknames that Reaney cites are the authentic Godwin Clawecuncte, John Prickehard, John Fillecunt, Richard Scittbagge, Robert Clevecunt, Ernald Pokestrong, John Strokelady and Roger Louestycke. He also ventures that, paradoxically, while 'Shitface' was 'strangely enough complimentary ... Shitpot [was] an aggressive nickname, expressive of dislike and contempt'.[44] While Reaney's list of names is predominantly sexual, Susan Signe Morrison's is entirely scatological: Rogero Drittecarle, John Drytecarle, Rob. atte Tordehelle, Augnes..uxor Walteri Muk, Thomas Turd and Thomas le Gangfurmer. 'In these cases the ... people are metonymically associated with something to do with muck, dung, dirt, or turds.'[45]

Norman Longmate has suggested that 'the sanitary idea' resulted from the cholera epidemic of the nineteenth century which led to the First Public Health Act of 1848 and an entirely new emphasis on hygiene, wash-houses and public sanitation.[46] The nineteenth-century association between sewage and mortal disease may, to some extent, account for the prudishness concerning lavatorial matters that is part of our Victorian legacy. To impose post-Victorian attitudes on Renaissance texts, however, can lead to serious misinterpretations and the assumption that scatological naming is necessarily insulting or distasteful reveals more about twenty-first-century mores than about Shakespeare's.

In the period when the writer's plays were being performed for the first time, the sight and the smell of excrement were part of the London landscape. Southwark was crossed with open rain ditches through which raw sewage flowed into the Thames.[47] John Stow's *A Survey of London* (1603) provides a vivid contemporary account:

In the yeare 1589. was graunted a fifteene, by a common Councell of the citie, for the cleansing of this Brooke or dike: the money amounting to a thousand markes was collected, and it was undertaken, that by drawing diverse springes about Hampsted heath, into one head & course, both the citie should bee served of fresh water in all places of want, and also that by such a follower as men call it, the channell of this brooke should bee scowred into the river of Thames, but much mony being therein spent, ye effect fayled, so that the Brooke by meanes of continuall incrochments upon the banks getting over the water, and casting of soylage into the streame, is now become woorse cloyed and [choken] than ever it was before.[48]

The disposal of sewage and refuse was a serious urban difficulty throughout the period and in 1628 the king, disgusted by the quantities of filth lying about the streets, ordered a complete repair of the pavements. The problem persisted at least until the eighteenth century (as Chapters 5 and 6 will demonstrate). Not until 1762 was the Westminster Paving Act passed.[49]

Peter Ackroyd has noted that this appalling state of the capital had been an ongoing problem since the reign of Henry III (1216–72):

In the pleas and memoranda of the Guildhall, for example, we read of the master of Ludgate putting dung into the Fleet to such an extent that the water was stopped in certain places; a common privy is 'diffectif' and 'the ordur therof rotith the stone wallys'. The taverners of St Bride's parish put their empty barrels, and slops, into the street 'to nusauns of all folk ther passyng'. There were complaints about defective paving in Hosier Lane, while in Foster Lane the fourteen households had the habit of casting from their windows 'ordure & vrine, the which annoyet alle the pepol of the warde'. The cooks of Bread Street were indicted for keeping 'dung and garbage' under their stalls, while a great stream of 'dong and water and other diverse filth' was known to pour down Trinity Lane and Cordwainer Street by Garlickhithe Street, and descend between the shops of John Hatherle and Richard Whitman before discharging itself into the Thames. A dung-hill in Watergate Street beside Bear Lane 'is noyowse to all the commune people, kasting out in-to this lane ordour of Prevees and other orrible sightis'.[50]

But such noisome risks to public health carried on for hundreds of years. In 1531 the Statute of Sewers was formulated to combat 'the outrageous Flowings, Surges and Course' of water and waste in London. Authority was granted 'to tax, assess, charge, distrain and punish' those liable for the upkeep of sewers and drains.[51] In the context of such living conditions and ignorance of the health risks, it is less surprising to discover a very different attitude to fecal language from that of our highly sanitised era.

Today's reader might be struck by the strangeness of the King's Men playing scripts that involve scurrility, but ought at the same time to note the production of royal entertainments such as Jonson's *Pleasure Reconciled To Virtue* of 1618 in which Comus the belly god and 'father of farts' enters in a state of thoroughly flatulent drunkenness, or *The Alchemist* (1610) which we know to have been first performed by 'the King's Majesty's Servants' with its bold opening line, 'Thy worst. I fart at thee'.[52] Thomas Nabbes's *Microcosmus. A Morall Maske* (1637) contains an account of the duties of the character, Smelling, which is hardly delicate:

> I am my Ladies Huntsmant and keepe some lesser beagles for her chamber-use to excuse the freenesse of her necessities eruptions. I play the Gardner likewise, and attend her alwaies when shee goes to pluck a Rose. My Mistresse *Cloaca* had a very stinking breath, before Misackmos perfum'd her, and she is now growne lesse common, then when her imperfections lay open.[53]

The gardener's euphemism is explained by the OED which defines 'plucking a rose' as 'of women, to visit the lavatory, to urinate or defecate', and it notes the earliest printed instance as Beaumont and Fletcher's *Knight of the Burning Pestle*. Though later, Robert Herrick's epigram 'Upon Umber' is an example of the way in which serious questions of mimesis and representation could be raised by delightfully ribald verse:

> Umber was painting of a lion fierce,
> And, working it, by chance from Umber's erse
> Flew out a crack so mighty that the fart
> (As Umber swears) did make his lion start.[54]

Henry Parrot's short poem tells of the embarrassment caused by a wooer's *faux pas*:

> As young *Renaldo* stood diuising best
> To please his Lady with some pretty tale,
> (Whose setled contenance thereto addrest
> And bashfull blushing did him then appale)
> He therewith coughing, chanc'd to let a fart
> Which euer since hath dasht him out of hart.[55]

Next to entertainments like these, Shakespeare's scripts seem positively tame.[56]

A further important counter-argument to the suggestion that Shakespeare named his low-life characters with lurid contempt, is the presence of characters of senior social status who, nevertheless, are named in accordance with this brazen sense of humour: Falstaff and Belch are both knights (albeit somewhat coarse examples of the species) and in *Henry V* the French generals include one Jaques Châtillion (III.v.43). Both Christian and surnames here have scatological overtones (for Jaques see below).[57]

The common characteristic of most examples of Shakespearean onomastic bawdy is their localised essence. The lewdness is often confined to a mere quip or indecency. Even when a character's name is rude, it is foregrounded for a short period only (as with the Pompey Bum example above). The joke is often explicit and usually contained. The most obvious exception to this tendency and the most sustained example of Shakespearean onomastic scatology is the name *Jaques* in *As You Like It* – 'jakes' (as is usually noted and rapidly passed over) was the Renaissance term for toilet. Shakespeare uses the word 'jakes' unequivocally to mean 'privy' in *King Lear*. When Kent loses his temper with Oswald, he threatens to tread the steward 'into mortar and daub the wall of a jakes with him' (II.ii.65). The term also appears less obviously towards the end of *Love's Labour's Lost* in the masque of the Nine Worthies where Nathaniel performs the role of Alexander the Great.

NATHANIEL	When in the world I lived I was the world's
(*as Alexander*)	commander.
	By east, west, north, and south, I spred my
	conquering might.
	My scutcheon plain declares that I am Alisander.
BOYET	Your nose says no, you are not, for it stands too
	right.
BIRON	Your nose smells 'no' in this, most tender-
(*to Boyet*)	smelling knight.
PRINCESS	The conqueror is dismayed. Proceed, good
	Alexander.
NATHANIEL	When in the world I lived I was the world's
(*as Alexander*)	commander.
BOYET	Most true, 'tis right, you were so, Alisander.
BIRON	Pompey the Great!
(*to Costard*)	
COSTARD	Your servant, and Costard.
BIRON	Take away the conqueror, take away Alisander.
COSTARD	O, sir, you have overthrown Alisander the
(*to Nathaniel*)	Conqueror. You will be scraped out of the
	painted cloth for this. Your lion that holds his
	pole-axe sitting on a close-stool will be given to
	Ajax. He will be the ninth Worthy. A conqueror
	and afeard to speak? Run away for shame,
	Alisander.

(V.ii.556–74)

This passage, like that of 'Pyramus and Thisbe' towards the end of *A Midsummer Night's Dream*, frames the well-intentioned and incompetent dramatic performance of the social inferiors within the contemptuous reactions of their superior audience. The jokes in this instance, with which Boyet and Biron interrupt the Masque of Worthies, highlight not only the physical disparity between Alexander and the actor representing him (Nathaniel's nose 'stands too right', i.e. his head is carried too straight to resemble that of the great warrior) but also the odorous difference between them. Alexander's skin, in the words of North's *Plutarch*, 'had a marvellous good savor, and ... his breath was very swete, insomuch that his body had so swete a smell of it selfe, that all the apparell he wore next unto his body, tooke thereof a passing delightfull savor, as if it had bene perfumed'.[58] Boyet's nose, as Biron quips, senses the fetid presence of Nathaniel and again disqualifies the actor from rendering a convincing performance of Alexander.[59] Costard's aspersion at the end of this section is enigmatic for a modern reader: 'Your lion, that holds his pole-axe sitting on a close-stool, will be given to Ajax.' In the middle ages, Alexander's coat of arms was taken to be a lion sitting on a chair, holding a battleaxe. The chair has been transformed here into a close-stool or commode while the coat of arms itself is proffered to a jakes.[60] Alexander's coat of arms is being presented to the privy and this joke is especially appropriate given Boyet's earlier observations on the reeking Nathaniel.

Shakespeare was evidently fond of this lavatorial pun. In *Troilus and Cressida*, Ajax rails at Thersites, calling him a 'stool for a witch' (II.i.43), that is, a low thing but also a close-stool or privy. Thersites retaliates by calling Ajax a 'thing of no bowels' (l. 50). Their vituperative anality is facilitated by the pun on Ajax's name. Later, Thersites remarks that, in anticipation of his fight with Hector, 'Ajax goes up and down the field, asking for himself' (III.iii.237) – that is, for a jakes or privy. In modern parlance, we might say that the Greek, for fear, is 'shitting himself'.

III

Love's Labour's Lost was probably written around 1594 and *Troilus* around 1602. Between the composition of these two plays, Sir John Harington utilised this common pun when, in 1596, he published his treatise on the flushing toilet entitled, *A Nevv Discovrse of a Stale Svbiect, Called The Metamorphosis of Aiax*.[61] The text is, in part, an enlightening work on sanitary plumbing; indeed, Harington suggests that a water closet could not 'but do her Majestie good service in her pallace of Greenwitch & other stately houses, that are oft annoyed with such savours, as where many mouthes be fed can hardly be avoided'.[62] The second section of the book, probably written and certainly illustrated by Thomas Combe (Harington's manservant), contains building plans with technical drawings as well as further advice.[63] For example, Harington notes that, 'If water be plentie, the oftner it [the W.C.]

is used and opened, the sweeter; but if it be scant, once a day is inough, for a need, though twentie persons should use it.'[64] While, by modern standards, this might sound pretty grim, Jonathan Kinghorn, who built Harington's toilet in the Gladstone Pottery Museum in 1981, according to the original plans, insists that 'The reconstruction of Harrington's [sic] design was, contrary to the belief of some, a very efficient and practical one.'[65]

As well as being an engineering manual about the construction of the toilet, the book is also an amusing exploration into what has become a forbidden subject. *The Metamorphosis* is a witty, ribald work with remarks about 'gongfarmers' with their 'beastly cart, laden with excrements',[66] those who forget the post-excretory rituals ('they that omit, their lawndresses shall finde it done in their linnen'[67]), and jokes about haemorrhoids.[68] At one point, Harington recounts the origins of the Caesarian proclamation allowing flatulence:

> This Claudius I say ... for his curtesie was greatly to be commended: for a Gentleman one day being talking with him, and falling suddenly into a grievous fit of the cholicke, the poore Gentleman would not for good maners sake breake wind, which might presently have eased him, and after the disease increased so sore on him that he died. The Emperour enformed of his death, was much grieved thereat, specially hearing of the cause, and immediatly thereupon made it be solemnly proclaimed, that if any man herafter should be troubled with the cholicke, it should not be taken for ill maners to break wind, though it were in the Emperours owne company.[69]

In places the book is erudite and allusive, in others it has a crude suggestive irony, while in yet others, it deals with 'in plaine English[,] a shyting place'.[70] Indeed towards the end, the book blesses its reader, 'God send you manie a good stoole.'[71]

But as well as its amusing and scatological content, Harington's work may have a further and more pressing concern. Indeed Rick Bowers has gone so far as to claim that Harington, lurking at the edge of power, is utilising toiletry engineering to address what he considered to be the corruptions of the Elizabethan State: 'His dominant satirical metaphor is *to clean things up*, to subdue the stench, to provide disclosure however uncomfortable or shaming.'[72] For Jason Scott-Warren it was precisely Harington's marginal position that provided this vantage point: 'The failure of so many of his bids for preferment only intensifies the sense in which he was a courtier, a privileged hanger-on, permanently "without portfolio".'[73] There is, insists Bowers, a deliberate inversion to Harington's satire through which the world of high politics is examined in the lowest setting of the privy: 'Harington constantly asserts ironic disjunctions and irreverent wordplay in service of a dominant democratizing metaphor of reversal – high is low, low is high; toilets are as important as politics; politics is in the toilet. It's time to clean up government.'[74] Sophie Gee also insists upon the ideological aims of Harington's satire: 'The subtext of *The Metamorphosis* was that the offical disposal of excrement was an allegory for England's social and political hygiene too.'[75] Will Stockton, too, is convinced by the earnestness of Harington's undertaking: '*The Metamorphosis of Ajax* stems from Harington's quite serious attempts at linguistic and social reform.'[76]

For our purposes, however, the book is important because of the playful onomastics of its title and its popularity. At the outset of *The Metamorphosis*, Harington illustrates the prevalence of the confusion between Jaques and jakes:

> There was a very tall & serviceable gentleman, somtime Lieutenant of the ordinance, called M. *Jaques Wingfield*; who coming one day, either of businesse, or of kindnesse, to visit a great Ladie in the Court; the Ladie bad her Gentlewoman aske, which of the *Wingfields* it was; he told her *Jaques Wingfield*: the modest gentlewoman, that was not so well seene in the French, to know that *Jaques*, was but *James* in English, was so bashfoole, that to mend the matter (as she thought) she brought her Ladie word, not without blushing, that it was M. *Privie Wingfield*; at which, I suppose the Lady then, I am sure the Gentleman after, as long as he lived, was wont to make great sport.[77]

This instance emphasises the ambiguity of the name and plays with the Cratylic debate, since the meaning of *Jaques* depends upon the speaker rather than any inherent or fixed definition. Indeed the whole book with its pseudo-classical title resembles the device in Shakespeare according to which unheroic characters (or

in this case a subject) are named after classically elevated heroes,
as was demonstrated above in the case of Pompey Bum. The
appearance of the 'Ajax/a jakes' pun in *Love's Labour's Lost* and
Troilus and the 'Jaques/jakes' pun here suggests the ubiquity of
the slang term and the alternative meanings and the range of
possible quibbles which surrounded it. John Davies, whose *Wits
Bedlam* contains a number of poems lauding Harington, offers us
another instance of the pun in an epigram '*On one called* Iaques':
'Fie out vp on't spue, spit, and cough; / A *Iakes* here lieth: Mary,
fough!' And later in the same collection, Davies uses the term
again in his epigram '*On one* Loue *a Gold-finder alias a Iakes-
Farmer*':

> If yee can smell,
> Then draw ye neere:
> And you'l soone tell
> Who lyeth heere.[78]

   The Metamorphosis of Aiax was extremely popular. In the year
of its publication it went through no fewer than four editions. The
anonymous reply, *Vlysses vpon Aiax*, went though two editions,
both in 1596. This latter text is often erroneously attributed to
Harington himself, though his authorship is unlikely since *Vlysses*
attacks *The Metamorphosis* on the grounds of its indecency: 'your
pen hath dropt excrements, and you cannot wipe them cleane
with your witte.'[79] Moreover, Davies's *Wits Bedlam* includes an
epigram which argues that Harington's wit is far in excess of
Vlysses' and this would seem to offer a powerful case against
Harington's authorship of the reply.

> I Dare not say your Wit was wisedome pointed,
> When you in *Aiax* had your Wit annoynted:
> Sith by no small Fooles, yet accompted wise,
> Such 'straines of Wit are held but Fooleries:
> But, this I say, and say what well I wot,
> *Vlisses* vpon *Aiax* plaid the Sot:
> For, what you put in *Aiax*, was more woorth,
> By odds, than what *Vlisses* then put forth.[80]

Another epigram, this time in Thomas Bastard's *Chrestoleros*, seems again to distinguish, via Homeric parody, between the intelligent authorship of *The Metamorphosis* and that of *Vlysses*:

> *Vlysses* hauing scapt the ocean floood. [*sic*]
> Twise ten yeares pilgrimage in foreyn landes.
> And the sweete deathes of *Syrens* tunde with blood,
> And *Cyclops* iawes, and *Circes* charming handes:
> Comes home, and seeming safe, (as he mistakes)
> He steps awrie, and fals in to *Aiax*.[81]

Whether or not Harington wrote the reply, *Vlysses* is full of the same kind of fecal humour for which it attacks *The Metamorphosis*. It offers us yet another instance of the 'Ajax/a jakes' pun. Citing the story of Iubile in France who was jostled around by some pages 'and suspecting Treason among them; sodainelie layde that you wot of in his britches, enough I warrant you to feast Aiax for one meale if he were a hungrie'.[82] Despite its declared aim, to criticise *The Metamorphosis*, it relishes the scatological – here, by citing a piquant instance of after-dinner repartee:

> Nicke *Beomond* (a wittie and pleasaunt gallant) being one day inuited to a rich gentlemans table, who tooke delight to heare himselfe speake, perceiuing manie matters begunne by him, and no man suffered to answere, at last (with a knocke or a hem to make the thing mannerlie) he let me a rounde cracke that was hearde throughout the companie, which the host stomaking and the rest merelie laughing at, tut tut saide he (to the gentleman) you must not be angerie, for if you will not heare vs at one ende you shall not chuse but both heare and smell vs at the other.[83]

In places *Vlysses* pretends to engage with the technical description of the toilet offered in *The Metamorphosis*, and to criticise it. Citing the following anecdote, it points out the potential hazard of omitting 'glasse windowes' from the privy. A certain gentleman who goes with 'his quiuer well furnished to offer on *Cloacinds* Alter', while sitting there, is interrupted by his maid who enters and, because she cannot see him, 'lets flie into her maisters lap at both endes, and sette both her winde-mill and water-mill a working. Out whore (quoth the Mayster) Alas, fie vpon me (quoth

the maid) new clothes cries he with a vengeance, away runnes she
bare arst without wiping.'[84]

Towards the end of the book, the author begins seriously and in
a sustained way to criticise Harington for the indecency of his
treatise. But on the penultimate page, he shows himself just
unable, as he confesses, to resist another funny story:

> But euen here in shutting vp of my letter, a merry iest incounters
> me, which I must needs tel you, Henry the 8, in his youth, a prince
> of famous memorie, riding a hunting in grasse time with certain
> nobles and familiars, by chance made toward a gentlemans parke
> of good estimation and reckoning whom he highly fauored; where
> (finding the parke gate lockt, and being very desirous to enter), he
> set his horne to his mouth, and merrily winded it to call the Keeper.
> Sir Andrew Flamocke (a valiant and quicke witted gentleman)
> standing hard behinde him (and that very instant troubled with
> the chollicke) euen at the very time the King drewe his horne from
> his mouth lets me flie a rouncing F. from his T. The King looking
> backe, and angerly asking who it was that durst be so beastly in his
> presence? Sir Andrew (after a long congee) made this answer: If it
> please your Maiestie, you blew for the Keeper, and I blew for Iohn
> the Keepers man.[85]

Vlysses goes on perfunctorily to moralise this anecdote by committing the kingly blast to those readers 'that kindely interpret,
courteously accept & friendly protect my pleasures', while to the
rest, 'I commit the filth, worse than Sir Andrew Flamoks fart, to
their digesting'.[86]

It was not only Vlysses who responded to *The Metamorphosis*.
Other writers showed that they were well aware of its existence
and substance. Thomas Nashe relished the scandalous nature of
this vile tract. In a letter to William Cotton (not earlier than
August 1596) he refers *The Metamorphosis* with histrionic
contempt:

> m[r] Harrington [of] late hath sett vp sutch filthy stinking iakes in
> pouls [ch]urchyard, that the stationers wold give any mony for a
> couer [fo]r it. what shold moue him to it I know not, except he
> [m]eant to bid a turd in all gentle readers teeth ... O it is detestable
> and abhominable, farre worse then ... Gillian a Braynfords [Wi]ll
> in which she bequeathed a score of farts amõgst her frends [&] able

to make any man haue a stinking breath that lookes [b]ut on the outside of it. . . . For my parte I pitty him & pray for him that he may haue many good stooles to his last ending, & so I wold wish all his frends to pray, for otherwise it is to be feared . . . he will dy with a turd in his mouth at his last gaspe & bee coffind vp in a iakes farmer tunne no otherwise nosewise christian, for his horrible *p*fume being able to come nere him.[87]

Incidentally, 'Gillian a Braynford' in the poetic version by Robert Copland ('Iyl of Brainfords Testament' written about 1535) actually bequeathed twenty-six and a half farts to, among others, the profligate, the rude, the impotent, the envious, the vain, promiscuous widows ('though mine ars ake', l. 110) as well as, more bizarrely, those that arrive at a dinner party without cutlery and the overly generous but, entirely properly, to those that avoid buying their round at the bar.[88] The odd half a fart comes about as she allows the Curate who is taking down her will a fart and a half in payment (l. 234). It is worth noting that Gillian had something of an unfortunate reputation. Vlysses condemns Rabelais (whom Harington cites as one of the influences of *The Metamorphosis*) by noting that he is 'a condempned Athiest [and the author of] some course fictions (as filthy as Iyllyan of *Braindfords* fartes)'.[89] There is a clear reference to 'the old woman of Brentford' (the disguised Falstaff) in *The Merry Wives* though her flatulance is not mentioned (IV.ii.77). When the great Victorian editor and literary scholar, Fredrick J. Furnivall, edited the poem in 1871 his foreword makes it clear that he had thought to reprint both *Jyl* and *The Wyll of the Deuyll*:

but had since thought of withdrawing in order to avoid possible annoyance to the [Early English Text] Society from any cantankerous puritan like the one who bothered me about the Percy-Folio Loose and Humorous Songs. Both tracts are of value as illustrating the manners and tone of the classes they treat of in Tudor days . . . None of us students of English antiquity are beasts or fools enough to want to possess such tracts because they contain a few coarse words; we want the whole of the getable evidence, whatever it may be, on the social condition of Tudor England, on our shelves, so that we may judge of it for ourselves.[90]

While Furnivall's edition was 'Printed for Private Circulation' and so testifies to Victorian prudishness, Nashe's disdain for *The Metamorphosis* in the letter to Cotton is clearly affected as, in the year of its publication, his *Haue with you to Saffron-walden* uses the term in its insulting description of the Harvey brothers as 'the most contemptible *Mounsier Aiaxes* of excrementall conceipts and stinking kennel-rakt vp inuention that this or anie Age euer afforded'.[91] Moreover, *Saffron-walden* contains a cartoon entitled '*The picture of Gabriell Haruey, as hee is readie to let fly vpon* Aiax' (see Illustration 2) with a figure delving into the back of his hose.[92] Despite the vehemence of Nashe's condemnation in the letter to Cotton, he clearly admired *The Metamorphosis*. In his 'The Prayse of The Red Herring', published in *Nashes Lenten Stvffe* (1599), he lauds the book, noting that Harington 'offers sacrifice to the goddesse *Cloaca*, and disportes himselfe very schollerly and

2 *The Picture of Gabriell Haruey, as hee is readie to let fly vpon* Aiax from Thomas Nashe, *Haue with you to Saffron-walden* (1596).

wittilie about the reformation of close stooles and houses of office, and spicing and embalming their rancke intrailes, that they stincke not'.[93] But such newfangled engineering did not meet with universal approval and Tommaso Garzoni regarded the construction of such edifices as the preserve of a growing number of eccentrics:

> Whoever saw so many od Mechanicks, as are at this day, who not with a geometrical spirite like *Archimedes*, but euen with arte, surpassing the profoundest Cabalistes, who instead of a pigeon loft, place in the garrets of houses, portable, and commodious Aiaxes, in stead of convenient fish ponds?[94]

But half a century later the idea seems to have caught on. John Cotgrave talks of 'the glorious *Aiax* of *Lincolns Inne* I saw in *London* [which] laps up naught but filth And excrements'.[95] For Henry Hutton, however, both apparatus and, more significantly, its having been written up, cause offence. He prescribes a fitting purpose for this toiletry book. Of he that 'pen[ned] a pithie tractate of *A-iax*', Hutton writes:

> I wish he would reserue A-iax in minde,
> 'Twill serue but for A-iax and come behinde:
> For men adiudge the volumes of this foole,
> Worthie no chayre, scarce to deserue the stoole.[96]

John Davies, on the other hand, is lavish in his praise of the volume. In his 'Papers Complaint, compild in ruthfull Rimes Against the Paper-spoylers of these Times', the voice of the poem is a piece of paper defiled by the work of writers and poets. The paper is careful to distinguish however, between the epic magnificence of *The Metamorphosis* and the ignorance of those whose opprobrium it aroused:

> An other comes with Wit, too costiue then,
> Making a Glister-pipe of his rare Pen:
> And through the same he all my Brest becackes,
> And turnes me so, to nothing but *Aiax*.
> Yet *Aiax* (I confesse) was too supreme
> For Subiect of my-his wit royalld *Reame*,
> Exposed to the rancor of the rude,

> And wasted by the witlesse Multitude.
> He so adorned me that I shall nere
> More right, for kinde, then in his Robes appeare.
> Whose Lines shall circumscribe vncompast *Times*:
> And, past the wheeling of the Spheares, his Rimes
> Shall runne (as right) to immortallity,
> And praisd (as proper) of Posterity.[97]

Jonson seems also to have been hospitable to *The Metamorphosis*. In his mock-heroic poem 'On the Famous Voyage', which deals with the subject of the appalling sanitary conditions in London, he gestures towards the classical epics while implicitly referring to Harington's book, 'My *Muse* had plough'd with his, that sung A-iax' (l. 196).[98] In *Epicœne*, La Foole asks Truewit to bring him 'a cold venison pasty, a bottle or two of wine and a chamber pot'. Truewit replies, 'A stool were better, sir, of Sir A-jax his invention.'[99] John Marston too seems to have been aware of the book. In *The Scourge of Villainye* (published two years after *The Metamorphosis*), he mentions the 'nastie lothsome brothell rime, / That stincks like *Aiax* froth, or muck-pit slime'.[100] John Day's play, *The Ile of Gvls*, refers to *The Metamorphosis* in such a casual way as to suggest that its audience would have been familiar with the volume:

> *Enter Demetrias a Prince, attyred like a wood-man, with him his Page*
> DEME Boy, how doost like me in this attyre?
> PAGE As the audience doe a bad play, scuruely.
> DEM Is it not strange a prince should be thus metamorphosed?
> PAGE Not so strange as the metamorphosis of *Aiax* and like your
>   grace.[101]

The fact that the allusion appears without elaboration as late as the play's 1633 edition is testament to the notoriety of Harington's work. In 1620, nearly a quarter of a century after the publication of *The Metamorphosis*, John Taylor applauds it in his *The Praise of Hemp-seed*:

> *A learned Knight, of much esteeme and worth,*
> *A pamphlet of a* Privy *did set forth,*
> *Which strong breath'd* Aiax *was well lik'd, because*
> *Twas writ with wit and did deserue applause.*[102]

Cyrus Day has suggested that the phrase 'Pills to Purge Melancholy' – a popular title for comic anthologies of the late seventeenth and early eighteenth centuries – was itself derived from the preface of *The Metamorphosis*.[103] The popularity of *The Metamorphosis* was anticipated by Harington himself who accounted for it as follows:

> If I had entituled the booke, *A Sermon shewing a soveraigne salve for the sores of the soule. Or, A wholsome haven of health to harbour the heart in. Or, A marvellous medicine for the maladies of the minde.* would you ever have asked after such a booke? would these grave and sober titles have wonne you to the view of three or foure tittles? much lesse three or foure score periodes. But when you heard there was one had written of A Jax, straight you had a mind to see what strange discourse it would prove, you made enquirie who wrote it, where it might be had, when it wold come forth. You prayed your friend to buy it, beg it, borow it, that you might see what good stuffe was in it. And why had you such a mind to it? I can tell you; you hoped for some meriments, some toyes, some scurrilitie, or to speake plaine English, some knaverie. and if you did so, I hope now your expectation is not altogether frustrate.[104]

In giving his book a title which employs a much-used dirty joke, Harington shows himself to be a shrewd marketing man.

IV

The popularity of *The Metamorphosis of Aiax* and the widespread use of the pun make the name *Jaques* in *As You Like It* (written only four years after the publication of Harington's text) inevitably a *double entendre*. The idea of Shakespeare's most pronounced introspective, bar one, being named after a popular slang term for a toilet is likely to cause offence to those who see Shakespeare as the high-poet-priest of the psyche. Yet, connotative naming is, as we have seen, often an economic way for the playwright to communicate a character's essence to the audience prior to speech. Modern audiences are usually quite happy to accept that Belch should be played as a bumbling and windy old sot, but the entry of Jaques onto the Elizabethan stage would have aroused a similar kind of expectation.[105] Indeed Murray J. Levith goes so far as to suggest that the olfactory connotations of the name might also influence the reception of Jaques's female equivalent: 'Jaquenetta, the damsel in *Love's Labor's Lost*, has a name which is a French feminine diminutive of "Jaques," and perhaps is meant to contain a reference to the smell of the country wench.'[106] Be that as it may, it is certainly the case that the by now well-established dramatic romanticisation of Jaques is, in part, the result of a squeamishness surrounding his name: 'Nineteenth-century players seem to have popularized the pronunciation Jakewiss or Jakeweez, because they and their audiences were all too conscious of the meaning of jakes.'[107]

A valuable clue in deciphering the peculiar motivation of Shakespeare in naming his solipsistic intellectual after a toilet may lie in the fact that Jaques is a melancholic.[108] On two occasions he is the 'melancholy Jaques' (II.i.26 and 41) and elsewhere Amiens warns him not to overdose on music, for 'It will make you melancholy, Monsieur Jaques' (II.v.10). Orlando renames him according to his most pronounced characteristic: 'Adieu, good Monsieur Melancholy' (III.ii.287). Melancholia, as Harington himself was well aware, was a problem of indigestion or constipation. In his *The Englishmans Doctor* (the first English translation of the important *School of Salernum*), he notes that as well as a humming of the left ear, thin urine and hallucinations, the symptoms of melancholia include 'bitter belches from the stomacke coming'.[109] It is no accident that the alternative titles that Harington could have given his toiletry book are to do with the mental health of its readers: '*A Sermon shewing a soveraigne salve for the sores of the soule.*, *A wholsome haven of health to harbour the heart in.* or *A marvellous medicine for the maladies of the minde.*' These suggest that Harington's scatological study could have been plausibly read under a title to do with the soul, the heart or the mind. The fact that he is dismissive of such titles, as indicated by his absurd alliteration, merely confirms the plenitude of such 'medical' tracts against which his satire is targeted.[110]

One such medical tract, albeit one published a quarter of a century later, is Robert Burton's *Anatomy of Melancholy* (1621), which makes explicit the connection beween what the modern reader might consider to be the distinctive psychological condition of depression and the all-too-physical problem of constipation. On the right of the title page is a picture of Hypocondriacus who, the accompanying poem tells us, 'leans on his arm, / Wind in his side doth him much harm, / And troubles him full sore, God knows, / Much pain he hath and many woes.'[111] In a chapter headed 'Retention and Evacuation a cause, and how', Burton notes, 'I may well reckon up costiveness, and keeping in of our ordinary excrements, which as it often causeth other diseases, so this of melancholy in particular.'[112] In this causal link between the bowel and the brain, Burton was following one of his most significant sources, Timothy Bright's *A Treatise of Melancholy* (1586), itself long thought to be a possible source of *Hamlet*.[113] Bright had 'advised evacuation of the melancholic humor, first through cleansing with a clyster [or enema], then by phlebotomy with some prior exercise to facilitate the flow of blood, by facilitiating the bleeding of hemorrhoids, and finally by purgings'.[114] The diagnosis and treatment for a variety of ailments resulting from trapped wind was carefully set out by Jean Feyens whose *A New and Needful Treatise of Wind Offending Mans Body* offered his personal suffering as its justification: 'Who would think that such deadly and cruel Symptoms should come from a little wind? But I know it to be so by long experience.'[115] Like Burton, Feyens has a chapter devoted to 'The Cure of the Windy Melancholy' which depends on enemas being administered 'valiantly'.[116] During the affliction called 'windy Melancholy', the body 'sends forth filthy vapours that are not easily discussed, and there are rumblings, and the breaking of wind'.[117]

Feyens's, Bright's and Burton's insistence on the connection of dietary and emotional disorders is a Renaissance commonplace. Menenius defers attempting to plead with Coriolanus until the warrior has eaten, and explains the failure of Cominius to sway the soldier by reference to his hunger: 'he had not dined. / The veins unfilled, our blood is cold, and then / We pout upon the morning, are unapt / To give or to forgive ... Therefore I'll watch him / Till he be dieted to my request, / And then I'll set upon him' (V.i.50–8). Rabelais's narrator informs us that pygmies 'are commonly very teastie and cholerick: the Physical reason whereof is, because their heart is near their spleen'.[118] Francis Bacon too notes the emotional effects of constipation: 'We know diseases of stoppings and suffocations are the most dangerous in the body; and it is not much otherwise in the mind', and Burton himself illustrates the principle with an example:

> A young merchant going to Nordeling fair in Germany, for ten days' space never went to stool; at his return he was grievously melancholy, thinking that he was robbed, and would not be persuaded but that all his money was gone; his friends thought he had some philtrum given him, but Cnelius a physician being sent for, found his costiveness alone to be the cause, and thereupon gave him a clyster, by which he was speedily recovered.[119]

Burton certainly knew Harington's *Metamorphosis*. His own signed copy of this source is still extant in the Bodleian Library, as is the manuscript listing it among those books endowed to the Bodleian upon his death.[120] Moreover the second section of Harington's work (which contains technical details and drawings of the water closet) is called 'An Anatomie of the Metamorpho-sed Ajax'. The similarity of Burton's own title, published over twenty years later, is probably more than coincidental.

I am not suggesting that Jaques is the victim of a particularly bad case of constipation, merely that his punning name and his disposition are of a piece with the Renaissance idea of melancholy as being intimately related to excretory irregularity. More important perhaps is the suggestion that Jaques's name would make him less the serious thinker that he has come to be in post-Renaissance productions of *As You Like It*, and rather more of a standing joke. Bearing his name and personality in mind, Jaques's philosophising is not merely fatuous but flatulent: 'I must have liberty / Withal, as large a charter as the wind, / To blow on whom I please ... Give me leave / To speak my mind, and I will through and through / Cleanse the foul body of th'infected world, / If they will patiently receive my medicine' (II.vii.47–61).[121] In the light of this misanthropic anality, Senior's otherwise rather odd observation begins to make some sense: 'I love to cope him in these sullen fits, / For then he's full of matter' (II.i.66–7). The *OED* defines 'matter' from about 1400 as 'the fluids of the body, excrementitious products etc. Often with qualifying adj., as in ... *fæcal*'. Thus

Senior's description of Jaques implies that he is not merely metaphorically but literally 'full of shit' and so the Duke's rather cavalier attitude to his melancholy ought not to be seen as symptomatic of aristocratic insensitivity, but rather as a clue to the manner in which Shakespeare expects his audience to respond to the costive courtier. The tantalising question arises as to whether Jaques is the playwright's portrait of Harington himself; after all, purgation, and the consequent restoration of corporeal well-being, are insisted upon by both Shakespeare's fictional and Elizabeth's real-life courtiers.[122]

The notion that Jaques's name may have a lavatorial resonance and that this is related to Shakespeare's representation of melancholy will of course have implications for other plays in the canon. At about the same time that he was writing *As You Like It*, Shakespeare brought his previously marginal melancholic stage centre in *Hamlet*. It is obviously too much to claim that the fecal overtones of the comedies contain all the answers to this most enigmatic play but I would point out the capacity of a reading of this nature to solve some of the play's more insistent mysteries surrounding the characterisation of its protagonist as a melancholic. As Feyens insisted, trapped wind 'disturbs the mind and reason, and causeth terrible dreams, melancholy, dotings, shakings of the head, and sometimes death'.[123] While the prince's eventual demise is down to Laertes's poisoned sword, the other symptoms listed here are conspicuously insisted upon by Shakespeare. Furthermore, Hamlet's symptoms are unlikely to be relieved by his weird and blustery diet: 'I eat the air' (III.ii.92).

Feynes's account of melancholy might be used as a description of the Prince of Denmark: 'sometimes a black vapour ariseth, and hurts the brain, causeth troublesome dreams, and disturbs the mind with doting'.[124] Hamlet draws attention to the sable of mourning, the 'black vapour' reified in his 'inky cloak [and] suits of solemn black' (I.ii.77–8). He is also concerned about his nightmares: 'I could be bounded in a nutshell and count myself a king of infinite space, were it not that I have bad dreams' (II.ii.256–8). For Bridget Gellert Lyons the form of the revenge tragedy is a function of its dramatisation of its prevailing medical condition and the soliloquy is symptomatic of melancholia:

The contemplativeness of the melancholy temperament received formal expression in the solitary meditations of the stage melancholic; delusions and madness in a particular kind of visionary speech; calculation and shrewdness in the machinations of the villainous plotter; discontent in the justified or unjustified alienation of the satirist or revenger.[125]

Like Feynes, she too could be talking specifically about Hamlet. The cure is simple: 'we revel by Clysters and Purges'.[126] It is at the point at which Shakespeare's Prince is about to accomplish the murder of Claudius that he himself uses the language of the enema: 'Am I then revenged to take him in the *purging* of his soul, / When he is fit and seasoned for his passage?' (III.iii.84–6, my emphasis). As Marcellus insists, 'Something is rotten in the state of Denmark' (I.iv.67); might that 'something' not be the prince himself?

At the climactic highpoint of the drama, as Hamlet and Laertes duel with one another, Gertrude makes the apparently unflattering and inappropriately comical observation that, 'He's fat and scant of breath' (V.ii.240). The first part of the line is, not surprisingly, given the glamour associated with the role, often cut in production (as was the case in the 1990 film version directed by Franco Zeffirelli and starring Mel Gibson or the stage production directed by Michael Grandage in 2009 at Wyndam's Theatre, London and starring Jude Law).[127] Gertrude's overcandid remark has required much rash explanation from the play's editors. John Dover Wilson (1934) writes, 'I have little doubt that "fat" simply means "sweaty"' though the *OED* offers no evidence for this.[128] It does, however, note that from its earliest instances, *fat* has both positive and negative connotations. Bernard Lott's edition (1968) claims that the description may have been 'inserted to suit a particular actor who took the part of Hamlet', but he is happier explaining the difficulty by blaming textual error: 'This is almost certainly a mistake for another word which cannot now be restored.'[129] Even more ingenious is the explanation of G. R. Hibbard in his Oxford edition (1987): 'It looks ... like a bit of maternal solicitude. Gertrude is eager to find an excuse for her son should he lose the match; and her solicitude becomes all the more evident if Hamlet is neither fat nor scant of breath.'[130] Laura

Keys's elucidation of the overweight prince is even more far-fetched. She argues that Hamlet is a fattened 'scapegoat' whose death is demanded to restore the kingdom to health: 'Hamlet, bloody, guilty, dying, and fat, is a microcosm of Denmark's ills.'[131] Surely, this is protesting too much.

Gertrude's comment is more likely to be another device for reminding the audience of Hamlet's melancholy. One of the anecdotes in *Vlysses vpon Aiax* reports the wish of a certain grocer's wife to 'laugh and be fat' which implies the same correlation between a plump frame and a cheerful disposition that Shakespeare himself had illustrated in Falstaff. Caesar is rightfully suspicious about malcontented Romans whose over-pensiveness is incarnate in their scrawny frames, 'Let me have men about me that are fat ... / Yon Cassius has a lean and hungry look. / He thinks too much. Such men are dangerous ... Would he were fatter!' (I.ii.193–9). If, by the time of the duel, Hamlet is 'fat', perhaps Gertrude is suggesting that her son has at last shaken off his debilitating melancholy and may be in a position to defeat Laertes.[132]

Earlier in the play, there are various references to Hamlet's physical 'transformation' (II.ii.5) since the death of his father, and Polonius's lengthy description of the change emphasises loss of appetite and weight:

And he, repulsèd [that is, rejected by Ophelia] – a short tale to make –
Fell into a sadness, then into a fast,
Thence to a watch, thence into a weakness,
Thence to a lightness, and, by this declension,
Into the madness wherein now he raves,
And all we wail for.

(II.ii.147–52)

In *I Henry IV*, Falstaff too claims to be waning away as a result of the humiliation suffered during the Gad's Hill robbery: 'am I not fallen away vilely since this last action? Do I not bate [i.e., abate or lose weight]? Do I not dwindle? Why, my skin hangs about me like an old lady's loose gown. I am withered like an old apple-john' (III.iii.1–4). The Renaissance association between melancholy and weight loss is neatly emphasised in what is also one of

Shakespeare's most explicit speeches on naming. In reply to
Richard II's bracing enquiry, 'How is't with agèd Gaunt?' (II.i.72),
John of Gaunt makes a speech that dwells obsessively on the
appropriateness of his name:

> O, how that name befits my composition!
> Old Gaunt indeed, and gaunt in being old.
> Within me grief hath kept a tedious fast,
> And who abstains from meat that is not gaunt?
> For sleeping England long time have I watched.
> Watching breeds leanness, leanness is all gaunt.
> The pleasure that some fathers feed upon
> Is my strict fast: I mean my children's looks.
> And therein fasting, hast thou made me gaunt.
> Gaunt am I for the grave, gaunt as a grave,
> Whose hollow womb inherits naught but bones.
>
>   (II.i.73–83)

Like Camden, Gaunt is playing with the Cratylic view that 'each
man's fortune is written in his name', and seems to imply that he
has at last fulfilled his eponymous destiny.[133] Even the usually
insensitive Falstaff notes the emaciated state of Gaunt and the
Cratylic quality of his name, 'I ... told John o' Gaunt he beat his
own name; for you might have trussed him and all his apparel into
an eel-skin' (II Henry IV, III.ii.314). The curt reply that Gaunt
receives from the King however, 'Can sick men play so nicely with
their names?' (l. 84), suggests that, in Richard's eyes, such
Cratylic confidence is merely fanciful and that Gaunt's views on
naming, as on everything else (notably chivalry and regal duties),
are anachronistic nonsense.

As with so many contentious issues, Shakespeare appears to
have been able to exploit both sides of the debate on naming. In
some of his work it seems, as Barton has argued, 'Shakespeare's
naming is fairly random',[134] but this is by no means the general
case, and while the pursuit of allegorical names may be largely
doomed to failure, there is ample evidence to suggest that many of
Shakespeare's characters were named with great care and that
their carefully chosen names, phallic, fecal and flatulent, may
provide a crucial clue to the way in which the bearer should be

perceived: 'A name cannot help being meaningful'.[135] Whether or not such clues can be adequately followed is, of course, another matter.

NOTES

1 William Camden, *Remaines Concerning Britian*, edited by R. D. Dunn (University of Toronto Press: Toronto and London, 1984), p. 52.
2 Camden, *Remaines*, p. 45.
3 Michel de Montaigne, *The Essayes of Michael Lord of Montaigne*, translated by John Florio (George Routledge and Sons: London, 1891), p. 138.
4 Montaigne, 'Of Glory', in *Essayes*, p. 317.
5 Montaigne, 'Of Names', in *Essayes*, p. 136.
6 Stephen Greenblatt, 'Towards a Poetics of Culture' in H. Aram Veeser (ed.), *The New Historicism* (Routledge: New York and London, 1989), 1–14, p. 5.
7 Thomas Hobbes, *Leviathan*, edited by C. B. Macpherson (Penguin: Harmondsworth, 1968), p. 106. Shakespeare makes much of this equivalence between naming and economic and social validity. In *The Taming of the Shrew*, Tranio persuades the pedant to disguise himself as Vincentio. The financial and the social rewards are inseparable, 'His name and credit shall you undertake' (IV.ii.108). In *As You Like It*, Jaques rejects Amiens's terminology for his stanzas by personifying them and exonerating them from debt: 'I care not for their names, they owe me nothing' (II.v.20).
8 Plato, *Cratylus*, translated by N. H. Fowler (Heinemann: London, 1926), p. 7 and p. 11.
9 François Rabelais, *Gargantua and Pantagruel*, translated by Sir Thomas Urquhart and Pierre Le Motteaux, introduced by Terence Cave (David Campbell: London, 1994), p. 369.
10 Michel Foucault, *The Order of Things: The Archaeology of Human Sciences* (Tavistock Publications: London, 1970), p. 17.
11 Foucault, *The Order of Things*, p. 36 and p. 17.
12 Roger Fenton, *A Treatise of Vsurie* (William Aspley: London, 1611), p. 4.
13 C. L. Whitby, 'Character Names in the Comedies of Shakespeare', unpublished MA dissertation, University of Birmingham, 1975, p. 7.
14 Camden, *Remaines*, p. 142.
15 The idea that the current vogue for writing about names reflects a secret longing to escape the absurdist incertitude of post-structuralism is an attractive possibility but, whatever the reasons, a good deal of academic energy has been spent in the pursuit of the epistemological foundations of early modern attitudes to semantics, especially in relation to the

'fitness' or otherwise of names. Writers on the subject include Robert Adger Law, 'On Certain Proper Names in Shakespeare', *Texas Studies in English*, 30 (1951), 61–5; G. Wilson Knight, 'What's in a Name?', in *The Sovereign Flower* (Methuen and Co.: London, 1958), 162–201; Harry Levin, 'Shakespeare's Nomenclature', in *Shakespeare and the Revolution of the Times: Perspectives and Commentaries* (Oxford University Press: Oxford, 1976), 51–77; Manfred Weidhorn, 'The Rose and Its Name: On Denomination in *Othello, Romeo and Juliet, Julius Caesar*', *Texas Studies in Language and Literature*, 11 (1969–70), 671–86; William Green, 'Humours, Characters, and Attributive Names in Shakespeare's Plays', *Names*, 20 (1972), 157–65; Lawrence Danson, 'Metonymy and *Coriolanus*', *Philological Quarterly*, 52 (1973), 30–42. More recent studies include Anne Ferry, *The Art of Naming* (University of Chicago Press: Chicago and London, 1988); John Leonard, *Naming in Paradise: Milton and the Language of Adam and Eve* (Clarendon Press: Oxford, 1990); Anne Barton, *The Names of Comedy* (Clarendon Press: Oxford, 1990); John Pitcher, 'Names in *Cymbeline*', *Essays in Criticism*, 43 (1993), 1–16; Laurie Maguire, *Shakespeare's Names* (Oxford University Press: Oxford, 2007).

16 Thomas Healy, *New Latitudes: Theory and English Renaissance Literature* (Edward Arnold: London, 1992), pp. 28–9.

17 Barton, *Names of Comedy*, p. 29.

18 Barton, *Names of Comedy*, pp. 121–30. She describes the overtones of the names thus: Iago – I-ego; Othello – hell; Emilia – ill; Desdemona – daemon; Cassio – ass. She also notes 'the chiming echo of "Iago" in the last two syllables of the name "Roderigo"', describing the effect as 'sinister' (p. 122).

19 Barton, *Names of Comedy*, p. 30.

20 On *Coriolanus* see Danson, 'Metonymy and *Coriolanus*'. Mamillius's name emphasises the closeness of maternal bonding in the latter play which is consistently remarked upon by other characters: e.g., II.iii.12, III.ii.194–7.

21 Barton, *Names of Comedy*, p. 91.

22 Wilson Knight, *The Sovereign Flower*, p. 164.

23 Barton, *Names of Comedy*, p. 66.

24 Barton, *Names of Comedy*, p. 97.

25 Levin, 'Shakespeare's Nomenclature', p. 56. Ironically, Levin, in his discussion of Wilson Knight's work on naming, gets the name of his book wrong. He calls *The Sovereign Flower, The Sovereign Flame*. Wilson Knight, of course, wrote another volume entitled *The Mutual Flame*.

26 Levin, 'Shakespeare's Nomenclature', p. 77.

27 Helge Kökeritz, 'Punning Names in Shakespeare', *MLN*, 65 (1950), 240–3.

28 For *Pistol* see Eric Partridge, *Shakespeare's Bawdy* (Routledge: London and New York, 1968), third edition, p. 161. For *Lance* see Partridge p. 132 and Gordon Williams, *A Glossary of Shakespeare's Sexual Language* (Athlone: London, 1997), p. 181. For the phallic nose see Mikhail Bakhtin, *Rabelais and his World*, translated by Hélène Iswolsky (Indiana University Press: Bloomington, 1984), p. 316.

29 The verb 'to do' meant to have intercourse. See *Measure for Measure*, Additional passage, I.ii.4–5 and *Macbeth*, I.iii.9. Ann Jennalie Cook cites the following proverb, which uses the same connotation of 'do', to illustrate the prevalence of premarital intercourse in the period: 'Courting and wooing bring dallying and doing' (*Making a Match: Courtship in Shakespeare and his Society* (Princeton University Press: Princeton, 1991), p. 193).

30 Wilson Knight, *The Sovereign Flower*, p. 186.

31 Jane appears in *II Henry IV*, III.ii.195, and Kate in *Measure for Measure*, III.i.458.

32 Edward Phillips, *The New World of English Words* (Nath. Brooke: London, 1658).

33 '*I* and *J* were first distinguished in the Shakespeare Folios in the Fourth Folio, F4, which was published in 1685' (Pitcher, 'Names in *Cymbeline*', p. 16).

34 The name appears as *Gobbo* in Q2, *Iobbe* in Q1 and F1 and *Job* in F3. *Iobbo* is the reconstructed form used by Wells *et al.* in *The Complete Works, Original Spelling Edition* (Oxford University Press: Oxford, 1986). J. Wright defines 'job' as 'ordure, excrement' and notes a widespread usage including Warwickshire (*English Dialect Dictionary*, 6 vols (Oxford University Press: Oxford, 1898–1905), III, 370). Wright's source, G. F. Northall's *A Warwickshire Word Book*, rather squeamishly Latinises its definition: *stercus* (English Dialect Society, no. 79 (London, 1896), p. 120). While the *OED* is less specific about the fecal possibility of 'job', it does list a definition, first found in 1400, which evokes this connotation though it does not directly correspond to it: 'A small portion of some substance; a piece, lump.'

35 Ben Jonson, *The Works of Ben Jonson*, edited by C. H. Herford and Percy and Evelyn Simpson, 11 vols (Oxford University Press: Oxford, 1925–51), VIII, 212. The explanation of Satanic anality (as discussed in Chapter 1 above), commonplace in the medieval drama, may be that the fart is a parodic inversion of the breath of life, 'And the LORD God formed man of the dust of the ground, & breathed into his nostrils the breath of life; and man became a liuing soule' (Genesis 2: 7).

36 Camden, *Remaines*, p. 114. *Cloacina*, from *cloaca*, Lat. for 'sewer'. For *Ajax*, see below. Percy Hide Reaney also notes the name and comments that, in 'another record he is called Roland *le Fartere*' (*The Origin of*

English Surnames (Routledge: London, 1967), p. 294). An analogue of this curious serjeanty appears in Rabelais's *Gargantua and Pantagruel* when the Lord Suckfist remarks about captains who 'play on the lute, and crack with their tailes, to make pretty little platforme leaps'. This was clearly a formulaic ritual as another example from the same work demonstrates, 'then forthwith rising up he [Panurge] gave a fart, a leap, and a whistle' (p. 211 and pp. 262–3).

37 John Florio, *Queen Anna's New World of Words* (Edw. Blount and William Barret: London, 1611), p. 374.

38 If the name were *Dagberry*, it would connote 'dags' or 'dag-locks' which the *OED* defines as 'Locks of wool clotted with dirt about the hinder parts of a sheep' – the first written instance being 1623 but undoubtedly the word was in common parlance with shepherds before this date. 'Dagging' is the process of removing the encrusted wool (and incidentally is still known by this name today, especially in Australia). As far as the second half of the name is concerned, Geoffrey Hughes notes the presence of the word 'fartleberries' in Francis Grose's *A Classical Dictionary of the Vulgar Tongue* (S. Hooper: London, 1785). The word was defined as 'excrement hanging about the anus' (Geoffrey Hughes, *Swearing: A Social History of Foul Language, Oaths and Profanity in English* (Blackwell: Oxford, 1991), p. 158).

39 Levin disapproves, writing of Belch's name that it 'is too often interpreted as a stage direction' ('Shakespeare's Nomenclature', p. 64).

40 Note the relevance here of Camden's remark, cited above: 'each mans fortune is written in his name' (*Remaines*, p. 142).

41 Wilson Knight, *The Sovereign Flower*, p. 171.

42 Montaigne, *Essayes*, p. 138.

43 Reaney, *The Origin*, pp. 290–1.

44 Reaney, *The Origin*, p. 294.

45 Susan Signe Morrison, *Excrement in the Late Middle Ages: Sacred Filth and Chaucer's Fecopoetics* (Palgrave: Houndmills, 2008), p. 18.

46 Norman Longmate, *King Cholera: The Biography of a Disease* (H. Hamilton: London, 1966), p. 143.

47 William Rendle, *Old Southwark and Its People* (W. Drewett: London, 1878), p. 2.

48 John Stow, *A Survey of London*, 2 vols (Clarendon Press: Oxford, 1971), I, 13.

49 For a social history of various urban pollutions see Emily Cockayne, *Hubbub: Filth, Noise and Stench in England* (Yale University Press: New Haven and London, 2007).

50 Peter Ackroyd, *London: The Biography* (Chatto and Windus: London, 2000), pp. 59–60.

51 Jonathan Gil Harris, 'This is Not a Pipe: Water Supply, Incontinent

Sources, and the Leaky Body Politic', in Richard Burt and John Michael Archer (eds), *Enclosure Acts: Sexuality, Property, and Culture in Early Modern England* (Cornell University Press: Ithaca and London, 1994), 203–28, p. 210.

52 *Pleasure Reconciled To Virtue* is reprinted in T. J. B. Spencer and Stanley Wells (eds), *A Book of Masques* (Cambridge University Press: Cambridge, 1967), p. 237. Bruce Boehrer goes as far as to suggest that the fictional Dapper is actually a version of Harington: 'As for Dapper, while he huddles in his outhouse awaiting the pleasure of his royal aunt, he seems almost deliberately designed to suggest the youthful Harington, whose exploits in the field of sanitary engineering established a particularly intimate connection between himself and his Faery godmother.' (Bruce Boehrer, 'The Privy and Its Double', in Richard Dutton and Jean E. Howard (eds), *A Companion to Shakespeare's Works*, 4 vols (Blackwell: Oxford, 2003), IV, 69–88, p. 76.) For discussion of Harington, see below.

53 Thomas Nabbes, *Microcosmus. A Morall Maske* (Charles Greene: London, 1637), D3^r. In noting the intervention of Misackmos, Nabbes is plainly illustrating the degree to which he has been influenced by Harington's *The Metamorphosis of Ajax*. Harington had assumed the pseudonymn 'Misackmos'; the name means 'hater of filth'. For a full discussion of *The Metamorphosis* see below.

54 Thomas Clayton (ed.), *Cavalier Poets* (Oxford University Press: Oxford, 1978), p. 123.

55 Henry Parrot, *Laquei ridiculosi: or Springes for Woodcocks, Caueat Emptor* (John Busby: London, 1613), D2^v.

56 If John Aubrey is to be believed then the Queen herself took delight in jokes involving flatulence: 'This Earle of Oxford, making of his low obeisance to Queen Elizabeth, happened to let a Fart, at which he was so abashed and ashamed that he went to Travell, 7 years. On his returne the Queen welcomed him home, and sayd, "My Lord, I had forgott the Fart."' *Brief Lives* cited by Hughes in *Swearing*, p. 103.

57 Perhaps one of the bluntest toiletry names for an aristocrat is *Don John*. The *OED* lists a published instance in accordance with the definition, still current in America, of 'john' as 'toilet' as early as 1735. Though it is unlikely that the word had not appeared in spoken English earlier, I cannot find any evidence of a lavatorial connotation for it before the eighteenth century. However, note that the toilet is refered to as 'Don A JAX house' in Sir John Harington, *The Metamorphosis of Ajax*, edited by Elizabeth Story Donno (Routledge and Kegan Paul: London, 1962), p. 195. *Jack* and *John* are used, as in the case of Falstaff, interchangeably. For *The Metamorphosis*, see below.

58 'The Life of Alexander the Great' in Plutarch, *Plutarch's Lives of the Noble Grecians and Romanes*, translated by Sir Thomas North, 8 vols (Clarendon

Press: Oxford, 1928), V, 168. Alexander's bodily freshness was evidently proverbial in the period. Montaigne begins his essay 'Of smels and odors' with just this example of personal fragrance: 'It is reported of some, namely of Alexander, that their sweat, through some rare and extraordinary complexion, yeelded a sweet smelling savour; whereof Plutarke and others seeke to find out the cause.' (*Essayes*, p. 156.) Sir Thomas Browne writes in his essay 'Of the Iewes', 'wee will not deny that particular men have sent forth a pleasant savour, as Theophrastus and Plutark report of Alexander the great' (*Pseudodoxia Epidemica*, edited by Robin Robbins, 2 vols (Clarendon Press: Oxford, 1981), I, 324).

59 Note that Casca's and Coriolanus's main objection to the mob is on the grounds of their 'stinking breath' (*Julius Caesar*, I.ii.246); 'their stinking breaths' and their 'stinking greasy caps' (*Coriolanus*, II.i.233 and IV.vi.139).

60 *Montaigne's Essayes* offers us an example of these terms for the toilet when discussing his use 'of a commodious aiax or easie close-stoole' (p. 557).

61 It is worth noting that as well as the pun on *Ajax*, Harington employs a contemporary connotation of *discourse* which the *OED*, citing an example from 1577, defines as 'flowing or running out': 'The riuer Tygris in the discourse of his currant maketh an Ilande.' Thus Harington's discourse on the jakes comes literally to mean something like, 'to pass water / solids on the toilet'. Incidentally, we know that Harington possessed a copy of *Loves labor lost* as well as a number of other quartos of Shakespeare's plays including *What yow will*, *K. Leir of Shakspear*, *Perocles* and *Hamlet* (see F. J. Furnivall, 'Sir John Harington's Shakespeare Quartos', *N & Q*, 7th series, 9 (1890), 382–3).

62 Harington, *The Metamorphosis*, p. 57.

63 See R. Hughey, 'The Harington Manuscript at Arundel Castle and Related Documents', *Library*, 15 (1934–5), 388–444. Of Harington and Combe, a reviewer in the *TLS* remarks that 'They must have made a genial pair of scamps' (Review of the 1927 edition of *The Metamorphosis*, edited by Peter Warlock and Jack Lindsay (Franfrolico Press: London, 1927) in *TLS*, 27 December 1928, p. 1022).

64 Harington, *The Metamorphosis*, p. 194.

65 Jonathan Kinghorn, 'A Privvie in Perfection: Sir John Harrington's [sic] Water Closet', *Bath History*, 1 (1986), 173–88, p. 187.

66 Harington, *The Metamorphosis*, p. 85. The carting 'Of noysome Garbage ... Dirt and Dung' was sometimes reserved for the inmates of Bridewell. (see E. D. Pendry, *Elizabethan Prisons and Prison Scenes*, 2 vols (Universität Salzburg: Salzburg, 1974), I, 42).

67 Harington, *The Metamorphosis*, p. 65.

68 Harington, *The Metamorphosis*, p. 87 and p. 159. Burton was later to

recommend the opening of haemorrhoids as a cure for melancholy. *The Anatomy of Melancholy* (William Tegg and Co: London, 1849), p. 447. For influence of Harington on Burton, see below.

69 Harington, *The Metamorphosis*, p. 122. Harington was plainly fascinated by this Claudian command. In his translation of the *Regimen Sanitatis Salernitanum*, a Latin poem of the twelfth century on the subjects of diet and indigestion which was published in 1607 as *The Englishmans Doctor*, he twice notes the liberated attitude of the Roman Caesar:

> Great harmes haue growne, & maladies exceeding
> By keeping in a little blast of wind:
> So *Cramps*, & *Dropsies*, *Collickes* haue their breeding,
> And *Mazed Braines* for want of vent behind:
> Besides we finde in stories worth the readiug, [*sic*]
> A certaine *Romane Emperour* was so kind,
> *Claudius* by name, he made a Proclamation,
> A *Scape* to be no losse of reputation. (Stanza 4)

> The *Turnep* hurts the stomack, winde it breedeth
> Stirres vrine, hurts his teeth theron that feedeth,
> Who much thereof will feed, may wish our Nation
> Would well allow of *Claudius* proclamation. (Stanza 25)

Unsurprisingly, Rabelais is aware of this tragic death, noting 'that bashfull Fool who by holding in his Wind, and for want of letting out a Bumgunshot dy'd suddenly in the presence of Emperor *Claudius*' (*Gargantua and Pantagruel*, p. 569). Claudius's indulgence in favour of farting seems also to have been well known. Milton's *Areopagitica* cites Suetonius who noted that the edict allowed 'the breaking of wind quietly or noisily at dinner parties' (John Milton, *Complete English Poems, Of Education, Areopagitica*, edited by Gordon Campbell (J. M. Dent and Sons: London, 1990), p. 584). Montaigne in his essay 'Of the force of Imagination' also refers to it when noting the 'indiscreet and tumultuous' character of the 'posterior'. Having discussed the blessed state of a person 'who could let tunable and organized ones, following the tune of any voice propounded unto his eares', he contrasts the more usual condition of limited sphincter control: 'And would to God I knew it but by histories, how that many times our belly, being restrained thereof, brings us even to the gates of a pining and languishing death: And that the Emperour, who gave us free leave to vent at all times, and every where, had also given us the power to doe it' (*Essayes*, p. 39). One of the principal early modern handbooks on farting also mentions Claudius's enlightened attitude: 'And *Claudius Caesar* made an Edict to give leave for any to fart at meat, because he knew one endangered by refraining through modesty' (Jean Feyens, *A New and Needful Treatise of Wind Offending Mans Body*, translated by William Rowland (Benjamin Billingsley: London, 1676), pp. 16–17).

70 Harington, *The Metamorphosis*, p. 56.

71 Harington, *The Metamorphosis*, p. 254.

72 Rick Bowers, *Radical Comedy in Early Modern England: Contexts, Cultures, Performances* (Ashgate: Aldershot, 2008), p. 58 (emphasis his).

73 Jason Scott-Warren, *Sir John Harington and the Book as Gift* (Oxford University Press: Oxford, 2001), p. 19.

74 Bowers, *Radical Comedy*, p. 70.

75 Sophie Gee, *Making Waste: Leftovers and the Eighteenth-Century Imagination* (Princeton University Press: Princeton and Oxford, 2010), p. 13.

76 Will Stockton, *Playing Dirty: Sexuality and Waste in Early Modern Comedy* (University of Minnesota Press: Minneapolis and London, 2011), p. 15.

77 Harington, *The Metamorphosis*, p. 82.

78 John Davies, *Wits Bedlam, Where is had Whipping-cheer, to cure the Mad* (James Dauies: London, 1617), L3^v, L6^v.

79 Anon., *Vlysses vpon Aiax* (Thomas Gubbins: London, 1596), A2^r.

80 Davies, 'To Sir Iohn Harrington. Epigram. 233', *Wits Bedlam*, G1^r.

81 Thomas Bastard, *Chrestoleros. Seuen bookes of Epigrames written by T B, 'in Vlyssem'* (Iohn Broome: London, 1598), p. 124.

82 Anon., *Vlysses vpon Aiax*, B5^v.

83 Anon., *Vlysses vpon Aiax*, B6^v. The length at which I am quoting *Vlysses* is justified by the lack of its availability. Since its first publication in 1596, only one edition (C. Whittingham: Chiswick, 1814) has been produced.

84 Anon., *Vlysses vpon Aiax*, D7^v.

85 Anon., *Vlysses vpon Aiax*, F3^r.

86 Flamock's flatulence was notorious and is mentioned by several early modern writers including George Puttenham. See Jonathan Goldberg, *Sodometries: Renaissance Texts, Modern Sexualities* (Stanford University Press: Stanford, 1992), pp. 49–51.

87 Thomas Nashe, *The Works of Thomas Nashe*, edited by Ronald B. McKerrow, 5 vols (A. H. Bullen: London, 1904–10), V, 195–6.

88 Robert Copland, *Poems*, edited by Mary Carpenter Erler (University of Toronto Press: Toronto, 1993). The fart arrives as follows: 'With that she groned as panged with pain / Griping her bely with her hands twain / And lift vp her buttok somwhat a wry / And like a handgun, she let a fart fly' (ll. 152–5).

89 Anon., *Vlysses vpon Aiax*, B4^r. The degree to which Rabelais influenced Harington is a topic of some dispute: 'whereas Rabelais lets loose literary

and, figuratively speaking, theological excrement, Harington's project is one of gathering it all together into one sanitized place, under a single head' (William E. Engel, 'Was Sir John Harington the English Rabelais?', in Barbara C. Bowen (ed.), *Rabelais in Context* (Summa Publications: Birmingham, Alabama, 1993), 147–56, pp. 153–4.) Harington's biographer is more confident about the influence though: 'Rabelais was clearly the model for the style of some of the liveliest parts of the *Metamorphosis*, and contributed to its richly allusive fantasy and giddyingly nimble syntax' (D. H. Craig, *Sir John Harington* (Twayne Publishers: Boston, 1985), p. 80).

90 Robert Copland, *Jyl of Breyntfords Testament*, edited by Frederick J. Furnivall (Printed for Private Circulation: London, 1871), pp. 3–4.

91 Nashe, *The Works*, III, 11.

92 Reproduced in Nashe, *The Works*, III, 38. Charles Nicholl informs me that the woodcut had been used elsewhere before being reproduced here and is probably therefore not a portrait of Harvey but an opportunisitic cartoon.

93 Nashe, *The Works*, III, 177.

94 Tommaso Garzoni, *The Hospitall of Incvrable Fooles*, translated by Edward Blount (Edward Blount: London, 1600), p. 7. The STC notes that the translation is 'also sometimes attributed to Thomas Nash'.

95 John Cotgrave, *The English Treasury of Wit and Language Collected Out of the Most, and Best of our English Drammatick Poems* (Humphrey Moseley: London, 1655), p. 16.

96 Henry Hutton, *Follie's Anatomie or Satyres and Satyricall Epigrams. With a Compendious History of Ixion's Wheele* (Mathew Walbanke: London, 1619), B4^{r-v}. It is possible that Hutton is writing of *Vlysses* and that 'this foole' is its author rather than Harington. The fact that he does not bother to discriminate, however, implies a non-specific disgust with the joke.

97 John Davies, *The Scourge of Folly. Consisting of satyricall Epigramms and others in honour of many noble and worthy Persons of our Land Together With a pleasant (though discordant) Descant vpon most English Prouerbes: and others* (Richard Redmer: London, 1611), p. 231.

98 Jonson, *The Works*, VIII, 89. For further discussion of the poem, see Andrew McRae, '"On the Famous Voyage": Ben Jonson and Civic Space', *Early Modern Literary Studies*, 3 (1998), 8.1–31. See also Chapter 6 below.

99 *Epicœne*, IV.v.180–1.

100 John Marston, *The Poems of John Marston*, edited by Arnold Davenport (Liverpool University Press: Liverpool, 1961), p. 171.

101 John Day, *The Ile of Gvls* (Iohn Hodgets: London, 1606), B4^{v}.

102 In his 'A Preamble, Preatrot, Preagallop, Prearacke, Preapace, or Preface; and Proface my Masters, if your stomackes serve', Taylor refers

to Ajax among the catalogue of 'such Authors or their Works, as have writ upon many poore obiects'. Others in the list include Erasmus, Aristotle, and Pliny. John Taylor, *The Praise of Hemp-seed* (H. Gosson: London, 1620), B1ᵛ.

103 Cyrus Day, 'Pills to Purge Melancholy', *Review of English Studies*, 8 (1932), 177–84, p. 182. 'Laugh and be fat', another popular title noted by Day, occurs in *Vlysses*.

104 Harington, *The Metamorphosis*, p. 181.

105 Perhaps the best modern example of the use of toiletry names occurs throughout the *Carry On* films. In *Carry On Screaming* for example, the toilet attendant was called Dan Dan the Sanitary Man and in *Carry On at Your Convenience* the owner of the toilet factory was W. C. Boggs. John Train's *Remarkable Names of Real People*, lists 'Crapper Limited, Toilets' of London and notes with glee that 'Thomas Crapper's biography is aptly titled *Flushed with Pride*' (Crown Publications: New York, 1977), p. 24. This biography, by Wallace Reyburn, was published in London in 1969. Reyburn is cognisant of Harington's pioneering book and a drawing from it is reproduced on p. 41.

106 Murray J. Levith, 'Juliet's Question and Shakespeare's Names', in Murray J. Levith (ed.), *Renaissance and Modern: Essays in Honor of Edwin M. Moseley* (Skidmore College: New York, 1976), 21–32, p. 29.

107 Agnes Latham, introduction to the Arden edition of *As You Like It* (Routledge: London, 1975), p. lxviii.

108 B. H. Newdigate boldly suggests that not merely did Shakespeare know *The Metamorphosis*, but that Harington 'is portrayed for us as the melancholy Jaques himself' (*TLS*, 3 January 1929, p. 12). Simon Cauchi discusses Falstaff as a version of Harington but the argument is not convincing ('Sir John Harington and Sir John Falstaff', *N & Q*, n.s., 35 (1988), 468–9).

109 Stanza 62. In *Everyman In His Humour*, Jonson emphasises the fecal aspects of melancholia when Matthew offers Stephen his study for the composition of melancholic love sonnets: 'your true melancholy breeds your perfect fine wit, sir'. Stephen's reply unconsciously puns on close-stool, 'I thank you sir ... Haue you a stoole there, to be melancholy vpon?' (III.i.91). On the anonymous *The School of Salernum* see the edition edited by Francis R. Packard and Fielding H. Garrison (Augustus M. Kelley: New York, 1970) as well as Henry E. Sigerist, 'An Elizabethan Poet's Contribution to Public Health: Sir John Harington and the Water Closet', *Bulletin of the History of Medicine*, 13 (1943), 229–43.

110 E.g. Thomas Cogan's *The Haven of Health* (William Norton: London, 1584). Harington is attacking such alliterative titles if not this one in particular.

111 Burton, *The Anatomy of Melancholy*, p. xix.

112 Burton, *The Anatomy of Melancholy*, p. 152.

113 On the contested status of Bright's treatise as a source of Shakespeare's play see *Hamlet*, edited by Harold Jenkins (Routledge: London and New York, 1982), pp. 106–8.

114 Stanley W. Jackson, *Melancholia and Depression: From Hippocratic Times to Modern Times* (Yale University Press: New Haven and London, 1986), p. 86.

115 Feyens, *A New and Needful Treatise*, p. 42.

116 Feyens, *A New and Needful Treatise*, p. 87.

117 Feyens, *A New and Needful Treatise*, p. 43.

118 Rabelais, *Gargantua and Pantagruel*, p. 263. The digestive proximity is more explicit in J. M. Cohen's translation: 'the physical reason for which is that they keep their bowels close to their hearts' (Penguin: London, 1955, p. 256).

119 Francis Bacon, *Essays*, edited by Michael J. Hawkins (J. M. Dent and Sons: London, 1973), p. 80; Burton, *The Anatomy of Melancholy*, p. 152.

120 'A note of Mr Robert Burton; books given to the library by his last will and Testament', 1639 (MS Selden Supra 80).

121 Frequently in performance the actor playing Jaques gives his song an anal twist (for instance, David Thacker's 1992 RSC production in which Jaques was played by Michael Siberry): 'If it should come to pass / That any man turn ARSE, / Leaving his wealth and ease ...' (II.v.46–8). The text of course has 'ass'.

122 On the possibility of Jaques representing Harington, see Juliet Dusinberre, 'As *Who* Liked It?', *Shakespeare Survey*, 46 (1994), 9–21, p. 12.

123 Feyens, *A New and Needful Treatise*, p. 34.

124 Feyens, *A New and Needful Treatise*, p. 44.

125 Bridget Gellert Lyons, *Voices of Melancholy: Studies in Literary Treatments of Melancholy in Renaissance England* (Routledge: London, 1971), p. 17.

126 Feyens, *A New and Needful Treatise*, p. 63.

127 Patricia Parker notes that 'Critics ... recoil from the notion of a corpulent Hamlet' (*Literary Fat Ladies* (Methuen: London, 1987), p. 22). Laurence Olivier's film version had 'He's hot and scant of breath' while that starring the svelte Richard Burton (directed by John Gielgud) amended it to 'He's faint and scant of breath'. Other film versions have kept the line though; these include Tony Richardson's 1969 production, Rodney Bennett's 1980 BBC version and Kenneth Branagh's 1996 epic.

128 William Shakespeare, *Hamlet*, edited by John Dover Wilson (Cambridge University Press: Cambridge, 1934), p. 255.

129 William Shakespeare, *Hamlet*, edited by Bernard Lott (Longmans: London, 1968), p. 218.

130 William Shakespeare, *Hamlet*, edited by G. R. Hibbard (Clarendon Press: Oxford, 1987), p. 348.

131 Laura Keyes, 'Hamlet's Fat', in Sidney Homan (ed.), *Shakespeare and the Triple Play: From Study to Stage to Classroom* (Associated University Presses: London and Toronto, 1988), 89–104, p. 97.

132 Compare *Laugh and be Fat, or An Antidote against Melancholy* (1700) and *Laugh and grow fat; or, A cure for Melancholy* (1797). Both listed by Day, 'Pills to Purge Melancholy', pp. 183–4.

133 Camden, *Remaines*, p. 142. Pitcher points out that 'Shakespeare borrowed several things from Camden's 1605 *Remains* ... [among which] his most important debt appears to have been the group of Anglo-Saxon names Edgar, Edmund, and Oswald, which he used in *King Lear*' ('Names in *Cymbeline*', pp. 10–11).

134 Barton, *The Names of Comedy*, p. 97.

135 Wilson Knight, *The Sovereign Flower*, p. 178.

3

M.O.A.I. 'What should that alphabetical position portend?': Shakespeare, Harington, Reynolds and the metamorphosis of scatology

I

Act II, scene v, the 'box-tree scene', is the comic climax of *Twelfth Night*, yet, despite its usually rapturous reception in the theatre, it contains a number of textual cruxes which, so far, have eluded satisfactory explanation. In the scene, the posturing Malvolio stumbles across the love-letter (forged by Maria) and, overlooked by Fabian, Toby and Andrew, attempts to decode its cryptic message. As I wish to discuss the episode in detail, it will be necessary to quote a sizeable extract:

SIR TOBY	O peace, and the spirit of humours intimate reading aloud to him.
MALVOLIO	(*taking up the letter*) By my life, this is my lady's hand. These be her very c's, her u's, and her t's, and thus makes she her great P's. It is in contempt of question her hand.
SIR ANDREW	Her c's, her u's, and her t's? Why that?
MALVOLIO	(*reads*) 'To the unknown belov'd, this, and my good wishes.' Her very phrases! By your leave, wax — soft, and the impressure her Lucrece, with which she uses to seal — 'tis my lady. To whom should this be? *He opens the letter*
FABIAN	This wins him, liver and all.

MALVOLIO   'Jove knows I love,
             But who?
             Lips do not move,
             No man must know.'
             'No man must know.' What follows? The numbers altered. 'No man must know.' If this should be thee, Malvolio?

SIR TOBY   Marry, hang thee, brock.

MALVOLIO   'I may command where I adore,
             But silence like a Lucrece knife
             With bloodless stroke my heart doth gore.
             M.O.A.I. doth sway my life.'

FABIAN   A fustian riddle.

SIR TOBY   Excellent wench, say I.

MALVOLIO   'M.O.A.I. doth sway my life.' Nay, but first let me see, let me see, let me see.

FABIAN   What dish o' poison has she dressed him!

SIR TOBY   And with what wing the staniel checks at it!

MALVOLIO   'I may command where I adore.' Why, she may command me. I serve her, she is my lady. Why, this is evident to any formal capacity. There is no obstruction in this. And the end — what should that alphabetical position portend? If I could make that resemble something in me. Softly — 'M.O.A.I.'

SIR TOBY   O ay, make up that, he is now at a cold scent.

FABIAN   Sowter will cry upon't for all this, though it be as rank as a fox.

MALVOLIO   'M.' Malvolio. 'M' — why, that begins my name.

FABIAN   Did I not say he would work it out? The cur is excellent at faults.

MALVOLIO   'M.' But then there is no consonancy in the sequel. That suffers under probation: 'A' should follow, but 'O' does.

FABIAN   And 'O' shall end, I hope.

SIR TOBY   Ay, or I'll cudgel him, and make him cry 'O!'

MALVOLIO   And then 'I' comes behind.

FABIAN   Ay, an you had any eye behind you you might see more detraction at your heels than fortunes before you.

MALVOLIO   'M.O.A.I.' This simulation is not as the former; and yet to crush this a little, it would bow to me, for every one of these letters are in my name.

(ll. 80–133)[1]

Maria's mock love letter has caused frustration for generations of Shakespearean scholars. The New Variorum is full of responses which are as far-fetched as they are plenteous.[2] In respect of her c's, u's, t's and P's, George Steevens noticed that neither 'c' nor 'P' appear in the superscription of the letter though he offered no explanation for their presence here. Edmond Malone proposed merely that 'This was perhaps an oversight in Shakespeare', though he was silent as to why the playwright may have chosen *these* four letters, two of which do and two of which do not appear in the address. J. Ritson postulated that the letters do not appear because Malvolio has not read all of it out. He supplies the following which he suggests was 'the usual custom of Shakespeare's age . . . "**T**o the **U**nknown belov'd, this, and my good wishes, with **C**are **P**resent."' W. A. Wright is sceptical though: 'If Ritson's supposition be correct, no more needs be said on the point; but I have grave doubts about it.' Arthur D. Innes also disapproved of Ritson's solution, opining that Malvolio's failure to read out the whole of the address 'would not fit well with so precise a character'. He continues rather vaguely, 'Probably Shakespeare merely named letters that would sound well, knowing that no audience would detect a discrepancy.' But the internal rhyme of 'c', 't' and 'P' is hardly significant in itself, nor does it explain the choice of the remaining letter 'u' which fails to rhyme with the others — why not 'b', 'd', 'e', 'g' or 'v', all of which do rhyme and all of which appear in the address?

Aguecheek's repetition of the sequence and its resulting emphasis implies that it is more than just a random collection of letters: 'Her c's, her u's, and her t's? Why that?' Clearly the audience is meant to be aware of this combination of letters in particular and as early as 1793 Blackstone commented queasily, 'I am afraid some very coarse and vulgar appellations are meant to be alluded to by these capital letters.'[3] For an audience listening to, rather than reading, the play, a word of three letters, spelt out, could easily be assimilated, and Andrew's repetition makes doubly sure: 'c', 'u', 't', or 'cut', as most recent editions acknowledge, was an early modern synonym for cunt. 'Cut' appears in Thomas Middleton's *A Chaste Maid in Cheapside* as a *double entendre* underlying Lady Kix's lament on her childlessness, 'Can any woman have a greater cut?'[4] In *Twelfth Night*, as Toby reassures Andrew that, provided he send for more cash, he will be successful in his wooing of Olivia, he declaims, 'Send for money, knight. If thou hast her not i'th'end, call me cut' (II.iii.175).[5] The lewd play on having her 'i'th'end' makes the prospective insult all the more fitting.

'Cut' was also used as a verb, signifying, euphemistically, sexual activity. Commonly it appears in the verb-phrase 'cut a caper' as in *Pericles*: Boult's advertising of the virginal Miranda so excites Monsieur Veroles (whose name derives from *vérole*, the French for 'pox') that 'He offered to cut a caper at the proclamation' (xvi.103). Dancing and dalliance were commonly linked as in Henry Hutton's account of a 'Letcher' which describes whoring in jigging terms: 'hee'l cut a caper, neately prance, / And with his Curtail some odde Galliard dance'.[6] In *The Sun's Darling* by Ford and Dekker, the Italian dancer is described lewdly as 'one that loves mutton so well, he alwaies carries capers about him; his brains lie in his legs, and his legs serve him to no other use then to do tricks, as if he had bought em of a Jugler'.[7] The dancer himself deploys dance jargon to brag of past conquests; he knows 'Corantoes, galliardaes [and] amorettaes dolche dolche to declamante do bona robaes de Tuscana.'[8] In *Twelfth Night*, as Toby and Andrew drink away the early hours boasting of their dancing prowess, their conversation thinly masks an obsession with sexual potency. Note the presence not only of the verb-phrase 'cut a caper' but the mention of the 'galliard' as a coded reference (as in the examples above) to fornication:

> SIR TOBY   What is thy excellence in a galliard, knight?
> SIR ANDREW Faith, I can cut a caper.
> SIR TOBY   And I can cut the mutton to't.
> SIR ANDREW And I think I have the back-trick simply as strong as
>   any man in Illyria.
>
>   (I.iii.112–16)

The sexual connotations surrounding 'galliard' (dalliance), 'cut' (cunt), 'caper' (copulate), 'mutton' (prostitute), and 'back-trick' (sexual mastery) thicken the lewd tone of the exchange.[9]

Given the scurrilous nature of her 'c's, her u's, and her t's', it is hardly surprising that 'makes she her great P's' can be glossed, in the words of the Oxford editors, as 'urinates copiously'.[10] Toby uses 'make' in the verb-phrase 'make water', meaning 'to urinate' (I.iii.122). But Aguecheek is oblivious to the sexual and urinary connotations of the words ('cut' and 'pee') formed by the letters Malvolio reads and his bafflement is of a piece with the practice throughout of demonstrating his ignorance by having him say or repeat things which the audience can, and he cannot, understand (compare his misprision over Mistress Mary Accost and, later, 'what is *Pourquoi*? Do, or not do?'). Despite the almost universal acceptance of 'P' for 'pee' in modern editions, it is worth pointing out that the *OED* lists the first printed instances of the word as 1902 (noun) and 1879 (verb). Contemporary evidence suggests that 'P' or 'P—' stands for 'prick', as in John Taylor's *A Common Whore* in which the letter appears alongside the rather obviously vaginal 'O': '[the whore] Hath much more vnderstanding of the *French*, / If she hath learn'd great P, O Per se O. / She'le quickly know *De morbo Gallico*.'[11]

It may be that 'P' is being used in *Twelfth Night* as a euphemistically abbreviated form of 'piss' which the *OED* cites as *c.*1386 (noun) and *c.*1290 (verb) but another possibility is that 'makes she her great P's' is a version of 'make-peace' defined by the *OED* as 'One who or something which makes peace' (1516). At the beginning of *Richard II*, for instance, Gaunt attempts to appease the belligerent Bolingbroke, 'To be a make-peace shall become my age. / Throw down, my son, the Duke of Norfolk's gage' (I.i.160–1). In the light of Shakespeare's pacific use of the term in *Richard II*, we might read 'These be her very c's, her u's, and her t's, and thus makes she her great P's' as a description of the ways in which Olivia deploys her sexual charms to appease or satisfy: 'Olivia cannot know that ... without her consent, her private parts will be on display for everyone's amusement.'[12] Neither, of course, is Malvolio portrayed as saying this consciously, but an audience hearing it would be able to contrast such a piece of crude gossip with Olivia's fugitive and cloistered virtue: 'like a cloistress she will veilèd walk' (I.i.27).

In her explanation of the riddle, Leah Scragg has suggested that a second-order quibble, which underlies the bawdy, is available for an especially acute audience member. She proposes that the letters spell out 'cut-p[urse]': 'While laughing at the incongruity of "cut" and "pee" ... the members of the audience are thus encouraged to visualize "cut-P----" and in doing so a seventeenth-century spectator may well have been prompted to transfer an anxious hand to his side.'[13] Despite the number of cases Scragg cites of pick-pocketing episodes from contemporary plays, the implication that an unruly Shakespearean comedy, the very title of which is suggestive of carnivalesque revelry, may be an early version of a neighbourhood watch scheme, seems dourly implausible.

The density of sexual reference during the scene makes the killjoy Malvolio and the idiotic Andrew objects of the audience's knowing scorn. They are ridiculed as the result of a conspiracy between a suggestive playwright and an alert audience. This ironic deflation of a character from their own mouths is the staple stuff of ribald comedy. As the joke becomes more sophisticated, so the danger grows that the audience will fail to pick it up and consequently the likelihood that it will get lost increases. Such has been the fate of 'M.O.A.I.' – a joke, as I will suggest, that was readily assimilable in its own day but which, since, has reduced modern commentators to the level of the bewildered Malvolio.

The critical fortunes of 'M.O.A.I.' have been even less illustrious than those of her 'c's, her u's, and her t's', which undoubtedly is the more readily solved riddle. James O. Halliwell-Phillipps casually proposed 'My Own Adored Idol, or some such words, or cipher ... imitated from similar enigmas which were current at the time.'[14] Other critics have surmised that Malvolio was a cipher for a real person. In 1884, F. G. Fleay, for instance, advanced the thesis that Malvolio was a coded version of John Marston: 'At any rate, there is a singular likeness between the names of Malevole [in Marston's *Malcontent*] and the steward Malvolio, and a still more singular agreement between **IO: MA:**, Marston's abbreviated signature, and the M.O.A.I. of the letter addressed to **MA**lvol**IO**.'[15] The proposed alliterative correspondence between Marston's abbreviated signature and the letters in Malvolio's name sounds tenuous, not least because the order in which the letters occur is quite different (and unexplained). In addition, the suggestion of intertextual influence is flawed by chronology. *The*

Malcontent, which was published in 1604, was not written before 1602, whereas *Twelfth Night* is usually dated to 1601. It would not, therefore, have been possible for Shakespeare to have modelled Malvolio on Marston's Malevole. Another more plausible identity behind the cryptogram was proposed by Percy Allen in 1937:

> Malvolio, attempting to link the letters 'Moai' with his own name, perceives that 'there is no consonancy in the sequel ... A should follow but O does.' Substitute the name 'Montaigne' for 'Malvolio,' and there *is* consonancy; because the letters Mo-ai are the first letters of the two syllables of *Mont-aigne*.[16]

Michel de Montaigne's own interest in onomastics, reflected in his essay 'Of Names' (see Chapter 2 above), might make him a particularly appropriate solution to this riddle though one wonders how easily it could have been picked up by an audience who had not yet had the benefit of John Florio's 'Englished' version of the *Essais* (published in 1603). Finally, Gabriel Harvey's 'admission that he was entranced with capital letters', suggests to J. J. M. Tobin that he lies behind the pedantic steward.[17] Harvey's *Ciceronianus* does indeed contain the bizarre confession, 'It is hard to believe how strangely fascinated I was by these emblems of capital letters', but whether that is enough to link Harvey to Malvolio (who does not seem at all interested in the letters for their own sake, let alone whether they are upper or lower case) is quite another matter. In addition, such an association suggests no plausible reason for Shakespeare's use of *these* capital letters rather than any others.

The enigma continues to draw unlikely solutions. In 1954 Leslie Hotson proposed that the letters refer to the four elements: 'To tease Malvolio, Maria has cleverly chosen those designations for the elements whose initials appear in his name: *Mare*-Sea, *Orbis*-Earth, *Aer*-Air, and *Ignis*-Fire. M.O.A.I.'[18] The Arden II editors are unimpressed, asking why *Mare* and *Orbis* have been used as opposed to the more usual *Aqua* or *Terra*?[19] Eight years later, Lee Sheridan Cox advanced another possibility: 'I suggest that M.O.A,I stands for I AM O (Olivia).'[20] This interpretation never explains the mis-ordering of all four letters beyond the inanity that 'Turning a phrase around is one of the oldest and

simplest riddle devices.'[21] Cox proposes that Fabian's '"O" shall
end, I hope' indicates that 'he trusts the steward will be completely
convinced that Olivia is the writer'. Usually glossed, since Samuel
Johnson's edition, as the hangman's noose (see both Arden II and
III as well as Riverside), the 'O' that Fabian is hoping for is also,
clearly, the 'Oh' of lament that he anticipates Malvolio making
when all is discovered. This is supported by Toby's insistence that
Malvolio will be made to wail, if not in sorrow then in pain: 'Ay, or
I'll cudgel him, and make him cry "O!"' Moreover, given the
proximity of Orsino's court, the abbreviation of Olivia's name to
their shared first initial is somewhat careless since there is nothing
to stop the initials reading 'I AM O (Orsino)'. And if it is appropriate that 'O' should come at the end (hence, according to Cox, the
significance of Fabian's line), then Orsino would be a better
candidate than Olivia. Given the importance of its terminal
position, Cox fails to explain why 'O' comes second in the original
sequence of four letters. Cox's over-elaborate deciphering has been
taken to task by R. Chris Hassel Jr who caustically opines, 'since
almost none of us could have deciphered Cox's riddle, we can
hardly laugh at Malvolio for his similar failure'.[22] If Hassel accuses
Cox of an overly intricate solution, his own is so blatant as to be
hardly worth noting: 'M.O.A.I. are simply the first, last, second,
and second from last letters in his name.'[23] There needs no critic
come from the page to tell us this since even Malvolio knows as
much: 'every one of these letters are in my name' (II.v.133).

The virtue of simplicity is something missing from other
attempts to decode the riddle. D'Orsay W. Pearson, for instance,
suggests that M.O.A.I. 'is the French pronoun *moy*, now *moi*,
which currently we pronounce as a single syllable: [*mwa*]'.[24]
Ingeniously, Pearson notes that Maria in F1 talks not of gulling
Malvolio into 'a nayword' (Oxford edition, II.iii.126) but into 'an
ayword' (i.e. an 'I-word'). The former reading is more usual as
'ayword' appears neither elsewhere in Shakespeare nor in the
OED.[25] Pearson's reading permits him to argue that Maria 'gulls
him with a first-person pronoun — *moai* = *moe* = *moy* = I
myself'.[26] Not only is Pearson's suggestion weakened by the
absence of *ayword* from any other source but it is undermined by
an alternative meaning of the prefix when it does appear. The *OED*

lists 'ay-lasting', 'ay-when' and 'aywhere'. In all of these cases the meaning of the prefix is 'ever' (thus 'everlasting', 'always', and 'everywhere'). This is the most common sense of 'aye' as illustrated by 'This world is not for aye', a proverbial tag uttered by the Player King in *Hamlet*.[27] Thus if F1 (and Riverside) are followed, the meaning of gulling Malvolio into 'an ayword' is more likely to be that he'll be permanently aware of his having been conned – in modern parlance – 'he'll never live it down'.[28]

Less plausible still is Inge Leimberg's suggestion, in *Connotations*, that '"M.O.A.I." is an anagram (and a very simple and obvious one at that) of Rev. 1: 8.'[29] The biblical text is of course, 'I am Alpha and Omega'. Leimberg's special pleading ought to arouse our scepticism. Even if we grant its transmutation to 'I'm A and Ω', eliding the verb in order to produce 'I' and 'M', the letters come in the wrong order and we are stuck with the extra word 'and'.[30] Leimberg supports her reading by reference to Erasmus's *Laus Stultitiae* in which a similar anagrammatic trick involving the letters 'A', 'M' and 'O' occurs. But a Greek solution via a Latin text in an English play might reasonably be thought to be beyond the capabilities of Shakespeare's audience (indeed beyond the playwright himself if we accept the word of Ben Jonson on Shakespeare's linguistic limitations). When Leimberg explains the ordering of the letters via a complicated number/letter coding, she becomes unconvincing, particularly as she prefaces her numerology with the cavalier remark, 'letters and numbers are interchangeable anyway'.

In a later number of the same journal, John Russell Brown answers Leimberg but his solution is again unsatisfactory. He rightly draws attention to the gnarled logic of Leimberg's essay: 'a good riddle has one solution which is blindingly obvious once it has been found ... Professor Leimberg's solution is not of this kind'.[31] Brown's explication is disarmingly simple and has the merit of effrontery. 'M' stands for Malvolio, 'O' stands for 'the Oh! of sexual anticipation, pleasure, and/or surprize ... The "A" of the riddle would be another exclamation, as resistance or hesitation is overcome: a more positive Ah! ... and "I" would ... represent Olivia giving her full assent.'[32] Brown continues, 'The whole riddle is thus a covert dramatisation of the sexual fantasy which

supposedly drives Olivia and "sways her life."' Faced with the
brazen logic of this account, according to which the riddle is
reduced to the grunting of sexual climax, the reader is entitled to
ask in what sense is it 'covert'?

One might have thought that an actor's perspective on the
problem would be germane here. After all, critics and editors can
avoid problems that elude them whereas an actor has to make
sense of every word or justify its being cut. Donald Sinden, who
played Malvolio for the Royal Shakespeare Company in 1969,
directed by John Barton, is illuminating in respect of her 'c's, her
u's, and her t's'. He notes how he 'Naughtily ... abbreviated the
original text' of 'and her t's' to ''n her t's', producing a letter 'n'
between the leading 'cu' and the final 't' and so updating the
Renaissance obscenity 'cut'.[33] On 'M.O.A.I.' though, his remarks
are less enlightening:

> I ask if the audience know the word – 'MO-AH-EE?' ... While
> Fabian and Sir Toby speak I try to work it out; '"MO-AH-EE doth
> sway my life." Nay, but first let me see, let me see'; the next two lines
> being cut [FABIAN What dish o' poison has she dressed him! SIR TOBY
> And with what wing the staniel checks at it!] he continues, '"I may
> command where I adore." Why, she may command me', he tells the
> audience, 'I serve her; she is may [sic] Lady. Why this is evident to
> any formal capacity, there is *no* obstruction in this' – spoken so
> quickly it elicits a laugh. 'What should that alphabetical position
> portend? If I could make that resemble something in *me*' ... "M"
> comma "O" comma "A" comma', and he shows the commas to the
> audience the while; what a fool he has been not to notice before! So
> what does it all mean? 'M', he queries. A great light dawns. The
> eyes pop. The 'M' dissolves into 'M' m M A L V O L I O', he ventures
> in a whisper. Don't they understand?' '"M" ... why, that begins MY
> NAME!' So that is clear for the 'M', 'but then there is no *consonancy*'
> (no consonants) 'in the sequel. That *suffers* under probation ... "A"
> *should* follow but "O" *does*! The [sic] "I" comes behind.' More
> thought: '"M.O.A.I."' etc.[34]

This prolix and confused commentary is clearly an attempt to
recreate the dawning of the idea on the puzzled steward but it also
unfortunately betrays Sinden's own ignorance of what it is he is
saying ('no *consonancy*', for example, means that there is no

coherence or consistency in what follows. It does not mean that there are 'no consonants'). His Malvolio moves from gibberish, 'MO-AH-EE', through a tortured attempt to make the letters 'resemble something in' him but by the end of the extract (and the paragraph ends here as the essay moves on to discuss 'here follows prose'), we have only secured a satisfactory explanation for the first letter. Sinden has nothing to say about 'O. A. [or] I'. His own failure to solve the riddle, or at least acknowledge its mystery, is betrayed by the limp 'etc.' with which the paragraph ends.

Given the difficulty of solving this conundrum, as illustrated by this survey of contrived explanations, the temptation is to leave well alone. The Arden II editors gloss 'M.O.A.I.' as 'a sequence of letters expressly designed to make Malvolio interpret them as he does, thus prolonging the comic scene'. And they advise sternly, 'Attempts to wring further meaning from them are misplaced.'[35] Arden III does survey some solutions in its introduction but its textual note here is similarly lacklustre: 'This *fustian riddle* ... has proved over the decades to be as much a trap for critics as for Malvolio.'[36] Cynthia Lewis shares this critical acquiescence. In a bizarre article which sets out her stall and then kicks it over, she notes that the character names (Viola, Malvolio, Olivia) are near anagrams of each other, then goes on to propose that they are no more than 'empty ruses'. 'M.O.A.I.' is simply a vacuous trick: 'Shakespeare's anagrammatic names ... are meant to challenge the audience in much the same way as M.O.A.I. challenges Malvolio ... the more we flatter ourselves that we see meaning in the anagrams, the closer we resemble the ludicrous Malvolio.'[37] Vincent F. Petronella is less defeatist, noting of the anagrammatic nomenclature that, 'By Act III of the play, the Malvolio–Olivia–Viola triangle is fully established, visually, emotionally, and onomastically. In the name of Malvolio is Olivia, and in the name of Olivia is Viola.'[38] Despite his clear-headed exploration of the analogous relationship between the anagram and the Renaissance fad for anamorphism in the visual arts, Petronella settles for the tortuously jargonistic diagnosis that Malvolio is 'acting out the Lacanian mirror stage' and thus the 'anagram is a conversion of one signifier into another signifier, and in this regard represents Lacanian "lack"'.[39] In spite of such

ingenuity, the overwhelming tendency of editors is either to admit
defeat (as in the case of Arden II) or to remain silent (Riverside).
Most disappointingly the Oxford editors completely ignore the
puzzle though peculiarly they take the trouble to gloss the unprob-
lematic verb which occurs in the same line: '**sway** rule'.[40]

II

It is important to observe that there is a notable hermeneutic
distinction between her 'c's, her u's, and her t's' and 'M.O.A.I.' In
the first case the joke arises from letters picked out of the superscription at random, as it were, by Malvolio (we have already seen
that two of the characters he picks are not even there). In the
second case, 'M.O.A.I.' is what he reads; in the story of the play,
Maria has written *these letters in this order*. This means that in the
first instance the joke arises from the dullness of Malvolio and
Andrew who unwittingly expose their own simple-mindedness by
failing to notice the obscenity that they are spelling out. In the
second case however, the joke originates from Maria whose letter
Malvolio is now reading. This has two implications. Firstly,
'M.O.A.I.' is less spontaneous; as Malvolio wrestles to make the
letters appropriate to him, so the audience are given time to
decode the joke for themselves – compare the duration of the
pondering over this combination of letters with that over her 'c's,
her u's, and her t's' which is only repeated once for the slower
members of the audience: in contrast, 'M.O.A.I.' or constituent
letters are repeated eighteen times. The second implication is that
because the characters are part of the main body of the letter, the
joke is mediated through an explicitly *written* text and is therefore
more literary.

As the first step in decoding the puzzle we need to establish
what kind of puzzle it is. In spite of Lewis's claim that the
anagrammatic quality of the names of the *dramatis personae* is an
irrelevance, evidence from the period demonstrates that naming
and anagrams were of particular importance to Renaissance
philosophers who were attempting to settle one of the most
profound of semantic questions: is language conventional or
absolute? That is, is the name for something a summation of its

being? As we saw in Chapter 2, the debate is rehearsed in Plato's *Cratylus*, which records the argument between the eponymous speaker, who is convinced 'that there is a kind of inherent correctness in names', and the sceptical Hermogenes, who argues that 'no name belongs to any particular thing by nature but only by the habit and custom of those who employ it and who established the usage'.[41]

William Camden's *Remaines of a Greater Worke Concerning Britaine* (1605) contains a chapter on 'Anagrammes' in which is demonstrated their talismanic efficacy. Camden writes:

> The onely *Quint-essence* that hitherto the *Alchimy* of wit coulde draw out of names, is *Anagrammatisme* ... which is a dissolution of a Name truly written into his Letters, as his Elements, and a new connexion of it by artificiall transposition, without addition, substraction, or chang [*sic*] of any letter into different words, making some perfect sence appliable to the person named.[42]

Camden cites over fifty examples of these lexical miracles in Latin, Greek and English including 'Charles Iames Steuart. CLAIMES ARTHVRS SEATE', and 'Elizabetha Regina Angliæ, ANGLIS AGNA, HIBERIÆ LEA [To England a lamb, to Spain a lion]'.[43] These puzzles were considered to be more than mere amusements. Larzer Ziff has noted the

> folk belief in the animism of language. The meaning of words on this level was not arbitrary but organically connected with the essence of the thing signified by the word. Adam had named the creatures of the earth after their kind, which meant that he did not indifferently call the leopard 'leopard' and the ant 'ant,' but that he saw the leopardness of the leopard and named it accordingly.[44]

This linguistic essentialism went all the way up to the highest of animals: as Camden puts it, 'names are divine notes, and divine notes do notifie future events ... each mans fortune is written in his name'.[45] It may be particularly appropriate, given Malvolio's much-disdained Puritanism (II.iii.130, 132, 136) that, according to Jeffrey Walker, this kind of linguistic fixation was especially characteristic of this particular religious group: 'the anagram and the acrostic were used alongside hymns, sermons, and ballads to provide some sense of order in the Puritan world'.[46] Maurice Hunt reads the episode in terms of popular anti-Puritanism: Malvolio's 'juggling the alphabetical letters of the code to suggest his own name reflects conformists' accounts of puritans willfully twisting the literal sense of biblical passages to create meanings justifying their narrow beliefs'.[47]

In *The Arte of English Poesie* (1589), George Puttenham had attributed a didactic role to anagrams: their purpose, he wrote,

> is to insinuat some secret, wittie, morall and braue purpose presented to the beholder, either to recreate his eye, or please his phantasie, or examine his iudgement, or occupie his braine or to manage his will either by hope or by dread ... and therefore giue them [that is, anagrams] no litle commendation.[48]

Puttenham also points out that the anagram has particularly romantic associations, functioning as a kind of code which can only be deciphered by the courtier and his lady. He notes the frequency of 'amorous inscriptions which courtiers vse to giue and also to weare in liuerie for the honour of their ladies, and commonly containe but two or three words of wittie sentence or secrete conceit till they be / vnfolded or explained by some inter-pretatiõ'.[49]

A number of points arise here which are especially significant for Malvolio. To begin with, Camden's principle that the anagram should fit the speaker 'without addition [or] substraction' contrasts humorously with the efforts of the desperate steward who is so eager to realise his fantasies that he is prepared 'to crush this a little'. In fact to make the inscription 'bow to' him, he has to ignore the order in which the characters occur as well as supplying the remaining letters of his name. A Renaissance audience in possession of a reasonable rate of literacy and accus-tomed to the onomastic fidelities of the anagram, would readily see the distinction between its inner magic and its crude deforma-tion here.[50] Secondly, whereas the anagram is supposed to 'examine his iudgement' and demonstrate the intelligence of the decoder, Malvolio's perversion of it is solely to 'please his phantasie'. The Horatian commonplace, 'to teach and to delight', which informs so many of the period's satires, both poetic and dramatic, is here distorted as Malvolio's imagination runs away with his reason. Finally the knowing confidence of the yellow-stockinged Malvolio's cryptic utterances, 'Some are born great ...' etc., is a parodic reworking of the intimacy associated with this kind of lovers' puzzle and their 'two or three words of wittie sentence or secrete conceit'. Malvolio behaves as every keen lover ought to. The fact that his instructions are a cruel hoax is something of which he is, at this stage anyway, blissfully unaware.

It is worth reminding ourselves that the object of Maria's letter is to effect in the stubborn Malvolio a kind of transformation, a mutation in terms of physicality and personality from the stiff resolve of the buttoned-up steward to the ecstatic fancy of the cross-gartered lover. The capacity of love to change identities is a constant motif in the works of Shakespeare and is foregrounded in the opening lines of *Twelfth Night*. As Orsino laments his own enforced transformation, he compares himself to the unfortunate Acteon:

> O, when mine eyes did see Olivia first
> Methought she purged the air of pestilence;
> That instant was I turned into a hart,
> And my desires, like fell and cruel hounds,
> E'er since pursue me.
>
> (I.i.18–22)

As is well known, the reference is to Ovid's *Metamorphoses*, that staple resource of Shakespearean myth and mutation. In book III, Ovid famously tells how the hunter Acteon caught sight of the bathing goddess Diana. To prevent him telling of her nakedness, she turns him into a stag and he is torn to pieces by his own hounds. Ovid calls Diana Titania, since she and her twin brother Phoebus, whom Ovid calls Titan, are the grandchildren of the Titans, Coeus and Phoebe. This is the source of Shakespeare's naming of his faerie queene in *A Midsummer Night's Dream* and the Ovidian pliancy of eroticism and bestiality is seen most fully in this play in the 'translat[ion]' (III.i.113) of Bottom the weaver. But it is also, albeit parodically, implicit in *Twelfth Night* as the box-tree plotters, just like Puck, relish the mischievous consequences of their practical joke. Their purpose is to 'make [Malvolio] an ass' (II.iii.157), an appropriate objective in the light of Maria's earlier

description of him as 'an affectioned ass' (l. 137) and one which is
anticipated in her petulant 'Go shake your ears' (l. 117). William
C. Carroll has identified the mulish metamorphosis as a symptom
of semantic confusion: the 'puzzles which Shakespeare stresses in
his comedies [occur] where language and action relentlessly
pursue logic into paradox. Questions of boundary, shape,
language, and identity inevitably arise when men become asses.'[51]
Carroll proposes that the perplexities of language are triggered by
desire and that alteration is the inevitable result: 'Each of
Shakespeare's comic lovers is transformed: some become more
generous, some more foolish, some more dangerous, one becomes
literally an ass, dozens become figurative asses.'[52] Desire, language
and shape-shifting are thus plaited together as is precisely illustrated by the cases of Bottom and Malvolio. Unlike Bottom's
supernatural transformation, however, Malvolio's is crushingly
unconsummated, a devastating con-trick without the ethereal
raptures of a liaison with the queene of faerie. That awaiting
Malvolio is a metamorphosis not of delicate poetry but of the
bleakest prose and it is initiated by a failure to recognise the trick-
eries of a Protean language.

It is in terms of a kind of linguistic metamorphosis that
Puttenham describes the instabilities of discourse, the medium
through which Malvolio's transformation is to be effected.
Language 'receaueth none allowed alteration, but by extraordinary occasions by little & little, as it were insensibly bringing in of
many corruptiõs that creepe along with the time'.[53] Language,
that is, both diachronically (though elaboration, amelioration,
etc.) and synchronically (through metaphor, figurative use, etc.),
is in a state of constant metamorphosis, uncertain, slippery,
anagrammatic: 'A sentence is but a chev'rel glove to a good wit,
how quickly the wrong side may be turned outward' (III.i.11–13).
Such a diction, effervescent with the absurdities of transparent
barricadoes, 'clerestories toward the south-north' (IV.ii.38), and
the crazy metempsychoses of avian grandams, is an idiom from
which the sombre steward is fittingly barred. Bound in a dark
house, he is desperate to petrify language, to arrest its incremen-
tal change by committing it to paper: 'help me to a candle and pen,
ink, and paper' (IV.ii.82). The letter he intends to write to his lady

is an attempt to fix the meanings of the one 'she' wrote to him: 'Entirely possessed by the letter, Malvolio can only reclaim himself by investing himself in writing.'[54]

The emotional distance between the intensity of Ovidian love, love which changes things, and the misplaced delusions of Malvolio whose outward affectations reveal rather than disguise his inward obduracy, is signalled by the distinction between the effortless and constant changing of the natural world and the forced and sudden transformation of Malvolio's speech and costume. For Ovid's Pythagoras, metamorphosis is as fundamental as life itself: 'Our bodies also ay / Doe alter still from time to time, and neuer stand at stay. / We shall not be the same we were to day or yesterday.'[55] Unlike the gentle gliding of one shape into another which occurs in the *Metamorphoses*, Malvolio's shape-shifting is laboured, even clumsy: 'This does make some obstruction in the blood, this cross-gartering' (III.iv.20). His pseudo-metamorphosis voices itself not in the sublime poetry of Ovid or Orsino but in asinine utterances, 'Sweet lady, ho, ho!' (III.iv.17), 'O ho' (l. 62), 'Aha' (l. 91), etc. It is no surprise to find that the linguistic correlative of his coarse physical transformation is wrenched and hammered until it fits Malvolio, the anagram 'crush[ed]' until it takes the shape of his name. The wrestling with the anagram is profoundly narcissistic as Malvolio dwells on the centrality of himself. His febrile self-regard is a kind of linguistic auto-eroticism as he toys with the letters which constitute his identity. Carroll writes, 'Reading ... becomes an effort to double oneself, to find in letters something that "resemble[s]" oneself ... There must be a text behind the text, then, but the other text is still just one's own reflection.'[56]

The infinitesimal shifting of language and form described by Puttenham and Pythagoras is battered by the mulish Malvolio into egotistical points of forced change. This particular point — 'M.O.A.I.' — offers the promise of a subtle and refined metamorphosis at the same time as an infamous dirty joke, as crude and obvious as Malvolio's yellow stockings. 'M.O.A.I.' too changes shape — not to an ill-ordered collection of letters which happen to be in Malvolio's name but, acronymically, to the title of a text which celebrates, as does *Twelfth Night*, the misprision and comedy of metamorphosis itself, *The **M**etamorphosis **O**f **A** I**AX**.*[57]

III

As we have seen in Chapter 2, about four years before *Twelfth Night* was first performed, Sir John Harington published his satirical tract on the flushing toilet, *A Nevv Discovrse of a Stale Svbiect, Called The Metamorphosis of Aiax*. The pseudo-Ovidian title is drawn from the Latin poet's account (which appears in book XIII of *Metamorphoses*) of the Grecian warrior's metamorphosis into a purple flower. Ajax had contended with Ulysses' superior rhetoric in an argument over who should inherit the armour of Achilles. After a bitter exchange, the captains decided to make the award to Ulysses. Ajax, unable to accept the loss of honor,

> drawes his sword and saies:
> Well: this is mine yet: vnto this one claime *Vlysses* laies.
> This must I vse against my selfe: this blade that heeretofore
> Hath bathed beene in Troiane bloud, must now his maister gore,
> That none may *Aiax* ouercome saue *Aiax*.[58]

Ovid tells how 'Anon the ground bestained where he stood, / Did breed the pretie purple flowre vpon a clowre of greene, / Which of the wound of *Hyacinth* had erst ingendred beene.' The story was well known; Shakespeare has York describe his intense rage: 'I am so angry at these abject terms; / And now, like Ajax Telamonius, / On sheep or oxen could I spend my fury.'[59] This moment of high tragedy is itself comically metamorphosed by Harington's farcical version:

> GReat Captaine AIAX, as is well knowen to the learned, and shall here be published for the vnlearned, was a warrier of Græcia; strong, headdy, rash, boisterous, and a terrible fighting fellow, but neither wise, learned, staide, nor Politicke. Wherefore falling to bate with Vlisses, & receiuing so fowle a disgrace of him, to be called foole afore company, and being bound to the peace, that he might not fight with so great a Counseller; he could indure it no longer, but became a perfit mal-content, viz. his hat without a band, his hose without garters, his wast without a girdle, his bootes without spurs, his purse without coine, his head without wit, and thus swearing he would kill & slay; first he killed all the horned beasts he met, which made Agamemnon and Menelaus now, more

affraid then Vlisses, whereupon he was banished the townes presently, and then he went to the woods and pastures, and imagining all the fat sheepe he met, to be of kin to the coward Vlisses, because they ran awaie from him, he massacred a whole flocke of good nott Ewes. Last of all hauing no bodie else to kill, poore man killed him selfe; what became of his bodie is vnknowen, some say that wolues and beares did eate it, and that makes them yet such enemies to sheepe and cattell. But his bloud as testifieth *Pouidius* the excellent Historiographer, was turnd into a Hiacint, which is a verie notable kinde of grasse or flower.[60]

Harington continues with a story, borrowed from Rabelais, of a 'young Gentleman' who, having self-administered several laxatives, 'commanded his man to mowe an halfe acre of grasse, to vse at the priuy'.[61] The owners of the field attempted to protect their hay by informing the gentleman that 'it was of that ancient house of A IAX' but the young man was unimpressed and 'in further contempt of his name, vsed a phrase that he had learned at his being in the low Countreys, and bad *Skite vpon AIAX*'. Mysteriously he is immediately 'strikê in his posteriorûs with S. Anthonies fier'. This embarrassing complaint is cured only after a voyage to Japan and the resolution not to use the grass of Ajax as toilet paper 'but rather, teare a leafe out of Holinsheds Chronicles'.[62] In reverence to the memory of the Grecian warrior, the gentleman 'built a sumptuous priuy, and in the most conspicuous place thereof, namely Iust ouer the doore; he erected a statue of AIAX, with so grim a countenance, that the aspect of it being full of terror, was halfe as good as a suppositor'. The place was called 'A-IAX: though since, by ill pronunciation … the accent is changed, and it is called a Iakes.'[63] Several pages later, Harington offers another ribald etymology. This time an old man 'being somewhat costiue, at the house groned so pittifully' that his friends asked him what ailed him.

> He told them, he ayled nothing, but onely according to the prouerbe, he complained, that age breedes aches … oh saith he, maisters make much of youth, for I tell you age akes, age akes. I feele it, age akes. Vpon which patheticall speech of his, deliuered in that place, the younger men that bare him speciall reuerence, termed the place age akes: which agrees fully in pronunciation,

though it may be since, some ill orthographers haue mis-written it,
and so now it passeth currant to be spoken and written A IAX.[64]

The transformations of the name of a Grecian warrior or a
platitude on old age into a term for the lavatory, offer instances of
the kinds of linguistic metamorphoses that animate Puttenham's
discussion and *Twelfth Night*. Like Feste, Harington is a 'corrupter
of words' (III.i.34).

Whatever its etymology (and the *OED* describes its origins as
'unascertained'), the word 'jakes/iakes/iax' was in common
parlance from at least the early half of the sixteenth century.[65]
Florio's translation of Montaigne offers us an example of the term
when discussing the use 'of a commodious aiax or easie close-
stoole'.[66] In Chapter 2 we noted Shakespeare's use of the term to
mean 'privy' in *King Lear*, *Love's Labour's Lost* and *Troilus and
Cressida*. *The Metamorphosis of A IAX*, as we have also seen in
Chapter 2, was extremely popular. In the year of its publication it
went through four editions. 'An Apologie' went through three, and
the anonymous reply, *Vlysses vpon Aiax*, went though two
editions, both in 1596. The book enjoyed a wide circulation and
references and allusions to it as well as parodies of it have been
found in the work of John Davies, Thomas Bastard, Thomas
Nashe, Henry Hutton, John Day, John Marston, Ben Jonson, John
Taylor and Thomas Nabbes (see Chapter 2). That a number of
these allusions occur over several (and, in some cases, many)
years, demonstrates the notoriety of Harington's text. Nabbes's
allusion comes in his *Microcosmus. A Morall Maske* which was not
published until 1637, over forty years after that of Harington's
work.[67] *The Metamorphosis of A IAX* was not only renowned
amongst contemporary and subsequent writers but, if Alan
Brissenden is correct, it was a text much worried over by censors,
politicians and even Elizabeth herself.

In his Oxford edition of *As You Like It*, Brissenden notes the
irregularities that surround its entry in the Stationers' Register.
The title is written on a fly-leaf and lacks the name of the stationer
or a record of the accompanying fee. Nor is the year recorded:
'there was no formal entry for *As You Like It*'.[68] Next to the group
of titles which includes *As You Like It* is written the instruction 'to

be staied', in other words the permission for printing these plays was to be delayed or prevented. Brissenden observes that of the four titles that appear in this group, the other three were all in print within a year. Only *As You Like It* remained unprinted (that is until its inclusion in F1 in 1623). While its non-appearance and the 'gagging-order' may be put down to the reluctance of the Chamberlain's Men to see the play in print and thus render it vulnerable to piracy by another company, Brissenden advances an altogether more compelling explanation. Harington, godson to Elizabeth, was a Captain of Horse in the army of the ill-fated Earl of Essex who, in July 1599, had left on the Irish campaign. Harington returned to court to report on the mission's failure and 'the Queen, furious, sent him packing'.[69] Brissenden notes how Harington's *Metamorphosis of A IAX* had already aroused the displeasure of the Queen and that, since its publication, Sir John Harington had become popularly known as 'Sir Ajax'. Sophie Gee is even more convinced of the work's notoriety: 'Harington's book met with a storm of criticism and anger. The court regarded his proposals as outrageous, and the treatise cost him his favor with the monarch.'[70] In the light of the Queen's personal and the court's widespread disapproval of Harington and the infamy and indecency of his book, the suppression of *As You Like It* can be attributed to no fewer than four reasons:

> first, the name Jaques itself, with its lavatorial / Harington associations; second, the fact that Harington was the Queen's godson; third, the satirical qualities of the role; fourth, the relationship of Harington with the Earl of Essex, who was out of favour with the Queen even before he went to Ireland.[71]

The prominence of Harington's text, attested by Brissenden's carefully argued case, has two major consequences for *Twelfth Night* (usually dated to the year after *As You Like It*) and especially Malvolio's acrostic: first, that Shakespeare's 'M.O.A.I.' was a deliberate echo of the title of *The Metamorphosis of A IAX* and second that he intended it to be recognised as such. The comic effect of the fastidious Malvolio alluding to a text that is not only scatological and shameless in the extreme but that is also, officially, the object of state and monarchical disapproval, is deviously fitting.

While he racks his brains over this mysterious anagram, he is
repeatedly spelling out the abbreviated title of one of the most
notoriously obscene works of the day.

The reluctance of modern criticism to see indecency in
Shakespeare's idyllic comedy has frequently been remarked upon.
Dympna Callaghan notes that 'the raw physical humour [of
Twelfth Night] often disconcerts critics who favour the ethereal
lyricism held to be the definitive characteristic of romantic
comedy'.[72] Brissenden echoes this: 'The more that is learned about
the meanings of words the clearer it becomes that Elizabethans
found bawdy punning publicly acceptable and entertaining in a
way lost by the nineteenth century but rediscovered in the
twentieth.'[73] In the box-tree scene, early modern obscenity fuses
with 'the Elizabethan love of verbal games and acrostics'[74] to
provide an answer to one of the most taxing of Shakespearean
conundrums. Harington's title supplies the only instance of the
letters M, O, A and I *in this particular order*. None of the elaborate
solutions surveyed at the outset of this chapter can claim as
much.

Finally the popularity of *Twelfth Night*'s acronymic games can
be illustrated in two plays which are clearly indebted to
Shakespeare's comedy. In 1607, Dekker and Webster's *West-ward
Hoe* was published. It contains the following exchange on the
handwriting of Mistress Honisuckle:

Iusti.	I trust ere few daies bee at an end to haue her fal to her ioyning: for she has her letters *ad vnguem*: her A. her great B. and her great C. very right D. and E. dilicate: hir double F. of a good length, but that it straddels a little to wyde: at the G. very cunning.
Houy [*sic*].	Her H. is full like mine: a goodly big H.
Iusti.	But her: double LL. is wel: her O. of a reasonable Size: at her p. and q. neither Marchantes Daughter, Aldermans Wife, young countrey Gentlewoman, nor Courtiers Mistris, can match her.
Hony.	And how her v.[75]

Peppered with the same sort of sniggering *double entendre* as her
'c's, her u's and her t's', the passage clearly recalls Malvolio's

pondering on his lady's handwriting. One year later in *The Famelie of Love*, the very same letters that so tax Malvolio reappear as Geradine attempts to seduce Maria (a name borrowed perhaps from the author of 'Olivia's' letter just seven years earlier):

> GER. Here me exemplify loues Latine word
> Together with thy selfe
> As thus, harts ioynd *Amore*: take *A* from thence,
> Then *more* is the perfect morall sence?
> Plurall in manners, which in thee doe shine
> Saintlike, immortall, spotles and diuine.
> Take *m* away, *ore* in beauties name,
> Craues an eternall Trophee to thy fame,
> Lastly take *o*, in *re* stands all my rest,
> Which *I*, in *Chaucer* stile, do terme a iest.[76]

What starts out as a macaronic and sophisticated language game, peters out into the Chaucerian ribaldry of 'tak[ing] *o*' and 'in *re* [i.e. 'thing'] stand[ing]', where 'o', 'thing' and 'stand' have obvious sexual meanings.[77] Again, the combination of bawdy and lexical manipulation is strongly reminiscent of *Twelfth Night*. The fact that the specified letters (A, M, O and I) are exactly the same as those that intrigue Olivia's steward and which have foxed generations of literary critics, suggests that the correspondence is more than a coincidence.

It is in his introduction to the philosophy of Saussure that Jonathan Culler describes the tantalising appeal of such linguistic games as well as the overwhelming desire of readers and audience to search for solutions:

> The most interesting semiotic objects are those which insistently intimate their relation to sign systems but are hard to place and resist easy interpretation. They don't quite fit the system's categories; they seem to escape it, to violate what one takes to be its rules. But since we are governed by the semiological imperative, *Try to make sense of things*, we struggle with the refractory or evasive object, straining and extending our notions of significance ... We encounter here a point ... about literature: if an explicit semiotic code provided interpretations for literary works, literature would have little interest.[78]

While we might comfort ourselves with Culler's 'semiological imperative' which justifies our determination to wrestle with such lexical puzzles as 'M.O.A.I.', we should also note the sobering analogy which arises between our mission in this and that of the love-sick Malvolio confronted with Maria's ingenious letter. In this way the greatest challenge of *Twelfth Night* might be to compel its audiences and commentators to reassess their knowing superiority to Shakespeare's foolish steward and to recognise in his metamorphosis a symbol of their own wavering interpretations. If, as Culler concludes, the significance of literature is in its refusal to comply with a single interpretative shape, *Twelfth Night*, which insists on the inevitability of metamorphosis, is literature indeed.

IV

If, as the last and current chapters have maintained, Harington's toiletry work was sufficiently scandalous to provide a readily discernible solution to the puzzles surrounding the melancholic characterisation of Jaques in *As You Like It* and the metamorphic naming of Malvolio in *Twelfth Night*, its subsequent disappearance from the literary radar is all the more unfortunate. Indeed, as I have argued, the increasingly far-fetched explications of 'M.O.A.I.' surveyed at the outset of this chapter are symptomatic of the disappearance of a text which, at one time, offered an obvious and straightforward solution to the acrostic riddle. As Jason Scott-Warren glumly declares: 'Harington's work has found so few readers even among students of Elizabethan literature.'[79] One such student who fittingly rivals Harington himself in terms of his obscurity today is the Quaker, peace activist, poet, journalist and political firebrand, Reginald Reynolds (1905–58).

Nowadays, Reynolds is probably best known as Mahatma Gandhi's special envoy, liaising with the English authorities during the controversies over Indian Independence and the era of Civil Disobedience. Indeed it was Reynolds who, in March 1930, travelled to Delhi to deliver to the Viceroy, Lord Irwin, the document that became known as 'Gandhi's Ultimatum'. In the letter, Gandhi stressed his pacific intentions and those of his English messenger: 'This letter is not in any way intended as a threat, but is a simple and sacred duty peremptory on a civil register. Therefore I am having it delivered by a young English friend who believes in the Indian cause and is a full believer in non-violence and whom Providence seems to have sent to me, as it were, for the very purpose.'[80] Reynolds was outspoken about the abuse of India at the hands of its British colonisers: 'British rule has destroyed the ancient system of village self-government. What else would you expect? A despotic central administration, conducted by foreigners in a foreign interest, has never been compatible with local autonomy.'[81] Gandhi later wrote to Reynolds: 'You I hold as a gift from God for the advancement of the work.'[82]

On his return to England, Reynolds was to publish several essays on the topic of Indian freedom and remained a fierce opponent of inequality in whichever form he encountered it. For nearly two decades (1940–58) he wrote satirical poetry for the New Statesman and he collaborated with George Orwell and A. J. P. Taylor on a two-volume anthology of British Pamphleteers (1948, 1950). Regarded as seditious, Reynolds was often the subject of surveillance. On one such occasion he directly addressed one of the plain-clothed policemen who was tailing him and offered him a complete list of the places he intended to visit and how long he expected to spend at each one.

It might be stretching a point to suggest that this mixture of humour and subversiveness is a quality Reynolds shared with Harington, yet we have already noted the awkward relationship between the Elizabethan poet and the Elizabethan State. Indeed, both writers share a similarly sceptical attitude towards the prevailing powers: compare Harington's 'On Treason' with Reynolds on a similar topic: 'Treason doth never prosper; what's the reason? / For if it prosper, none dare call it treason.' Citing Blake in an essay of 1941, Reynolds expresses virtually the same sentiment: 'The hand of Vengeance found the bed / To which the Purple Tyrant fled: / The iron hand crush'd the Tyrant's head / And became a tyrant in his stead.'[83] Harington's contempt for the predatory world of high politics is shared by Reynolds who, in 1945, wrote to a friend of his belief that 'Until a new humanity can be created, politics will be a cynical game – and sinister.'[84] Elsewhere, Reynolds was to formulate his disappointment with his country's leaders in roundly scatological terms: 'The politicians pass, the jakes remain.'[85]

Though Reynolds never abandoned his punishing regime of political journalism, writing and speaking engagements – he died in Australia in 1958 while, among other topics, he was 'gathering material on the plight of the Australian Aborigine'[86] – he also demonstrated throughout his work a concern for environmental issues which, with hindsight, establishes him as one of the prophets of modern ecological debate. In particular, he was frustrated that the recycling of human waste as fertiliser, though still common in his blessed India, was regarded as primitive in the West and had given place to 'one of the worst *rackets* in the world, by which I mean the trade in chemical fertilisers.'[87]

Registered as a Conscientious Objector, Reynolds joined the Chelsea Borough Civil Defence, driving for a Mobile Hospital Unit and later training sniffer dogs used in the recovery of buried bomb victims. It was during this exhausting period that he researched and wrote *Cleanliness and Godliness* which was published in 1943. The book's full title makes explicit Reynolds's gleeful debt to Harington: *Cleanliness and Godliness or The Further Metamorphosis: A Discussion of the Problems of Sanitation raised by Sir John Harington, together with Reflections upon Further Progress recorded since that Excellent Knight, by his Invention of the Metamorphosed Ajax, Father of Conveniences, revolutionised the System of Sanitation in this country but raised at the same time fresh Problems for Posterity which are discussed in all their implications, with numerous digressions upon all aspects of Cleanliness by the author Reginald Reynolds.* In Chapter 2 we saw Harington's own satirical take on the protracted and often alliterative titles of early modern medical tracts. Reynolds's title is similarly facetious. Note the alliteration – *System of Sanitation* and *Problems for Posterity* – and the use of the Posterity/posterior pun. At one point, Reynolds discusses his reliance on Harington's work:

> Let us return to fundamentals and resurrect among the Elizabethan giants the figure of AJAX, but for whose appearance at this time the title of this book would have no meaning and my book itself would never have been brought to birth. Lend force and sweetness to my words, Stercutius and Cloacina, Baal-Peor and

Tlaçolteotl, deities of sanitation and fertility; and rise, ye genii, banished from Mohammed's paradise, who frequent the smallest chambers of our houses; for I would pay the neglected tribute of an ungrateful nation to the greatest of its sons, the foremost of its inventors, the most accomplished and versatile genius since the Moorish Zaryab, saving only Leonardo da Vinci.[88]

Reynolds's mock-Tudor language, his Faustian invocation of the fecal deities and the eulogistic admiration of Harington, whom he goes on to call 'the sanitary messiah', deliberately evoke the mock-epic register of *The Metamorphosis*. Yet there remains a serious claim – that an ungrateful culture has overlooked the pioneering sanitary achievements of 'the greatest of its sons'.

While *Cleanliness and Godliness* is concerned with the wasteful-ness of European civilisation and fulminates against the manufacture of chemical fertilisers, particularly at a time of national hardship, it attempts to excavate Harington's radical vision from the embarrassed and euphemistic prudishness of a post-Victorian sensibility. Reynolds laments how, during Victorian times, 'the functions of the closet were considered such a shameful secret that to be seen entering or leaving the smallest room in the house was sufficient to cover with confusion the delin-quent caught *in flagrante delicto*'.[89] Unfortunately, however, although reduced, the force of such a taboo is still intact, nowhere more so than in the Western hemisphere. Reynolds argues that such proscription on the discussion of fecal matters is

peculiarly Puritan in origin, and for this reason of a specifically Anglo-Saxon character, a *taboo* found principally in Britain and the United States of America, not against dirt itself or filthy habits but *against any mention of things relating to excretion*. Thus, the writing of this book is a breach of this particular *taboo* because society conspires to pretend that the principal objects of discussion do not exist.[90]

In his autobiography, *My Life and Crimes*, published just two years before his death, Reynolds noted how his choice of subject matter was responsible for his guarded reception by publishers whose usual difficulties were exacerbated by the paper shortage brought about by the Second World War. They were, Reynolds writes, 'unwilling, very naturally, to speculate on writers with unpopular views who had not even established themselves'.[91]

Recovering in hospital after falling off his bicycle, Reynolds – 'an unemployed cripple' – entered and won a writing competition.[92] The publisher, Philip Unwin, read the piece and wrote to Reynolds inviting him to write a book. In Reynolds's own account of this exchange there is a hint of incredulity that Unwin should have overlooked the churlish tone of Reynolds's initial response:

> The gist of my reply to Philip Unwin was that I was, indeed, a writer of books, but that I was really a serious political writer, whose views were unpopular at the moment. I had – so I told him – no expectation of seeing any book, of the type I should like to have written, published during the war. Then, in a final flourish (remembering those notes begun at Storrington for the hypothetical project known as *Ajax*), I said that if I wrote a book at all it would be a history of the water closet, as I had come to the conclusion that the best part of mankind went down the drain.[93]

In fact, Unwin was enthusiastic and his faith was well placed. *Cleanliness and Godliness* 'sold out rapidly' and was later to result in Reynolds's first American book deal with Doubleday and Company.[94]

While Reynolds was to consider *Cleanliness and Godliness* 'my first non-political book, which was to be quite an important milestone for me', the work is far from apolitical.[95] Reviewers cited the work of Robert Burton and Laurence Sterne as influences, though Reynolds confessed to 'have read very little of either'.[96] Rather, Reynolds acknowledged that his own '"Shandian" efforts' ostensibly, at least, diluted the work's political imperative and that his research for the project was 'held together by sheer exuberance as the project got under way; and much of that exuberance came from the delight in words, not as a means to a political end, but as things to play with'.[97] But it would not be long before Reynolds himself acknowledged that his own fecopolitics placed him in a line of Humanist humorists whose scatological satire is, as we are discovering repeatedly throughout these chapters, a mechanism for exposing all kinds of political or social corruption. Edwin Chadwick, zealous champion of public health and president of the Association of Sanitary Inspectors, is discussed as both a disciple of Harington and a political figure: 'a most worthy gentleman and (in his own Victorian fashion) an apostolic successor of Sir John, carrying into the realm of politics and the administrative battle-field the brave escutcheon of Ajax'.[98] While the mock-Falstaffian language arouses a humorous response, the political implications are deadly serious. Unsurprisingly, two further names Reynolds mentions are Rabelais and Swift. Describing his meeting with the melancholic George Orwell who, Reynolds noted, 'already saw the world through tired eyes', Reynolds offers an analysis of the humour in *Animal Farm*: 'Even the wit was like that of Swift, who laughed at humanity because he despaired of it. The laughter of Rabelais and of Chesterton is confident and boisterous – that of Swift and Orwell is like a jest on the scaffold.'[99]

While *Cleanliness and Godliness* inherits the 'confident and bois-terous' laughter of Rabelais who, as we have seen, was Harington's inspiration, the book roundly confronts the environ-mental damage caused by the use of chemical fertilisers. Thus, in Reynolds's own words, it straddles the two stools of scatological comedy and political censure: *Cleanliness and Godliness* 'had been begun in a mixture of levity and cynicism [but] had ended with a passionate indictment of human folly and the reckless improvi-dence of "civilisation" as urban life became increasingly detached from the roots of its own food'.[100] Indeed, not only does Reynolds concede that, on one level, *Cleanliness and Godliness* is anything but apolitical, but he goes on to remark upon the curiously positive response of those readers whose ideological positions were directly opposed to his own: 'among the first and keenest admirers of the book were people whose political principles I abhorred'.[101] What the radical Reynolds shared with 'the Toryism of (approximately) the eighteenth century' was a concern for the maintenance of the soil's fecundity.[102] While the 'feudal interests' of a degraded aristocracy cast the egalitarian Reynolds in an alter-native, indeed entirely opposed, political camp, their shared anxiety that the fertility of the farmland was fast being depleted made them into strange bedfellows.

Moreover, *Cleanliness and Godliness* is contemptuous of profes-sional politicians. With Orwellian despair Reynolds was to give up on former political allies including the No More War Movement, of which he had been General Secretary.[103] In *Cleanliness and Godliness* this loathing is invigorated with a Swiftian and then Byronic scatology:

> Put not your trust in princes, and still less in politicians. Swift's secret code of the people of Tribnia, or Langden, where a close-stool signified a privy council, and a running sore, the administration, still serves to describe them; nor is there a statesman living for whom I would not write such an epitaph as Byron wrote for Castlereagh:

> *Posterity will ne'er survey*
> *A nobler grave than this:*
> *Here lie the bones of Castlereagh.*
> *Stop, traveller ...*

> But I trust we are of one mind.[104]

But such opprobrium belies the book's informed, eloquent and, given their currency in the twenty-first century, proleptic attitudes to green issues. *Cleanliness and Godliness* is underpinned by a progressive outlook which is both organic and holistic: the cause of physical weakness 'should be sought first *in our food and the manner in which our food is grown*'.[105] Reynolds's attack on industrialised farming sounds weirdly like today's Local Food Movement – broadly speaking the aspiration to consume foods grown locally rather than those imported from overseas with their concomitantly large environmental 'footprint'. Reynolds champions 'the return to an economy where the people of little towns eat the produce of neighbouring fields in all its freshness, and unspoilt by the preservative processes, returning to these same fields their rich heritage of fertile humus'.[106] In fact modern China is currently 'piloting bold experiments, using human waste as a source of fuel' while among the objectives of the Earth Institute is 'the conversion of solid waste into useable energy'.[107] Elsewhere Reynolds espouses strikingly similar ideals to those of the opponents of genetically modified crops:

> The religion of the future ... will attack the sale of adulterated and devitalised food, demanding that the people should have vitamins, and have them more abundantly. It will be concerned with the

needs of the soil, with the limitation of population to a reasonable figure (consistent with the resources of each country) to avoid the evils which we have described; and it will pursue justice and freedom and the Good Life, where men are good because they are happy and satisfied.[108]

The spiritual dimension of this Utopian vision is explicit in Reynolds's green version of the Lord's Prayer: 'Thy Will Be Dung'.[109]

In these ways *Cleanliness and Godliness* is weirdly prescient. Reynolds is unabashed by filth, arguing for it being a pollutant in relative rather than absolute terms: 'dirt is matter misplaced'.[110] Not till nearly a quarter of a century later was the influential anthropological treatise of Mary Douglas's *Purity and Danger* to demonstrate exactly this: 'dirt is essentially disorder. There is no such thing as absolute dirt: it exists in the eye of the beholder.'[111] Alongside its political immediacy and its environmental urgency, *Cleanliness and Godliness* displays a spirited, Haringtonesque scatology. Reynolds relishes his literary inheritance and, just like Harington, runs ancient and modern together. For example, at one point he talks of the lack of toilet paper caused by the privations of the current World War at the same time as name-dropping his literary masters: 'a long trench is poor comfort and wretched hospitality, with army form blanks chopped up *pour torcher le cul* in a manner the Reverend Rabbles (as Sir John calls him) would have justly scorned'.[112] Indeed, Reynolds is adept at ventriloquising the very voice of Harington:

> For I happening to demand of a dear friend of mine, concerning a great companion of his, whether he were religious or no, and namely if he used to pray, he told me that to his remembrance he never heard him ask anything of God, nor thank God for anything: except it were at a jakes, he heard him say, he thanked God he had had a good stool. Thus you see a good stool might move as great a devotion in some man as a bad sermon; and sure it suits very well that *Quorum Deus est Venter, eorum templum sit cloaca*. He that makes his belly his god, I would have him make a jakes his chapel.[113]

Harington is both the stimulus and the presiding spirit of Reynolds's own work: 'Harington was the great revolutionary of his age, the most practical Utopian of the Renaissance, the true prophet of what little progress we can claim.'[114] We have no choice but to follow in Harington's footsteps: 'Whoever will search the scriptures at this time will find that Sir John Harington has been there before him and claimed this whole Empire for Ajax, planting his flag alike upon both testaments with all reverence.'[115] *Ulysses upon Ajax* also appears as well as *The Englishmans Doctor, or The School of Salerne*, Harington's 'Englished' version of *Regimen Sanitatis Salernitanum* – yet another source for Reynolds: 'some excellent precepts [are] to be found in this work concerning the use of the closet'.[116] Given the obscurity of Harington's *Metamorphosis* nowadays, Reynolds's admiration may seem peculiarly intense: 'Thousands of patients will bless his name, their eyes moist with the tears of sincerest gratitude, and great Sir John himself will keep him a place among the Immortals.'[117]

As well as the ubiquitous presence of Harington, Reynolds's work is allusive to a host of other artists. There is mention of Thomas Malory, Samuel Pepys, John Gay, Jonathan Swift, Ned Ward, Tobias Smollett, James Boswell, Samuel Johnson, William Hogarth, John Dryden, Jane Austen, William Wordsworth, John Keats, James Joyce, Rudyard Kipling, George Orwell, Robert Graves and Aldous Huxley. But *Cleanliness and Godliness* is saturated in particular with allusions to early modern writers: Thomas More, Francis Bacon, Thomas Browne, William Camden, King James I, Robert Burton, John Donne, John Florio, Robert Herrick, John Marston, Thomas Dekker, John Taylor and, unsurprisingly, William Shakespeare. In Chapter 2 we considered the masque of the Nine Worthies in *Love's Labour's Lost*. Reynolds uses the same passage to finish his penultimate chapter with a Shakespearean flourish:

> Then at last will Ajax return to the proper dignity which ancient heraldry afforded him, when it attributed to the great Alexander the arms described by Shakespeare in a passage which we have already noticed; and I do not mean where it is written *this love is as mad as Ajax: it kills sheep*; for the metamorphosed Ajax will nourish them, and you may have the wool and the mutton. But I speak of the painted cloth where the lion holds his poll-axe sitting on a close-stool; and if this was a good enough device for one of the

> Nine Worthies, and a conqueror at that, the British Lion might find
> a worse seat and a new world to conquer into the bargain.[118]

The passage, given that the date is 1943, is extraordinary in its contemporaneity. Indeed the mock-Tudor language is frequently punctured by a sudden awareness of the dangers of the present time: 'This very day on which I am writing, Japan declared war upon Great Britain and America.'[119] 'Signor Mussolini and Herr Hitler' appear several times and Reynolds describes how Mr Chamberlain 'turned all four cheeks to Herr Hitler'.[120] Elsewhere he elaborates on the relations between contemporary international politics and hygiene in a fascinating passage:

> If Stalinism has failed to bring sanitation to Russia, or even a better conception of cleanliness, Fascism has done as little for other countries. Always a cleanly people (since the era of plumbing began in Europe), the Germans are neither more nor less so under the Third Reich; while the Italians, who formerly ranked among the dirtiest people in Europe, have held the title under Il Duce.[121]

This glancing at contemporary politics while maintaining the book's literary allusions is typically Haringtonesque. In particular, Shakespeare's texts seep into the foundations of the work: Reynolds uses phrases such as 'sermons in stones' (As You Like It); 'my fortunes are not in one bottom trusted' (The Merchant of Venice); 'Uneasy lies the head that wears a crown' and later, 'uneasily their heads may lie' (II Henry IV); 'The master, the swabber, the boatswain, and I' (The Tempest); 'Alas, poor Yorick!' (Hamlet).[122] He also talks of Falstaff and the 'knightly gauntlets in the Fourth Act of Richard II', while he explicates the title of his book with reference to the magic of The Tempest: 'How rightly ... have we called this book The Further Metamorphosis, that treats of changes more miraculous even than those of which Ariel sang to the disconsolate Ferdinand.'[123] Unsurprisingly the titbit that Shakespeare's father was fined for dumping sewage also appears.[124]

Although Harington's 1596 and Reynolds's 1943 scatological tracts are separated by just under three and a half centuries, there can be no doubt that The Metamorphosis proved to be a vital inspiration to Reynolds and allowed him to reinvigorate the

Elizabethan Humanist's satirical discourse. This cocktail of politics, literary sources, contemporary history and copious erudition deserves a greater readership. The fact that Reynolds and Harington before him were leading exponents of an English scatology which has now been almost entirely eclipsed is the sad proof of just how easy it is to slip between two stools.

NOTES

1 William Shakespeare, *Twelfth Night*, edited by Roger Warren and Stanley Wells (Oxford University Press: Oxford, 1994), pp. 145–9; cited hereafter as Oxford edition. All quotations from *Twelfth Night* (except otherwise indicated) are from this edition.

2 William Shakespeare, *Twelfe Night*, edited by Horace Howard Furness (J. B. Lippincott Company: Philadelphia and London, 1901), p. 166. Cited hereafter as Variorum.

3 William Shakespeare, *Twelfth Night*, edited by J. M. Lothian and T. W. Craik (Methuen and Co.: London, 1975), p. 67. Cited hereafter as Arden II edition.

4 Thomas Middleton, *The Collected Works*, edited by Gary Taylor and John Lavagnino (Clarendon Press: Oxford, 2007), II.i.138. The Oxford editors of *Twelfth Night* also cite Webster's Induction to *The Malcontent* (ll. 25–6) for another instance of this pun, p. 146. The proverbial formulation 'come cut and long-tail' meaning 'in any circumstances' (referring to animals with cropped and long tails, i.e. all animals) is also evocative of female and male genitals (see *The Merry Wives of Windsor*, III.iv.46).

5 Both Arden II and Arden III (edited by Keir Elam (Cengage Learning: London, 2008)) as well as Oxford editions note that 'cut' here may also mean a gelded horse. The *OED* notes the insult but is not decisive in relation to its etymology, 'It is doubtful whether the sense is "cut-tail horse" or "gelding".'

6 Henry Hutton, *Follie's anatomie. Or satyres and satyricall epigrams* (M. Walbanke: London, 1619), B 1.

7 John Foard [*sic*] and Tho[mas] Decker [*sic*], *The Sun's Darling: A Moral Masque* (Andrew Penneycuicke: London, 1656), pp. 12–13.

8 Foard and Decker, *The Sun's Darling*, p. 13.

9 For 'mutton' see *Measure for Measure* in which Lucio nudgingly remarks that the Duke 'would eat mutton on Fridays' (III.i.440). For 'back-trick' see M. P. Tilley, *A Dictionary of the Proverbs in England in the Sixteenth and Seventeenth Centuries* (University of Michigan Press: Ann Arbor, 1950), S842 who cites 'steel to the back' as a euphemism for 'sexually potent'. In *The Merry Wives of Windsor*, Falstaff justifies his sexual appetite:

'When gods have hot backs, what shall poor men do?' (V.v.11). Note also 'the beast with two backs' as an image of copulation (*Othello*, I.i.118).

10 Oxford edition, p. 146.

11 John Taylor, *A common whore with all these graces grac'd, Shee's very honest, beautifull and chaste* (H. Gosson: London, 1635), A 6. For the vaginal 'O', see *Romeo and Juliet*, III.iii.88–90.

12 Dympna Callaghan, '"And all is semblative a woman's part": Body Politics and *Twelfth Night*', *Textual Practice*, 7 (1993), 428–52, p. 437.

13 Leah Scragg, '"Her C's, her U's, and her T's: Why That?": A New Reply for Sir Andrew Aguecheek', *Review of English Studies*, n.s., 42 (1991), 1–16, p. 5. Despite its proximity, Scragg has nothing to say on 'M.O.A.I.'.

14 Variorum, p. 168.

15 Variorum, p. 168.

16 Percy Allen, *Times Literary Supplement*, 1859 (18 September 1937), p. 675.

17 J. J. M. Tobin, 'Malvolio and His Capitals', *American Notes and Queries*, 23 (1985), 69–71, p. 70.

18 Leslie Hotson, *The First Night of Twelfth Night* (Hart Davis: London, 1954), p. 166.

19 Arden II edition, p. 68.

20 Lee Sheridan Cox, 'The Riddle in *Twelfth Night*', *Shakespeare Quarterly*, 13 (1962), 360, p. 360. The irregular punctuation is Cox's.

21 Cox, 'The Riddle in *Twelfth Night*', p. 360.

22 Chris R. Hassel Jr, 'The Riddle in *Twelfth Night* Simplified', *Shakespeare Quarterly*, 25 (1974), 356, p. 356.

23 Hassel, 'The Riddle in *Twelfth Night* Simplified', p. 356.

24 D'Orsay W. Pearson, 'Gulled into an "I"-word, or, Much Ado About a Pronoun', *Journal of the Rocky Mountain Medieval and Renaissance Association*, 8 (1987), 119–30, p. 121.

25 'Ayword' is however retained by the Riverside edition which notes that the sense attached to 'nayword' when it is used in *The Merry Wives of Windsor* (II.ii.122 and V.ii.5) 'seems to be "password"' (p. 418). That sense appears to be inappropriate here.

26 Pearson, 'Gulled into an "I"-word', pp. 122–3.

27 Tilley, *A Dictionary of the Proverbs*, W 884. *Hamlet*, III.ii.191.

28 Another possibility arises from the fact that 'an ayword' on stage would sound like 'an eye-word' as demonstrated by the quibbling at 'Ay, an you had any eye behind you …'. Although the *OED* has no entry for 'eye-word' there may be a *double entendre*, sexual or anal, on the idea of a backward eye. This would make Malvolio's 'let me see, let me see, let me see', especially ironic. Urine was used to alleviate problems with the eye which would link with 'thus makes she her great P's'. (Note Surly's sardonic expression of disbelief, 'if my eyes do cozen me so … I'll have /

A whore, shall piss 'em out, next day', Ben Jonson, *The Alchemist*, edited
by F. H. Mares (Methuen: London, 1971), II.i.43–5.) Finally the assumption that a knowledge of French 'was widespread in the last quarter of
the sixteenth century' (p. 125), upon which Pearson's explanation must
rely, is far from safe. Pistol in IV.iv of *Henry V* and even the King in the
wooing scene, seem painfully ignorant of the language.

29 Inge Leimberg, '"M.O.A.I.": Trying to Share the Joke in *Twelfth Night* 2.5
(A Critical Hypothesis)', *Connotations*, 1 (1991), 78–95, p. 85.

30 In a subsequent article, Leimberg insists that 'the original "and" in
"M.O.A.I." is very often, or even usually, lacking in iconography ... and
therefore will not be missed' ('Maria's Theology and Other Questions
(An Answer to John Russell Brown)', *Connotations*, 1 (1991), 191–6,
p. 192).

31 John Russell Brown, 'More About Laughing at "M.O.A.I." (A Response to
Inge Leimberg)', *Connotations*, 1 (1991), 187–90, pp. 187–8.

32 Brown, 'More About Laughing', pp. 189–90.

33 Donald Sinden, 'Malvolio in *Twelfth Night*', in Philip Brockbank (ed.),
Players of Shakespeare (Cambridge University Press: Cambridge, 1985),
41–66, p. 55. Eric Partridge anticipates Sinden's elision of 'and': 'Note
that Shakespeare has not, after all, omitted the n ... cunt is spelt out
clearly enough' (*Shakespeare's Bawdy* (Routledge: London and New York,
1947), pp. 160–1).

34 Sinden, 'Malvolio in *Twelfth Night*', p. 57. The inconsistent punctuation
is Sinden's/Brockbank's.

35 Arden II edition, p. 68.

36 Arden III edition, p. 243. Among the solutions Elam surveys is this
present one though he merely rehearses my argument rather than eval-
uating it one way or the other.

37 Cynthia Lewis, '"A Fustian Riddle"?: Anagrammatic Names in *Twelfth
Night*', *English Language Notes*, 22 (1984–5), 32–7, pp. 37, 35. More
recently, Lewis has revisited the conundrum objecting to the solution
which follows here. An earlier version of this chapter appeared as an
article in *Renaissance Quarterly*, 51 (1998), 1199–224 of which Lewis
writes, 'In a 25–page article that sneers at all others' speculation while
advancing his own, Peter J. Smith argues that ...' ('Whodunit? Plot,
Plotting, and Detection in *Twelfth Night*' in James Schiffer (ed.), *Twelfth
Night: New Critical Essays* (Routledge: London, 2011), 258–72,
p. 266).

38 Vincent Petronella, 'Anamorphic Naming in Shakespeare's *Twelfth
Night*', *Names*, 35 (1987), 139–46, p. 139.

39 Petronella, 'Anamorphic Naming', pp. 143, 142.

40 Oxford edition, p. 147.

41 Plato, *Cratylus*, translated by N. H. Fowler (Heinemann: London, 1926),

pp. 7, 11. For a discussion of the Cratylic debate see Chapter 2 above.

42 William Camden, *Remaines of a Greater Worke Concerning Britaine* (Simon Waterson: London, 1605), p. 150.

43 Camden, *Remaines*, pp. 153, 154.

44 Larzer Ziff, *Puritanism in America: New Culture in a New World* (Viking Press: New York, 1973), p. 119.

45 Camden, *Remaines*, p. 150. Onomastic revelations were not always fortunate. Governor Thomas Dudley was the recipient of a poem which tactlessly insisted on the brevity of his life – the anonymous poet reassembling the letters of his name to form the glum 'Ah old, must dye' (Cited in Ziff, *Puritanism in America*, p. 119).

46 Jeffrey Walker, 'Anagrams and Acrostics: Puritan Poetic Wit', in Peter White (ed.), *Puritan Poets and Poetics: Seventeenth-Century American Poetry in Theory and Practice* (Pennsylvania State University Press: Pennsylvania and London: 1985), 247–57, p. 256.

47 Maurice Hunt, 'Malvolio, Viola, and the Question of Instrumentality: Defining Providence in *Twelfth Night*', *Studies in Philology*, 90 (1993), 277–97, p. 282.

48 George Puttenham, *The Arte of English Poesie*, edited by Gladys Doidge Willcock and Alice Walker (Cambridge University Press: Cambridge, 1936), p. 108.

49 Puttenham, *The Arte of English Poesie*, p. 102.

50 Julia Briggs estimates that the literacy rate among males in London was over fifty per cent (*This Stage-Play World: English Literature and Its Background, 1580–1625* (Oxford University Press: Oxford, 1983), p. 109). The Reformation stress on the Word of God, the collapse of the ecclesiastical monopoly on literary and religious texts that followed the dissolution of the monasteries and the growth of private libraries all support this estimate. For further evidence see Heidi Brayman Hackel, '"Rowme" of its Own: Printed Drama in Early Libraries', in John D. Cox and David Scott Kastan (eds), *A New History of Early English Drama* (Columbia University Press: New York, 1997), 113–30 and Barbara M. Mowat, 'The Theater and Literary Culture', in the same volume, 231–48.

51 William C. Carroll, *The Metamorphosis of Shakespearean Comedy* (Princeton University Press: Princeton, 1985), p. 5.

52 Carroll, *The Metamorphosis*, p. 31.

53 Puttenham, *The Arte of English Poesie*, p. 144.

54 Jonathan Goldberg, 'Textual Properties', *Shakespeare Quarterly*, 37 (1986), 213–17, p. 217.

55 Ovid, *The xv. Bookes of P. Ouidius Naso, Entituled Metamorphosis* [sic], translated by Arthur Golding (John Windet and Thomas Judson: London, 1584), p. 190^v.

56 Carroll, *The Metamorphosis*, pp. 89–90.

57 In the British Library copy (shelved at c. 21. a. 5) the name appears on the title page as AIAX. Subsequently it appears both as AIAX and A IAX (for example at B 4^v, B 5, D 5, D 8^v as well as the header on F 6, etc.). In the Bodleian copy which is shelved at MAL 509 (and is used for this chapter) the title is clearly printed as A IAX on the title page, the headings on pages A 8 and 1, and the majority of the running headers on the recto leaves. (Whether printed AIAX or A IAX, the word(s) would consist of two syllables.)

58 Ovid, *The xv. Bookes*, p. 166.

59 *II Henry VI*, V.i.25–7.

60 Sir John Harington, *A New Discourse of a Stale Subject, Called the Metamorphosis of Aiax* (Richard Field: London, 1596), A 8–8^v.

61 Harington, *A New Discourse*, B 1.

62 Harington, *A New Discourse*, B 1^v.

63 Harington, *A New Discourse*, B 2.

64 Harington, *A New Discourse*, B 4^v.

65 The *OED* lists instances up to 1969 including one from Joyce's *Ulysses*. On the interchangeable use of 'i' and 'j', the *OED* notes, 'In Dictionaries, the I and J words continued to be intermingled in one series down to the 19th c.' In Shakespeare's work, the letters were not distinguished until the publication of F4 in 1685 (see John Pitcher, 'Names in *Cymbeline*', *Essays in Criticism*, 43 (1993), 1–16, p. 16).

66 Michel de Montaigne, *The Essayes of Michael Lord Montaigne*, translated by John Florio (George Routledge and Sons: London, 1891), p. 557.

67 Thomas Nabbes, *Microcosmus. A Morall Maske* (Charles Greene: London, 1637), D 3.

68 William Shakespeare, *As You Like It*, edited by Alan Brissenden (Oxford University Press: Oxford, 1994), p. 2.

69 Shakespeare, *As You Like It*, edited by Brissenden, p. 3.

70 Sophie Gee, *Making Waste: Leftovers and the Eighteenth-Century Imagination* (Princeton University Press: Princeton and Oxford, 2010), p. 13.

71 Shakespeare, *As You Like It*, edited by Brissenden, p. 3.

72 Callaghan, '"And all is semblative a woman's part": Body Politics and *Twelfth Night*', p. 435.

73 Shakespeare, *As You Like It*, edited by Brissenden, p. 35.

74 Oxford edition, p. 50.

75 Tho [mas] Decker [*sic*] and Iohn Webster, *West-Ward Hoe* (John Hodgets: London, 1607), B 4v.

76 Anon., *The Famelie of Love* (John Helmes: London, 1608), D 2–2^v. While G. K. Hunter and Andrew Gurr attribute the play to Thomas Middleton, the editors of *Middleton's Collected Works* have not included it. See G. K. Hunter, *English Drama, 1586–1642* (Clarendon Press: Oxford, 1997), p.

562; Andrew Gurr, *The Shakespearian Playing Companies* (Clarendon Press: Oxford, 1996), p. 352; Gary Taylor and John Lavagnino (eds), *Thomas Middleton and Early Modern Textual Culture* (Clarendon Press: Oxford, 2007), p. 444.

77 For 'O', see note 11 above. For 'thing' as euphemism for genitals in Chaucer, see *Wife of Bath's Prologue*, ll. 121 and 510 (Geoffrey Chaucer, *The Riverside Chaucer*, edited by Larry D. Benson (Oxford University Press: Oxford, 1988), pp. 106, 112). In *Twelfth Night*, see III.iv.290–1. In *Macbeth* the Porter quibbles over 'stand' when he describes the influence of alcohol on sexual potency: it 'makes him stand to and not stand to' (II.iii.33).

78 Jonathan Culler, *Saussure* (Fontana/Collins: London, 1976), pp. 115–16.

79 Jason Scott-Warren, *Sir John Harington and the Book as Gift* (Oxford University Press: Oxford, 2001), p. 59.

80 Quoted in Robert Huxter, *Reg and Ethel: Reginald Reynolds, His Life and Work and His Marriage to Ethel Mannin* (Sessions Book Trust: York, 1992), p. 56.

81 Reginald Reynolds, *Cleanliness and Godliness* (George Allen and Unwin: London, 1943), p. 121.

82 Huxter, *Reg and Ethel*, p. 57.

83 John Harington, *Letters and Epigrams of Sir John Harington*, edited by Norman Egbert McClure (University of Pennsylvania Press: Philadelphia, 1930), p. 255 and Huxter, *Reg and Ethel*, p. 141. The quotation is from Blake's 'The Grey Monk', *William Blake's Writings*, edited by G. E. Bentley, 2 vols (Clarendon Press: Oxford, 1978), II, 1311.

84 Huxter, *Reg and Ethel*, p. 3.

85 Reynolds, *Cleanliness*, p. 97.

86 Huxter, *Reg and Ethel*, p. 230.

87 Reynolds, *Cleanliness*, p. 260.

88 Reynolds, *Cleanliness*, pp. 61–2.

89 Reynolds, *Cleanliness*, p. 167.

90 Reynolds, *Cleanliness*, p. 167.

91 Reginald Reynolds, *My Life and Crimes* (Jarrolds: London, 1956), p. 185.

92 Reynolds, *Life*, p. 185.

93 Reynolds, *Life*, p. 186.

94 Reynolds, *Life*, p. 186.

95 Reynolds, *Life*, p. 92.

96 Reynolds, *Life*, p. 186.

97 Reynolds, *Life*, p. 187.

98 Reynolds, *Cleanliness*, p. 86. Chadwick features in the *DNB*, edited by Sir Leslie Stephen and Sir Sidney Lee (Oxford University Press: London, 1917), XXII, 406–8.

99 Reynolds, *Life*, pp. 212, 213.
100 Reynolds, *Life*, p. 201.
101 Reynolds, *Life*, p. 201.
102 Reynolds, *Life*, p. 202.
103 Reynolds, *Life*, pp. 96, 140.
104 Reynolds, *Cleanliness*, p. 226.
105 Reynolds, *Cleanliness*, p. 215.
106 Reynolds, *Cleanliness*, p. 251.
107 Kerry Brown, Review of *When a Billion Chinese Jump: How China will Save Mankind – or Destroy It* by Jonathan Watts, *Times Higher Education*, 1955 (8 July 2010), 48–9, p. 48 and Martin Cohen, 'Profits of Doom', *Times Higher Education*, 1958 (29 July 2010), 34–9, p. 36.
108 Reynolds, *Cleanliness*, p. 262.
109 Reynolds, *Cleanliness*, p. 201.
110 Reynolds, *Cleanliness*, p. 217.
111 Mary Douglas, *Purity and Danger: An Analysis of the Concept of Pollution and Taboo* (Routledge: London, 2002), first published 1966, p. 2.
112 Reynolds, *Cleanliness*, p. 136.
113 Reynolds, *Cleanliness*, p. 194.
114 Reynolds, *Cleanliness*, p. 10.
115 Reynolds, *Cleanliness*, p. 21.
116 Reynolds, *Cleanliness*, pp. 16, 36.
117 Reynolds, *Cleanliness*, p. 117.
118 Reynolds, *Cleanliness*, p. 251.
119 Reynolds, *Cleanliness*, p. 130.
120 Reynolds, *Cleanliness*, p. 209.
121 Reynolds, *Cleanliness*, pp. 129–30.
122 Reynolds, *Cleanliness*, pp. 17, 68, 41, 97, 53.
123 Reynolds, *Cleanliness*, pp. 254, 200, 217–18.
124 Reynolds, *Cleanliness*, p. 55.

4

Cavalier scatology between two stools: Rochester, Mennes, Pepys, Urquhart and the sense of dis-ordure

[Rochester's] verses cut and sparkle like diamonds.[1]

I

Published in his *Poems* of 1680, Rochester's 'Song' typifies the debauched excess of the 'Cavalier':

> I Rise at Eleven, I Dine about Two,
> I get drunk before Seven, and the next thing I do;
> I send for my *Whore*, when for fear of a *Clap*,
> I Spend in her hand, and I Spew in her *Lap*:
> There we quarrel, and scold, till I fall fast asleep,
> When the *Bitch*, growing bold, to my Pocket does creep;
> Then slyly she leaves me, and to revenge th'affront,
> At once she bereaves me of *Money*, and *Cunt*.
> If by chance then I wake, hot-headed and drunk,
> What a coyle do I make for the loss of my *Punck*?
> I storm, and I roar, and I fall in a rage,
> And missing my *Whore*, I bugger my *Page*:
> Then crop-sick, all *Morning*, I rail at my *Men*,
> And in Bed I lye Yawning, till Eleven again.

> (ll.1–14)[2]

This diurnal round of eating, drinking, molestation, quarrelling, theft and exploitation seems, at first sight, to be brazenly and aggressively self-determined. The day starts when the narrator wakes and ends when he sleeps. His selfishness is inscribed on every clause; every line contains at least one use of the first-person pronoun and in no fewer than nine lines it appears twice or more. The narrator of the poem (could that be Rochester?) is unbound by any social protocols, sexual proprieties or cultural niceties.[3] Only his fear of disease influences his behaviour, ejaculating in his mistress's hand instead of her vagina.[4] He sleeps in (surely a rebuttal of the Puritan work ethic), dines late and gets drunk early. He spends the evenings with his whore and if she is unavailable, he will turn to the nearest alternative and bugger the page. The perfunctory nature of this alternative is symptomatic of the speaker's egocentricity – others exist only to satisfy his pleasure, whether they be his servants against whom he rails, his whore with whom he quarrels, or the pageboy. But the boy is only a quiet, passive receptor of the speaker's sexual appetites and, we might add, fluids. Paul Hammond writes, 'The act seems to be produced more by anger and frustration than by desire, an assertion of power rather than an act of love.'[5] Obviously the page's consent is unsolicited and unrequired as he exists merely to satisfy and, in so doing, pacify his master, called upon when all other options have proved unavailable.[6] The boy 'is not simply an inferior but a dependant: in no sense sharing in pleasures or admitted to the status of a friend, he is there entirely to provide physical relief'.[7] Of all the secondary figures in the poem, it is the page who is treated most dismissively, most anonymously and most cavalierly. His being compulsorily sodomised is the final demonstration of the fiercely abusive character of the Cavalier – a term which denotes a level of courtly sophistication but which has come to connote, typified by conduct like the above, haughtiness, nonchalance, disdain, even superciliousness. Peter Porter suggests that such cavalier arrogance thinly masks the political uncertainties of the Caroline Restoration: Rochester and his ilk 'were the sons and heirs of long-exiled cavaliers [Rochester's own father died in exile], men and women distrustful even of their own legitimation. Behind their masks of fashion, their charades to relieve boredom and their sexual preditoriness, was a Hobbesian anxiety about the state itself ... What came back with King Charles was anxiety as well as idleness and horseplay.'[8]

This trepidation is discernible in the description of the daily

THE SENSE OF DIS-ORDURE

routine of this spoiled and soiled patrician: his customary diversions rapidly take on an air of hollowness. The poem's largely paratactic grammar lists his reiterated daily activities in a banal inventory which intimates ennui rather than gratification. In a letter (1675–7?) to Henry Savile, Rochester finds nothing left remarkable beneath the visiting moon: 'The world, ever since I can remember, has been still so insupportably the same that 'twere vain to hope there were any alterations, and therefore I can have no curiosity for news.'[9] For his part, Savile too was unimpressed with the world: 'from the rising of the Sun to the setting thereof, I see noething that pleases my eyes, nor heare noething but what grates my eares'.[10] For the libertine of 'Song', in spite of his Epicurean pursuit of the good life, what he describes is a world that turns tediously around the sating of appetites – appetites which will require just as much assuaging the very next day. The poem makes its end where it began – 'I Rise at Eleven ... till Eleven again' – and this orbital continuity implies that this dissolution constitutes nothing more than a vicious circle of addiction inside of which the Cavalier eats, drinks, spews and fucks his way to oblivion. As Warren Chernaik argues, 'lust becomes indistinguishable from rage'.[11]

When, in Rochester's poetry, satisfaction does come, it is only ever fleeting: 'If I by miracle can be / This livelong Minute true to Thee / Tis' all that Heaven allowes.'[12] Carole Fabricant insists on the ephemeral nature of erotic gratification: 'in instance after instance Rochester's poetry is characterized, not by the exultation of sexuality as commonly assumed, but by an unequivocal demonstration of the latter's transience and futility'.[13] As well as being short-lived, there is nothing sensual or erotic about the Cavalier's sexual exploits, nothing savoury or satisfying about the food or wine. Melissa E. Sanchez terms these cavalier sexual encounters 'gallingly deficient' and proposes that while satisfaction depends on (self-)deception – 'The perfect Joy of being well deceaved', as the poet has it in 'Artemiza to Chloe' (l. 115) – 'Rochester's poetry insists that we can never be well deceived enough, that the joy provided by delusion, like all other human enjoyment, remains decidedly inadequate.'[14] This is a life of conspicuous but nugatory consumption which eludes satisfaction and stumbles drunkenly towards despondency and melancholy. Jeremy Lamb reads this decline in biographical terms: 'as the 1660s ticked by, [Rochester's] alcoholism ensured that the once steady stream of euphoria which drink had brought him evaporated into shorter, darker, costlier bursts, finally culminating in suicidal thoughts'.[15] Along with the vanity of the Cavalier's lifestyle, his very identity is swamped with craving. The process of satisfying his appetite is little more than mechanical as the egocentricity, which we noted above, is transmuted into bleak solipsism in the alembic of despair.

This then is the inverse of the Cavalier as royal courtier, as heroic, curly-locked swaggerer, as gifted poet and diplomat, as sensual lover. In her suggestively entitled essay on Rochester, 'The Sense of Nothing', Barbara Everett shows how the radiance of Caroline surface gives way, in Rochester's poetry, to a vacuum: 'even his most elegant verse often resounds with the crash of breaking glass; or where there is no crash, a startled reader will find himself glimpsing a void beneath the bright surface, a vacancy beneath the brilliant style'.[16] This hollowness is masked by Caroline ostentation, the equestrian portraits of King Charles or the relaxed splendour of Sir Anthony van Dyck's dynastic groupings. Miles away from the luxuriant pastorals of Sir Peter Lely, or the voluptuous eroticism of poets like Sir John Suckling or Thomas Carew, Rochester's is a world, in Vivian de Sola Pinto's phrase, 'of ugliness, cruelty, and filth'.[17] This tripartite Hobbesian formulation is no accident even though critics are divided on the contribution of Hobbes to Rochester's work. For Stephen Clark for instance, Hobbes acts as a stimulant on the poet: 'The libertine recuperation of Hobbes ... provokes a spendthrift pursuit of immediate and intense sensation.'[18] It is among others, argues Pinto, on the other hand, the influence of Hobbes with his 'mechanico-materialistic universe' which brings about the ontological crisis giving rise to physical impotence, theological confusion, intellectual despair and religious doubt.[19] 'After Death, nothing is, and nothing Death, / The utmost limit of a Gasp of Breath. / ... Devouring Time swallows us whole; / Impartial Death confounds Body and Soul.'[20] His bedside confessor and first biographer, Gilbert Burnet, records that, even in prose, Rochester formulated this nihilism with disarming simplicity: 'He said, They were happy that believed: for it was not in every man's power.'[21]

In this dystopia, caustic dissatisfaction turns readily into self-loathing, shame and disgust, frequently animated by a savage intensity. Ken Robinson opens his pertinently entitled essay, 'The Art of Violence in Rochester's Satire' with the bald sentence: 'Rochester's poetry is often violent.'[22] Rochester's various poems about masculine impotence rail at his human frailty and mire his suave, cavalier aesthetic in brutal obscenity. Cephas Goldsworthy accounts for this violence in terms of Rochester's personal impotence: 'For many years Rochester's amorous powers had been failing. The reasons were many: mercury poisoning causes impotence, as do the later stages of syphilis. All the curses he had called down upon his recalcitrant member eventually arrived to plague him.'[23] For Graham Greene, Rochester's impotence is the spur to his jealousy: 'The age of impotence had come upon him early, and those who can no longer give pleasure themselves are prone to believe that pleasure will be sought elsewhere.'[24] Admonishing his limp manhood in 'One Writing Against his Prick', Rochester challenges its obdurate failure via a series of savage rhetorical questions: 'Did shee not raise thy drooping head on high / As it lay Nodding on her wanton thigh? / Did shee not clap her leggs aboute my back / Her Porthole open? Damn'd Prick what is't you lack?' (ll. 11–14) and the poem ends with a rigid warning: 'Hence forth stand stiff and gaine your creditt los't / Or I'le nere draw thee, but against A Post' (ll. 15–16).[25] Again, in 'Song' ('Bless me you stars!...'), the frustration of sexual impotence is powerfully conveyed by the blunt and trashy pornographic descriptions of his mistress: 'Her Leggs stretcht wide, her Cunt to me did show' (l. 6). Yet in spite of the unabashed nature of this peep show, he is unable to attain an erection: 'Yea thô she took it in her warm moyst hand / And Crammed it in (Dul Dog) it would not stand' (ll. 17–18).[26] The libertine is alienated from that which defines him, his own predatory sexuality, symbolised in his own phallic appetites. His penis is now an object of his denunciation as 'Frustration leads to aggression, and aggression is vented on the offender.'[27] This is the Cavalier as hollow man, pox-ridden, drunk, violent and impotent.

For David Farley-Hills, Rochester's verdict on love is as 'a

degraded experience and, therefore, an archetypal situation for
demonstrating the fatuousness, the essential meaninglessness,
of all human experience'.[28] While Farley-Hills captures the
poignant incoherence of Rochester's vision, his use of 'archetypal' and the generalisation of 'all human experience' erases
the historic specificity of the poetry. Rochester's is not a
universal disgust, not, as Ronald W. Johnson would have us
believe, an expression of his 'bleak vision of mankind', but, as
the many references to his contemporaries testify, the result of
a precise set of historical and political circumstances.[29] As David
M. Vieth insists, Rochester's poetry needs to be read decisively
in terms of the 'radical metamorphoses that occurred in English
language and literature during the early years of the
Restoration'.[30] He goes on:

> The decade and a half following the restoration of Charles II
> probably marks the most traumatically rapid set of cultural
> changes the English-speaking peoples have ever experienced.
> Under the impact of events of the mid-century, earlier notions of
> unity, authority and hierarchical relationship gave way to those of
> multiplicity, disparity, and toleration. A theoretically holistic
> culture was replaced by what was in fact a fragmented society, with
> a social and political dynamic actuated by vectors of special-
> interest groups.[31]

This emphasis on the traumatic nature of local historical circumstances in the aftermath of the English Civil War has been restated
more recently. Writing of Rochester and Ned Ward, Mona Narain
avers that 'both writers remain deeply concerned with the
ongoing traumatic changes in class and social structure put in
motion by the Restoration, which continued for decades till the
close of the seventeenth century'.[32] Citing such luminaries as A. J.
Smith and C. V. Wedgwood, Howard Erskine-Hill suggests that the
post-Civil War aristocratic subject articulates 'the voice of fagged
out Royalism'.[33] The popularity of Rochester's poetry, composed
during the Interregnum, is among those newly disempowered by
their dislocation from the centre of politics following the arrival,
as a political force, of the middling sort: 'Rochester's verse ...
appealed to the affluent, culturally disoriented, alienated youth of
the 1670s.'[34] Such dislocation is visible in Rochester's scathing

opinion of those now in power – eager, he claims, to serve their own ambitions rather than their country: 'They who would be great in our little government seem as ridiculous to me as school-boys who with much endeavour and some danger climb a crab-tree, venturing their necks for fruit which solid pigs would disdain if they were not starving.'[35]

Greene ascribes this sense of contempt to the disappointments of the Restoration:

> The sombre desperate mood in which his poetry seems usually to have been composed was aided by the general disillusionment of the time. So much had been expected of the Restoration and so little had come of it; so much had been expected of the war with Holland, and it brought only disgrace. Vast hopes disappointed are apt to leave an overmastering weariness behind, and war is not usually followed by peace of mind. The excitement of war is a drug that we miss in the dull days after. Spleen was the disease which ran through the literature of the succeeding quieter years ... Disillusionment, monotony, boredom preyed worst on the finest spirits.[36]

Notice the way in which Greene describes political turmoil in relation to physical illness. The entire culture of the day, according to Greene, was splenetic and Savile actually uses this word of his own demeanour when, writing to Rochester in June 1678, he declares, 'I am troubled with spleenetick vapours that make mee dislike the world as much as ever I approved it.'[37] In the introduction to his magisterial *Dictionary of Sexual Language and Imagery in Shakespearean and Stuart Literature*, Gordon Williams attributes this Restoration spleen to the humiliation of Republican victory in the English Civil War. Rochester's poetry with all its pornographic and scatological content is physically scarred by the experience of defeat: 'What the sexual language of Restoration court society illustrates above all is a maimed elite, still reeling from the shock of being challenged – and defeated – by a bunch of farmers and shopkeepers.'[38] More pertinent still, for our purposes, is Williams's description of the nauseating aesthetic that follows the overthrow of the royalist body politic: 'there is a new dimension to the harping on natural emissions, which become the repulsive suppurations of disease'.[39] Fittingly, this 'harping on natural emissions' is evident in Burnet's descriptions of Rochester's own decrepitude:

> He had not been long in the Country when he thought he was so well, that being to go to his Estate in *Somersetshire* he rode thither Post. This heat and violent motion did so inflame an Ulcer, that was in his Bladder, that it raised a very great pain in those parts: Yet he with much difficulty came back by Coach to the Lodge at *Woodstock-Park*. He was then wounded both in Body and Mind: He understood Physick and his own Constitution and Distemper so well, that he concluded he could hardly recover: For the Ulcer broke and vast quantities of purulent matter passed with his Urine. But now the hand of God touched him, and as he told me, It was not only a general dark Melancholy over his Mind, such as he had formerly felt; but a most penetrating cutting Sorrow. So that though in his Body he suffered extream pain for some weeks, Yet the Agonies of his Mind sometimes swallowed up the sense of what he felt in his Body.[40]

Here Burnet insists on the contiguity of physical and mental maladies; bodily disease is inseparable from spiritual and emotional dis-ease. As Burnet later reports, 'In this disposition of Mind did he continue all the while I was with him, four days together; He was then brought so low that all hope of Recovery was gone. Much purulent matter came from him with his Urine, which he passed always with some pain; But one day with unexpressible torment.'[41]

The force of the metaphor of the body politic is evident in Edward Hyde's description of the displaced aristocracy. The Earl of Clarendon thought Restoration boorishness and acerbity were viscerally motivated: 'The tenderness of bowels, which is the quintessence of justice and compassion, the very mention of good nature, was laughed at and looked upon as the mark and character of a fool; and a roughness of manners, or hardheartedness and cruelty, was affected … much of the malignity was transplanted, instead of being extinguished, to the corruption of many wholesome bodies, which, being corrupted, spread the diseases more powerfully and more mischievously.'[42] Clarendon's metaphor had, for the seventeenth century, a physical cause. Thomas Hearne recalled that the young Rochester 'had a natural

Distemper upon him which was extraordinary, & he thinks might be one occasion of shortening his Days, which was that sometimes he could not have a stool for 3 Weeks or a Month together'.[43] Rochester's own corporeal decline as well as the cruelty of his demeanour and that of his social equals are reified in a disorder of the guts. It is as though he figures forth in the concoction of pus and piss, the crisis of the aristocracy displaced from the centres of power by the middling sort.

As Jeffrey C. Persels has noted in respect of an earlier period, 'the proper functioning of the body human has direct bearing on the proper functioning of the body politic ... The body, the intestines, excrement and their relative health thus prove to be so many evident metaphors for social order.'[44] This of course is only half the story, as the health of the nation is just as likely to be vehicle as tenor of the metaphor. Physical affliction need not just be symbolic of social disharmony, but it can be *symbolised by* social disharmony. Rochester's depiction of the body politic being subjected to the whims and incontinences of the body natural (as in the much-vaunted debauchery of Charles II himself) becomes then a discourse of political critique and issues from within its own ranks. Proximity to the centre makes the realisation that it cannot hold all the more disturbing. As Pinto puts it, 'The criticism is all the more effective because it comes from one who is within the society which is criticized and who possesses its virtues of easy sureness of tone and diction and poise of gesture and rhythm.'[45] Simon Dentith agrees:

> In social and historical terms, Rochester may be seen as symptomatic of a wider crisis of authority ... This crisis of authority manifests itself in a distrust of any secure language whatsoever, though this distrust is itself articulated in a tone of linguistic authority derived from the assumption of aristocratic ease.[46]

It is precisely this undermining of his own cavalier position which makes Rochester such a scourge both to himself and his contemporaries.[47] As Everett writes, 'a work of art is recognised by its incapacity to be absorbed wholly by the society which produces it, and which it represents so admirably'.[48] A similar internal tension is recognised by Richard Harries: 'Satire, however scurrilous or

scatological, gets its energy not only from the views it attacks but
from the sense of corresponding virtues which are betrayed.'[49]
Such a regime, Rochester insists self-consciously, has lost its
potency and cavalier corporeality becomes infused with the
despondency of failure, riddled with the disfiguring diseases of
political disgrace. Rochester's lampoon on the literary efforts of
John Sheffield, Earl of Mulgrave, '*My Lord* All-Pride', is typically
scatological:

> Bursting with pride the loath'd Impostume swel's,
> Prick him he shed's his venom straight and smel's,
> But 'tis so lewd, a Scribler that he writes
> With as much force to nature as he fights.
> Harden'd in shame, 'tis such a baffled Fop
> That every School-boy whips him like a Top.
> And with his arm and heart his brain's so weak,
> That his starv'd fancy is compell'd to rake
> Among the excrements of others wit
> To make a stinking meal of what they shit.
> So Swine for nasty meat to dunghill run,
> And toss their gruntling Snouts up when they've done.
>
> (ll. 1–12)[50]

Unsurprisingly, the kind of personalised scatological attack we
find in Rochester is of a piece with the poet's misanthropic
darkness of tone.

Often, the scatology is indistinguishable from the kinds of
sexual disgust we have already witnessed. Rochester stages a
poetic exchange between Louise de Keroualle, Duchess of
Portsmouth, and Nell Gwyn (both mistresses of Charles II) in
which they rail vituperatively at each other and agree only in their
joint damnation of Hortense Mancini, duchesse de Mazarin, who,
following her arrival in December 1675, was also vying for the
King's attentions:

> NELL: When to the King I bid good Morrow,
>   With Tongue in Mouth, and Hand on Tarse,
>   Portsmouth may rend her Cunt for Sorrow,
>   And *Mazarine* may kisse myne *Arse*.

PORTS: When Englands *Monarch*'s on my Belly
           With Prick in Cunt, thô double Cramm'd,
           Fart of mine Arse, for small whore Nelly
           And Great Whore *Mazarine* be damn'd.

                                                      (ll. 1–8)[51]

This obscene dialogue exemplifies the mutual assimilation of
sexual and scatological disgust. The poem vacillates between the
brusque anality of Nell's and Portsmouth's curses ('kisse myne
Arse' and 'Fart of mine Arse') and the casually gross descriptions
of sexual activity. Yet the poem is more than mere bathos. It would
seem to demonstrate the historically specific abjection and
despondency which Greene, Williams, Porter, Sanchez, Vieth,
Pinto *et al.* describe and which we have seen writ large in 'Song' ('I
Rise at Eleven ...'). Nell, Portsmouth and the absent Mazarin are
the unfortunate heirs of a tradition of literary misogyny seen at its
most vicious in the tragic dramas of the Jacobeans and, like the
women in Tourneur or Webster, they are synechdochic figures of
a historically localised cultural anxiety. Their filthy language,
straddling the two stools of sexual and scatological, fuses one
orifice with another: cunt and arse become synonymous as their
corruption is figured both front and back. Elsewhere, the speaker
of 'The Advice' encourages the shepherd to abjure the company of
women on the grounds that they are more trouble than they are
worth. The female capacity to provide release from sexual tension
is nothing more than 'Easing us of an Excrementish Load' (l.
15).[52] While the term 'excrement' could refer to different kinds of
innocuous physical product such as hair, nails or even feathers,
the word was also being used to refer specifically (according to
OED at least since 1533) to fecal matter.[53] Rochester's use of
'Excrementish Load' draws together vaginal and anal as the
ultimate destination of the shepherd's ejaculate. As Will Stockton
points out, 'the discourse of sodomy conflates and confuses the
anus and the vagina, female and male bodies, and threatens
sexual difference'.[54]

But perhaps the most explicit superimposition of front and
back orifices and one which is most conspicuously suggestive of
the recent civil strife, occurs in a lyric of eight stanzas which

recounts the double penetration of Phillis 'In the *Fields* of *Lincolns Inn*'.[55] While Coridon's penis is 'fitted, / To her less frequented Arse' (l. 12), Strephon's is thrust 'into her *Cunt*' (l. 16). What follows is an extraordinary account of a penile battle which, within the body of Phillis, rehearses the imbroglio of political disorder:

> Now for Civil *Wars* prepare,
> Rais'd by fierce intestine bustle,
> When these *Heroes* meeting justle,
> In the *Bowels* of the fair.
>
> They tilt, and thrust with horrid pudder,
> Blood, and slaughter is decreed;
> Hurling Souls at one another,
> Wrapt in flakey *Clotts* of *Seed*.
>
> (ll. 17–24)

This internal dissension, strife within the '*Bowels* of the fair', figures forth the historic as hysteric (in its Greek sense of 'belonging to the womb'). The 'fierce intestine bustle' literalises the metaphor of the body politic so that Phillis's vagina/anus becomes the battle ground – the site of 'Civil *Wars*' – for the clashing weapons of her suitors. But note also the martial aspect of the struggle: the heroes jostle one another, tilting, thrusting with horrid pudder, and the inevitable products of battle, blood and slaughter, are fatally determined while the spilling of souls, manifest in their emissions, both vaginally and anally, is simultaneously an image of death and the little death of orgasm.[56] The role of Phillis in the performance is worth examining. Though she initiates the activity – the second stanza informs us that it is she who 'Lay most pensively contriving, / How to Fuck with *Pricks* by pairs' (ll. 7–8) – once the shepherds take up battle stations, she is pretty much absent, merely the field on which the combat is being fought. Her absence turns the business into something very like a homoerotic exchange or at least a homosocial encounter, a tournament between knights for the honour of an observing but passive lady, rather than a sexual feat in which she takes an active role.[57] In this way the poem again draws together vagina and anus; if the battlefield is a level one (though Strephon's prick 'was a handful longer' (l. 13)), Phillis becomes merely the provider of two apertures rather than an erotic or aroused presence in her own right. Oddly, at this point, the poem insists on a kind of internal propriety which prevents the mutual annihilation of the two warriors. Nature's barrier, the wall of the vagina, ensures that martial strife remains only metaphorical. For all the vigour of their warfare, both pricks live to fight another day:

> *Nature* had 'twixt *Cunt* and *Arse*,
> Wisely plac'd firm separation;
> God knows else what desolation
> Had ensu'd from *Warring Tarse*.
>
> (ll. 25–8)

Nature's mission is to protect the warring tarses (or as Rochester has the plural, '*Tarse*') no matter which hole they have occupied.[58] But the vaginal wall is not intended to forbid or even discourage anal intercourse; rather its role is to pacify the warring cocks and guarantee their future potency. Even as the poem insists on the separation of front and back, then, this is not the primary objective. In fact, the conclusion of the poem delineates a mutual satisfaction without identifying a victor. All are sated no matter where they have been: 'The *Nymph* was sorely *Ballock* beaten, / Both the *Shepherds* soundly tir'd' (ll. 31–2). The fact that the shepherds are undifferentiated implies the interchangeablility of their coital destinations – while they may be divided from each other, front and back are equivalent targets. In the words of Farley-Hills, 'Nature as a cruel and blind jest centres our sexual instruments in the places of excrement.'[59] Yet, as the specificity of 'Civil *Wars*' implies, the agent of this confusion is not universal Nature but particular mid-seventeenth-century History. As Fabricant insists, 'Throughout Rochester's writings, delineations of a perfect sexuality are carefully, even emphatically, distanced from everyday Restoration reality.'[60]

The metaphor of war standing in for frantic sexual activity appears several times in *Sodom*. Addressing his catamite

Pockinnello, King Bolloxinian remarks on the conflict between his
reason and his desire, the latter of which compels him to prefer
sodomising his servant to sleeping with his queen (Cuntagratia):

> Yoᵣ Charms more great then Cuntagratias are
> And euery glance prognosticates a warre,
> Warre t'wixt my reason & its pleasing sence
> That is o' th' Buggering the Gods from hence.
>
> (III.i.85–8)[61]

Later an exhausted Buggeranthes suggests that 'toyles of C[un]t
are more then toiles of warre' (III.iv.35). Sexual and martial
striving are confused and stand in for one another as the social
and political uncertainties of the age are imaged as orgiastic
gropings which defy conventional sexual taxonomies.

Another example of the unification of sexual and fecal occurs
in Rochester's 'On Mrs Willis'. The fifth stanza runs together the
erotic and the scatological: 'Bawdy in thoughts, precise in Words,
/ Ill natur'd though a Whore, / Her Belly is a Bagg of Turds, / And
her Cunt a Common shore' (ll. 17–20).[62] *OED* defines 'common-
shore' specifically as a channel for effluent: 'being originally the
"no-man's-land" by the water side, where filth was allowed to be
deposited for the tide to wash away' and cites *Pericles*: 'Emptie olde
receptacles, or common-shores of filthe' (IV.vi.186). *OED* also
cites Florio who links it with a toilet and a sewer: 'a common shore
iakes or sinke'. In James William Johnson's opinion, the viciousness of the poem can only result from Rochester's present agony:
'The scatological and misogynistic qualities of the satire are so
graphic as to suggest it was vented during one of Rochester's
diseased relapses.'[63] For Robinson the poem is animated by
'seething torrents of raw vehemence', and he goes on to describe
how Rochester 'reveals the nasty physical facts of the last two
lines with their gross literalization of the metaphor of Willis's cunt
as a sewer'.[64] Within such vehemence he finds what he describes
as 'a Hamlet-like proclivity to generalize under the pressure of
extreme disenchantment'.[65] Peculiarly, however, the Hamletic
hysteria Robinson alludes to is not present here; in fact, the
language is disarmingly platitudinous, almost axiomatic. The
body's interior, that which should be numinous as the location of

the soul, is here graphically described as the seat of the body's corruption, but there is none of Hamlet's excessive frenzy. There is no 'Now could I drink hot blood' (III.iii.60) about it; rather Rochester's disgusting analogy is grounded in a literary tradition stretching back to the middle ages and beyond.

Drawing on the medieval *contemptus mundi* motif, the body is seen to be nothing more than a site of constant decay – 'Remember oh Man that dust thou art and unto dust shalt thou return.' In *Christs Teares over Ierusalem*, Thomas Nashe provides an especially malignant example of this trope when he apostrophises London prostitutes: 'ô yee excrementall vessels of lust', and his aggressive questioning of the whores metamorphoses them into lavatories: 'What are you but sincks and priuies to swallow in mens filth?'[66] The likening of prostitutes to toilets is entirely conventional. Chaucer has his Parson fulminate against 'harlotes that haunten bordels of thise fool wommen, that mowe be likned to a commune gong [public lavatory], where as men purgen hire ordure'.[67] Unsurprisingly the same trope is found in Rochester; in '*Broad Side against Marriage*' he refers to a whore as the 'Close stool to Venus, Natures comon shore' (l. 76) running together ideas of arousal and defecation as though both are in similar need of release.[68] This homology, according to which front and back orifices are rendered synonymous, is the final demonstration of the inherent corruption of mankind born '*inter urinas et faeces*'. As Nicholas Culpeper notes, 'The neck of the womb is seated between the passage of Urin and the right Gut, to shew fond man what little reason he hath to be proud and domineer, being conceived between the places ordained to cast out excrements, the very sinks of the Body' – figuratively that is, between two stools.[69] This vehicle for religious self-abasement (the motif can be traced back to the writings of the biblical exegetes) is secularised by Rochester. The poet is clearly less interested in ethical meditation or spiritual crusading than he is in damning his political enemies and using them to represent more specifically historical flaws. The corruptions of city life (see Chapter 6 below) are symbolised by the confusion of female genitalia and the effluent of the metropolis: 'When your lew'd *Cunt*, came spewing home, / Drencht with the Seed of half the *Town*, / . . . / Full gorged

at another time, / With a vast *Meal* of Nasty Slime' (ll. 113–18).[70]
For Narain, 'Corinna's vagina *is* the sewage system of the city.'[71]
What was a convention of medieval religiosity is here transformed
into a malevolent barb against London itself; Rochester's assimilation and transformation of this scatological device is, in every
sense of the word, cavalier.

The contrast between this Restoration disgust and earlier carnivalesque scatology can be seen in the distance – in substance and
levity – between Rochester's employment of the device, and the
birth of Gargantua. In Sir Thomas Urquhart's translation of
Gargantua and Pantagruel, Gargamelle's anal prolapse appears as
follows:

> a little while after she began to groane, lament and cry, then
> suddenly came the midwives from all quarters, who groping her
> below, found some *peloderies*, which was a certaine filthy stuffe, and
> of a taste truly bad enough; this they thought had been the childe,
> but it was her fundament, that was slipt out with the mollification of
> her *streight intrall*, which you call the *bum-gut*, and that meerly by
> eating of too many tripes, as we have shewed you before: whereupon
> an ugly old trot in the company, who had the repute of an expert she-
> Physician, and was come from *Brispaille* near to Saint *Gnou*
> three-score years before, made her so horrible a restrictive and
> binding medicine, and whereby all her *Larris*, arse-pipes and
> conduits were so opilated, stopped, obstructed, and contracted, that
> you could hardly have opened and enlarged them with your teeth,
> which is a terrible thing to think upon ... by this inconvenient the
> *cotyledons* of her matrix were presently loosed, through which the
> childe sprung up and leapt, and so entering into the hollow veine, did
> climbe by the diaphragm even above her shoulders, where that veine
> divides it self into two, and from thence taking his way towards the
> left side, issued forth at her left eare.[72]

Paradoxically, while Rabelais relishes the details of the prolapse,
and the foul-smelling and evil-tasting excrescences which result
therefrom, the baby is not borne *inter urinas et faeces*. Instead, in a
parody of the birth of Athene from the head of Zeus, he issues
from Gargamelle's left ear, untainted by the stench and soil
pouring from his mother's lower bodily strata. This is a miraculous
birth: 'as soone as he was borne, he cried not as other babies use

to do, *miez, miez, miez, miez*, but with a high, sturdy, and big voice
shouted aloud, Some drink, some drink, some drink, as inviting all
the world to drink with him'.[73] Gargantua's instant invitation to
'all the world' contrasts with the private consumption of the
Rochesteresque courtier.

On the one hand, Rochester consumes food, wine and boy in
the privacy of his own room while he voids himself secretly in the
appropriately named 'privie'. In Rabelais, on the other hand, as
Mikhail Bakhtin notes, the banquet images constitute a 'popular-
festive form . . . This is no commonplace, privately consumed food
and drink, partaken by individuals. This is a popular feast, a
"banquet for all the world".'[74] Even Gargamelle's evacuation is a
riotous public spectacle. As Bakhtin insists, carnival is collective,
commensal and all embracing: 'Carnival laughter is the laughter
of all the people.'[75] Moreover, it is the reader of the novel or the
spectator of the drama who is embraced and folded in by the world
of carnival: 'Carnival does not know footlights, in the sense that it
does not acknowledge any distinction between actors and spectators . . . Carnival is not a spectacle seen by the people; they live in
it, and everyone participates because its very idea embraces all the
people.'[76] Rabelaisian scatology, as Bakhtin is at pains to point out,
is a version of fecundity because excrement 'is linked to the generating force and to fertility'.[77] The birth of Gargantua illustrates a
'material bodily affluence, a generating and growing superabun-
dance'.[78] Anus and vagina are linked in their productivity as two
places from whence the body can demonstrate its productiveness.
Bakhtin proposes that in the early modern period, 'Excrement was
conceived as an essential element in the life of the body and of the
earth in the struggle against death. It was part of man's vivid
awareness of his materiality, of his bodily nature, closely related to
the life of the earth.'[79] Little wonder then that the excrement
Gargamelle expels is so readily taken for the new-born babe.

Cavalier poetry, by contrast, runs together back and front, male
and female in an orgy of confusion and degradation: 'Since Fucking
is not, as 'twas wont, / The Ladyes have got a new Trick, / As an
Arsehole serves for a Cunt / Soe a Clitoris serves for a Prick' (ll. 9–
12).[80] This sexual and fecal imbroglio, as I have suggested, is a sign
of the times, these lines appearing in a poem which opens, 'Oh! what

a damn'd Age do we live in' (l. 1). Evidently this opinion of the age
was shared by Rochester's circle of friends. In a letter to him of
1676, Henry Bulkeley attributes the Earl's current difficulties to

> an Age when fooles are ye most powerfull Enemyes, & the few Wise
> wee have either cannott or will not befreind vs, since ye Fop is the
> only fine Gentlman of the Times, & a committee of those able
> Statesmen assemble dayly to talke of nothing but fighting &
> fucking at Locketts [a tavern in Charing Cross], & will never be
> reconciled to men who speake sense & Reason.[81]

Writing fewer than eighty years after Rochester's death, the
Scottish philosopher, David Hume, attributes the poet's obscenity
to the depravity of his age: 'The very name of Rochester is
offensive to modern ears; yet does his poetry discover such energy
of style and such poignancy of satyre, as give ground to imagine
what so fine a genius, had he fallen *in a more happy age* and
followed better models was capable of producing.'[82] The jubilant
kind of anality and sexual fecundity which we witness in Rabelais
is extirpated as Rochester's focalised hostility directs it to a local
satirical target – his own peers, his own society, and even particular named individuals, as we have seen. Cavalier scatology is
infused with a political specificity which is less pronounced in that
of the earlier period.

Commonly in Rochester, the anus and the vagina are blurred
together in the act of sodomy. In 'Song' (beginning 'I Rise at
Eleven . . .'), as we have already seen, the poet will sodomise his
page if his whore is unavailable. 'The Disabled Debauchee' is
almost indifferent to the identity of his sexual partner as he, his
mistress Cloris, and the link-boy (that is, a torch bearer) satisfy
themselves on each other indiscriminately: 'Nor shall our Love-fits
Cloris be forgot, / When each the well-look'd Linkboy strove
t'enjoy; / And the best Kiss was the deciding Lot, / Whether the
Boy Fuck'd you, or I the Boy' (ll. 37–40).[83] This sexual permissive-
ness is, in Sarah Wintle's opinion, 'partly induced by the
conditions of the war itself' – the chaos of indiscriminate fucking
is thus an index to the turmoil of the times.[84] The rake's disinter-
ested attitude makes whore and boy equal as sites of (vaginal or
anal) penetration.

Occasionally, such alternative methods of sexual release may be necessitated by the inconveniences of menstruation. In *Sodom*, for instance, monthly 'termes' may prompt anal or oral sex: 'In tyme of termes she offers him her Arse / Or with her mouth sucks jelly from his Tarse' (I.ii.77–8).[85] But they may also prompt further variations: 'In tyme of terme we frig or thrust / Twixt Breast or Armes to quench our lust' (III.i.10–11). The most widespread (in both senses) destination for the Rochesterian tarse is the anus – male and female. The 'plot' of *Sodom* is predicated on the interchangeability of vagina and anus. In his prologue, King Bolloxinian declares that the wily prostitute 'is the Cheat, twas this made me retire / From humid C[un]t to humaine Arse all fire'. The play dramatises the consequences of the King's edict outlawing vaginal intercourse and demanding buggery: 'Cunt tyr'd out he shall to Arse repaire'. In fact, any port is suitable to enter in the storm of sexual licence which, implicitly, the play equates with the febrile atmosphere of the court of Charles II. The outrageous association of Bolloxinian with the restored monarch leads Johnson to assume that the King knew nothing of the satire: 'Considering its overt assault on him, Charles II was doubtless unaware that the travesty existed.'[86] Repeatedly in *Sodom* the two orifices are coupled as penetrative targets: 'May plentifull Delight of C—t & Arse / Be neuer wanting to yor Roiall Tarse' (I.i.17–18); 'Gase on the Charmes of C—t & Arse / And thrust to heauen yor standing tarse' (III.i.7–8); 'Here prostrate at yor feet you may Comand / My C—t or Arse when ere yor Pr[ick] does stand' (III.iii.113–14). For all the text's explicit obscenity, it nevertheless equates such licentiousness with transgression. Bolloxinian phrases his quintessentially libertine rhetorical question in orthodox religious terms: 'How can I leave my old beloved sin / That has so long my Deare Companion been?' (IV.vi.49–50) and there is more than a hint of Tamburlaine about his defiance of the Gods: 'Let Heavens descend & sett ye world on fire! / Wee to some darker Caverne will retire; / There on thy Bugger'd A[rs]e I will Expire' (IV.vi.83–5). As Marlowe's warrior slips quietly away he is, in spite of his charted conquests, resigned to disappointment: 'And shall I die, and this unconquered?' (V.iii.150).[87] Similarly, Rochester's King must face his limitations: 'And must I fall? then

farewell royall sport / Of Cunt & arse & gorgeous pomp of Court'
(III.i.170–1). Just as the final pathetic demise of Tamburlaine
suggests, though not without ambiguity, that Marlowe the atheist
may have endorsed an orthodox religious position, so
Bolloxinian's audacious but fated buggery implies that Rochester
was fully aware of, and antipathetic towards, the moral bank-
ruptcy of the Stuart court. Indeed Hammond goes so far as to
conclude that Rochester's depiction of homosexual relations is
ultimately reactionary, even condemnatory: 'It is a way of concep-
tualising sex between men which would surely have satisfied the
most censorious Restoration divine.'[88] Rochester's disgust with
contemporary political depravity epitomises the self-loathing we
have discussed above – he is, after all, a member of that Court – it
also typifies the difficulty of confidently separating private and
public spheres.

Elsewhere the fusion of orifices extends to the blending of their
respective products. Discharge from either opening might make
intercourse, whether vaginal or anal, ill-advised: 'By all *Loves* soft,
yet mighty *Pow'rs* / It is a thing unfit, / That *Men* shou'd Fuck in
time of *Flow'rs* / Or when the *Smock*'s beshit' (ll. 1–4).[89] The 'nasty
Nymph' is implored to use 'Paper still behind, / And Spunges for
before' (ll. 7–8). But in a much more disturbing poem we hear of
a mysterious witch:

> deep red in Charms, and Spells;
> *Philters*, and *Potions*, that by *Magick* skill,
> Can give an *Eunuch* Stones, and *Cunt* its fill.
> *Babes*, at her call fly from the breeding *Womb*,
> With *Neighbor Turd*, in loathsome *Jakes* to roame.
>
> (ll. 21–5)[90]

The hag, a back-street abortionist, deposits '*Babes*' and '*Neighbor
Turd*' in the '*Jakes*' (or toilet) so that the kind of anal Rabelaisian
fertility we considered above is here horribly perverted. The poem
goes on to detail how unforthcoming women will be revenged by
having one bodily orifice transformed into the other in a metamorphosis of staggering obscenity: '*For this abuse, the*
Rump-fed-Runts *shall mourn, / Till slimey Cunt, to grimey Arse hole
turn*' (ll. 71–2).[91] What we see in Rochester's cavalier scatology is

the deliberate obfuscation of sexual categories and a refusal to preserve the distinctions between comic scatology and bleak, predatory sexuality. While for Edward Burns 'Reading Rochester ... is always an unsettling experience', Michael Davies is rightfully more forthright: 'Restoration decadence does not come more comprehensively or more forcefully than this.'[92]

II

It is over a quarter of a century since Francis Barker, catching Pepys, in the privacy of his own chamber (like the Cavalier's private place), masturbating over a lewd book, developed his groundbreaking formulation about the emergence of bourgeois subjectivity.[93] This act of repression, what Barker calls the 'enclosure of the Pepysian moment', forces subjectivity in upon itself and superimposes autonomy and solitude:

> The diagram of the text [that is, the *Diary*] is as a series of concentric circles at the furtive heart of which is the secret declivity of the soul itself. The I surrounded first by discourse, then by the *domus*, the chamber, and finally by the public world, is placed at the heart of its own empire, in silence and very largely in terror. The *Diary* for all the fullness of its days, despite being so richly populated with others and with the furniture of gossip and events, is thus the record of a terrible isolation.[94]

This isolation, which results in the self-loathing of Rochester's Cavalier is, as we have already seen, and as Barker asserts once more, the outcome of recent historical upheaval: 'individuation is historically produced – this situation is the result of the revolutionary process that preceded it. The political upheaval of the mid-century established, as all revolutions must if they are to be thoroughgoing, a new set of connections between subject and discourse, subject and polity.'[95] For our purposes, the most significant aspect of this epistemological shift was the establishment of 'new images of the body and its passions [which] were a crucial, if increasingly occluded, element'.[96] How fitting that such new cultural repression of corporeal operation should find expression through the form of the diary.[97] As Norman O. Brown puts it, 'only repressed life is in time, and unrepressed life would be timeless or in eternity'.[98] The diary is the most rigorously ordered genre chronologically and, in Pepys, as Barker demonstrates, it charts the very moment 'when the division between the public and the private is constructed in its modern form'.[99]

It is in terms of the treatment of his own digestion that Pepys voices this historically novel attitude to the body – an attitude which, not surprisingly, sounds very like anxiety. On the morning of 7 October 1663 Pepys woke with a 'pain that continued on me mightily, that I keeped within all day in great pain, and could break no wind nor have any stool after my physic had done working. [Later that day] having a good fire in my chamber, I begun to break six or seven small and great farts; and so to bed.'[100] This contentment (like sexual satisfaction in Rochester's work) is short-lived. We hear only two days later that 'I could neither have a natural stool nor break wind, and by that means still in pain and frequent offering to make water. [I] do not think myself likely to be well till I have a freedom of stool and wind.'[101] The pains are not only anal but genital (in an uncanny analogue of Rochester's amalgamation of back and front, the other side of the *jouissance* that is Freud's 'polymorphous perversity'): 'the greatest of my pains I find to come by my straining to get something out backwards, which strains my yard and my cods, so as to put me to a great and long pain after it ... After supper to bed as I use to be, in pain, without breaking wind and shitting.'[102] Pepys resolves to tackle this constipation, 'I see I must take, besides keeping myself warm, to make myself break wind and go freely to stool before I can be well.' To this end, he calls upon his wife to administer an enema:

> Anon about 8 a-clock, my wife did give me a Clyster which Mr. Hollyard directed, *viz.*, A pinte of strong ale, four ounces of Sugar, and two ounces of butter. It lay while I lay upon the bed above an hour, if not two. And then, thinking it quite lost, I rose; and by and by it begun with my walking to work, and gave me three or four most excellent stools and carried away wind – put me into excellent ease; and taking my usual wallnutt quantity of Electuary at my going into bed, I had about two stools in the night – and pissed well. Voided some wind.[103]

THE SENSE OF DIS-ORDURE

The delayed effects of the enema offer an instance of the puzzle-ment caused by the bowel. While digestion is extensively theorised as the centre of bodily health, Pepys assumes the worst, that nothing will come of it, he thinks it 'quite lost'. The eventual farts and movements come as a pleasant surprise (hence his use of 'excellent' to describe his stools).[104] If on the one hand the body is beginning its trajectory towards individuality and even privacy (at its extreme a Rochesteresque solipsism), it is still sufficiently 'other' to elude the control of its narrator.

This inability to regulate the body makes Pepys reliant on his doctor and his wife and even at the mercy of divine intervention: 'I have by my wife's good advice almost brought myself, by going often and leisurely to the stool, that I am come almost to have my natural course of stool as well as ever, which I pray God continue to me.'[105] Pepys is also happy to consult his work-mates and evidently felt no embarrassment seeking the advice of high-ranking civil servants and Admiralty bigwigs:

> I did however make shift to go to the office, where we sat; and there Sir J. Mennes and Sir W. Batten did advise me to take some Juniper water, and Sir W. Batten sent to his Lady for some for me, strong water made of Juniper. Whether that, or anything else of my draught this morning did it, I cannot tell, but I had a couple of stools forced after it and did break a fart or two.[106]

The first of the colleagues mentioned here, Sir John Mennes (to whose own poetry we shall shortly turn) seems to have taken a keen interest in matters scatological. On 25 September 1662, Pepys records how Mennes 'told us, among many other things, how in portugall they scorn to make a seat for a house of office. But they do shit all in pots and so empty them in the river.'[107] But it was to Pepys especially that Mennes offered his advice about bowel movements, sometimes, if we are to believe Pepys's irritated tone, with officiousness: 'Up and to my office, where all the morning – and part of it Sir J. Mennes spent as he doth everything else, like a fool, reading the Anatomy of the body to me.'[108] Mennes, born in Kent at the end of the 1590s and thirty-five years Pepys's senior, typified the culture from which the new subjectiv-ity was in the process of emerging; in Barker's words, he hailed

from the 'older sovereignty of the Elizabethan period' which,
following the upheaval of the Civil War, had been 'disassem-
bled'.[109] Mennes thus provides an ideal test case against which to
try the hypothesis that changing attitudes to scatology are symptomatic of a shift in sensibility brought about by the crisis of the
embattled aristocracy. Thus, if Pinto, Vieth, Narain, Greene,
Williams and Barker are correct, albeit in their various ways, in
asserting that post-Restoration obscenity is torridly intensified by
the overthrow of the Cavalier cause, then we might expect to find
a less pessimistic – more Rabelaisian – scatology in the years
leading up to the Republican triumph.

Turning to *Musarum Deliciae or the Muses Recreation* which
appeared a quarter of a century before Rochester's *Poems*, such a
hypothesis does indeed seem to be borne out. *Musarum Deliciae*,
published in London in 1655, is, nowadays, a little-known collection. Its compilers, Mennes (Pepys's unofficial proctologist) and
James Smith are literary nonentities save for the excellent study on
Cavaliers, Clubs and Literary Culture by Timothy Raylor in which he
takes this text as exemplifying the processes of collaborative
composition which typified the literary scene in mid-century
London. Raylor suggests that modern critical indifference to
Cavalier poetry is directly a result of its obscure topicality or
political interestedness and, indeed, we have seen this to be the
case in respect of Rochester's verse: 'the literature of the period
has generally been dismissed by critics as too timebound and
partisan to be worthy of serious attention'.[110]

In the remainder of this chapter, I consider the kinds of
scatology that appear in *Musarum Deliciae* in order to demonstrate
that it partakes more of the Rabelaisian spirit than the
Rochesteresque; that it is a more benign, comic form of scatology
without direct political targets. *Musarum Deliciae* contains the
ribald mock-epic entitled '*To a friend upon a journey to* Epsam *Well*',
impossible to cite here in full as it runs to over 120 lines, though
in what follows its unavailability justifies extensive quotation. The
purgative effects of Epsom salts have been well known for some
time: 'Epsom and Glauber salts ... act mainly by increasing
osmotic pressure, but perhaps also by irritating the secretory cells
of the intestinal lining.'[111] In his *Diary* entry for 21 August 1664

Pepys records, 'So up and drunk three bottles of Epsum-water, which wrought well with me.'[112] In the poem two friends undertake a journey to Epsom to take the waters ostensibly for medicinal purposes:

> 'Tis here the people farre and neer
> Bring their Diseases, and go clear.
> Some drink of it, and in an houre,
> Their Stomach, Guts, and Kidneyes scower:
> Others doe Bathe, and Ulcers cure,
> Dry Itch, and Leprosie impure;
> And what in Lords you call the Gout,
> In poor the Pox, this drives all out.
>
> (ll. 23–30)[113]

We should note in passing the poem's awareness of the manner in which different social classes are stigmatised differently. While the poor are acknowledged to have the pox, Lords have the same condition euphemised as 'the gout'. The poem then moves on to describe the place, while the miraculous powers that reside there are quickly eclipsed by the description of fecal surroundings:

> Close by the Well, you may discerne
> Small shrubs of *Eglantin* and *Fern*,
> Which shew the businesse of the place;
> For here old *Ops* her upper face
> Is yellow, not with heat of Summer,
> But safroniz'd with mortall scumber.
>
> (ll. 31–6)

The yellow stains of the place are but a foreshadowing of the debris and detritus that will remain after the patients have left. But the allusion to 'old *Ops*' (a Roman goddess of fertility) infuses the atmosphere with a classical seriousness which is to be debunked by the mention of 'scumber', which *OED* defines as 'Of a dog or fox: To evacuate the fæces. Also *jocularly* of a person.' The coupling of the classical deity with animal discharge (intensified by the use of 'mortall') bathetically deflates the pastoral setting, traditionally taken to be a place of spiritual contemplation, with its 'Small shrubs of *Eglantin* and

Fern'. This comic rupturing of the classical precedent (and, along with it, the world of Humanist emulation of the classical ideal) continues. In particular, the most distinguished classical sources are reduced to bumwipe (possibly an allusion to Gargantua's experiments with different abstergent objects in chapter 13 of book I of *Gargantua and Pantagruel*):

> But then the pity to behold
> Those ancient Authors, which of old
> Wrote down for us, Philosophy,
> Physick, Musick, and Poetry,
> Now to no other purpose tend,
> But to defend the fingers end.
> Here lies *Romes Naso* torn and rent,
> New reeking from the Fundament:
> *Galens* old rules could not suffice,
> Nor yet *Hippocrates* the wise.
> Not teaching, how to clense, can doe,
> Themselves must come and wipe it too.
> Here did lye *Virgil*, there lay *Horace*,
> Which newly had wip'd his, or her Arse.
> *Anacreon* reeled too and fro,
> Vex'd, that they us'd his papers so.
> And *Tully* with his Offices,
> Was forc'd to doe such works as these.

(ll. 37–54)

The debasement and befouling of classical sources symbolises the potential degradation of all that mattered to Renaissance Humanism; there is something humbling about seeing this library reduced to toilet paper. However, the tone is in stark contrast to Rochester's mordant vision. For instance, '*Tully* with his Offices' – a reference to *De Officiis* by Marcus Tullius Cicero, one of the models of Humanist rhetoric – is clearly a scatological joke since the *OED* defines 'offices' as 'The function or action of discharging excrement' (dating from 1386). There is a deliberate ambiguity being sustained between the rarefied cultural capital of the sources cited and the lowliness of their fate, piled on a dunghill, having been used merely 'to defend the fingers end'.

Even the efforts of the contemporary lover, his protestations and sonnets, end up on the midden:

> Here lies the Letter of a Lover,
> Which piece-meale did the thing discover
> Sonnets halfe written could not stay,
> But must necessity obey.
> This made us for a while to think,
> The Muses here did seldome drink:
> But hap what would, we light from stirrup,
> And streight descend to drink the syrrup.

(ll. 55–62)

These Orlando-like sonnets, which had enjoyed their heyday over half a century earlier, demonstrate the presumption of the lover and confirm the sad irony of Yeats's claim that 'Love has pitched his mansion in / The place of excrement' (ll. 15–16).[114] But in placing the letter of a lover down the toilet, the poem is self-consciously re-enacting the comic intrigue of Chaucer's *The Merchant's Tale*. Lovesick for the beautiful but unfortunately already-married May, Damian writes her a love letter which she hides until she has convenient opportunity to read it. Waking in the middle of the night, after her repulsive elderly husband, January, has kissed her all over, she feigns the need to go to the toilet:

> She feyned hire as that she moste gon
> Ther as ye woot that every wight moot neede;
> And whan she of this bille hath taken heede,
> She rente it al to cloutes atte laste,
> And in the pryvee softely it caste.

(ll. 1950–4)[115]

'Epsam *Well*' thus underlines its affinity with the Chaucerian spirit of farcical scatology we saw in our discussion of his fabliaux in Chapter 1. Indeed, as we will see, *Musarum Deliciae* is explicitly imitative of the author of *The Canterbury Tales* in a style which is carnivalesque rather than cavalier. In order to demonstrate this contrast, compare Rochester's 'An Epistolary Essay' in which bad poetry is not merely used to wipe the arse but becomes fecal in itself, consolidated into fart and shit:

> Perhaps ill Verses ought to be confind,
> In meer good breeding, like unsav'ry wind:
> Were reading forc't, I shoud be apt to think,
> Men might no more write scurvily then stink;
> But 'tis your choice whether you'l read or no.
> If likewise of your smelling it were so:
> I'd fart just as I write, for my own ease
> Nor shoud you be concernd, unless you please.
> Il'e own that you write better then I do,
> But I have as much need to write as you:
> What tho'th'Excrements of my dull brain
> Runs in a harsh insipid strain,
> Whilst your rich head, eases itself of wit,
> Must none but Civit Catts have leave to shit?
>
> (ll. 30–43)[116]

The contrast is fundamental: in 'Epsam *Well*' the function of poetry at the present time is 'to defend the fingers end' (l. 42) and so artistic ambition, erudition and classical precedent are fondly mocked. Intellectual achievement offers physical comfort but the lavatorial reification of artistic insight is humorous and bathetic, in the style of Chaucer. In Rochester, on the other hand, artistic inspiration is quite simply 'th'Excrements of my dull brain': poetic achievement is shit, pure and simple. Writing, like farting, provides alleviation, 'I'd fart just as I write, for my own ease', while his addressee's head 'eases itself of wit'. Moreover, evacuation is a natural necessity: 'I have as much need to write as you'. Commenting on Rochester's satires, David Farley-Hills recognises the significance of this equivalence: 'Poetry is both sublime and absurd, it is [the] psychological equivalent of ejaculation or defecation.'[117]

Returning to 'Epsam *Well*', the speaker and his companion next make their way towards the source of the spring where they are greeted and waited on by one of the ancient sentries:

> The good old Father takes a cup,
> When five times wash'd, he fills it up
> With this priz'd Liquor, then doth tell

> The strange effects of this new Well.
> Quoth he, my friends, though I be plaine,
> I have seen here many a goodly train
> Of Lords and Ladies, richly clad,
> With Aches more than ere I had:
> These having drunk a week, or so,
> Away with health most jocund go:
> Mean while the Father thus did prate,
> We still were drinking as we sat;
> Till Gut by rumbling, us beseeches,
> My Boyes, beware, you'l wrong your Breeches.
> Ah, doth it worke? the old man cryes,
> Yonder are brakes to hide your thighes.
> Where, though 'twere neer we hardly came,
> Ere one of us had been too blame.
>
> (ll. 63–80)

In the nick of time they feel the effects of the purgative waters and, in a parody of the ancient epic games, they take part in a defecation derby encouraged by the achievements of ancestral generations:

> Here no Olympick games they use,
> No wrestling here, Limbs to abuse,
> But he that gaines the glory here
> Must scumber furthest, shite most clear.
> And, for to make us emulate,
> The good old Father doth relate
> The vigour of our Ancestors,
> Whose shiting far exceeded ours.
> ...
> This speech of his me netled;
> With that my head I straightway put
> Between my knees, and mounting scut,
> At chiefest randome, forty five,
> With Lyon's face, dung forth I drive,
> The ayre's divided, and it flyes,
> Like *Draco volans* through the skies.
> Or who had seen a Conduit break,
> And at the hole with fury reak:
> Had he but hither took the paine

> To come, had seen it once againe.
> Here *Colon* play'd his part indeed,
> And over-shit the stones a reed.
> Whereat the Father, all amaz'd,
> Limps to the place, where having gaz'd
> With heav'd up hands, and fixed eyes,
> Quoth he, dear, let me kisse those thighes
> That prop the taile will carry hence
> Our glory and magnificence.
>
> (ll. 81–112)

The poem ends in triumph and a celebration in the pub.[118]

Such festive revelry is reminiscent of *The Canterbury Tales* and indeed *Musarum Deliciae* not only alludes to Chaucer, as we have just seen, but contains several poems written in imitation of him. In '*Partus Chauceri Posthumus*', early modern English masquerades as that of the late middle ages. In addition, the poem deliberately mimics Chaucer's idiolect. It begins: 'Listen you Lordlings to a noble game, / Which I shall tell you, by thilk Lord S. *James* / Of a lewd Clerk, and of his haviour bold, / He was I trow, some three-score winters old' (ll. 1–4).[119] Unlike the dark mixture of scatology and sexuality that typifies the poetry of Rochester, these mock-Chaucerian poems are characterised by an ebullient, farcical carnality juxtaposed with a fabliaux-like flatulence: 'A lusty Runnyon ware he in his hose, / Lowd could he speak, and crackle in the Nose' (ll. 9–10). In fact 'runnion' is early modern rather than late medieval slang for a penis; *OED* lists this very example as the earliest printed use meaning 'the male organ'. *Musarum Deliciae* is thus affecting a Chaucerian grammar while articulating it through a contemporary vocabulary. Such occupation of late medieval syntax with early modern lexis is indicative of a fluency with Chaucerian style and, as such, is symptomatic of the true enthusiast: Raylor informs us, 'Mennes has been regarded as instrumental in keeping Chaucer's reputation alive in the seventeenth century ... In his later years, given the opportunity, Mennes would while away whole afternoons entertaining his colleagues at the Navy Office by reading from Chaucer and other early English poets.'[120] Mennes's familiarity with his master is demonstrated by his allusion to *The Merchant's Tale* not only in

'Epsam *Well*' as we have already seen, but in '*Imitatio Chauceri altera, In eundum*'. Towards the end of the poem he describes his protagonist: 'Lustfull he was, at Forty needs must wed, / Old *Ianuary* will have *May* in Bed, / And live in glee, for, as wise men have sayn, / Old Fish, and young Flesh, would I have fayn, / And thus he swinketh' (ll. 47–51).[121] The allusion to January and May reminds us of Mennes's source while the Chaucerian 'swinketh', meaning '[he] labours' is not only sexually charged but readily resonates with 'swyveth', meaning '[he] copulates with'. Compare this innocuous punning on the term with Rochester's outrageous employment of same, the word being emphasised by its terminal position (this is the closing section of '*A Ramble in St.* James's Park'). Condemning his mistress for her promiscuity with other lovers, Rochester threatens to have her lover torn from her 'While she whines like a *Dog-drawn Bitch* ... / *And may no* Woman *better thrive, / That dares prophane the* Cunt *I Swive*' (ll. 160–6).[122] The distance between Mennes's inoffensive jesting and Rochester's scabrous curse could not be greater. In addition, the scatology is similarly distinct. In '*Imitatio Chauceri*' Mennes remarks of a flock of sheep, 'Sir *Iohn* of them, must alwaies taken keep, / A shitten Sheepherd cannot make clean sheep' (ll. 25–6). The lines are light-hearted and proverbial, unlike Rochester's excoriating and vituperative scatology such as we have seen in poems like '*My Lord* All-Pride' or '*On Mrs Willis*'.

It would appear that *Musarum Deliciae* is without the vicious rantings of Rochester's poetry, relishing scatology rather than condemning it – wallowing in fecal matter as opposed to berating it. Indeed, *Musarum Deliciae* is without the kind of localised scatological satire that we have witnessed in Rochester's work. Even when *Musarum Deliciae* does allude to particular figures, it does so in a way which is harmless and good-humoured. In perhaps one of the most infamous examples of political facetiousness ever composed, *Musarum Deliciae* documents the famous parliamentary fart let by Sir Henry Ludlow in 1607, nearly half a century earlier. '*The Fart Censured in the Parliament House*' is a poem running to over two hundred lines and mentioning by name over eighty MPs.[123] As Michelle O'Callaghan has pointed out, the poem exists in many variants

and was clearly circulated widely.[124] A brief extract will provide
a flavour:

> Puffing down coms grave antient Sir *Io. Crook*,
> And reads his message promptly without book.
> Very well, quoth Sir *William Morris*, so;
> But *Harry Ludlows* foysting Arse cry'd no.
> Then starts up one fuller of devotion
> Then eloquence, and says, *An ill motion*.
> Nay, by my Faith, quoth Sir *Henry Ienkin*,
> The motion were good, wer't not for stinking.
> Quoth Sir *Henry Pool*, 'Tis an audacious trick,
> To Fart in the Face of the body Politick.
>
> (ll. 1–10)[125]

The humour is puerile to say the least, the verse couplets clunky
and the punning poor: the overall effect is of a harmless jest. For
instance, 'one fuller of devotion / Then eloquence' (ll. 5–6) refers
to Nicholas Fuller who sat in the House in the 1593, 1604 and
1614 Parliaments. The poem's verdict on him refers mockingly to
his Puritan sensibilities which lead him on several occasions to
challenge the royal prerogative. However, the critique is slight and
implicit rather than vituperative or belligerent as Rochester would
have had it. Fuller's pronouncement on Ludlow's fart puns on the
terminology for parliamentary protocol as well as fecal matter as
he declares it '*An ill motion*': this is school-boy humour. The poem
goes on to document the various reactions of further MPs:
'Swooks quoth Sir *Iohn Lee*, is your Arse in dotage? / Could you not
have kept this breath to cool your pottage?' (ll. 52–3); 'In
compasse of a thousand miles about, / Sir *Roger Owen* said, such a
Fart came not out' (ll. 98–9). The poem's rough and ready prosody
is indicative of a collaborative composition and, indeed, Raylor
notes how 'verses were continually added to it, introducing new
members.'[126] O'Callaghan points to the poem's popularity in
manuscript (its inclusion in *Musarum Deliciae* was its first appearance in print). This prevalence, she argues, is a result of its
'inherent conviviality', and she goes on to opine that the poem
partakes in what she calls a 'politics of jesting' which it inherits
from 'the ludic traditions championed by Erasmus and More'.[127]

The improvisatory, playful and popular quality of this poetic composition could not be further from Rochester's perfectly formed and elegant obscenity.

These extracts from *Musarum Deliciae* serve to demonstrate a definite tonal affinity with Urquhart's Rabelais and a corresponding distance from Rochester, in the light of which it is surely more than coincidental that Urquhart's translation of *Gargantua and Pantagruel* was published in 1653, only two years before *Musarum Deliciae*, while there remained a further twenty-five years before the publication of Rochester's *Poems*. R. J. Craik describes the gleeful delight of Urquhart's prose which makes it antithetical in spirit to Rochester's acrid poetry: 'Urquhart's translation is a gloriously unembarrassed sweep which suggests exuberant spontaneity throughout, and his uncertainties, such as they are, are concealed by his enthusiasm.'[128] For James H. Magan, 'It was the combination of out-of-the-way learning, scatological fantasy, verbal exuberance and wild narrative that Urquhart shows in his other works which made him the ideal translator for Rabelais ... the eccentric bachelor-cavalier was most inventive when sexual or scatological suggestions are concerned.'[129] Nicholas McDowell has forcefully demonstrated that Urquhart's exuberant translation of Rabelais is a residual part of an Interregnum struggle against the Puritan authorities: 'Urquhart's translation of the first two books of Rabelias looks like a statement of Cavalier allegiance and anti-Puritan defiance.'[130] Throughout the period, 'European translation displayed the urbane, cosmopolitan mentality of the Cavaliers while emphasizing the blinkered provincialism of their Puritan rulers.'[131] But this is a mirthful kind of Cavalier outlook, one which is diametrically opposed to the despondent Rochester's. Dying in the year of the Restoration, reportedly in a laughing fit at the news that Charles II had been welcomed back, Urquhart did not live long enough to feel the longer-term effects of the Cavalier defeat.

Curiously, but just like Rabelais (or Urquhart), the knock-about humour of *Musarum Deliciae* implies a popular audience while the literary pastiche, the mock-epic and the epic catalogue of bumwipe authors suggest an educated or, at least, erudite one. But this tension between low and high cultural forms is also one of the

distinguishing features of Urquhart's translation and one of the
most significant achievements of *Gargantua and Pantagruel*: as
Raymond Oliver puts it, 'one of the hallmarks of Rabelais's style,
which Urquhart recreates in English, is a kind of irony based on
the clash between high and low diction or between high words
and low actions'.[132] Raylor notes the same quality in *Musarum
Deliciae* and suggests that the catalogue of classical authors in
'Epsam *Well*' 'establishes a disjunction between the assumed value
of the classics and their actual employment', although he goes on
to argue that there is no threat to the status of the classics; the
passage takes for granted their elevated status and is comic
'precisely because it is an aberration'.[133] The epic form, epic
authorities and all that they stand for in terms of Humanist aspiration are never undermined. Raylor concludes that 'Epsam *Well*' is
typical of the collection in that it is 'predicated upon a commit-
ment to concepts of ceremony, classicism, good-fellowship, and
social order'.[134] It would be difficult to find a more obvious
contrast with Rochester in terms of tone and ethical value. For
Peter Porter, Rochester's fecal poetry is qualitatively different from
that of his peers: 'their scatological works are customarily set
apart from their main output, and are seen as deliberate relief
from high-mindedness. Rochester's case is different: his main
compositions and even his more deliberately decorous writings
are likely to break into scatology at any moment.'[135] Raylor's
description of the division between pre- and post-Restoration
Cavalier poetry acts as an ideal summary of the contrasts we have
witnessed in the comparison of *Musarum Deliciae* and Rochester's
work: 'The tone of Restoration society, conditioned by the long
years of exile and poverty, involved an obscenity more vulgar, a
cynicism more bitter, and a vandalism more fundamental and
skeptical than anything ever dreamt up by the Order of the Fancy
[the group to which Mennes and Smith belonged].'[136]

Between the farcical scatology of *Musarum Deliciae* and the
bleak anality of Rochester's *Poems* occurred an irrevocable shift in
sensibility. This perhaps is most clearly seen in the anxieties voiced
by Pepys's *Diary* which contains, cheek by jowl, both a candid
openness about matters scatological as well as an incipient
embarrassment. *Musarum Deliciae* offers perhaps the last articula-

tion of what we might think of as a golden age of 'innocent scatology' which looks back ultimately to Chaucer. Once that innocence is lost, and Rochester's work signals its final extinction, the introduction of a sharper political agenda lends the scatology a darker tone which looks forward ultimately, of course, to the writings of Jonathan Swift.

NOTES

1 William Hazlitt, *Lectures on the English Poets*, in David Farley-Hills (ed.), *Rochester: The Critical Heritage* (Barnes & Noble: New York, 1972), p. 214.

2 John Wilmot, *The Works of John Wilmot, Earl of Rochester*, edited by Harold Love (Oxford University Press: Oxford, 1999), pp. 274–5. All further references to Rochester's work are to this edition.

3 Michael Davies has noted the immanence of Rochester in his own work. Citing one of the poems which names Rochester in the final line, he writes, 'No matter how self-ironizing a poem like "To the Post Boy" might finally be, nevertheless it presents a portrait of Rochester's decadence which is simultaneously laughable in its outrageousness and horrifying in its depravity.' ('"Bawdy in Thoughts, Precise in Words": Decadence, Divinity and Dissent in the Restoration', in Michael St John (ed.), *Romancing Decay: Ideas of Decadence in European Culture* (Ashgate: Aldershot, 1999), 39–63, p. 46.) Writing of 'Ramble in St James's Park', David Farley-Hills asserts that 'poet and protagonist are clearly related' (*Rochester's Poetry* (Bell and Hyman: London, 1978), p. 204).

4 On the dangers of venereal disease, see Rochester's '*Advice to a Cuntmonger*' which begins: 'Fucksters you that would bee happy / Have a care of *Cunts* that Clapp yee' (ll. 1–2, Wilmot, *Works*, pp. 269–70).

5 Paul Hammond, 'Rochester's Homoeroticism', in Nicholas Fisher (ed.), *That Second Bottle: Essays on John Wilmot, Earl of Rochester* (Manchester University Press: Manchester and London, 2000), 47–62, p. 59.

6 The cynical use of the pageboy darkly anticipates that of the typist in Eliot's grim epic as 'the young man carbuncular ... / Endeavours to engage her in caresses / Which still are unreproved, if undesired' (*The Waste Land*, ll. 231–38 in *Collected Poems, 1909–1962* (Faber: London, 1974), p. 72). Note how Eliot has parodically embedded this sordid seduction within the form of an English sonnet (ll. 235–48).

7 Warren Chernaik, '"I loath the Rabble": Friendship, Love and Hate in Rochester', in Fisher (ed.), *That Second Bottle*, 7–19, p. 13.

8 Peter Porter, 'The Professional Amateur', in Jeremy Treglown (ed.), *Spirit of Wit: Reconsiderations of Rochester* (Basil Blackwell: Oxford, 1982), 58–74, p. 59.

9 John Wilmot, *The Letters of John Wilmot, Earl of Rochester*, edited by Jeremy Treglown (Basil Blackwell: Oxford, 1980), p. 117.

10 Wilmot, *Letters*, p. 196.

11 Chernaik, "I loath the Rabble", p. 13.

12 Wilmot, *Works*, p. 26.

13 Carole Fabricant, 'Rochester's World of Imperfect Enjoyment', *Journal of English and Germanic Philology*, 73 (1974), 338–50, p. 343.

14 Melissa E. Sanchez, 'Libertinism and Romance in Rochester's Poetry', *Eighteenth-Century Studies*, 38 (2005), 441–59, 555–6, p. 555. For 'Artemiza to Chloe' see Wilmot, *Works*, p. 66.

15 Jeremy Lamb, *So Idle a Rogue: The Life and Death of Lord Rochester* (Sutton: Stroud, 2005), p. 99.

16 Barbara Everett, 'The Sense of Nothing', in Treglown (ed.), *Spirit of Wit*, 1–41, p. 7.

17 Vivian de Sola Pinto, 'John Wilmot, Earl of Rochester', in Boris Ford (ed.), *The Pelican Guide to English Literature*, 7 vols (Penguin: Harmondsworth, 1965), IV, 142–55, p. 147.

18 Stephen Clark, '"Something Generous in Meer Lust"?: Rochester and Misogyny', in Edward Burns (ed.), *Reading Rochester* (Liverpool University Press: Liverpool, 1995), 21–41, p. 23.

19 Pinto, 'John Wilmot, Earl of Rochester', p. 149.

20 Wilmot, *Works*, pp. 45–6.

21 Gilbert Burnet, *Some Passages of the Life and Death of Rochester*, in Farley-Hills (ed.), *Rochester: The Critical Heritage*, 47–92, p. 65.

22 Ken Robinson, 'The Art of Violence in Rochester's Satire', *Yearbook of English Studies*, 14 (1984), 93–108, p. 93.

23 Cephas Goldsworthy, *The Satyr: An Account of the Life and Work, Death and Salvation of John Wilmot, Second Earl of Rochester* (Weidenfeld & Nicolson: London, 2001), p. 145.

24 Graham Greene, *Lord Rochester's Monkey* (Penguin: New York, 1974), p. 166.

25 Wilmot, *Works*, pp. 264–5.

26 Wilmot, *Works*, p. 266.

27 Reba Wilcoxon, 'Pornography, Obscenity, and Rochester's "The Imperfect Enjoyment"', *Studies in English Literature*, 15 (1975), 375–90, p. 382.

28 Farley-Hills, *Rochester's Poetry*, p. 105.

29 Ronald W. Johnson, 'Rhetoric and Drama in Rochester's "Satyr against Reason and Mankind"', *Studies in English Literature*, 15 (1975), 365–73, p. 371.

30 David M. Vieth, 'Rochester and the Restoration: An Introductory Note and Bibliography', *Papers on Language and Literature*, 12 (1976), 260–72, p. 262.

31 Vieth, 'Rochester and the Restoration', p. 263.
32 Mona Narain, 'Libertine Spaces and the Female Body in the Poetry of Rochester and Ned Ward', *English Literary History*, 72 (2005), 553–76, p. 570.
33 Howard Erskine-Hill, 'Rochester and Falstaff', in Fisher (ed.), *That Second Bottle*, 35–45, p. 37.
34 Vieth, 'Rochester and the Restoration', p. 261.
35 Wilmot, *Letters*, p. 119.
36 Greene, *Lord Rochester's Monkey*, p. 74.
37 Wilmot, *Letters*, p. 195.
38 Gordon Williams (ed.), *Dictionary of Sexual Language and Imagery in Shakespearean and Stuart Literature*, 3 vols (Athlone: London, 1994), I, viii–ix.
39 Williams (ed.), *Dictionary*, I, ix.
40 Burnet, *Some Passages*, p. 79.
41 Burnet, *Some Passages*, pp. 85–6.
42 Cited in Henry Craik, *The Life of Edward Earl of Clarendon*, 2 vols (Smith, Elder & Co.: London, 1911), II, 32–3.
43 Thomas Hearne, *Remarks and Collections of Thomas Hearne*, edited by C. E. Doble, 11 vols (Clarendon: Oxford, 1884–1918), III, 263.
44 Jeffrey C. Persels, '"Straitened in the Bowels", or Concerning the Rabelaisian Trope of Defecation', *Etudes Rabelaisiennes*, 31 (1996), 101–12, p. 105.
45 Pinto, 'John Wilmot, Earl of Rochester', p. 146.
46 Simon Dentith, 'Negativity and Affirmation in Rochester's Lyric Poetry', in Burns (ed.), *Reading Rochester*, 84–97, p. 88.
47 The dedicatory epistle to the first volume of *Familiar Letters* (1697) describes Rochester as 'a Scourge to all Blockheads, by what Names or Titles soever dignified, or distinguish'd' (Wilmot, *Letters*, p. 261).
48 Everett, 'The Sense of Nothing', p. 3.
49 Richard Harries, 'Rochester's "Death-Bed Repentance"', in Fisher (ed.), *That Second Bottle*, 191–6, p. 191.
50 Wilmot, *Works*, p. 93
51 Wilmot, *Works*, p. 91.
52 Wilmot, *Works*, p. 271.
53 See for instance Shakespeare's non-fecal use of the term in *Comedy of Errors*, II.ii.79, and, more ambiguously, *Love's Labour's Lost*, V.i.98.
54 Will Stockton, *Playing Dirty: Sexuality and Waste in Early Modern Comedy* (University of Minnesota Press: Minneapolis and London, 2011), p. xix.
55 Wilmot, *Works*, p. 275.
56 Shakespeare too dwells with prurience on this conflation of spirit and ejaculate in Sonnet 129: 'Th'expense of spirit in a waste of shame ...' (l. 1).

57 'It can, of course, be argued that Rochester's verse at all times presup-
   poses a homosocial bonding' (Clark, '"Something Generous in Meer
   Lust"?: Rochester and Misogyny', p. 51).
58 *OED* defines 'tarse' as 'the penis', deriving from OE. Williams notes that
   in Rochester's *Sodom*, 'The king of Gomorrah ... is named Tarsehole;
   and the author of *Juvenalis Redivivus* (1683) resolves to "quit *Tarsander's*
   Praise", commenting: *"Those that have read* E. *of* R. *Poems, know very well
   what I mean by* Tarsander".' (*Dictionary*, III, 1366.) In *Sodom* Rochester
   uses the plural form, *tarses* (II.ii.92, Wilmot, *Works*, p. 309).
59 Farley-Hills, *Rochester's Poetry*, p. 204.
60 Fabricant, 'Rochester's World of Imperfect Enjoyment', p. 340.
61 Wilmot, *Works*, p. 312.
62 Wilmot, *Works*, p. 37. Clark wonders whether, in the description of the
   belly as a 'Bagg of Turds', if there is 'perhaps an oblique glance at the
   poet's constipation' ('"Something Generous in Meer Lust"?: Rochester
   and Misogyny', p. 36).
63 James William Johnson, *A Profane Wit: The Life of John Wilmot, Earl of
   Rochester* (University of Rochester Press: Rochester, NY, 2004), p. 316.
64 Robinson, 'The Art of Violence', pp. 106, 107.
65 Robinson, 'The Art of Violence', p. 106.
66 Thomas Nashe, *Christs Teares over Ierusalem* (James Roberts: London,
   1593), V1^v, V2^v.
67 *The Parson's Tale*, l. 884.
68 Wilmot, *Works*, p. 273.
69 Cited in Gail Kern Paster, *The Body Embarrassed: Drama and the Disciplines
   of Shame in Early Modern England* (Cornell University Press: Ithaca, NY,
   1993), p. 211.
70 Wilmot, *Works*, p. 79.
71 Narain, 'Libertine Spaces', p. 562.
72 François Rabelais, *Gargantua and Pantagruel*, translated by Sir Thomas
   Urquhart and Pierre Le Motteux, introduced by Terence Cave
   (Everyman: London, 1994), p. 37. One of Urquhart's most incisive and
   sympathetic commentators, Roger Craik, is unapologetic about the
   standard of Urquhart's earlier work: 'what accounts for the fascination
   of Urquhart's works before his last, his translation of Rabelais, is their
   eccentricity, their untrammelled enthusiasm for unworthy subjects and,
   above all, their lack of promise' ('Sir Thomas Urquhart's *Apollo and the
   Muses*', *Yale University Library Gazette*, 70 (1996), 135–42, p. 137). Of
   the translation of Rabelais, however, critical opinion is more kind.
   Huntington Brown's still influential study claims that 'the earliest and
   greatest of all the translations of [Rabelais's] work was made by a
   Scottish Cavalier' (*Rabelais in English Literature* (Harvard University
   Press: Cambridge, MA, 1933), xi).

73 Rabelais, *Gargantua and Pantagruel*, pp. 37–8.
74 Mikhail Bakhtin, *Rabelais and His World*, translated by Hélène Iswolsky (Indiana University Press: Bloomington, IL, 1984), p. 278.
75 Bakhtin, *Rabelais*, p. 11.
76 Bakhtin, *Rabelais*, p. 7.
77 Bakhtin, *Rabelais*, p. 175.
78 Bakhtin, *Rabelais*, p. 221.
79 Bakhtin, *Rabelais*, p. 224.
80 Wilmot, *Works*, p. 279.
81 Wilmot, *Letters*, p. 125.
82 David Hume, *History of Great Britain*, in Farley-Hills (ed.), *Rochester: The Critical Heritage*, p. 200. My emphasis.
83 Wilmot, *Works*, p. 45.
84 Sarah Wintle, 'Libertinism and Sexual Politics', in Treglown (ed.), *Spirit of Wit*, 133–65, p. 143.
85 Wilmot, *Works*, p. 308.
86 Johnson, *A Profane Wit*, p. 395.
87 Christopher Marlowe, *Tamburlaine the Great*, edited by J. S. Cunningham (Manchester University Press: Manchester, 1981), p. 313.
88 Hammond, 'Rochester's Homoeroticism', p. 62.
89 Wilmot, *Works*, p. 37.
90 Wilmot, *Works*, p. 81.
91 Wilmot, *Works*, p. 83.
92 Burns, 'Introduction', in *Reading Rochester*, p. 3 and Davies, '"Bawdy in Thoughts, precise in Words": Decadence, Divinity and Dissent in the Restoration', p. 47.
93 The capacity of Rochester's verse to excite lust is evident in William Hogarth's *Before* (1736). On the rake's dressing table is a volume which bears Rochester's name. We know that Pepys had a collection of Rochester's poetry which he had bound in a single volume with Burnet's *Life and Death of Rochester* in such a way that only Burnet's title is visible on the spine (Samuel Pepys, *The Diary of Samuel Pepys*, edited by Robert Latham and William Matthews, 11 vols (G. Bell and Sons: London, 1970–83), X, 488. All subsequent references to the *Diary* are to this edition). On Pepys's secret edition of Rochester, see Wilcoxon, 'Pornography, Obscenity, and Rochester's "The Imperfect Enjoyment"', p. 375.
94 Francis Barker, *The Tremulous Private Body: Essays on Subjection* (Methuen: London and New York, 1984), pp. 9–10.
95 Barker, *Tremulous Private Body*, p. 10.
96 Barker, *Tremulous Private Body*, p. 10.
97 Incidentally, the *Diary* contains several references to Rochester, none of them complimentary. Pepys is scandalised by Rochester's abduction of

Elizabeth Malet, an episode which landed the errant Earl in the Tower. See entry for 28 May 1665 (VI, 110). On 17 February 1669 Pepys records how Rochester gave T. Killigrew 'a box on the ear in the King's presence' and is offended that the King readily pardoned Rochester, noting sternly that it is 'to the King's everlasting shame to have so idle a rogue his companion' (IX, 451–2). On another occasion Pepys overhears the court gossip – 'a story of my Lord of Rochester's having of his clothes stole while he was with a wench, and his gold all gone but his clothes found afterward, stuffed into a feather-bed by the wench that stole them' (2 December 1668, IX, 382).

98 Norman O. Brown, *Life Against Death: The Psychoanalytic Meaning of History* (Wesleyan University Press: Middletown, CT, 1950), p. 93.

99 Barker, *Tremulous Private Body*, p. 14.

100 Pepys, *Diary*, IV, 327.

101 Pepys, *Diary*, 9 October 1663, IV, 328. Three years earlier, Pepys records a bizarre account of how he was able to make water, all too well: 'This night I had a strange dream of bepissing myself, which I really did; and having kicked the clothes off, I got cold and found myself all muck-wet in the morning and had a great deal of pain in making water, which made me very melancholy' (28 May 1660, I, 162).

102 Pepys, *Diary*, 11 October 1663, IV, 329–30. Pepys's testicles seem to have caused him some problems: 'One evil more I have, which is that upon the least squeeze almost, my cods begin to swell and come to great pain, which is very strange and troublesome to me; though upon the speedy applying of a poultice, it goes down again and in two days I am well again' (26 March 1664, V, 98).

103 Pepys, *Diary*, 12 October 1663, IV, 332.

104 The inability to fart is a prognosis of discomfort: 'a sure præcursor of pain, I find, is sudden letting off of some farts; and when that stops, then my passages stop and my pain begins' (20 June 1664, V, 183). On the other hand, too much wind is also a nuisance: 'My health pretty well, but only wind doth now and then torment me about the fundament extremely' (31 May 1662, III, 97).

105 Pepys, *Diary*, 11 December 1663, IV, 414.

106 Pepys, *Diary*, 10 October 1663, IV, 329. At the end of the month, Pepys sums up his physical health, lamenting his over-reliance on laxatives: 'Myself in pretty good health now, after being ill this month for a week together. But cannot yet come to shit well, being so costive, that for this month almost, I have not had a good natural stool; but to this hour am forced to take physic every night, which brings me neither but one stool, and that in the morning as soon as I get up – all the rest of the day very costive' (31 October 1663, IV, 358). This problem seems to have persisted. Four years later Pepys records, 'I find myself to be full of wind,

and my anus to be knit together, as it is always with cold' (16 August 1667, VIII, 388). Then again, diarrhoea can also cause problems, especially in an unfamiliar house: 'in the night was mightily troubled with a looseness (I suppose from some fresh damp Linnen that I put on this night); and feeling for a chamber pott, there was none, I having called the maid up out of her bed, she had forgot I suppose to put one there; so I was forced in this strange house to rise and shit in the Chimny twice; and so to bed and was very well again' (28 September 1665, VI, 244).

107 Pepys, *Diary*, 25 September 1662, III, 205.

108 Pepys, *Diary*, 14 October 1663, IV, 334.

109 Barker, *Tremulous Private Body*, p. 10. Mennes was appointed to Comptoller of the Navy in 1661 – a post he held for ten years. Pepys was frequently insulting about the generation gap between them, referring to Mennes as 'the old foole', *Diary*, 7 April 1663, IV, 98; 'the old coxcomb', 23 May 1663, IV, 152; suggesting that Mennes deserved to 'be pitied for his dotage', 12 March 1664, V, 80; describing how he went 'to the fleet like a doting fool, to do no good but proclaim himself as asse', 16 September 1665, VI, 226; calling him 'a simple weak man', 17 September 1665, VI, 228 and 'worse then nothing', 27 September 1666, VII, 300. On one occasion Pepys laments 'how ill all the Controller's business is likely to go as long as ever Sir J. Mennes lives', 4 December, 1668, IX, 384.

110 Timothy Raylor, *Cavaliers, Clubs and Literary Culture: Sir John Mennes, James Smith and the Order of the Fancy* (Delaware University Press: Newark, NJ, 1994), p. 19.

111 Ralph A. Lewin, *Merde: Excursions into Scientific, Cultural and Socio-Historical Coprology* (Aurum Press: London, 1999), p. 104.

112 Pepys, *Diary*, V, 249.

113 S[i]r J[ohn].M[ennes]. and Ja[mes]: S[mith]., *Musarum Deliciae: or The Muses Recreation* (Henry Herringman: London, 1655), p. 4.

114 'Crazy Jane Talks With the Bishop', in W. B. Yeats, *Yeats's Poems*, edited by A. Norman Jeffares (Macmillan: London, 1989), p. 375.

115 Geoffrey Chaucer, *The Riverside Chaucer*, edited by Larry D. Benson (Oxford University Press: Oxford, 1988), p. 162.

116 Wilmot, *Works*, p. 99.

117 Farley-Hills, *Rochester's Poetry*, p. 204.

118 Raylor suggests that Mennes may have accompanied William Davenant and Endymion Porter to the Cotswold Games in 1630. In the wake of the ideological contentions surrounding *The Book of Sports*, such attendance would have political implications which may underlie Mennes's inclusion of the games in this poem (*Cavaliers, Clubs and Literary Culture*, p. 39).

119 Mennes and Smith, *Musarum*, p. 85.

120 Raylor, *Cavaliers, Clubs and Literary Culture*, p. 31.
121 Mennes and Smith, *Musarum*, p. 75.
122 Wilmot, *Works*, p. 80.
123 A full and modernised text of the poem appears at www.earlystuartlibels.net. It is edited by Michelle O'Callaghan.
124 The fart is mentioned in *The Alchemist*, the editor of which asserts that, since the poem 'was written before 1610 ... it cannot be original to Sir John Mennis and James Smith, who put it out in the 1656 volume'. Ben Jonson, *The Alchemist*, edited by F. H. Mares (Revels Plays: London, 1967), p. 55.
125 Mennes and Smith, *Musarum*, p. 65.
126 Raylor, *Cavaliers, Clubs and Literary Culture*, p. 74.
127 Michelle O'Callaghan, 'Performing Politics: The Circulation of the "Parliament Fart"', *Huntingdon Library Quarterly*, 69 (2006), 121–38, pp. 121, 122.
128 R. J. Craik, *Sir Thomas Urquhart of Cromarty (1611–1660): Adventurer, Polymath, and Translator of Rabelais* (Mellen Research University Press: Lewiston/Lampeter, 1993), p. 153.
129 James H. Magan, 'Verbal Excess and Sexual Abstinence: The Legacy of Sir Thomas Urquhart', *Logophile*, 3 (1979), 1–7, pp. 5, 6.
130 Nicholas McDowell, 'Urquhart's Rabelais: Translation, Patronage, and Cultural Politics', *English Literary History*, 35 (2005), 273–303, pp. 283–4.
131 McDowell, 'Urquhart's Rabelais', p. 297.
132 Raymond Oliver, 'Urquhart's *Rabelais*', *Southern Humanities Review*, 8 (1974), 317–28, p. 323.
133 Raylor, *Cavaliers, Clubs and Literary Culture*, p. 131. Magan quotes Urquhart who accuses the Roundhead soldiers of destroying his notes towards the formulation of an Adamic language. These, Urquhart claims, were used for pipe-lighters, packing materials and 'for what Urquhart coyly calls "posterior purposes"' ('Verbal Excess', p. 4).
134 Raylor, *Cavaliers, Clubs and Literary Culture*, p. 135.
135 Porter, 'The Professional Amateur', p. 62.
136 Raylor, *Cavaliers, Clubs and Literary Culture*, p. 210.

5

Swift's shit: poetic traditions and satiric effects

The professors are as full of shit on the stand as the druggist and the cop. Shakespeare was a great street artist. Proust was a great street artist. And so on. He was going to compare me and my act to Jonathan Swift. The professors are always schlepping in Swift to defend some *farshtunkeneh* nobody.[1]

> Because I am by nature blind,
> I wisely choose to walk behind;
> However, to avoid disgrace,
> I let no creature see my face.
> My words are few, but spoke with sense:
> And yet my speaking gives offence:
> Or, if to whisper I presume,
> The company will fly the room.
> By all the world I am oppressed,
> And my oppression gives them rest.[2]

I

At the end of his discursive satire, 'Tunbridge Wells', Rochester throws his hands up in horror at the ubiquity of human depravity:

> Bless me thought I what thing is man that thus
> In all his shapes he is rediculous:
> Our selves with noise of reason wee do please
> In vaine; Humanity's our worst disease.

> Thrice happy beasts are, who because they be
> Of reason void, are so of Foppery.
> Faith I was so asham'd that with remorse
> I us'd the insolence to mount my horse
> For he doing only things fitt for his nature
> Did seem to me, by much, the wiser Creature.[3]

The contemptuous pondering on the futility of man's estate ('what thing is man') is reminiscent of Hamlet's nihilistic 'What a piece of work is a man!', a speech which having listed humanity's achievements and virtues concludes, in the best tradition of *contemptus mundi*, that mankind is nothing more than the 'quintessence of dust' (II.ii.305–10). But what for Shakespeare was a meditation on death, a fatalistic realisation of mortality, is refocused by Rochester. What worries Rochester here is not the decline of life – that, simply, is the way of all flesh; indeed Rochester seems to have been passive, almost nonchalant, about his own corporeal deterioration. In a letter to his wife for instance, written in October 1677, he describes how 'my Rheumatisme begins to turn to an honest gout, my pissing of blood Doctor Wetherly say's is nothing My eyes are almost out but that hee says will nott doe mee much Harme'.[4] In the same month he addresses a short note to his mistress, Elizabeth Barry, in which he describes himself as a 'cripple' and, in a post-script, adds movingly 'This is all my hand would write, but my heart thinks a great deal more.'[5] In 'Tunbridge Wells' Rochester seems unconcerned with his own or mankind's *physical* decay, unlike Swift (as we shall see). Instead, the passage explores the propensity for us to abrogate intelligence and judgement, to behave irrationally and self-deceptively.[6] Despite protesting our capacity for reason, we act unreasonably: 'Our selves with noise of reason wee do please'. It is not merely that all coherence is gone for Rochester – due to the causes, political and epistemological, that we explored in Chapter 4 – rather that humanity's assumption of a rational position is mere 'noise', pretence, empty gesticulating. In 'Tunbridge Wells', overwhelmed by human stupidity, bestial instinct takes on the mantle of feral intelligence; the steed is 'the wiser creature' acting in accordance with its own proper 'nature'.[7]

This clash of equine wisdom and human idiocy is re-enacted most famously in the fourth voyage of Lemuel Gulliver who, in his journey to Houyhnhnmland, sees for himself the inferiority of the humanoid Yahoos and the calm rational superiority of their quadruped masters. But this is more than a case of 'four legs good, two legs bad' since Gulliver notes that, in humiliating contrast to the barbaric and primitive Yahoos, the Houyhnhnms are capable of the highest achievements in art:

> In *poetry* they must be allowed to excel all other mortals; wherein the justness of their similes, and the minuteness, as well as exactness of their descriptions, are indeed inimitable. Their verses abound very much in both of these, and usually contain either some exalted notions of friendship and benevolence, or the praises of those who were victors in races, and other bodily exercises.[8]

Houyhnhnm poetry is a combination of epic subject matter (the achievements of athletes and adulation of individuals) and a literary style to which we used to refer as 'metaphysical'. Much of Swift's own poetic work comprises panegyric and concrete detail. The 'justness of [the Houyhnhnms'] similes, and the minuteness, as well as the exactness of their descriptions' recalls the ingenious conceits of the school of Donne and perhaps it is no surprise that Swift, graduate of Hart Hall (now Hertford College), Oxford, High Church Anglican and Dean of St Patrick's, should be aware of the work of another student of Hart Hall, High Church Anglican and Dean of St Paul's.[9] The poets share a searing honesty, rigour and courage in the face of traditionally 'unpoetic' subjects, such as physical functions. John M. Aden may just as well be describing Donne when he imputes to Swift, 'an instinctive or intuitive sense of humor (or comedy) in the pursuit of ultimately serious purpose'.[10] Both Donne and Swift are authors of poems about nudity and the comedy of sexuality, both bracingly sceptical towards sentimentality and traditions of love poetry which aim to erase the awkward realities of jealousy, physical decline and corporeal disappointment.

While it may be objected that Donne is never explicitly mentioned by Swift, this in no way precludes the influence of the earlier poet. One striking image, though not unknown to other poets, suggests that Swift may have read Donne's *Songs and Sonnets*. In 'A Valediction: forbidding Mourning', Donne compares the lovers to 'stiff twin compasses':

> Thy soul the fixed foot, makes no show
> To move, but doth, if th'other do.
>
> And though it in the centre sit,
> Yet when the other far doth roam,
> It leans, and harkens after it,
> And grows erect, as that comes home.
>
> (ll. 27–32)[11]

In *A Tale of a Tub*, Swift compares the brothers Peter and Jack: 'we may look on them as two pair of compasses, equally extended, and the fixed foot of each remaining in the same centre; which, though moving contrary ways at first, will be sure to encounter somewhere or other in the circumference'.[12] While the geometry is slightly different, the overall effect is conspicuously alike. But in any case, as Heinz J. Vienken reminds us, 'it needs pointing out that many a modern critic has drawn attention to the fact that Swift must or could have known a variety of authors, who are neither present in his library nor mentioned in his works. Reasons for these attributions are heterogeneous; they may lie in the affinity of contents and ideas or motifs and sources.'[13]

Both classically minded poets write on 'Going to Bed' – Donne in a celebratory elegy with this title, Swift, parodically, in 'A Beautiful Young Nymph Going to Bed'. In his version Swift combines Rochester's atrabilious intensity with Donne's rhetorical potency. But Swift goes further than Donne and extends the casting off of costume in an exaggerated manner to the casting off of prosthetics. Having returned home 'the lovely goddess' (l. 23) takes off her wig and removes her glass eye, 'wipes it clean, and lays it by' (l. 12). She removes the padding from her cheeks then 'Untwists a wire; and from her gums / A set of teeth completely comes. / Pulls out the rags contrived to prop / Her flabby dugs, and down they drop' (ll. 19–22). Though Donne's is erotically charged while Swift's is viciously parodic, both poems share a firm rejection of the etherealised version of romantic love.

Donne's tough intellectual ardour (used in his mock-elegy as well as in poems like 'The Flea' in order logically, almost litigiously, to justify sexual congress) is exceeded by Swift's unflinching vehemence. This produces the kinds of detail which characterise, in Gulliver's opinion, the poetry of the Houyhnhnms, detail which serves in this case to expose in the most graphic, Swiftian manner, the ghastly flaws in the decaying and pox-ridden whore with her 'shankers, issues, running sores; / Effects of many a sad disaster' (ll. 30–1). Ulcerated by venereal illness, the nymph is the dazzling, nude mistress of Donne's poetry abused, infected and discarded by the diseased Cavalier of Rochester's predatory verse.[14]

While significantly Donne's conquest was unnamed, the anonymous object of a desire which is focused solely on its own masculine satisfaction, Swift's nymph is specified in the very first words of the poem: 'Corinna, pride of Drury Lane ...' (l. 1). One possible source of the name is the final line of Rochester's 'The Imperfect Enjoyment' in which the speaker, addressing his limp penis, desires that his premature ejaculation be put right by those that come after him: 'And may Ten Thousand abler Pricks agree / To doe the wrong'd *Corinna* Right for Thee'.[15] But Swift's nymph is also identified by her location; in eighteenth-century London, Drury Lane was known as a place of prostitution. In his 'Trivia, or the Art of Walking the Streets of London', for instance, John Gay writes of the street-walker who is said to 'trudge demure the Rounds of *Drury-Lane*' (III, 20).[16]

Corinna is thus identified not only nominally but geographically and hence professionally as an anti-pastoral reincarnation of that bucolic goddess of the same name who gathers flowers and sings country songs in the pre-lapsarian world of Robert Herrick. But even there, in the garden of the *Hesperides*, physical decay is never far away. While 'Corinna's *going a Maying*' celebrates natural fecundity with its 'Dew-bespangling Herbe and Tree' (l. 6) and its budding boys and girls (l. 43), the *carpe diem* is underlined by the poem's conclusion: 'We shall grow old apace, and die / Before we know our liberty. / Our life is short; and our dayes run / As fast away as do's the Sunne' (ll. 59–62).[17] Surprising as it may appear, Herrick too punctuates his ethereal garden with the dungy landscapes that will later characterise the work of Swift. In

his 'Upon *Skoles*', Herrick includes the kind of scandalous anality
that Swift will later raise to an art-form:

> *Skoles* stinks so deadly, that his Breeches loath
> His dampish Buttocks furthermore to cloath:
> Cloy'd they are up with Arse; but hope, one blast
> Will whirle about, and blow them thence at last.[18]

Writing a generation after Donne, Herrick's pastoral ideal is
shattered by the realisation of human anality. 'There are no
pastoral nymphs, figures of the body without bodily needs.'[19] This
urgent knowledge of physicality and the immanence of its decline
– 'the irreducible demands of a body that stubbornly insists on its
need to piss and fart' – is Herrick's poetic bequest to Swift through
his descendent, Abigail Erick, Swift's mother.[20]

Fittingly, it was in his manifesto on the composition of poetry,
entitled 'On Poetry: A Rhapsody' and first published in 1733, only
seven years after the publication of *Gulliver's Travels*, that Swift
exclaimed, like Rochester before him, on the rationality so evident
in the animal kingdom and the absence thereof in the case of
mankind:

> What reason can there be assigned
> For this perverseness in the mind?
> Brutes find out where their talents lie:
> A bear will not attempt to fly:
> A foundered horse will oft debate,
> Before he tries a five-barred gate:
> A dog by instinct turns aside,
> Who sees the ditch too deep and wide.
> But man we find the only creature,
> Who, led by folly, combats nature;
> Who, when she loudly cries, 'Forbear',
> With obstinacy fixes there;
> And, where his genius least inclines,
> Absurdly bends his whole designs.
>
> (ll. 11–24)

Again the horse (along with the bear and the dog) demonstrates a
ratiocination which is far closer to the prudence expected of a

rational being than a bestial one.[21] Moreover, Swift's use of the word 'debate' implies a logical working through of pros and cons (here of jumping the gate), if not orally, as is the case in the General Assembly of the Houyhnhnms (see chapters 8 and 9 of book IV), then at least mentally. Man is the only perverse creature who 'combats nature', who obstinately flouts his self-preservation.

It is to these twin themes, physical decay and persistent stubbornness, that Swift frequently returns. In the advertisement to 'The Beasts' Confession to the Priest', written about the same time as 'On Poetry: A Rhapsody', Swift remarks 'upon the universal folly in mankind of mistaking their talents; by which the author doth a great honour to his own species, almost equalling them with certain brutes; wherein, indeed, he is too partial, as he freely confesseth'.[22] Again Rochester's theriophilic admiration as well as his despair at the degradation of humanity, the uniquely obdurate giddiness of mankind, is clearly visible: 'Creatures of every kind but ours / Well comprehend their natural powers; / While we, whom reason ought to sway, / Mistake our talents every day' (ll. 203–6). Unsurprisingly it is Aesop who is called upon to witness the inferiority of human imbecility in comparison with animal understanding:

> Our author's meaning, I presume, is
> A creature *bipes et implumis*;
> Wherein the moralist designed
> A compliment to humankind:
> For, here he owns, that now and then
> Beasts may *degenerate* into men.
>
> (ll. 215–20)

The moronic and macaronic rhyming of ll. 215–16 reinforces the faintly absurd (though accurate) description of humanity as biped and unfledged so that the Latin diction comes dangerously close to inflated pomposity. For Swift's classically educated reader the implicit irony of *homo sapiens*, meaning 'wise' or 'judicious', would be especially sardonic. As Pat Gill asserts, 'Rochester's Hobbesian conception of the bestial nature of man and Swift's religious perception of post-lapsarian man afford similarly gloomy views of the precarious future of humankind.'[23] Geoffrey Hill is less convinced that Hobbes influences Rochester and Swift along the same lines but sounds persuaded that the philosopher was a presiding genius over both poets: 'it is difficult not to be in sympathy with those critics who cite the "agony and indignation" of Rochester's major satires as a precedent for Swift's own work in the genre and hard not to suppose that the Dean had read them, perhaps with mixed feelings about their "Hobbesian" views but with a professional attention to detail'.[24] The influence of Hobbes is widespread in Swift's writings. At the opening of *The Battle of the Books*, Swift talks of 'the Republic of Dogs' and notes satirically how if 'some leading dog' divides his food among a few other dogs, 'then it falls into an oligarchy [but if the dog] keeps it to himself . . . then it runs up to a tyranny'. At the beginning of *A Tale of a Tub*, Swift talks about how *Leviathan* 'tosses and plays with all schemes of Religion and Government, whereof a great many are hollow, and dry, and empty, and noisy, and wooden'.[25] In 'On Poetry: A Rhapsody', Swift sounds convinced by the philosopher's theory of internecine pessimism: 'Hobbes clearly proves that every creature / Lives in a state of war by nature' (ll. 335–6).[26]

Both Swift and Rochester despair at the awful predilection of men and women to lower themselves down the chain of being. This satirical tradition reaches back most famously in English letters to Jonson's *Volpone* (a play included in the Folio, a copy of which Swift owned) but whereas the characters of this play are metamorphosed into scavengers, parasites, birds of prey, etc. in order to represent human propensities towards opportunism, avarice, viciousness and so on, in Swift and Rochester the beastliness of mankind is reified rather than symbolic. This is why Jonson's savage but ebullient comedy is so difficult to find in either Rochester or Swift. As Gill insists, 'Both Rochester and Swift disclose a poetic concern with proper and improper arrangements, and this concern, as well as the rhetorical strategies and metaphorical images they employ to elaborate it, seem particularly anal in their insistence and intensity.'[27] Jonson's moral lessons, projected into the audience, demand that we recognise and acknowledge our own cupidity. We acquit Face with our applause at the end of *The Alchemist* even though in doing so we render ourselves vulnerable to the con-men that greet us as we leave the theatre (it is no accident that the play is set in the Blackfriars in 1610 and was first performed in the Blackfriars in 1610; it is literally a 'play for today'). But while Jonson with characteristic truculence and cussedness scourges contemporary moral vices, Rochester's filthy violence is, as we have seen, little more than the dying whimpers of the broken aristocrat, jostled and usurped by the champions of the new Commonwealth: 'waste is always *made*, not found – created by political and social processes'.[28] Jonson's persistent didacticism lends his Aesopian allegory a moral urgency which Rochester has long since abandoned. Christopher Hill has shown how the troops in Cromwell's New Model Army 'tended to be of the middling sort'.[29] The Cavalier is no longer his horse's master but, usurped by the new riders in Cromwell's disciplined cavalry, the victors of the English Civil War, he has become its Yahoo.[30]

These Whigs (as they became by the time Swift was writing), opposed to the court and Royal prerogative, and including Dissenters and Enthusiasts, represented Swift's worst nightmare: Dr Johnson remarks that, 'In the reign of Queen Anne he turned the stream of popularity against the Whigs, and must be confessed to have dictated for a time the political opinions of the English nation.'[31] Lady Mary Wortley Montagu, herself a Whig, writing to her sister in November 1726, savaged *Gulliver's Travels* (published earlier that year) with reference to the sensational *News from Colchester. Or, A Proper New Ballad of Certain Carnal Passages betwixt a Quaker and a Colt* (1659):

> Great Eloquence have they [she suspected the authors of *Gulliver's Travels* to be Pope and Arbuthnot as well as Swift] employ'd to prove themselves Beasts, and show such a veneration for Horses, that since the Essex Quaker no body has appear'd so passionately devoted to that species; and to say truth, they talk of a stable with so much warmth and Affection I can't help suspecting some very powerfull Motive at the bottom of it.[32]

Montagu's scurrilous joke attempts to defuse Swift's dangerous satire with an accusation of bestiality but the significance of his political reputation and weight can be seen in the remarks (a full decade later) of the Duchess of Marlborough whose increasing marginalisation resulted from the enmity of Swift's Tory allies: 'He has certainly a vast deal of wit; and since he could contribute so much to the pulling down the most honest and best-intentioned ministry that ever I knew … I could not help wishing that we had had his assistance in the opposition; for I could easily forgive him all the slaps he has given me and the Duke of Marlborough, and have thanked him heartily whenever he would please to do good.'[33]

Richard Tighe, the outspoken Whig and member of the Irish Privy Council, was the subject of a number of poetic attacks by Swift, the most notable being 'Mad Mullinix and Timothy' which has him posturing to Molyneux (or Mullinix), a Dublin beggar, about his intrepid achievements: 'I fart with twenty ladies by; / They call me beast, and what care I? / I bravely call the Tories Jacks, / And sons of whores – behind their backs' (ll. 151–4). He fulminates against his Tory opponents in grand gestures of eructation and flatulence: 'And while this vital breath I blow, / Or from above, or from below, / I'll sputter, swagger, curse and rail, / The Tories' terror, scourge and flail' (ll. 73–6). However, when it is pointed out to him that he furnishes the Tories with more amusement than discomfort, he determines to abandon politics and devote himself to gossip and street-cleaning along with those who 'purge the air' of 'noxious steams' (l. 240). He resolves (and the poem ends), 'God damn the Whigs and Tories too' (l. 272). The point of this apparent conversion is clear – a Whig is more use carting dung than as a political opponent while the ease with which Tighe is shown to abandon his convictions is indicative of the loathing Swift has for him and them. In 'Dick, a Maggot', Tighe is likened to a 'fresh turd just dropped on snow' (l. 14), while in 'Clad All in Brown', he is apostrophised directly, 'Foulest brute that stinks below / Why in this brown dost thou appear?' (ll. 1–2). Here his physical pollution is indicative of an interior moral failing:

> 'Tis not the coat that looks so dun,
> His hide emits a foulness out,
> Not one jot better looks the sun
> Seen from behind a dirty clout:
> So turds within a glass enclose,
> The glass will seem as brown as those.

> Thou now one heap of foulness art,
> All outward and within is foul;
> Condenséd filth in every part,
> Thy body's clothéd like thy soul.
> Thy soul, which through thy hide of buff,
> Scarce glimmers, like a dying snuff.
>
>   (ll. 7–18)

Swift insists that hypocrisy is no more able to mask corruption than a glass jar can conceal the feces within it. Subtitled 'Imitated from Cowley', 'Clad All in Brown' is a parodic reworking of Abraham Cowley's 'Clad All in White' in which he compares his mistress to the pure white of the lily:

> 'Tis not the *Linnen* shews so fair:
> Her skin shines through, and makes it bright;
> So *clouds* themselves like *Suns* appear,
> When the *Sun* pierces them with Light:
> So *Lillies* in a glass enclose,
> The *Glass* will seem as white as those.
>
>   (ll. 7–12)[34]

It is as if the lilies of Cowley's mistress have decayed into the detritus of Tighe's moral and political vacillations. Nothing is as bad as a decayed lily, as Shakespeare (not unbeknownst to Swift) had insisted upon: 'For sweetest things turn sourest by their deeds: / Lilies that fester smell far worse than weeds'.[35] As we have seen above in the allusions to Herrick and possibly to Donne, Swift's scatological satire relies as much upon a parodic inversion of other poetic traditions as it does on its own shocking and explicit effects. It is upon its allusions to Cowley and, further in the background, Shakespeare, that 'Clad All in Brown' depends. In this way, scatological comedy is intensified by being set alongside and operating in conversation with pastoral, the sonnet and other forms: Swift 'inherited his scatology as a conventional literary device from many skillful predecessors'.[36] Jens Martin Gurr regards Swift's scatological poems as 'transgressive of established poetic conventions and sub-genres'.[37] Consequently, fecal satire is as learned and allusive as those other modes of literature. Yet, like all great artists, Swift works both within and against the traditions and, as Brean Hammond has argued, in this he was probably more adept than anyone else: 'In his use of inherited literary traditions, Swift is probably the most subversive writer in his, or possibly in any, literary period.'[38]

Swift's Tory allegiances, though not unambiguous, are undeniable and frequently the cause of embarrassment among his admirers, such as Michael Foot, forced to concede, 'Yes, the hard impeachment cannot be denied: the fellow *was* a Tory.'[39] Although Swift was to seek the sponsorship of those of Whiggish persuasion (the most obvious being his long-term mentor, Sir William Temple), temperamentally his work can be best understood by placing it in the traditions represented by Rochester. While transparently anachronistic, there is some truth in George Orwell's insistence on Swift's elitism: 'No doubt he hates lords, kings, bishops, generals, ladies of fashion, orders, titles and flummery generally, but he does not seem to think better of the common people than of their rulers, or to be in favour of increased social equality, or to be enthusiastic about representative institutions.'[40] Gill echoes this and asserts, moreover, that this is another Rochesterian inheritance: 'Swift and Rochester converge in their scathing depictions of social adulteration.'[41] This is why Edward W. Said can use such an apparently oxymoronic formulation in his description of Swift's work as 'Tory Anarchy', a formulation anticipated by Carole Fabricant who writes of 'the ironic tensions between the "Tory" and the "anarchist" elements that are ever present in Swift'.[42] Said writes, 'In no author do the regulations of order and the challenging anarchy of dispersion cohabit with such integrity.'[43] Intellectually in Swift there is an admission of the necessity of social order while constitutionally his writings are wholly opposed to governance.[44] In this latter quality, his debt to Rochester is again clear. This debt is both profound and politically aligned.

In the year of its publication, *Gulliver's Travels* was recognised to have been inspired by Rochester's contempt for mankind. The anonymous author of *A Key, being Observations and Explanatory Notes, upon The Travels of Lemuel Gulliver* sees in the Yahoos personifications of Rochester's despondency: 'Here, Rochester's Remark's made good, at least, / Man differs more from Man, than

Man from Beast'.[45] Of Rochester's 'Satyr against Mankind', Vivian
de Sola Pinto shows how the poem demonstrates that 'mankind as
a whole is indefensible. The central passage of the poem, a
comparison between man and the beasts, is one of the most
searching pieces of moral realism in English poetry. It owes much
to Montaigne and *probably influenced Swift considerably.*'[46] More
recently David Farley-Hills has noted both the effect of Rochester
on Swift together with the latter's disavowal: 'References to
Rochester over the period [the early eighteenth century] are more
common in popular than in polite literature, but it is strange that
Swift makes no references to him, because his work shows
Rochester's influence.'[47] In fact, Harold Williams has noted the
existence of a commonplace book, supposedly in Swift's handwriting, in which Rochester's 'Upon Nothing' and 'On Rome's
Pardons' appear.[48] Even more convincing is Swift's 1712 'A Letter
of Thanks from My Lord Wharton to the Lord Bishop of S. Asaph'
which reads, 'O! the irresistible Charm of the Word Such! Well,
since Erasmus wrote a Treatise in Praise of Folly; and my Lord
Rochester an excellent Poem upon Nothing, I am resolved to
employ the Spectator, or some such of his Fraternity, (Dealers in
Words) to write an Encomium upon SUCH.'[49] More recently
Swift's popular biographer notes the influence of Rochester as
well as the bizarre difference between them: 'Rochester's poems
were full of pricks and cunts. Swift never mentioned them.'[50] But
for all this distinctiveness in the appearance or not of the organs
themselves, 'Swift and Rochester make women's private parts
public.'[51]

    In summing up the despair at the heart of *Gulliver's Travels*,
Said comes closest to recognising the affinities between the
defeated Cavalier and the disenchanted Tory (though Said is
writing of the latter, the description could refer to either author).
He writes of 'a measure of Swift's general disenchantment with
society, a disenchantment that in the end presents us with
minimal options for a satisfactory life ... nothing of human life is
left for Swift to take pleasure in, so he attacks it all'.[52] A couple of
times in *Gulliver's Travels* the narrator is confronted by Swift's own
despondent verdict on humanity. It is on these occasions that the
author, with telling irony, exposes the flawed admiration Gulliver

voices for his country and his countrymen. But in spite of its
fantasy setting, the horrors Gulliver describes are specifically
those of the English Civil War, the episode that (as we have seen in
Chapter 4) destroyed the cavalier dream:

> He [the King of Brobdingnag] was perfectly astonished with the
> historical account I gave him of *our affairs during the last century,*
> protesting it was only an heap of conspiracies, rebellions, murders,
> massacres, revolutions, banishments, and very worst effects that
> avarice, faction, hypocrisy, perfidiousness, cruelty, rage, madness,
> hatred, envy, lust, malice, and ambition could produce.[53]

The casual understatement ('it was *only* an heap ...', my
emphasis) demonstrates a ghastly insensitivity to the horrors of
war and the reader senses the author's numbed disappointment
beneath the vaunting triumphalism of the King's condemnation: 'I cannot but conclude the bulk of your natives, to be the
most pernicious race of little odious vermin that Nature ever
suffered to crawl upon the surface of the earth.'[54] By the fourth
voyage, the rationality and pacifism of the Houyhnhnms seems
to be rubbing off. Gulliver condemns the violent Yahoos who,
unable to find adversaries from other herds, 'return home, and
for want of enemies, engage in what I call a civil war among
themselves'.[55] But the satirical technique, which relies on a gap
between Gulliver's self-awareness and our awareness of him, is
used again in the same voyage as Gulliver explains the reasons
for his crew's enthusiasm towards exile despite the dangers of
a sailor's life:

> I said, they were fellows of desperate fortunes, forced to fly from the
> places of their birth, on account of their poverty or of their crimes.
> Some were undone by lawsuits; others spent all they had in
> drinking, whoring, and gaming; others fled for treason; many for
> murder, theft, poisoning, robbery, perjury, forgery, coining false
> money, for committing rapes or sodomy, for flying from their
> colours, or deserting to the enemy, and most of them had broken
> prison; none of these durst return to their native countries for fear
> of being hanged, or of starving in a jail; and therefore were under
> a necessity of seeking a livelihood in other places.[56]

Interestingly, Gulliver's equine master 'was wholly at a loss to know what could be the use or necessity of practising those vices. To clear up which I endeavoured to give him some idea of the desire of power and riches, of the terrible effects of lust, intemperance, malice and envy.'[57] Gulliver continues with unintended irony, 'he at last arrived at a competent knowledge of what human nature in our parts of the world is capable to perform'.[58] We have come full circle – an animal failing to comprehend the iniquities of human nature while demonstrating in its astonishment and incomprehension the unreasonableness of human behaviour. For Swift, and Rochester before him, it is not merely that 'Man's life is cheap as beast's', rather that man's life is worth considerably less.[59]

Given the similarity of Swift's political orientation as well as his shared sense of human turpitude, it is not surprising to find him participating in Rochester's scatological vision. In fact, as Coleridge notes, there seems to be a natural affinity between disappointment in the realisation of the omnipresence of human iniquity and scatological imagery: 'In Swift's writings there is a false misanthropy grounded upon an exclusive contemplation of the vices and follies of mankind, and this misanthropic tone is also disfigured or brutalized by his obtrusion of physical dirt and coarseness.'[60] Swift's use of the scatological is both more developed and more disturbing than Rochester's; for despite the splenetic vehemence, obscenity even, of the anality and sexual perversion in Rochester's poetry, these features were synechdochic of a larger human depravity. In Swift's work, on the other hand, scatology is a defining feature of mankind for good or (more frequently) ill.

II

Critics are divided over Swift's use of the scatological. Aldous Huxley in 1929 asserted that 'Swift hated bowels with such a passionate abhorrence that he felt a perverse compulsion to bathe continually in the squelchy imagination of them ... Swift's greatness lies in the intensity, the almost insane violence of that "hatred of the bowels" which is the essence of his misanthropy and which underlies the whole of his work.'[61] Huxley considers this to be 'subhumanly childish' and imputes it to arrested development: 'That the hatred of bowels should have been the major premiss of his philosophy when Swift was fifteen is comprehensible, but that it should have remained the major premiss when he was forty requires some explanation.'[62] Swift's anality must stem, writes Huxley, from sexual hang-ups:

> That any man with a normal dosage of sexuality could have behaved quite so oddly as Swift towards the women he loved seems certainly unlikely. We are almost forced by the surviving evidence to believe that some physical or psychological impediment debarred him from making love in the ordinary, the all too human manner.[63]

But those 'seems certainly' and 'We are almost forced . . .' give the game away. Despite suffering from Ménière's Syndrome, a physical ailment which caused Swift to be declared 'of unsound mind and memory and not capable of taking care of his person and fortune' in August 1742, there is no biographical evidence whatever of impotence. Nevertheless, the myth of Swift's sexual dysfunction is an abiding one: 'Most scholars agree that Swift never married and that he was threatened by female sexuality.'[64] Quite the opposite, as I will demonstrate with reference to Swift's poetry, is actually the case. Even David Ward, in spite of a generally sympathetic reading, goes further than Huxley, writing of Swift's 'horrified obsession with natural physical processes which would be symptomatic of some dangerous problems in a child of six, but in a grown man and an ordained priest is evidence of a terrible and pathetic sickness'.[65] He later adds that Swift 'was more than usually sick . . . The sickness goes far beyond an excessive interest in excrement; it is really a blindness to some of the possibilities of human life and emotion.'[66] Surprisingly it is that great freedom fighter and democrat, George Orwell, who, taking Huxley's lead, pruriently links Swift's scatological imperative to the slur of sexual inadequacy: 'Swift was presumably impotent and had an exaggerated horror of human dung' – much virtue in that 'presumably'![67]

Nor is this merely the prudish reaction of an overly cosseted modern age. Contemporary responses to Swift also indicate that he had overstepped the mark.[68] Laetitia Pilkington sounds baffled by a writing so intense that it could serve as a powerful emetic: 'with all the reverence I have for the Dean, I really think he sometimes chose subjects unworthy of his Muse, and which could serve for no other end except that of turning the reader's stomach, as it did my mother's, who, upon reading the "Lady's Dressing Room", instantly threw up her dinner'.[69] Sophie Gee argues that Swift's obscene reputation even compromised his professional standing: 'For his contemporaries, Swift's preoccupation with excrement, discarded matter, and bodily waste seemed to disqualify him from serious consideration as a cleric or theologian.'[70] William Makepeace Thackeray's response to Swift's scatology is a textbook illustration of Victorian repression: 'horrible, shameful, unmanly, blasphemous … filthy in word, filthy in thought, furious, raging, obscene'.[71] As recently as 2006, Derek Mahon is lazily dismissive of Swift's scatology, identifying it as anomalous and attributing its composition to bereavement: 'Not too much need be made of the scatological poems, few in number, written in the period of disorientation following Stella's [Esther Johnson's] death; they might even be ascribed, paradoxically, to the good influence of her living presence, now withdrawn.'[72]

On the other hand, a number of critics are not merely unoffended by Swiftian scatology but are eager in their defence of it. As a mark of his intellectual independence from the overwhelming constraints of stifling High Victorianism, as well as the (usual) distance between him and Thackeray, Charles Dickens, in a letter to John Forster (18 March 1841) relishes his new edition of the complete Swift, cutting pages and 'looking into it with a delicious laziness in all manner of delightful places'.[73] This critical tradition of defending Swiftian scatology is as old as Swift himself. In the year of publication of A Tale of a Tub (1704) William King satirises the oversensitivity of Swift's offended readers by affecting the satirical persona of a fastidious gong-farmer or night-soil collector: 'Sir, pardon me, if I fancy you may, by what I have said, guess at my profession: but I desire you not to fear, for I declare to you that I affect cleanliness to a nicety. I mix my ink with rose or orange-flower-water, my scrutiore [that is writing desk or bureau] is of cedar-wood, my wax is scented, and my paper lies amongst sweet bags.'[74] This urban(e) gong-farmer describes how, 'as I was returning from my *nightly* vocation, which, beginning between eleven and twelve in the evening, generally employs me till the dawn of the succeeding morning', he encountered a book-seller fly-posting the title pages of the newly published *Tale of a Tub*. This he took 'to be a satire upon my profession' and 'ordered one of my myrmidons to attack' him.

> [At] last the fellow, being of a ready wit, as having to do with all sorts of Authors, promised to go to Mr Nutt's for one of the copies; and that, if he did not convince me that it was a more scandalous libel upon the Author of that foolish Tale, than it could be upon anyone else, he would engage that I should set him astride upon one of my barrels, whenever I should meet him publishing any thing printed from the same Stationer.[75]

The prospect of being sat atop a barrel of feces demonstrates the lack of seriousness with which King treats the accusation of obscenity against Swift's work. His horror and shock is pure affectation: 'so stuffed [is the work] with curses, oaths, and imprecations, that the most profligate criminal in New-prison would be ashamed to repeat it'.[76] There is more than a little of Joe Orton's outraged, suburban Edna Welthorpe (Mrs) in this mock-rant: 'Men ... are obliged by necessity to make use of uncommon expressions, yet have an art of making all appear decent; but this Author, on the other side, endeavours to heighten the worst colours, and to that end he searches his ancient Authors for their lewdest images, which he manages so as to make even impudence itself to blush at them.'[77] Among the ancient authors cited by the erudite night-soil man is none other than 'Mr Harrington [*sic*]; that great commonwealth's-man, in his incomparable treatise of *The Metamorphosis of A-Jax*.'[78] By placing Swift in the tradition of this great Humanist scatologist, King signals his approval of the work; in the light of which the choice of his persona, a gong-farmer, indicates his own flirtation with the scatological tradition.

Norman O. Brown's influential defence of Swiftian scatology begins with an unabashed admission of its conspicuousness: 'Any reader of Jonathan Swift knows that in his analysis of human nature there is an emphasis on, and attitude toward, the anal function that is unique in Western literature.'[79] Brown distinguishes Swift's scatology from that of Aristophanes or Rabelais (the carnival tradition) because whereas for them anality 'is part of life, for Swift it becomes the decisive weapon in his assault on the pretensions, the pride, even the self-respect of mankind'.[80] Brown argues that anality in Swift has suffered nothing less than a critical *repression*. The analogy with psychoanalysis is a telling one; indeed Brown asserts that 'if we are willing to listen to Swift we will find startling anticipations of Freudian theorems about anality, about sublimation, and about the universal neurosis of mankind'.[81] Brown rightly attacks the critical propensity to read Swift's scatological vision as a facet of his later mental collapse, demonstrating that his apparent illness occurred nineteen years after the composition of the fourth voyage.[82] However, the real significance of Brown's account is in his careful distinction between Swift's point of view and that of his personae. Unlike Orwell, who lazily runs them together – 'it is difficult not to feel that in his shrewder moments Gulliver is simply Swift himself' – Brown is insistent on the ironic distance between the author and the voice of the text.[83]

In 'The Lady's Dressing Room', for instance, the poem that caused the hideous vomiting of Laetitia Pilkington's mother, the third-person narrator describes how Strephon sneaks into Celia's room and 'took a strict survey, / Of all the litter as it lay' (ll. 7–8). Of course, just as in the case of Iachimo in Innogen's bedchamber in Shakespeare's *Cymbeline*, this masculine intrusion into a private, female space and the voyeuristic examination of intimate articles of dress and make-up is an act of violation. At first Strephon finds Celia's smock, stained under the arms and, as the narrator ashamedly implies, beshitten: 'In such a case few words are best, / And Strephon bids us guess the rest; / But swears how damnably the men lie, / In calling Celia sweet and cleanly' (ll. 15–18). (Incidentally, here is another instance of the influence of Rochester on Swift as of course we are reminded of Rochester's nasty axiom: 'By all *Loves* soft, yet mighty *Pow'rs* / It is a thing unfit, / That *Men* shou'd Fuck in time of *Flow'rs* / Or when the *Smock's* beshit' (ll. 1–4).[84]) In Swift's poem it is not that the narrator is unable to mention the condition of the smock, rather that custom, decorum, good manners, forbid him doing so. Indeed this censorship seems to be at the behest of Strephon himself since it is *he* who 'bids us guess the rest'. There is then a refusal to name what is clearly there. Celia's stains may be unutterable, but they are no less there for all that. This then is an example of what Brown sees as Swift's capacity to illustrate the repression of his poetic characters: 'what is exposed is the illusion in the head of the adoring male, the illusion that the goddess is all head and wings, with no bottom to betray her sublunary infirmities'.[85] Though lacking Brown's Freudian apparatus, John Boyle, Earl of Orrery, writing in 1752, also sees the poem as an attempt to disabuse the youth who assumes his mistress is divine:

> *The Lady's Dressing Room* has been universally condemned, as deficient in point of delicacy, even to the highest degree. The best apology that can be made in its favour, is to suppose, that the author exhibited his Celia in the most hideous colours he could find, lest she might be mistaken as a goddess, when she was only a mortal. External beauty is very alluring to youth and inexperience; and Swift, by pulling off the borrowed plumes of his harpy, discovers at once a frightful bird of prey, and by making her offensive, renders her less dangerous and inviting.[86]

In spite of this attempted exculpation, Orrery is forced to conclude that Swift 'too frequently forgets the politeness and tenderness of manners, which are undoubtedly due to human kind'.[87]

What exercised the mother of Laetitia Pilkington upwards, acts (in the story of the poem) upon Strephon downwards. His prurient examination of Celia's personal effects causes him stomach gripes: 'But oh! it turned poor Strephon's bowels, / When he beheld and smelt the towels; / Begummed, bemattered, and beslimed; / With dirt, and sweat, and ear-wax grimed' (ll. 43–6). Having opened her laundry chest which released more evils than Pandora's box, Strephon is overcome by the sensual evidence of Celia's bodily processes. The poet, by way of an epic simile, describes the stench issuing from Celia's close-stool. ('To plump' is defined by *OED* as 'expressing a sound and action akin to those of *plop v.*, but with more distinct expression of the liquid "gulp" made by water when a body falls into it'):

> So things which must not be expressed,
> When *plumped* into the reeking chest,
> Send up an excremental smell
> To taint the parts from which they fell:
> The petticoats and gown perfume,
> And waft a stink round every room.
>
> (ll. 109–14)

Notice again the mock-squeamishness of 'things which must not be expressed' while the next few lines make certain that the reader is fully aware of the plop and the arising 'excremental smell'. Confronted with her close-stool, Strephon's disappointment becomes euphemistic: 'O! ne'er may such a vile machine / Be once in Celia's chamber seen! / O! may she better learn to keep / "Those secrets of the hoary deep"' (ll. 95–8). As a note in the 1735 edition makes clear, this quotation comes from Milton. In *Paradise Lost*, as Satan takes his leave from Hell, Sin opens the gate for him and 'Before their eyes in sudden view appear / The secrets of the hoary deep' (II, 890–1). Chaos, which lies beyond the threshold, is Satan's immediate destination. The relevance of this citation to Swift's poem is two-fold. Most obviously, Strephon is, like Satan, all but overwhelmed by the realisation of his situation. Celia's close-stool forces him to redefine not merely his relationship with her, but the definition of woman to which he has (erroneously) clung until this point. Secondly, the presence of Sin, Satan's daughter and his incestuous bride, means that the word 'hoary' is loaded with connotations of 'whorey'. Sin, once full of 'attractive graces' and 'perfect' (ll. 762–4) in Satan's sight, is now so deformed by sexual abuse – Death, her son, has raped her – that she is unrecognisable. Similarly, Celia, once prized by her lover is now the object of his revulsion.

Unable to continue his examination of the chamber, Strephon is forced to formulate a terrible conclusion: 'Thus finishing his grand survey, / The Swain disgusted slunk away, / Repeating in his amorous fits, / "Oh! Celia, Celia, Celia shits!"' (ll. 115–18). Strephon's gloomy mantra is paradoxically a function of 'his amorous fits' – in other words, Swift insists, as with so much of the more disturbing of Rochester's poetry before him, not to mention the work of Freud after him, the excremental and the sexual are intimately related: '"[a]morous fits" meshes perfectly, in terms of rhyme and stress, with "Celia shits"'.[88] This realisation is too much for Strephon to handle. From now on, all women are allied, in his mind, to the stench of the close-stool: 'His foul imagination links / Each dame he sees with all her stinks: / And, if unsavoury odours fly, / Conceives a lady standing by' (ll. 121–4). Like Gulliver, squeamish of the odours of his wife and preferring the smell of his horses, not to mention the aroma of his groom – 'for I feel my spirits revived by the smell he contracts in the stable' – the finicky reaction is shown to be absurd and the dainty manners which necessitate the poem's euphemistic approach (around which the narrator so skilfully skirts) are held up for ridicule.[89]

Such criticism of physical fastidiousness is, unsurprisingly by now, not without literary precedent. Most notably, Swift is following Shakespeare's lead. As Hotspur gives Henry IV an account of the battle, he dwells on the effete nature of the royal envoy sent to demand his prisoners:

> When I was dry with rage and extreme toil,
> Breathless and faint, leaning upon my sword,
> Came there a certain lord, neat and trimly dressed,
> Fresh as a bridegroom, and his chin, new-reaped,
> Showed like a stubble-land at harvest-home.
> He was perfumèd like a milliner,
> And 'twixt his finger and his thumb he held
> A pouncet-box, which ever and anon
> He gave his nose and took't away again –
> Who therewith angry, when it next came there
> Took it in snuff – and still he smiled and talked;
> And as the soldiers bore dead bodies by,
> He called them untaught knaves, unmannerly
> To bring a slovenly unhandsome corpse
> Betwixt the wind and his nobility.
> With many holiday and lady terms
> He questioned me.
>
> (I.iii.30–46)

Hotspur is excusing his petulant rejection of the King's command to relinquish his prisoners. The dainty and effeminate manner of the King's perfumed and pomaded messenger is, in itself, enough to arouse the hostile reaction of Hotspur who, fresh from battle, is 'dry with rage and extreme toil'. This is a war in which soldiers lose their lives but for the Osric-like emissary, the corpses offend his sense of smell. Soldiers, especially dead soldiers, cannot help stinking – neither can sailors. Rescued from a desert island, having been banished by the Houyhnhnms, Gulliver's only response to the Portuguese Captain, in spite of all the latter's civility, is a foppish insistence on his bodily odour: 'I was ready to faint at the very smell of him and his men.'[90] Gulliver tells us that gradually he is allowing his wife back into his company in order to dine, 'Yet the smell of a Yahoo continuing very offensive, I always keep my nose well stopped with rue, lavender, or tobacco leaves.'[91] The reactions of Strephon, alienated from his mistress by her natural functions, and Gulliver, dining with his wife with his nostrils full of herbs, are shown to be ridiculous and prissy. As the narrator of 'The Lady's Dressing Room', referring to the birth of Venus from the waves, concludes rhetorically, 'I pity wretched Strephon, blind / To all the charms of womankind; / Should I the queen of love refuse, / Because she rose from stinking ooze?' (ll. 129–32).

The idea that Celia, whose name means 'heavenly', should actually shit, defies the philosophical conventions of Platonic tradition in which love is so pure it lies outside carnal appetites, beyond the body (as in, for example, Donne's 'The Ecstasy'). In literary terms, it empties out the claims of Petrarchism according to which the mistress is idealised and any physical imperfections or unpalatable natural functions are air-brushed out of the picture. Yet in Swift the assertion that 'Celia, Celia, Celia shits!' is so significant, it occurs more than once. As well as in 'The Lady's Dressing Room', the line appears in exactly the same form as the climax of 'Cassinus and Peter' which is subtitled with mischievous hyperbole: 'A Tragical Elegy'. In this poem, two Cambridge under-graduates confer over the mysterious melancholy of Cassinus who sits inconsolable in his room with classic Hamletic symptoms – his greasy stockings disordered (l. 12) and 'His breeches torn exposing wide / A ragged shirt, and tawny hide' (ll. 15–16).[92] His half-smoked pipe is discarded while his chamber pot or 'jordan stood in manner fitting / Between his legs, to spew or spit in' (ll. 21–2). While Cassinus is (again, like Hamlet) self-dramatising, the ordinarily named Peter functions as a foil for his self-regarding mourning. Peter and Cassinus deliberate upon the latter's love problems in the manner of Renaissance courtiers discussing the passionate destruction inflicted by the cruel Petrarchan mistress. Palamon and Arcite (in Shakespeare's *The Two Noble Kinsmen*) or Romeo and Benvolio (in *Romeo and Juliet*) are typical examples of companions sharing the homosocial intimacies that result from the confiding of love too passionate to divulge to anyone except the closest male friend. Swift's deliberate employment of this tradition is signalled in Peter's several guesses at the reasons for his comrade's sadness. All are typical flaws in the Petrarchan mistress: that she is dead; that she is unfaithful; that she is ungrateful. Cassinus responds that Celia is both alive and well and innocent of all of these charges. Yet, he tells Peter, 'My purest passion [she] has betrayed' (l. 58) and accordingly his tombstone should read: 'Here Cassy lies, by Celia slain, / And dying, never told his pain' (ll. 77–8). Mystified by the cause of Cassinus's sorrow, Peter demands 'by friendship's sacred laws' (l. 91) that he be told the reasons for his confidant's melancholy. He recommends an eminently practical medical solution: 'Dear Cassy, thou must purge and bleed' (l. 89). The cure of voiding the bowel adumbrates ironically the climax of the poem. After much euphemistic reference to classical legend and warnings to Peter of the dire consequences of spreading the news throughout Cambridge, lest he be haunted by Cassinus's vengeful ghost, Cassinus breaks the news: 'Nor, wonder how I lost my wits; / Oh! Celia, Celia, Celia shits' (ll. 117–18). It is in the light of the poem's mock subtitle ('A Tragical Elegy') that we should acknowledge Jae Num Lee's pronouncement that these poems 'through the scatalogical elements broadly suggest the potentially tragic consequences of one's inability to come to terms with reality'.[93]

In 'The Lady's Dressing Room', Strephon's precious sensitivities towards natural bodily functions are the object of the poem's satire. Celia's soiled laundry is the evidence of her humanity, her natural appetites, both sexual and dietary, and the reader is compelled to side with the narrator and to concede the force of his rhetorical final question about sleeping with Venus. In 'Cassinus and Peter' the immediacy of the female, her sensual presence, is removed and the reader is faced with an exchange between two anxious male adolescents. Thus the focus shifts as the poem interrogates not the fastidiousness of an inexperienced lover but the well-established conventions of Petrarchan love poetry which are seen to be naïve and foolishly idealistic. Again the important thing to notice is how the poet employs a persona; the anxieties and neuroses belong to Cassinus, not to Peter, not to the poem's narrator, and *definitely* not to Swift himself. Though understated, Ward's remark on Swift's personae is important here: 'They are . . . the vehicles by which Swift manoeuvres the reader into a new way of seeing.'[94]

Confronted by the conventionally alluring prospect of female nudity, Gulliver is surprised by his own aversion: 'I was placed on their toilet directly before their naked bodies, which, I am sure, to me was very far from being a tempting sight, or from giving me any other emotions than those of horror and disgust.'[95] Moreover, Gulliver is overcome by the quantity of their urine – 'at least two hogsheads, in a vessel that held above three tuns'.[96] Such scatological moments dramatise not merely profound masculine anxieties in relation to female bodily actuality, but they enact the powerful conflicts between the reality of physical functions and idealising, literary traditions. They satirise not merely the looming etiquette of an increasingly 'polite civilisation' – what the sociologist David Inglis has called the emergence of the 'modern faecal habitus' – but they pillory the artificialities of a romanticised and finally unreal approach to poetic representation.[97] Brown considers this social and artistic satire to be one and the same thing, a reaction against knowledge which Freud would label 'repression': 'It is of course not ignorance but repression of the anal factor that creates the romantic illusions of Strephon and Cassinus and makes the breakthrough of the truth so traumatic.'[98] The mysophobia that Huxley, Orwell *et al.* have attributed to Swift is not his, but rather belongs to his many and varied personae. These critics have fallen directly into the trap Swift has set them. Ellen Pollak describes the erroneous conflation of author and narrator which occurs the first time she introduces

Swift's poetry to her undergraduate students: 'They will point to passages in several of the poems ... which suggest that *both* Swift and his narrator think that, as imperfect as female art is, women should keep up the fiction of their divinity because the reality it masks is so unbearable.'[99] In an essay to which Pollak's is indebted, Margaret Anne Doody has demonstrated that a clutch of contemporary female poets not only admired Swift but were influenced by him: 'Swift liked women, and that feeling was reciprocated.'[100] The tradition of criticism which maintains the figure of Swift as a misanthrope or misogynist following Huxley, Orwell *et al.*, ought to know better. Donald Greene claims that Swift is quite unpossessed by a mordant fecal fixation, rather that Strephon and Cassinus are: '*This* is madness; this is obsession; this is "the excremental vision", which makes a fetish of the routine, trivial, and harmless fact of human excretion; and this is what the poem pillories.'[101] According to this analysis then, anality in Swift does not connote contamination, but rather genuineness, accuracy, even precision and it is this paradox which is responsible for the slipperiness of these poems: 'The sheer difficulty of explaining how Swift's satires work dramatizes the way they trick us into experiencing the madness he represents.'[102]

The relationship between anality and sexuality, central to the work of Rochester and of essential importance to Freudian theory, is explored in another of Swift's comically excremental poems, 'Strephon and Chloe'. While Celia's name has celestial overtones as we have seen above, Chloe's may well evoke Cloacina, the goddess of sewage, whom John Gay describes as 'Goddess of the Tide / Whose sable Streams beneath the City glide'.[103] While the Celia poems reel from the shock of discovering the earthy nature of a heavenly goddess, Chloe's excretory behaviour is shown ultimately to valorise terrestrially her celestial (but fictional) reputation. That is, the poem celebrates the collapse of the illusion of female perfection in favour of a realistic and fundamentally more truthful sense of identity which permits a relationship based not on the niceties of social mores but on 'sense', 'wit', 'decency', 'prudence', 'esteem', 'love' and 'friendship' (ll. 307–12). The poem describes a goddess-like Chloe who, prior to her nuptials, appears in the poetic descriptions of her

admirers as 'of no mortal race' (l. 8). Indeed she is so perfect that
'No humours gross, or frowzy steams, / No noisome whiffs, or
sweaty streams, / Before, behind, above, below, / Could from her
taintless body flow' (ll. 11–14). While negating it, the poem
accents a rampant physicality by echoing the fervid entreaty of
Donne's aroused libertine: 'Licence my roving hands, and let them
go / Behind, before, above, between, below' (ll. 25–6).[104] Sexuality
and anality become fungible: Donne's persona is talking about
groping his girlfriend's body, Swift's about the excrementitious
products flowing from Chloe's various bodily apertures.[105] The
contrast with Donne's eroticism insists that Chloe, for all the ideal-
isation of her poetic admirers, is a human, not a divine, presence
and this is spelt out for us later in the poem, when the Donnish
phrase reappears with reference to her need to piss and fart
following too many cups of tea. Lying in her wedding bed, she
reaches out for the chamber pot: 'The nymph oppressed before,
behind, / As ships are tossed by waves and wind, / Steals out her
hand by nature led, / And brings a vessel into bed' (ll. 169–72).

Up until this point, Chloe has been the construction of
masculine conventions, a male fantasy like the goddesses of
modern advertising or the catwalk. In a sly mention of her father,
the poet demonstrates the extent to which Chloe has been subject
to patriarchal control; she has had no choice about her own
marriage: 'The bashful nymph no more withstands, / Because her
dear papa commands' (ll. 43–4). Yet it is physical necessity which
transforms her from a fictional goddess to a real woman. As she
begins to urinate, her husband is forced to confront the illusory
nature of her divinity. She is made incarnate through micturient
and flatulent necessity:

> Strephon who heard the foaming rill
> As from a mossy cliff distil;
> Cried out, 'Ye gods, what sound is this?
> Can Chloe, heavenly Chloe piss?'
> But when he smelt a noisome steam
> Which oft attends that lukewarm stream;
> (Salerno both together joins
> As sovereign medicines for the loins)
> And, though contrived, we may suppose

To slip his ears, yet struck his nose:
He found her, while the scent increased,
As *mortal* as himself at least.

(ll. 175–86)

In Chapter 2 we came across *The School of Salernum* translated by Sir
John Harington, the author of *The Metamorphosis of A-Jax* cited by
King's recondite gong-farmer. A handbook of practical medicine, it
advises particular diets in accordance with the Galenic humoral
theories popular from the middle ages. It also insists on the
foolishness of holding in farts for the sake of social nicety: 'Great
harmes haue growne, & maladies exceeding, / By keeping in a little
blast of wind: / So *Cramps* & *Dropsies*, *Collickes* haue their breeding, /
And *Mazed Braines* for want of vent behind'.[106] Swift had a copy of
this work in his library and demonstrates, in 'Strephon and Chloe',
the wisdom of following its advice.[107] In the 1735 edition of *The
Works of J.S., D.D.* the poem is glossed with the following note citing
The School of Salernum: '*Mingere cum bumbis res est saluberrima
lumbis*', meaning 'To urinate with farts is the most wholesome thing
for the loins'. The medical school at Salerno, Harington and now
Swift insist on the deleterious consequences of costiveness. This is a
lesson that Strephon, 'Inspired with courage from his bride' (l. 189)
takes readily on board. Finding his new wife 'As *mortal* as himself' (l.
186), Strephon is now able to discharge his own bladder and bowels:

But, soon with like occasions pressed,
He boldly sent his hand in quest,
(Inspired with courage from his bride,)
To reach the pot on t'other side.
And as he filled the reeking vase,
Let fly a rouser in her face.

(ll. 187–92)

OED, citing this instance as its first usage, defines 'rouser' as 'a
loud noise' though Pat Rogers, in his edition of Swift's poems, goes
further: 'it seems to mean, rather, "a real humdinger", "a particularly strong jet".'[108] The idea of farting in someone else's face
obviously picks up the tremendous and infamous fart from *The
Miller's Tale*, but it is seen here to be a good thing and to lead to the

exorcism of idealised and therefore inevitably false images of the beloved. Consequently the poem goes on to demonstrate the vanity of the pastoral ideal:

> Adieu to ravishing delights,
> High raptures, and romantic flights;
> To goddesses so heavenly sweet,
> Expiring shepherds at their feet;
> To silver meads, and shady bowers,
> Dressed up with amaranthine flowers.

(ll. 197–202)

The mythical, never-fading amaranth flower is shown to be an illusion and there is a sense of relief that such cloying and fraudulent imagery has been replaced with something more earthy and genuine. The verdant appeal of pastoral poetry, with its inspirational dynamic, is shown to be merely an idle dream and has to give way to the realities of bodily functions: 'How great a change! how quickly made! / They learn to call a spade, a spade. / They soon from all constraints are freed; / Can see each other *do their need*' (ll. 203–6). This scatological epiphany, argues the poem, emancipates the couple from the tyrannical imposition of social protocol as well as the artificialities of Petrarchan and pastoral traditions: 'No maid at court is less ashamed, / . . . / Than she, to name her parts behind, / Or when abed, to let out wind' (ll. 215–18). The poem is as good as its word and refuses to shy away from the actual business of defecating. In fact it ironically adopts the squeamish disposition of Cassinus or the other Strephon (from 'The Lady's Dressing Room') in order to describe explicitly the strained facial expressions of Chloe on the toilet.[109] Had her prospective husband peeped through the cranny in the privy door, he would have spied

> In all the postures of her face,
> Which nature gives in such a case;
> Distortions, groanings, strainings, heavings;
> 'Twere better you had licked her leavings,
> Than from experience find too late
> Your goddess grown a filthy mate.

(ll. 239–44)

Of course, had he peeped in such a surreptitious way, Strephon would be no better than the other Strephon rifling through the intimate laundry of his mistress's chest in 'The Lady's Dressing Room'. The narrator's insistence that it would have been better to have licked Chloe's turds, to have ingested them coprophagically, than to find her exposed as human, is evidently sarcastic; there is nothing beneficial to be gained by maintaining a false idea(l) of the beloved. As Thomas B. Gilmore Jr states so succinctly, 'the couple pass their married life exchanging farts'.[110] The poem's conclusion is that passion founded upon 'sense and wit' (l. 307) will far outlive that founded upon a false ideal: 'a mutual gentle fire, / Shall never but with life expire' (ll. 313–14).

In the poem, the idealised image of the goddess-like bride, which appears in the first half, is illusory. When the reality of human excrement arrives in the second section, the bridegroom *and the reader* are brought into contact with the actualities of bodily functions. Greene asks rhetorically, 'Is not a description of the physiology of human excretion a trivial matter by comparison with the anatomy of such vicious self-deception and negation of life?'[111] Once again, Swift harks back to Donne, this time to 'Elegy Seven: On His Picture' in which the youthful ideal of the courtier is set aside in favour of a rugged, grey-haired and broken-boned old man, returning to his mistress after years of naval service. The infatuations of young love are succeeded by an emotional attachment which is more than merely skin-deep: 'That which in him was fair and delicate, / Was but the milk, which in love's childish state / Did nurse it: who now is grown strong enough / To feed on that, which to disused tastes seems tough' (ll. 17–20). In both poems passionate devotion occurs not in spite of but rather because of unadorned physicality.

In 'Strephon and Chloe' the exchange of farts takes place in the nuptial bed, thus binding together the anal and the genital, the scatological and the sexual. Not all combinations of the two are happy ones however. In 'The Problem', Swift attacks Henry Sidney, Earl of Romney, who reneged on a promise he had made to William Temple that he would help Swift towards a prebend of Canterbury or Westminster. The poem is ostensibly an investigation into the reasons why Romney continually farts during periods of sexual arousal: 'Love's fire, it seems, like inward heat, / Works in my Lord by stool and sweat: / Which brings a stink from every pore, / And from behind, and from before' (ll. 7–10). Again the distant echo of Donne's 'Behind, before, above, between, below' emphasises the poem's brazen physicality, while the substitution of a beautiful, naked and yielding mistress with a flatulent, sweating and profligate Lord is both vile and parodic. A secondary allusion, this time to Andrew Marvell's seduction poem, 'To his Coy Mistress', insists on the discontinuity between her amorous perspiration and Sidney's sweaty skin. Marvell's zealous speaker implores his nubile lover to sex, confident that her skin registers her arousal: 'Now therefore, while the youthful hew / Sits on thy skin like morning dew, / And while thy willing Soul transpires / At every pore with instant Fires ...' (ll. 33–6).[112] While her soul issues through her pores in a sublime and erotic manner, Sidney's 'inward heat' 'brings a stink from every pore'. The contrast is simultaneously comedic and disgusting: to repeat Hammond's assertion cited above, 'In his use of inherited literary traditions, Swift is probably the most subversive writer in his, or possibly in any, literary period.' Swift's poem advances several explanations for Sidney's flatulence: that according to the laws of nature, passions will 'ferment' (l. 15) and 'Work out' (l. 16) right up the chain of being. So a weasel will exude a smell when excited just as kings 'who in a fright, / Though on a throne, would fall to shite' (ll. 19–20).[113] Yet the preferred solution is an outlandish cosmological one:

> Beside all this deep scholars know,
> That in the mainstring of Cupid's bow,
> Once on a time, was an ass's gut,
> Now to a nobler office put,
> By favour or desert preferred
> From giving passage to a turd.
>
> (ll. 21–6)

This account – somewhere between astronomy, astrology and excremental myth – is clearly designed to produce a comic effect as well being an attack on the intellectual pretensions of the 'deep scholars' rather in the manner of the 'projectors' in Lagado, one of whom was attempting to 'reduce human excrement to its original food' and who, in order to conduct his experiments, 'had a weekly allowance from the Society of a vessel filled with human ordure'.[114] Of even greater relevance here is the medical research taking place in the Academy on a cure for colic which consisted of the insertion of a pair of bellows 'eight inches up the anus, and drawing in the wind [the scientist] affirmed he could make the guts as lank as a dried bladder'.[115] Yet in spite of this scatological satire, it is important to note that in the poem, the processes of nature intermingle or fuse at some mock-mythical level both sexual and fecal functions. Moreover there seems to be a natural affinity which still governs over the affairs of men:

> But still, though fixed among the stars,
> [The ass's gut] Doth sympathize with human arse.
> Thus, when you feel an hard-bound breech,
> Conclude Love's bow-string at full stretch,
> Till the kind looseness comes, and then
> Conclude the bow relaxed again.
>
> (ll. 27–32)

The stretched bow-string refers concurrently to a state of sexual arousal and the need to defecate since the phrase 'hard-bound breech' simultaneously connotes the firmness of tumescence as well as the filled posterior of the breeches. In *A Tale of a Tub*, during Swift's brilliant parody of the sacred armour of Christ, he compares religion to a cloak and honesty to a pair of shoes, 'worn out in the dirt'.[116] Conscience, he continues, is 'a *pair of breeches* which, though a cover for lewdness as well as nastiness, is easily slipped down for the service of both.'[117] Once again the sexual and the fecal are superimposed. The remainder of 'The Problem' describes the race between Romney's various mistresses to be the first 'to catch a fart! / Watching the first unsavoury wind, / Some ply before and some behind' (ll. 36–8) – note that echo of Donne again, while the motif of many sharing the single fart of another takes us back to the ingenious division of the fart in *The Summoner's Tale*. The poem ends with the ladies sharing the farts and so concluding that 'My Lord's an universal lover' (l. 60); of course, the implicit consequence must be that he is also an universal farter.

In conclusion, this sampling and examination of Swift's scatology has demonstrated a barbed and personally targeted satire against Whiggish opponents, as well as the more general follies of particular social and political systems. Both the *ad hominem* and systemic scatological vitriol hardly comes as a surprise in the light of Rochester's influence on Swift, both of whom, like Gulliver, voyage into the Fart of Darkness. More lasting and finally more interesting, however, is Swift's adroit exploitation of genres such as pastoral, traditions, such as Petrarchism and even individual poets, such as Shakespeare or Rochester, from whom he derives literary patterns which he then undermines. As Hammond insisted above, Swift's subversion derives from and is energised by his use of these 'inherited literary traditions'. But what of the literature of the eighteenth century whose scatological imperative was derived not from the library but from the streets?

NOTES

1 Philip Roth, *Sabbath's Theater* (Vintage: London, 1996), pp. 318–19.

2 Jonathan Swift, *The Complete Poems*, edited by Pat Rogers (Penguin: Harmondsworth, 1983), p. 303. The blind anus has already figured in Rochester's *Sodom*. As Pockennello offers his arse as a temporary spouse to Bolloxinian he remarks, 'That Spows shall, mighty S^r, altho' itts blind, / Proue to my Lord both dutyfull & kind' (John Wilmot, *The Works of John Wilmot, Earl of Rochester*, edited by Harold Love (Oxford University Press: Oxford, 1999), p. 305).

3 Wilmot, *Works*, pp. 53–4.

4 John Wilmot, *The Letters of John Wilmot, Earl of Rochester*, edited by Jeremy Treglown (Blackwell: Oxford, 1980), pp. 155–6.

5 Wilmot, *Letters*, p. 156.

6 In a letter to Savile of June 1678 Rochester writes, 'most human affairs are carried on at the same nonsensical rate, which makes me (who am now grown superstitious) think it a fault to laugh at the monkey we have here when I compare his condition with mankind' (Wilmot, *Letters*, pp. 193–4).

7 At the opening of 'A Satyre against Reason and Mankind', Rochester wishes he could be 'a Dog, a Monky, or a Bear. / Or any thing but that vain Animal / Who is so proud of being Rational' (Wilmot, *Works*, p. 57).

8 Jonathan Swift, *Gulliver's Travels*, edited by Peter Dixon and John Chalker, introduced by Michael Foot (Penguin: Harmondsworth, 1967), pp. 321–2.

9 Donne matriculated at Hart Hall in 1584. Swift took his MA there in 1692.

10 John M. Aden, 'Corinna and the Sterner Muse of Swift', *English Language Notes*, 4 (1966), 23–31, p. 26.

11 John Donne, *John Donne: The Oxford Authors*, edited by John Carey (Oxford University Press: Oxford, 1990), p. 121.

12 Jonathan Swift, *A Tale of a Tub and Other Works*, edited by Angus Ross and David Woolley (Oxford University Press: Oxford, 1986), p. 97.

13 Heinz J. Vienken, 'Swift's Library, His Reading, and His Critics', in Christopher Fox and Brenda Tooley (eds), *Walking Naboth's Vineyard: New Studies in Swift* (University of Notre Dame Press: Notre Dame, 1995), 154–63, p. 163. Donne's satires were certainly known to Pope who wrote 'versified' versions of them.

14 The street-walker is, in the opinion of a number of commentators, sympathetic. For Aden, 'Swift cannot alter the facts of Corinna's life; he can only (at least he will only) show them and let them witness whatever the pity of it is, the pity she's a whore. Nor in doing so does he make fun of the "wretched" creature: her way of life makes fun of itself, and that is part of its pity' ('Corinna and the Sterner Muse of Swift', p. 31). Thomas B. Gilmore Jr writes that Swift's 'harsh comedy allows us to wrest from its total effect a sentiment less common and less easily won: something akin to respect ... that he himself perhaps felt for Corinna' ('The Comedy of Swift's Scatological Poems', *PMLA*, 91 (1976), 33–43, p. 35).

15 Wilmot, *Works*, p. 15.

16 John Gay, *John Gay: Poetry and Prose*, edited by Vinton A. Dearing and Charles E. Beckwith, 2 vols (Clarendon Press: Oxford, 1974), I, 168.

17 Robert Herrick, *The Poetical Works of Robert Herrick*, edited by L. C. Martin (Clarendon Press: Oxford, 1956), pp. 68–9.

18 Herrick, *Poetical Works*, p. 226.

19 Margaret Anne Doody, 'Swift Among the Women', *The Yearbook of English Studies*, 18 (1988), 68–92, p. 85.

20 Doody, 'Swift Among the Women', p. 89. Swift's other use of the name is similarly sour. In the poem entitled 'Corinna' the eponymous heroine is an author of scurrilous and licentious verse. Having, at the age of six, caught the butler and the lady's maid *in flagrante*: 'She made a song, how little Miss / Was kissed and slobbered by a lad: / And how, when Master went to piss, / Miss came, and peeped at all he had' (ll. 21–4).

21 Pope of course makes a similar point, contrasting the variety of animal virtues with the ambitions of Man to appropriate them. 'An Essay on Man', I.vi, in Alexander Pope, *Alexander Pope: The Oxford Authors*, edited by Pat Rogers (Oxford University Press: Oxford, 1993), p. 277.

22 Swift, *The Complete Poems*, p. 508.

23 Pat Gill, '"Filth of All Hues and Odors": Public Parks, City Showers, and Promiscuous Acquaintance in Rochester and Swift', *Genre*, 27 (1994), 333–50, p. 345. David Ward notes that 'Swift, born seven years after the restoration of the monarchy, lived in an age in which Hobbes's vision of the terror of anarchy still seemed all too real' (*Jonathan Swift: An Introductory Essay* (Methuen: London, 1973), p. 62).

24 Geoffrey Hill, 'Jonathan Swift: The Poetry of "Reaction"', in Brian Vickers (ed.), *The World of Jonathan Swift* (Basil Blackwell: Oxford, 1968), 195–212, p. 198. The quotation, 'agony and indignation' comes from John Wilmot, *Poems of John Wilmot, Earl of Rochester*, edited by Vivian de Sola Pinto (Routledge and Kegan Paul: London, 1953), p. xxix where Pinto talks of 'the agony and indignation of a man who had sought for "felicity and glory" in the world of pleasure and had found that it was an illusion concealing ugliness, folly, hypocrisy and injustice.'

25 Swift, *A Tale of a Tub and Other Works*, pp. 105 and 18.

26 Swift, *The Complete Poems*, p. 530.

27 Gill, '"Filth of All Hues and Odors"', p. 339.

28 Sophie Gee, *Making Waste: Leftovers and the Eighteenth-Century Imagination* (Princeton University Press: Princeton and Oxford, 2010), p. 9.

29 Christopher Hill, *God's Englishman: Oliver Cromwell and the English Revolution* (Penguin: Harmondsworth, 1972), p. 64. First published 1970.

30 By 1700 the reputation of the Cromwellian fighting force seems to have suffered. Ned Ward remarks upon seeing 'an old Oliverian trooper farting upon a trumpet', *The London Spy*, edited by Paul Hyland (Colleagues Press: East Lansing, MI, 1993), p. 114.

31 *The Lives of the Poets*, in Kathleen Williams (ed.), *Swift: The Critical Heritage* (Routledge and Kegan Paul: London, 1970), p. 202.

32 *Complete Letters of Lady Mary Wortley Montagu*, in Williams (ed.), *Swift: The Critical Heritage*, p. 65. In *Sodom* the rational stallion refuses to mount a woman. Buggeranthes recounts her story: 'I strokt his maine, / Pittyd his daily labour & his paine, / When on a sudden from his scabard flew / The statelyest yard y[t] ever mortall drew, / Which Clinging to his Belly stiffe did stand. / I tookt & graspt itt wth my loveing hand / And in a passion movd it to my C—t; / But hee, to womankind not being wont, / Drew back his Engine tho' my C—t cou'd spare / Perhapps as much Roome as his Lady mare. / Att last I found his Constancy was such / That hee woud none but his deare M[rs] touch' (Wilmot, *Works*, pp. 324).

33 *Memoirs of Sarah, Duchess of Marlborough*, in Williams (ed.), *Swift: The Critical Heritage*, p. 101.

34 Abraham Cowley, *The Collected Works of Abraham Cowley*, Volume II, part I, edited by Thomas O. Calhoun, Laurence Heyworth and J. Robert King

(University of Delaware Press: Newark, 1993), p. 34.

35 Sonnet 94, ll. 13–14.

36 Jae Num Lee, *Swift and Scatological Satire* (University of New Mexico Press: Albuquerque, 1971), p. 62.

37 Jens Martin Gurr, 'Worshipping Cloacina in the Eighteenth Century: Functions of Scatology in Swift, Pope, Gay, and Sterne', in Stefan Horlacher, Stefan Glomb and Lars Helier (eds), *Taboo and Transgression in British Literature from the Renaissance to the Present* (Palgrave Macmillan: New York, 2010), 117–34, p. 121.

38 Brean Hammond, 'Swift's Reading', in Christopher Fox (ed.), *The Cambridge Companion to Jonathan Swift* (Cambridge University Press: Cambridge, 2003), 73–86, p. 82.

39 Swift, *Gulliver's Travels*, p. 26.

40 George Orwell, 'Politics vs Literature: An Examination of *Gulliver's Travels*', in Sonia Orwell and Ian Angus (eds), *The Collected Essays, Journalism and Letters of George Orwell*, 4 vols (Penguin: Harmondsworth, 1970), IV, 241–61, p. 251. First published 1946.

41 Gill, '"Filth of All Hues and Odors"', p. 344.

42 Carole Fabricant, *Swift's Landscape* (Johns Hopkins University Press: Baltimore and London, 1982), p. 37.

43 Edward W. Said, *The World, the Text and the Critic* (Vintage: London, 1991), p. 54. First published 1983.

44 Rochester's own rebellious nature was well attested. As Gill reminds us, 'Rochester's careless defiance and scurrilous compositions cause him a good deal of trouble that he never tried to avoid' ('"Filth of All Hues and Odors"', p. 341).

45 Cited in Williams (ed.), *Swift: The Critical Heritage*, p. 10.

46 Vivian de Sola Pinto, 'John Wilmot, Earl of Rochester', in *The Pelican Guide to English Literature*, 7 vols (Penguin: Harmondsworth, 1966), IV, 150 (my emphasis). First published 1957.

47 David Farley-Hills (ed.), *Rochester: the Critical Heritage* (Barnes and Noble: New York, 1972), p. 13.

48 Jonathan Swift, *The Poems of Jonathan Swift*, edited by Harold Williams, 3 vols (Clarendon Press: Oxford, 1958), second edition, III, 1059. Love includes 'On Rome's Pardons' in his section devoted to Rochester's 'Disputed Works' (Wilmot, *Works*, p. 247).

49 Jonathan Swift, *Prose Works of Jonathan Swift*, edited by Herbert Davis, 14 vols (Basil Blackwell: Oxford, 1939–68), VI, 153.

50 Victoria Glendinning, *Jonathan Swift* (Hutchinson: London, 1998), p. 256.

51 Gill, '"Filth of All Hues and Odors"', p. 342.

52 Said, *The World, the Text and the Critic*, p. 89.

53 Swift, *Gulliver's Travels*, p. 172, my emphasis.

54 Swift, *Gulliver's Travels*, p. 173.

55 Swift, *Gulliver's Travels*, p. 308.

56 Swift, *Gulliver's Travels*, p. 290.

57 Swift, *Gulliver's Travels*, p. 290.

58 Swift, *Gulliver's Travels*, p. 291.

59 *The Tragedy of King Lear*, II.ii.441.

60 *The Literary Remains of Samuel Taylor Coleridge*, in Williams (ed.), *Swift: The Critical Heritage*, pp. 331–2.

61 Aldous Huxley, *Do What You Will: Essays* (Chatto and Windus: London, 1929), pp. 94 and 99. Indicative of the post-Victorian repression of his own time is Huxley's squeamishness about quoting the line 'Celia, Celia, Celia shits'. Instead he nervously cites it as 'Celia, Celia, Celia …' and continues, 'The monosyllabic verb, which the modesties of 1929 will not allow me to reprint, rhymes with "wits" and "fits"' (p. 94).

62 Huxley, *Do What You Will*, pp. 105 and 104.

63 Huxley, *Do What You Will*, pp. 104–5.

64 Ellen Pollak, 'Swift Among the Feminists', in Peter J. Schakel (ed.), *Critical Approaches to Teaching Swift* (AMS Press: New York, 1992), 65–75, p. 72.

65 Ward, *Jonathan Swift*, p. 3.

66 Ward, *Jonathan Swift*, p. 86 and p. 6.

67 Orwell, 'Politics vs Literature: An Examination of *Gulliver's Travels*', IV, 254. Incidentally, Said notes that 'Orwell's essay belongs to the period of his growing disenchantment with modern politics' (*The World, the Text and the Critic*, pp. 75–6).

68 Miss W——— responded in kind though with a poem called 'The Gentleman's Study, In Answer to [Swift's] The Lady's Dressing Room' which castigates males for poor personal hygiene. A milliner, Mrs South, goes to visit the chambers of Strephon and sees that 'some stocks lay on the ground, / One side was yellow, t' other brown; / And velvet breeches (on her word), / The inside all bedaubed with t—d, / And just before, I'll not desist / To let you know they were be-pissed: / Four different stinks lay there together, / Which were sweat, turd, and piss, and leather.' Later she hides behind a screen as Strephon returns home drunk: 'overcome with stink of fart, / And after, then came thick upon it / The odious, nauseous one of vomit, / That pourèd out from mouth and nose / Both on his bed, and floor, and clothes; / Nor was it lessened e'er a bit, / Nor overcome, by stink of s—t' (ll. 45–52 and 140–6, in Roger Lonsdale (ed.), *Eighteenth-Century Women Poets: An Oxford Anthology* (Oxford University Press: Oxford and New York, 1989), pp. 131 and 133).

69 Cited in Glendinning, *Jonathan Swift*, p. 252.

70 Gee, *Making Waste*, p. 101.

71 Cited in Glendinning, *Jonathan Swift*, p. 253.

72 Derek Mahon, 'Reveller at Life's Feast', *The Guardian*, 4 March 2006, p. 22.

73 Paul Schlike (ed.), *Oxford Reader's Companion to Dickens* (Oxford University Press: Oxford, 1999), p. 558. Keith Crook, citing Gulliver's description of the sophistry of lawyers whose hair-splitting is profitable only to themselves, notes, 'Dickens was to make the same charge as a leading theme in his novel, *Bleak House*' (*A Preface to Swift* (Longman: London and New York, 1998), p. 210).

74 'Some Remarks on *A Tale of a Tub*', in Williams (ed.), *Swift: The Critical Heritage*, p. 32.

75 'Some Remarks', p. 32.

76 'Some Remarks', p. 32.

77 'Some Remarks', p. 33.

78 'Some Remarks', p. 31. Incidentally, Harington's text is also mentioned in Huxley's essay, p. 103.

79 Norman O. Brown, *Life Against Death: The Psychoanalytical Meaning of History* (Wesleyan University Press: Middletown CT, 1959), p. 179.

80 Brown, *Life Against Death*, p. 179.

81 Brown, *Life Against Death*, p. 186.

82 This is Sir Walter Scott, for instance, whose edition of Swift's works was published in 1814 and who remarked thus on Swift's apparent mental illness: 'This unfortunate propensity [Swift's grossness] seems nearly allied to the misanthropy which was a precursor of his mental derangement.' Such misanthropy 'marks an incipient disorder of the mind, which induced the author to dwell upon degrading and disgusting subjects, from which all men, in possession of healthful taste and sound faculties, turn with abhorrence' (Williams (ed.), *Swift: The Critical Heritage*, p. 296). Orwell is even more forthright and incorrect: 'Swift ultimately blew everything to pieces in the only way that was feasible before the atomic bomb – that is, he went mad' ('Politics vs Literature: An Examination of *Gulliver's Travels*', IV, 257).

83 Orwell, 'Politics vs Literature: An Examination of *Gulliver's Travels*', IV, 242.

84 Wilmot, *Works*, p. 37.

85 Brown, *Life Against Death*, p. 186.

86 *Remarks on the Life and Writing of Dr Jonathan Swift*, in Williams (ed.), *Swift: The Critical Heritage*, p. 121.

87 *Remarks*, in Williams (ed.), *Swift: The Critical Heritage*, p. 121.

88 Gee, *Making Waste*, p. 110.

89 Swift, *Gulliver's Travels*, p. 339. Laetitia Pilkington recounts how Swift called her husband a fool for marrying her when, for the same cost, he could have kept a horse which 'would have given him better Exercise and more Pleasure than a Wife'. A. C. Elias, Jr. notes of this remark: 'This is

wonderful material – though not to be taken *too* seriously' ('Laetitia Pilkington on Swift: How Reliable Is She?', in Fox and Tooley (eds), *Walking Naboth's Vineyard*, 127–42, p. 131).

90 Swift, *Gulliver's Travels*, p. 335.

91 Swift, *Gulliver's Travels*, p. 345.

92 Will Stockton asks of this description, 'Has Hamlet dragged his stockings on the ground, or, just perhaps, has Hamlet soiled himself?' (*Playing Dirty: Sexuality and Waste in Early Modern Comedy* (University of Minnesota Press: Minneapolis and London: 2011), p. ix).

93 Lee, *Swift and Scatological Satire*, p. 83.

94 Ward, *Jonathan Swift*, p. 15.

95 Swift, *Gulliver's Travels*, p. 158.

96 Swift, *Gulliver's Travels*, p. 158.

97 David Inglis, *A Sociological History of Excretory Experience: Defecatory Manners and Toiletry Technologies* (Edwin Mellen Press: Lampeter, 2000).

98 Brown, *Life Against Death*, p. 188.

99 Pollak, 'Swift among the Feminists', pp. 72–3.

100 Doody, 'Swift Among the Women', p. 90. Doody's influence on Pollak is clear in the echoing titles of their essays.

101 Donald Greene, 'On Swift's "Scatological" Poems', *Sewanee Review*, 75 (1967), 672–89, p. 677.

102 Gee, *Making Waste*, p. 99.

103 'Trivia or the Art of Walking the Streets of London', in Gay, *Poetry and Prose*, I, 146. This section of Gay's poem tells of Cloacina's affair with a night-soil man and her giving birth to a shoe-shine boy. The other gods bring gifts of a brush, polish and a tripod and, having gratefully received these gifts, Cloacina 'downward glides, / Lights in *Fleet-ditch*, and shoots beneath the Tides' (I, 167–8). The editors note, though the Fleet 'was officially a channel or canal and it was navigable, it was in Gay's time already essentially a sewer. The whole river is now a covered sewer' (II, 558).

104 Donne, *John Donne: The Oxford Authors*, p. 13.

105 Pollak describes 'Swift's obsessive association of the female with bodily fluids and excess' ('Swift among the Feminists', p. 71).

106 Anon., *The School of Salernum*, translated by Sir John Harington, edited by Francis R. Packard and Fielding H. Garrison (Augustus M. Kelley: New York, 1970), p. 79.

107 Swift, *Poems*, second edition, II, 589.

108 Swift, *The Complete Poems*, p. 833.

109 Swift may be remembering Sejanus's discussion of female lavatorial girning when the Roman soldier asks Eudemus, 'who makes hardest faces on her stool?' (Ben Jonson, *Sejanus His Fall*, edited by W. F. Bolton (Ernest Benn: London, 1966), p. 21). The following lines are strikingly

similar to Swift's catalogue of discarded prosthetics in 'A Beautiful Young Nymph Going to Bed': 'Which lady sleeps with her own face, a' nights? / Which puts her teeth off, with her clothes, in court? / Or, which her hair? which her complexion? / And, in which box she puts it?' (I.i.307–10).

110 Gilmore, 'The Comedy of Swift's Scatological Poems', p. 37.

111 Greene, 'On Swift's "Scatological" Poems', p. 682.

112 Andrew Marvell, *The Poems and Letters of Andrew Marvell*, edited by H. M. Margoliouth, 2 vols (Clarendon Press: Oxford, 1952), I, 27. Hammond points out that Swift owned a copy of Marvell's *The Rehearsal Transpros'd* of 1672 ('Swift's Reading', p. 81).

113 The allegorical figure who represents James I in *A Tale of a Tub* 'claimed great Honnour for his Victorys, tho' he oftimes beshit himself when there was no danger' (Swift, *A Tale of a Tub and Other Works*, p. 144). Reginald Reynolds cites a story recounted by Sir Roger L'Estrange regarding King James's enthusiasm for hunting: 'such was his absorption in this sport that he would not leave the saddle even to relieve himself, so that his servants had a pretty mess to clean up at the day's end' (*Cleanliness and Godliness* (George Allen and Unwin: London, 1943), p. 253).

114 Swift, *Gulliver's Travels*, p. 224.

115 Swift, *Gulliver's Travels*, p. 226.

116 Swift, *A Tale of a Tub and Other Works*, p. 36.

117 Swift, *A Tale of a Tub and Other Works*, p. 36.

6

A palpable shit:
topology, religion and science

He takes the air upon dung-hills, in ditches, and common-shoars
[that is, sewers], and at my Lord Mayor's dog-kennel. In short,
almost every part has a tincture of such filthiness, as renders it
unfit for the worst of uses.[1]

The contemplation of the horrid or sordid or disgusting, by an
artist, is the necessary and negative aspect of the impulse toward
the pursuit of beauty. But not all succeed as did Dante in expressing the complete scale from negative to positive. The negative is the
more importunate.[2]

I

It is with reference to the unflinching attentions of Swift to the
realities of human bodily processes that Carol Houlihan Flynn
defends what we might call 'shiterature'. Persuasively she
analyses the fervid trepidation brought into existence by a modern
sense of corporeality during the early eighteenth century. Her
starting point is the assertion that 'When Defoe and Swift
employed strategies to contain or escape from the body, they
reflected the struggle against materiality that characterized their
age.'[3] Jens Martin Gurr, too, insists that the palpable nature of
scatology is designed to undermine the more complacent asser-
tions about human potentiality advocated by the Enlightenment:
'much eighteenth-century writing uses the physical to deflate the
claims of the spiritual and intellectual side of humankind', and he
concludes, 'The insistence upon anality, excrement, human

stench, and bestiality can thus be read as a direct response drasti-
cally countering the period's ideal of humans as remarkably
non-corporeal, purely intellectual or purely sentimental beings.'[4]
But this scepticism towards Enlightenment idealism is made
particularly acute by the concrete, material conditions inhabited
by these scatological writers. While Gurr opines that the scatological imperative is effected by a reaction against 'the overly
optimistic assessments of human moral and intellectual capabilities expounded in the philosophical and literary writings of the
early Enlightenment', it is also, in a more mundane though
concomitantly profound way, derived from the conditions of lived
experience.[5] The scatology of the period is as anti-urban as it is
anti-urbane: 'what has generally been ignored is the fact that
Swift actually lived in a landscape in which excrement was a
prominent – not to mention highly visible and necessarily
obtrusive – feature'.[6]

New economic structures and a hastily developing consumer
culture, together with the distension of London as a seat both of
poverty and disease caused by new levels of population density
and consequent overcrowding and filth, led to the declaration of
hitherto unexpressed anxieties. The very name of Dublin's fair
city is a derivation of the Irish *Dubh Linn*, meaning 'black pool'.
Cities were not known for their sweetness or light. The country
gentleman of Ned Ward's *The London Spy* (1698–1700) is overwhelmed by the crush of the populace: 'I thought my entrails
would have come out of my mouth, and I should have gone
shitten home. I was so closely imprisoned between the bums and
bellies of the multitude that I was almost squeezed as flat as a
napkin in a press.'[7] The population of the capital in 1670 was
around 0.37 million, almost doubling to 0.67 million within
thirty years. 'One in ten of all English people lived in London by
the mid-eighteenth century, and one in six are thought to have
spent some time in it. No other European city grew so fast.'[8] The
consequences of this surge in population included poorly
regulated building on hitherto open spaces. Since bricks were
heavy and expensive to transport, brick kilns sprang up in the city
itself: John Evelyn cited Bank-Side and St Paul's as particularly
noisome while the Duke of Chandos – himself a property

developer – lamented that his own house in Cavendish Square was 'poisoned with the brick kilns and other abominate smells which infect these parts'.[9]

Pepys's account of a road accident features both the narrowness of the streets and the plenitude of the crowd: 'driving through the backside of the Shambles in Newgate Market, my coach plucked down two pieces of beef into the Dirt; upon which the butchers stopped the horses, and a great rout of people in the street – crying that he had done him 40s. and 5l worth of hurt; but going down, I saw that he had done little or none'. Pepys's compensation is characteristically stingy: 'I gave them a Shilling for it and they were well contented, and so home.'[10] It is not likely that the soiled meat was destroyed; in all probability, it was put straight back on the hook. Ward complained that the pork sold in a London shop tasted 'nurs'd up in T[ur]d and Mire'.[11] Vegetables 'are produced in an artificial soil, and taste of nothing but the dunghills from whence they spring'.[12] By the time Pepys's fish supper was served up, it had already gone off: 'my stomach was turned when my sturgeon came to table, upon which I saw very many little worms creeping, which I suppose was through the staleness of the pickle'.[13] Perhaps Pepys's fish had come from Billingsgate, an area of town noted for its cramped streets and dodgy surroundings: 'By this time we were come to Billingsgate, and in a narrow lane, as dark as a burying-vault, which stunk of stale sprats, piss and sir-reverence, we groped about like a couple of thieves in a coal-hole.'[14]

The effects of overcrowding, poor hygiene, rotten food and uncomfortable living conditions were often, and unsurprisingly, the cause of physical illness – in Pepys's case, as we have seen in Chapter 4, predominantly to do with his bowels (on the same day as he received his lousy fish, he noted that he 'took phisique ... to loosen me, for I am bound'). For others, the effects of the ambient oppression were more psychological. Arriving in London in 1762, James Boswell noted down his own misgivings: 'I began to be apprehensive that I was taking a nervous fever, a supposition not improbable, as I had one after such an illness when I was last in London. I was quite sunk.'[15] Swift himself was born only one year after the cessation of the worst instance of plague ever visited on the city. Peter Ackroyd's intense description captures and is animated by the collective paranoia which made the disposal of sewage a matter of life and death:

> No one was ever safe. No one was ever entirely well in a city 'full of pits and sloughs, very perilous and noyous', dirty and filled with 'corrupt savours'. London itself had become a sink of disease. Yet nothing in its history could have prepared its citizens for the events which unfolded between the fated and fateful years of 1664 and 1666.[16]

Pepys provides a vivid and moving description of London during this fatal period:

> I walked to the Tower. But Lord, how empty the streets are, and melancholy, so many poor sick people in the streets, full of sores, and so many sad stories overheard as I walk, everybody talking of this dead, and that man sick, and so many in this place, and so many in that. And they tell me that in Westminster there is never a physitian, and but one apothecary left, all being dead.[17]

Westminster's streets were especially narrow, which caused it to suffer more than other areas in terms of the spread and effects of the plague. In exactly the same year, 1665, Marchamont Needham published his *Medela medicinæ: a plea for the free profession and a renovation of the art of physick*. It is this source which *OED* cites as containing the first printed use of the word 'miasma'. Although Needham uses the term to describe impurities of the blood and humours, it is not long after this that miasmatic theory begins to develop – a theory which postulates that aerial pollution is responsible for the transmission of epidemics. David Inglis writes, 'As a result of such a view of the nature of disease, various types of odour were increasingly deemed by medical and scientific professionals as being life threatening. Particular attention was given to odours given off by the human body and its effluvial products.'[18] In a mock-medical pamphlet of 1732 which is sometimes attributed to Swift, miasmatic infection is blamed for piles. The pamphlet advises

> never to make Use of a publick *Bog-House;* for that the unwholesome Vapours settled on the Seats at Churches, and which arise from the fetid Odure [sic] in *Bog-Houses,* penetrated the *Anus,* at

that time expanded by performing its Office; that a Corrosion being
made on the *Anus*, by certain pointed nitrous Particles in vitiated
Air, forcibly impelled upon that tender Part, made it susceptible of
the lubricating Moisture, which in the Explosion attends the
Excrement, and being of a saline or acrimonious Quality, (in Taste
like Tobacco-Juice, as I have been told by curious Enquirers into
Nature,) very often occasion'd those Tumours, which the Learned
call the *Piles*.[19]

More seriously, in 1750 several high-ranking Old Bailey officials
died after disease spread from Newgate Prison. Contemporary
accounts blamed 'a very Noisome Smell' and it was thought that
the 'putrid *Effluvia* which the prisoners bring with them in their
Cloaths, &c. especially where too many are brought into a
crowded Court together, may have fatal effects on People who are
accustomed to breath better Air'.[20] For Flynn this metropolitan
squalor and Swiftian scatology are inseparable; but she suggests
that Swift revels in rather than fears it and her conclusion is
succinct and unexpectedly triumphant: 'To discover the allure of
filth is to become Swift.'[21]

It is certainly the case that other writers of the period were less
sanguine about metropolitan depravities. Tobias Smollett's epistolary persona voices his disapproval of the new urban sprawl (it is
undoubtedly significant that Smollett was, himself, a physician):

> In the space of seven years, eleven thousand new houses have been
> built in one quarter of Westminster, exclusive of what is daily
> added to other parts of this unwieldy metropolis. Pimlico and
> Knightsbridge are now almost joined to Chelsea and Kensington;
> and if this infatuation continues for half a century, I suppose the
> whole county of Middlesex will be covered with brick . . . the capital
> is become an overgrown monster; which, like a dropsical head, will
> in time leave the body and extremities without nourishment and
> support.[22]

While brick is fire-resistant, we have already noted the deleterious
effects of its manufacture. Indeed, the demand for the material
was so substantial that, in order to increase the bulk of its
substance, composites including sifted ash, grit, dirt and even
human dung were added. 'The Frenchman Pierre Jean Grosley,
touring London in 1772, described humble houses fabricated

from "the first earth that comes to hand, and only just warmed at the fire". Grosley peered down his nose at bricks that were bulked out by the "excrements taken out of necessary houses".[23]

This of course is post-Fire London and the opportunity for a new beginning was being squandered: 'For reasons both practical and symbolic, Londoners maintained a loyalty to filth that postfire planners had not considered.'[24] Nicholas Hawksmoor, Christopher Wren's Clerk of Works and designer of St Alphege, Greenwich, and Christchurch, Spitalfields (among others), lamented that London's projects were marred by 'Lakes of Mud and Rills of Stinking mire'.[25] The city's capital function as the head of the body politic is failing and the metaphorical disease, imaged by Smollett as its oedematose swelling, is a symptom of corruption and disorder – both politically and morally. The city spirals out of control, generating its own waste and crime: 'London being an immense wilderness, in which there is neither watch nor ward of any signification, nor any order or police, affords them [criminals] lurking-places as well as prey.'[26] Other symptoms of urban corruption are claustrophobia and pollution – here, the omnipresence of smog and ordure:

> I am pent up in frowzy lodgings, where there is not room enough to swing a cat; and I breathe the steams of endless putrefaction; and these would, undoubtedly, produce a pestilence, if they were not qualified by the gross acid of sea-coal, which is itself a pernicious nuisance to lungs of any delicacy of texture ... If I would drink water, I must quaff the maukish contents of an open aqueduct, exposed to all manner of defilement; or swallow that which comes from the river Thames, impregnated with all the filth of London and Westminster – Human excrement is the least offensive part of the concrete, which is composed of all the drugs, minerals and poisons, used in mechanics and manufacture, enriched with the putrefying carcases of beasts and men; and mixed with the scourings of all the wash-tubs, kennels [gutters], and common sewers.[27]

Just four years before the 1726 publication of *Gulliver's Travels*, Daniel Defoe's *Journal of the Plague Year* was published. This fictionalised account of the epidemic 'documents' the burial of the plague dead and actually equates them with fecal matter: 'The

Distemper sweeping away such Multitudes, as I have observ'd, many, if not all the out Parishes were oblig'd to make new burying Grounds ... the dead Bodies were disturb'd, abus'd, dug up again, some even before the Flesh of them was perished from the Bones, and remov'd like Dung or Rubbish to other Places.'[28] John Oldham stigmatises the city as 'the Common-shore, / Where *France* does all her Filth and Ordure pour' (ll. 87–8) and he notes that the 'dangers of the Night' include 'emptied Chamber-pots [which] come pouring down / From Garret Windows: you have cause to bless / The gentle Stars, if you come off with Piss'.[29] William Hogarth's *Night* from his series, *Four Times of Day* (1738), is dominated by a shower of urine cascading from an emptied chamber-pot, running off the roof of a bay window and gushing into the tricorn hat of a drunken magistrate, while in the background, a tapster tops up a tun from a small barrel, visually evoking the idea that consumption of liquid will inevitably result in such torrential evacuations (Illustration 3).

   John Gay's 'Trivia, or the Art of Walking the Streets of London', warns the walker how the gathering storm, once broken, will cause the overflow of the drains: 'you'll hear the Sounds / Of whistling Winds, e'er Kennels break their Bounds; / Ungrateful Odours common Sewers diffuse, / And dropping Vaults distil unwholesom Dews' (book I, 169–72). In the second book we hear of the shoe-shine boy who, having woken up, 'leaning o'er the Rails, he musing stood, / And view'd below the black Canal of Mud, / Where common Sewers a lulling Murmur keep, / Whose Torrents rush from *Holborn*'s fatal Steep' (ll. 171–4). Gay's georgic parody with its gods and goddesses and its mythological classicism appears to animate the cityscape itself. Effluent seems to flow as part of the animus of London rather than its inhabitants. Only at one point does the narrator reproach its citizens for causing the sewage in the first place when he exhorts the reader to seek a privy for the purposes of urination: 'The thoughtless Wits shall frequent Forfeits pay, / Who 'gainst the Centry's Box discharge their Tea. / Do thou some Court, or secret Corner seek, / Nor flush with Shame the passing Virgin's Cheek' (ll. 297–300). Human excrement, as we have seen, is part of the urban landscape but in *The London Spy* it is so bad that even heavenly phenomena are

3 *Night*, one of four views by Hogarth (1697–1764), The Vyne,
The Chute Collection (National Trust).

occluded: 'The wonderful eclipse … was invisible to us at London by reason of a stinking fog that arose from reeking dunghills, distillers' vats, and piping-hot close-stool pans.'[30] The defilement of ordure and the miasmatic pollution which arises from the densely packed dwellings become synonymous.

Swift works within this fecal scenery but (as we have seen in the case of some of the poems considered in Chapter 5) displays a fascinated charm with it rather than a disgust or daintiness towards it. In his 'Digression Concerning Critics' he likens the textual commentator wading through books and pamphlets, 'the nauseous, the fulsome, the dull, and the impertinent', to a man wandering the streets of a populous city (here Edinburgh) 'in a morning, who is indeed as careful as he can to watch diligently and spy out the filth in his way; not that he is curious to observe the colour and complexion of the ordure, or take its dimensions, much less to be paddling in or tasting it, but only with a design to come out as cleanly as he may'.[31] Typically, as in the case of Celia's stained smock (which we considered in the last chapter), Swift's language negates the object while envisioning it in the most graphic terms. The idea of measuring or even tasting fecal matter would not occur to the squeamish reader who is placed in the exact role of the tiptoeing man. Swift's palpable description, however, ensures that we have our noses rubbed in it. This close attention to the size, shape and smell of feces finds its comic extreme in a passage from *An Examination of Certain Abuses, Corruptions, and Enormities in the City of Dublin*:

> Every Person who walks the Streets, must needs observe the immense Number of human Excrements at the Doors and Steps of waste Houses, and at the Sides of every dead Wall; for which the disaffected Party hath assigned a very false and malicious Cause. They would have it that these Heaps were laid there privately by *British Fundaments*, to make the world believe, that our *Irish* Vulgar do daily eat and drink; and consequently, that the Clamour of Poverty among us, must be false; proceeding only from *Jacobites* and *Papists*. They would confirm this, by pretending to observe, that a *British Anus* being more narrowly perforated than one of our own Country; and many of these Excrements, upon a strict View appearing Copple-crowned, with a Point like a Cone or Pyramid,

are easily distinguished from the *Hibernian*, which lie much flatter, and with less Continuity. I communicated this Conjecture to an eminent Physician, who is well versed in such profound Speculations; and at my Request was pleased to make Trial with each of his Fingers, by thrusting them into the *Anus* of several Persons of both Nations; and professed he could find no such Difference between them as those ill-disposed People alledge. On the contrary, he assured me, that much the greater Number of narrow Cavities were of *Hibernian* Origin ... I had almost forgot to add, that my Friend the Physician could, by smelling each Finger, distinguish the *Hibernian* Excrement from the *British*; and was not above twice mistaken in an Hundred Experiments; upon which he intends very soon to publish a learned Dissertation.[32]

The pseudo-science of what we might call eugenic proctology, and the deference to the 'eminent Physician' is reminiscent of the Academy of Lagado in its stercoraceous absurdity, but in addition, as Gulliver notes of Laputa, while these experiments take place, the country lies in ruins: 'The only inconvenience is, that none of these projects are yet brought to perfection, and in the meantime the whole country lies miserably waste, the houses in ruins, and the people without food or clothes.'[33] *Certain Abuses* argues that the widespread distribution of British turds is thought to be a propaganda trick to demonstrate the unfoundedness of Irish complaints of famine and poverty. In this way *Certain Abuses* echoes *A Modest Proposal*, published three years earlier, in its mingling of gross physicality (there the roasting and eating of babies) and a serious political sub-text – that Ireland is racked by starvation and is being brutally exploited by the English.

Swift's poetic parallel to this moment, and his most obviously nauseating vision of urban pollution, occurs in 'A Description of a City Shower', and it is this poem Gay has in mind when he acknowledges in the prologue to 'Trivia' '*among many other Obligations, I owe several Hints of it to Dr Swift*'.[34] In Chapter 5 we noted Swift's indebtedness to Jonson's *Volpone* and ought to mention at the outset that 'City Shower' is a reworking of the excremental epic, 'On the Famous Voyage' (the poem which, as we saw in Chapter 2, refers by name to Sir John Harington's *Metamorphosis of Ajax*). Jonson's poem describes a journey down the foul Fleet to the Thames. This mock-heroic expedition likens the effluent-filled landscape of London to the horrors of the underworld with its 'filth, stench, noyse [where] / Arses were heard to croake, in stead of frogs' (ll. 9–13).[35] The mud stirred up by the oars is as bad as the cargoes of the assembled night-soil men: 'an ayre, as hot, as at a muster / Of all your night-tubs, when the carts doe cluster, / Who shall discharge first his merd-urinous load' (ll. 43–5). The horrid genius of the shore, Cocytus, threatens to 'beshite us. / No matter, stinkards, row. What croaking sound / Is this we heare? of frogs? No, guts wind-bound, / Over your heads' (ll. 70–3). The dank landscape is haunted by 'sev'rall ghosts / ... of farts, but late departed' (ll. 104–5) and the heroes' nostrils are beset with smells that result from clerks eating 'Laxative lettuce, and such windie meate' (l. 147) while their voyage has taken place at a time 'when each privies seate / Is fill'd with buttock' and 'the walls doe sweate / Urine, and plaisters' (ll. 148–50). In Jonson's poem the city is one huge running sewer and though Swift is writing nearly a century later, nothing much (witness the gong-farmers) seems to have changed.[36] If anything the increased population has added to the volume of waste. One of the most revolting symptoms of the flood in Swift's cityscape is the over-flowing domestic sewer (which of course was the one which required emptying by the night-soil man): 'Returning home at night you find the sink / Strike your offended sense with double stink' (ll. 5–6). As Smollett's description above indicates, the water supply and drainage were persistent problems and indeed it is probably to this couplet that Swift is referring when, in a letter of 8 November 1710, he writes to Stella, 'Impudence, if you vex me, I'll give ten shillings a week for my lodging; for I am almost st[un]k out of this with the sink, and it helps me to my verses in my *Shower*.'[37] The storm acts not merely on the body of the city but upon the body of the citizen, giving rise to a series of symptoms of its imminent approach: corns become painful, aches in limbs and rotting teeth occur as well as 'spleen' (ll. 9–12) which, as Boswell's bewilderment illustrates, could mean melancholia, depression or boredom. The storm is anthropomorphised so that its rain is like vomit and its wind like flatus: the dust 'aided by the wind, fought still for life; / And wafted with its foe [water drops] by violent gust' (ll. 24–5). The poem climaxes in an apocalyptic vision of smells, sounds and sights – a synaesthetic vortex:

> Now from all parts the swelling kennels flow,
> And bear their trophies with them as they go:
> Filths of all hues and odours, seem to tell
> What streets they sailed from, by the sight and smell.
> They, as each torrent drives with rapid force
> From Smithfield, or St Pulchre's shape their course;
> And in huge confluent join as Snow Hill ridge,
> Fall from the conduit prone to Holborn Bridge.
> Sweepings from butchers' stalls, dung, guts, and blood,
> Drowned puppies, stinking sprats, all drenched in mud,
> Dead cats and turnip-tops come tumbling down the flood.
>   (ll. 53–63)[38]

The details of local geography contrast with the elemental forces of nature. 'On the Famous Voyage' also included mention of 'Bread-streets Mermaid', 'Bride-well', 'Paris-garden', 'Fleet-lane', and (as here) 'Hol'borne'. The references to specific locations ground the repugnance of the descriptions *in lived experience*; despite Jonson's mock-heroic frame and frequent classical references, despite Swift's epic similes and mention of the Trojan horse (ll. 47–52), recognisable place names serve to underscore the dreadful palpability of their dystopian visions.

Of Swift's magnificent closing rhyming triplet, David Ward writes, 'the comic stretching both of rhyme and rhythm gives the verse a welcome irregularity and flexibility of movement. The tumbling effect produced mimics precisely the flooding sweep of water and offal and rubbish into the river.'[39] Jonson's poem also 'ran grease, and haire of meazled hogs, / The heads, houghs, entrailes, and the hides of dogs / ... / Cats there lay divers had beene flead, and rosted, / And, after mouldie growne, againe were tosted' (ll. 125–30). But in Swift's catalogue of detritus there is more than just death; notice, for instance, how 'guts' occurs between 'dung' and 'blood' as though the term is intermediate between death and life. Despite the sickening effect of this tidal wave of debris, there is, as Ward implies, a curiously dynamic force to the flow, as though the city has been purged for its own good: 'at the end of the storm all sorts of inanimate and indiscriminate filth are swept away by the flood'.[40] Notice that use of the word 'inanimate' – in other words, the flood is life-giving in as much as it purges death and waste from the streets. It is neither a destructive nor a negative agent.[41] Writing of Swift's source, Jonson's 'The Famous Voyage', Andrew McRae insists on its unexpectedly positive outlook: 'The poem's mobilisation of the grotesque, within the civic body, facilitates a strain of satire remarkable for its understated sense of vitality and regeneration ... The "Famous Voyage," with its singular blend of learning and buffoonery, urbanity and jest, constructs a spatiality of intermeshed dissolution and creativity in the very guts of early modern London'.[42] But exactly the same assertion could be said to apply to 'City Shower'. Moreover, the mysterious joining of images of life and death at the conclusion of 'City Shower' justifies Flynn's optimistic pronouncement, cited above, that 'To discover the allure of filth is to become Swift.' The river, flowing water, the stream – all are symbolic of shape shifting, of something constantly coming into being, while the deluge or the flood are archetypal signifiers of a new beginning.

Writing of Rabelais, Mikhail Bakhtin explains how excrement can be considered a force for good: 'Excrement was conceived as an essential element in the life of the body and of the earth in the struggle against death. It was part of man's vivid awareness of his materiality, of his bodily nature, closely related to the life of the earth.'[43] As we have seen, Swift's poetry is vividly aware of its own materiality as well as its changing shape. This constant metamorphosis is characteristic of a progressive dynamic, as Bakhtin explains: 'The last thing one can say of the real grotesque is that it is static; on the contrary it seeks to grasp in its imagery the very act of becoming and growth, the eternal incomplete unfinished nature of being.'[44]

Whether crowded into shops like the women pretending to examine goods (ll. 33–4) or the dapper beau sheltering in a sedan chair (l. 43), the Londoners attempt to stay out of the rain and well clear of the running sewage. While in real life we shun fecal evidence, in fantasy, the realms of the psychoanalytical and in Bakhtinian carnival, we can find ourselves up to our knees in it. In chapter 5 of the second voyage, Gulliver is confronted with a giant turd: 'There was a cow-dung in the path, and I must needs try my activity by attempting to leap over it. I took a run, but unfortunately jumped short, and found myself just in the middle up to my knees.'[45] Unsurprisingly the reaction of the Brobdingnagians was one of merriment: 'the Queen was soon informed of what had passed, and the footmen spread it about the Court, so that all the mirth, for some days, was at my expense'.[46] In spite of the serious point – that Gulliver's attempted leap emblematises humanity's thwarted efforts to rise above its earth(l)y station – the comedy is crudely scatological and obvious. Contrast this comedic and fictional account with Pepys's much less amused (it goes without saying) actual occurrence of same: 'This morning one came to me to advise with me where to make a window into my cellar in lieu of one that Sir W. Batten had stopped up; and going down into my cellar to look, I put my foot into a great heap of turds, by which I find that Mr. Turners house of office is full and comes into my cellar, which doth trouble me.'[47] But carnivalesque shiterature is amusing precisely because, in Bakhtinian terms, it represents life and fecundity: 'Excrement is gay matter; in the ancient scatological images ... it is linked to the generating force and to fertility.'[48]

The Yahoo government comprises a dominant male who is more hideous than all the rest and a sidekick whose job it is to '*lick his master's feet and posteriors, and drive the female Yahoos to his kennel*; for which he was now and then rewarded with a piece of ass's flesh'.[49] The juxtaposition of anal rimming and the procuring of females for mating illustrates what is by now a familiar combination of the scatological and the sexual. According to this analysis then, fecal matter takes on fecund characteristics; excrement comes to symbolise life-giving properties. It is for this reason that the Yahoos actually administer fecal medicines to one another, compounding their emetics and their enemas from (among other things) 'seaweed, excrements, barks of trees, serpents, toads, frogs, spiders, dead men's flesh and bones' so that things usually associated with poison or death take on life-saving properties.[50] The generic cure for the disease known as '*hnea-Yahoo*, or the *Yahoo's-evil* ... is a mixture of *their own dung* and *urine* forcibly put down the Yahoo's throat'.[51] Moreover, the inversions characteristic of carnival occur in the administering of these drugs: 'the body must be treated in a manner directly contrary, by interchanging the use of each orifice, forcing solids and liquids in at the anus, and making evacuations at the mouth'.[52] In Yahoo culture, a culture which Gulliver shuns but which Swift metaphorically embraces, excrement is more than mere waste, it is a source of goodness, health and even ritualistic integrity. No wonder then that Norman O. Brown can find such symbolic import, such talismanic efficacy in the scatological rites of this nation. The (excre)mentality of the Yahoo, he explains, 'is substantially identical with the psychoanalytical doctrine of the extensive role of anal eroticism in the formation of human culture'.[53]

The archetypes of psychoanalysis are not always necessary though. In the diurnal world, Ned Ward offers a potent instance of the way in which farting can actually inspire social cohesion:

> Of all the fantastical Clubs that ever took Pains to make themselves stink in the Nostrils of the Public, sure no ridiculous Community ever came up to this windy Society, which was certainly establish'd by a Parcel of empty Sparks, about Thirty Years since, at a Public House in *Cripplegate* Parish, where they used to meet once a Week to poison the neighbouring Air with their unsavory *Crepitations*, and were so vain in their Ambition to out Fart one another, that they used to diet themselves against their Club-Nights with Cabbage, Onions and Pease-Porridge, that every one's Bumfiddle might be the better qualify'd to sound forth its Emulation.[54]

But amid the apparent chaos of Fart Club, there is a pronounced etiquette. Loud farts are called for but accidents are to be punished:

> An old Alms-Woman [gave] her constant Attendance in the next Room, and if any Member was suspected of a Brewers Miscarriage, he was presently sent in to be examined by the Matron, who, after searching his Breeches, and narrowly inspecting the hind Lappet of his Shirt, thro' her crack'd Spectacles, made her Report accordingly; if unsoil'd, then a Spank on the Bum was given to the Looby, as a Token of his Cleanliness; but if the nasty Bird had befoul'd his Nest, then *Beshit upon Honour*, was her return to the Board, and the laxative Offender was amerc'd for his Default.[55]

Remarkably a false prophet comes into their midst – one who 'by clapping his right Hand under his left Arm-pit, where he would gather Wind, and discharge it so surprizingly ... would give you a Lady's Fart, an old Woman's Slur, or a Maiden Fizzle, &c. so very tunably and natural, that they should entertain the Ears without offending the Nostrils'. But before he is exposed as a fraud, he is 'kindly embrac'd, with all the Marks of Favour, as if they took him to be a God of the Winds, and his Arse to be a Miracle'.[56] In Chapter 1 we noted the morphing of Divine Flatus into human flatulence in Chaucer's work. Over three centuries later, the motif reappears.

II

In the same way that anality and sexuality are exchangeable, so ecstasy, erotic and spiritual, links ideas of anality to religious intensity – scatology to eschatology. As Brown puts it, 'The psychoanalytical theory of infantile sexuality and its sublimation insists that there is a hidden connection between higher spiritual activity and lower organs of the body.'[57] In the light of this it is no accident that Gulliver, chained in 'an ancient temple' in Lilliput and finding himself 'extremely pressed by the necessities of nature' is forced to excrete in a sacred place.[58] Having shut the gate, 'I went as far as the length of my chain would suffer, and discharged my body of that uneasy load.'[59] Instantly Gulliver is overcome with remorse about his violation of the temple and is determined to justify his behaviour: 'this was the only time I was ever guilty of so uncleanly an action; for which I cannot but hope the candid reader will give some allowance, after he hath maturely and impartially considered my case, and the distress I was in'.[60] But just as Gulliver has breached a taboo about defecating in a place of worship, so he has breached a taboo about describing such behaviour in his account. Polite literature, Swift implies, allowing Gulliver to labour the point, is not the place for such descriptions: 'I would not have dwelt so long upon a circumstance, that perhaps at first sight may appear not very momentous, if I had not thought it necessary to justify my character in point of cleanliness to the world; which I am told some of my maligners have been pleased, upon this and other occasions, to call

in question.'[61] Of course this is a case of protesting too much, so that
the embarrassed insistence on the scatological descriptions serves to
rupture the pretence of good manners. Just as in the case of the man
dodging the effluence in the Edinburgh streets, the reader is dragged
through Gulliver's mire. Gulliver leaves the temple 'having occasion
for fresh air' and 'From this time my constant practice was, as soon
as I rose, to perform that business in open air, at the full extent of my
chain.'[62]

This epiphanic movement to the outside world from the claustrophobic privy is a significant topos in Swift. Four years later, in
an extraordinary poem, Swift offers a mythological account of the
repression of Cloacina's altars. In 'A Panegyric on the Dean, In the
Person of a Lady in the North', Swift adopts the voice of Lady
Anne Acheson, an affectionate acquaintance, to describe how the
Dean erected, over a period of five months, two toilets on her
estate, Market Hill:

> Here, gentle goddess Cloacine
> Receives all offerings at her shrine.
> In separate cells the he's and she's
> Here pay their vows with bended knees:
> (For, 'tis prophane when sexes mingle;
> And every nymph must enter single;
> And when she feels an *inward motion*,
> Comes filled with *reverence* and devotion.)
> The bashful maid, to hide her blush,
> Shall creep no more behind a bush;
> Here unobserved, she boldly goes,
> As who should say, *to pluck a rose*.
>
> (ll. 205–16)[63]

The scatological punning insists on the parallel between defecation and religious ritual. Not only is defecating like praying (both
require bended knee), but the turds are offerings at Cloacina's
'shrine'; she is a 'gentle goddess'. '[V]ows' are paid in separate
'cells', a word often denoting a monastic chamber. The separation
of male and female is indicative of a modesty suited to religious
ritual. Indeed Smollett remarks that 'the worship of Cloacina, in
temples which admitted both sexes, and every rank of votaries

promiscuously, was a filthy species of idolatry that outraged every
idea of delicacy and decorum'.[64] The '*inward motion*' is both a
moment of spiritual ecstasy and a contraction of the bowel;
'*reverence*' or more commonly 'sir-reverence', implies respect for
the holy place but it is also defined by *OED* (from 1592) as 'human
excrement' or 'a piece or lump of this'.[65] While '*pluck[ing] a rose*'
might be considered to be a suitably pious gesture of consecration
or devotion in a church or shrine, it also appears in *OED* as a
euphemism: 'of women, to visit the lavatory, to urinate or
defecate'. Those who use the toilets or, in the religious vocabulary
of the poem, 'who frequent this hallowed scene' are urged to wipe
themselves with one of Swift's own poems 'or Smedley's lay, / Or
billet-doux, or lock of hay: / And, O! may all who hither come, /
Return with unpolluted thumb' (ll. 221–4). (Unsurprisingly
Jonathan Smedley's vehement Whig position aroused Swift's
contempt and he referred to him as 'that rascal Smedley'.[66])

The poem develops into a mythological history of the incarcer-
ation of Cloacina: 'Thee bounteous goddess Cloacine, / To temples
why do we confine? / Forbid in open air to breathe; / Why are thine
altars fixed beneath?' (ll. 229–32). The poem answers that in the
Golden Age, defecation occurred in the most pastoral of settings
'in some flowery vale [where] many a flower abstersive grew, / Thy
favourite flowers of yellow hue' (ll. 247–50). During the usurpa-
tion of Saturn by Jove, Gluttony was released from hell and
gobbled up the offerings made to Cloacina, confining her to a cell.
Sloth, Dropsy, Gout, Asthma and Ease have ensured that defecation takes place in the claustrophobic privy:

> None seek thee [Cloacina] now in open air;
> To thee no verdant altars rear;
> But, in their cells and vaults obscene
> Present a sacrifice unclean;
> From whence unsavoury vapours rose,
> Offensive to thy nicer nose.
> Ah! who in our degenerate days
> As nature prompts, his offering pays?
> Here, nature never difference made
> Between the sceptre and the spade.

>   (ll. 281–90)

Outdoor feces only remain in the countryside, a pleasure Lady Acheson finds by unfortunate accident, as she steps in it or soils her dress, 'Unweeting gild the tarnished lace: / Here, by the sacred bramble tinged, / My petticoat is doubly fringed' (ll. 312–14). As in the case (cited above) of Gulliver failing to jump clear of the cow-dung obstruction, the consequences of pastoral as opposed to urban excrement are harmlessly amusing (contrast Pepys's cellar experience).

Swift's comic poem offers a version of the Fall of Man. The world of the Golden Age, in which defecating was both public and outdoors and took place in Edenic landscapes (hence the convenient proximity of 'many a flower abstersive'), was a period in which religious and bodily functions were indivisible. In its post-lapsarian state, excrement brings shame 'and thus a separation of the spiritual and the physical [as well as] an exaggeration of the significance of defecation'.[67] Such harmony between body and soul is a coprophilic paradise; but it is a paradise lost and therefore too immaculate to be contemplated:

> But, stop ambitious muse, in time;
> Nor dwell on subjects too sublime.
> In vain on lofty heels I tread,
> Aspiring to exalt my head:
> With hoop expanded wide and light,
> In vain I tempt too high a flight.

(ll. 319–24)

Musing on such greatness is nothing less than Icarian. Lacking here is the certitude of Milton's epic determination and Swift points this up by echoing the opening invocation of *Paradise Lost* in which the poet declares that his song will 'soar / Above th' Aonian mount, while it pursues / Things unattempted yet in prose or rhyme' (I, 14–16). But Milton's song is aided by the Holy Spirit who 'dost prefer / Before all temples th' upright heart and pure' (ll. 17–18). The now-polluted and claustrophobic privy is a degenerate version of the previous Arcadian landscape and Swift's parodic invocation to Cloacina cuts short further contemplation of this innocent world, a fecal utopia without the repressions and taboos of accommodated man.

This epic dimension, infused with a religious ardour, underlies 'The Gulf of all Human Possessions'. The privy contains all human deeds, good and bad:

> Here lie deposited the spoils
> Of busy mortals' endless toils:
> Here, with an easy search we find
> The foul corruptions of mankind.
> The wretched purchase here behold
> Of traitors who their country sold.
>
> The gulf insatiable imbibes
> The lawyer's fees, the statesman's bribes.
> Here in their proper shape and mien,
> Fraud, perjury, and guilt are seen.
>
> (ll. 13–22)[68]

Yet in spite of its being a sink of all human depravity, the privy is a great leveller. All are drawn there by 'Necessity' (l. 23) and for all of them, evacuating is a peculiarly spiritual process: 'The vigorous youth, and aged sire: / Behold, the coward, and the brave, / The haughty prince, the humble slave, / Physician, lawyer, and divine, / All make oblations at this shrine' (ll. 26–30). Just as in 'A Panegyric on the Dean', the activity of defecating is equated with making a religious offering – note the use of the sacred word, 'shrine'. But as we have also seen in 'A Description of a City Shower', a deluge of excrement precedes a new beginning, and in 'The Gulf', this all-too-physical donation presages a spiritual benefaction:

> Yet from this mingled mass of things,
> In time a new creation springs.
> These crude materials once shall rise,
> To fill the earth, and air, and skies:
> In various forms appear again
> Of vegetables, brutes, and men.
>
> (ll. 89–94)

Defecating is part of a larger cycle of existence and the resurrection of feces, in the form of fertiliser for vegetables on which animals and humans will feed, makes it part of the creative order / ordure of things. It thus acquires, as these poems insist, a fecund, even a spiritual dimension.

It is in his account of the strange religious sect known as the Æolists in *A Tale of a Tub* (also the title of Jonson's last complete play) that Swift had earlier relished the comedy of bodily wind in religious terms.[69] Of course, the section is a satire on the Enthusiasts whom Swift detested and scourged for their hetero-doxies of opinion and ritual. Nonetheless, his account is jubilant and farcical and the Æolists' religious observance, though being sent up, is strangely vitalised by its scatological reverence: 'For whether you please to call the *forma informans* of man by the name of *spiritus, aminus, afflatus*, or *anima*, what are all these but several appellations for *wind*, which is the ruling *element* in every compound and into which they all resolve upon their corrup-tion?'[70] The flatulent parody of Pentecost which we examined in *The Summoner's Tale* (see Chapter 1) illustrates how well estab-lished is the tradition which Swift draws on here. In *A Tale of a Tub* the *Spiritus Sanctus*, the life breathed into Adam by God the Creator is employed as a warranty of (albeit misguided) religious wisdom: 'The learned Æolists maintain the original cause of all things to be *wind*, from which principle this whole universe was first produced.'[71] *OED* defines 'enthusiasm' at about this time as meaning 'fancied inspiration' and Swift plays with the etymology of the word 'inspiration' (from the Latin *inspirare*, meaning 'to breathe in') so that the Æolists inflate themselves in order to preach. The priesthood 'were to be seen several hundreds linked together in a circular chain, with every man a pair of bellows applied to his neighbour's breech, by which they blew each other up to the shape and size of a *tun*'.[72] Eructation takes part in the creative breath of the universe and so is associated with sagacity: 'the wise Æolists affirm the gift of BELCHING to be the noblest act of a rational creature ... therefore the choicest, most edifying, and most enlivening *belches*, were very wisely conveyed through that vehicle [the nose] to give them a tincture as they passed'.[73] The more nidorous the belch, the more divine. The narrator describes how, on feast days, the priest connects himself by means of a 'secret funnel ... from his posteriors to the bottom' of a barrel which contains wind; thus 'the sacred Æolist delivers his oracular *belches* to his panting disciples; of whom some are greedily gaping after the sanctified breath, others are all the while hymning out the praises of the *winds*, and, gently wafted to and fro by their own humming, do thus represent the soft breezes of their deities appeased'.[74] In an outrageously comic moment, the narrator compliments female divines for their extra capacity. In females, the

> organs were understood to be better disposed for the admission of those oracular *gusts*, as entering and passing up through a receptacle of greater capacity, and causing also a pruriency by the way, such as with due management hath been refined from a carnal into a spiritual ecstacy. And, to strengthen this profound conjecture, it is further insisted that this custom of *female* priests is kept up still in certain refined colleges of our *modern* Æolists, who are agreed to receive their inspiration, derived through the receptacle aforesaid, like their ancestors the Sybils.[75]

While the satire is aimed locally at the religious sects, such as the Quakers, who permitted female preachers, the process of refining 'a carnal into a spiritual ecstasy' illustrates what Brown has called the 'hidden connection between higher spiritual activity and lower organs of the body'.[76]

This association is used by Swift to exaggerate the corruption and the bluster of the Papacy. Punningly he animates the papal 'bulls' into a herd of wild cattle sent forth by the Pope to gather gold on his behalf: 'they would *roar*, and *spit*, and *belch*, and *piss*, and *fart*, and snivel out *fire*, and keep a perpetual coil, till you flung them a bit of *gold*'.[77] The line between divine inspiration and the bulls' furious flatus is indeed a narrow one so that, at one point, the narrator can mockingly insist on the homogeneity of all gases: 'Mists arise from the earth, steams from dunghills, exhalations from the sea, and smoke from fire; yet all clouds are the same in composition as well as consequences, and the fumes issuing from a jakes will furnish as comely and useful a vapour as incense from an altar.'[78] Thus misplaced inspiration, that is, according to Swift's orthodox terms, any which deviates from the creed of High Anglicanism, is equivalent to a kind of ecstatic miasma so that the 'same spirits which, in their superior progress, would conquer a kingdom, descending upon the *anus* conclude in a *fistula*'.[79] Enthusiastic religion, conducted in the name of the same God and with equal devotion, is, notwithstanding, to Anglicanism what flatus is to the Holy Spirit. Jack, the egotistical individualist and religious radical, would drop to his knees in the gutter and fall to his prayers 'and whenever curiosity attracted strangers to laugh or to listen, he would of a sudden, with one hand, out with his *gear* and piss full in their eyes, and with the other all to-bespatter them with mud'.[80]

III

Just as the plurality of Swift's personae was identified, in Chapter 5, as a vital feature of his poetry, the contradictory nature of *A Tale of a Tub*'s treatment of flatulence (on one hand a token of albeit sullied inspiration, on the other the symptom of a spiritual confusion) parallels the text's arbitrariness of form and its fragmentation. It is, in this way, perhaps closer to Laurence Sterne's *The Life and Opinions of Tristram Shandy, Gentleman* with its rambling and apparently random composition than the tightly patterned *Gulliver's Travels* with its neat, serialised accounts of each voyage following one after the other. The difficulties of religious interpretation with which *A Tale of a Tub* irreverently deals are seen to parallel the difficulties of textual interpretation presented by the *Tale* itself. The text constitutes a hermeneutic challenge to its reader as it dramatises the contest over religious authority. As Nigel Wood has pointed out: 'So various is the *Tale* in its digressions (not just those announced in chapter-headings) that it forces interpretative choice on the reader.'[81] Swift is fully conscious of this and, at the *Tale*'s conclusion, remarks how his reader is capable of switching between a profound text and a nugatory one, just as a '*fly* driven from a *honey-pot* will immediately, with very good appetite, alight and finish his meal on an *excrement*'.[82]

This shifting of interpretation is highlighted in 'The Epistle Dedicatory' which is addressed to 'His Royal Highness Prince Posterity'. At one point, the narrator gestures towards a number of animal-shaped clouds: 'there is a large cloud near the *horizon* in the form of a *bear*, another in the *zenith* with the head of an *ass*, a third to the westward with claws like a *dragon* [but] in a few minutes think fit to examine the truth, 'tis certain they would all be changed in figure and position'.[83] These varying, unreliable cloudscapes, like those from *Hamlet* (III.ii.365), *Antony and Cleopatra* (which include a dragon and a bear, IV.xv.2) or even *The Tempest* (IV.i.156), insist once more on metamorphosis and the difficulty of establishing interpretative certitude. After all, insists the author, the addition to the *Tale* of explanatory notes which have reached publication unseen by him may provide the text's originator with 'twenty meanings which never entered into his imagination'.[84] This denial of responsibility for the final shape of the text, as well as its several lacunae, marked by asterisks (and so anticipating their use in *Tristram Shandy*) and the phrase '*Hiatus in MS*', make a coherent critical response all the more difficult.[85] The text, like the fart, has left its creator and must go its own way: 'Books, like men, their authors, have no more of one way of coming into the world, but there are ten thousand to go out of it and return no more.'[86] What is being raised here, as the Enlightenment struggles to determine the relationship between humanity and the world that surrounds it, to comprehend and explain the authority not merely of books – the Scriptures, Classical and Humanist knowledge, and so on – but of the natural world, is the issue of the reliability or otherwise of sensory experience. The epistemology of the fart raises nothing less profound than the question of 'science', in its etymological meaning of 'knowledge'. The ambiguity of Swift's text deliberately challenges the optimism of Enlightenment confidence. Science, like faith, is less straightforward than it may appear.

This anarchic impulse underlies one of Swift's most crudely comical achievements. Anonymously published (like nearly all of Swift's work), *The Benefit of Farting Explain'd* (1722) is generally attributed to him (for instance by the catalogue of the British Library) and certainly it has thematic and stylistic features in common with other of Swift's works.[87] However, Swift himself maintained that the 'slovenly pages' were the work of 'one Dobbs a surgeon', though given the spoof nature of the work, we might treat this denial with caution.[88] In any case, the short pamphlet is a mock-proctological text which purports to explain the cause of farting as excessive costiveness (a case of which we have already seen in 'Strephon and Chloe', discussed in Chapter 5). It sets out to investigate, in the words of the title page: 'The Fundament-all *Cause* of the *Distempers incident to the* Fair Sex Inquir'd into: Proving *à posteriori* most of the *Disordures* in-*tail'd* on *'em* are owing to *Flatulencies* not *seasonably vented*. Wrote in *Spanish*, by Don *Fart in hando Puff-in dorst*, Professor of *Bumbast* in the University of *Craccow*. And Translated into *English*, at the Request and for the Use of the Lady *Damp-Fart*, of *Her-fart-shire*.' In the light of the scatological satire against religious dissenters found in *A Tale of a Tub*, it is interesting to note that here the fart has 'been assigned as the first Cause of Quakerism, and Enthusiasm', while costiveness leads to Æolian epiphany: 'if supprest, it [the fart] upward flies, / And vents itself in Prophecies'.[89] Moreover, the pamphlet goes on to pose the question, 'Whether a FART be a spiritual or a material Substance?' The arguments of the opposing scientific camps are set out:

> The Professors of MetaPhyz-icks have argued warmly for its Spirituality; but the Naturalists as strongly oppose them. The famous Mr. *Boyle* brings it in as an Example to prove the vast Subtility [*sic*] of Matter, since a FART, which in the *Hydrostatical Ballance* does not weigh the Thousandth part of a Grain, shall, in one Minute, expand itself so far, as to occupy the whole Atmosphere of a large Drawing Room.[90]

Robert Boyle (1627–91), who both pioneered the theory of chemical elements and postulated the existence of atoms, had already been the butt of Swift's satirical attacks, having earned Swift's enmity as an intellectual antagonist of his patron, Sir William Temple. *A Meditation upon a Broomstick* was composed, according to Lord Orrery writing in 1752, 'in derision of the style and manner of MR ROBERT BOYLE'.[91] The intrusion of specific individuals as satirical targets is typically Swiftian – Dryden is mentioned more than once in *A Tale of a Tub*.[92] The narrator goes on to define a fart using the new scientific vocabulary, promulgated by those such as Boyle, in a passage strongly reminiscent of the 'projectors' in Lagado:

> I therefore define a FART to be, 'A Nitro-aerial Vapour, exhal'd from an adjacent Pond of Stagnant Water of a Saline Nature, and rarified and sublimed into the Nose or a Microcosmical Alembic, by the gentle Heat of a STERCORARIOUS Balneum, with a strong Empyreuma, and forc'd through the Posteriours by the Compressive Power of the expulsive Faculty.'[93]

This pseudo-science, reminiscent of the canting, scatological chemistry of Subtle and Face in Jonson's *The Alchemist*, displays the kind of crazy verbal dexterity at which *A Tale of a Tub* excelled. What in Jonson's play is its protagonists' virtuoso capability to improvise around new obstacles is quite simply the forerunner of Swift's restless inventiveness with language. The absurd elevation of the fart through the technical terminology, the attempt to unmask its very essence, is reminiscent of the reading of turds in Laputa for signs of political insurgence:

> Another professor showed me a large paper of instructions for discovering plots and conspiracies against the government. He advised great statesmen to examine into the diet of all suspected persons ... with which hand they wiped their posteriors; to take a strict view of their excrements, and from the colour, the odour, the taste, the consistence, the crudeness or maturity of digestion, form a judgment of their thoughts and designs. Because men are never so serious, thoughtful, and intent, as when they are at stool.[94]

Those who contemplate assassinating the King will pass green stools, we are told, those who plan to burn the city will pass another colour. Of course the extrapolation of diagnoses from stool samples and especially the casting of urine (which occasionally included tasting) had been a common and respected medical practice since ancient times.[95] What is different (and absurd) here is the search of feces for symptoms not of a physical ailment but a political intent.

As the Æolian preachers illustrate, there is a world of difference between male and female flatus. While trapped wind will lead in men to melancholia and ill health, 'in Women of a more strong Constitution, it vents itself intirely in Talkativeness; hence we have a Reason, why Women are more Talkative than Men'.[96] On the other hand, if the patient becomes over-reliant on enemas, she might run short of breath (or as *A Tale of a Tub* would have it, 'inspiration'), as is illustrated by the case of the late Widow Fartwell, 'for having her Posteriours much dilated and relaxed by a too frequent Use of Clysters in her Younger Days, was so debilitated in her retentive Faculty, that the Wind passing too freely that Way, there wanted a sufficient Supply to set the Wind-Mill of her Tongue a going'.[97] *The Benefit* takes up the Æolian faith in the potency of wind. At one point its author attributes natural disasters to gusts 'When in the Bowels of the Earth confin'd' which will destroy 'Whole Towns and People in the wide Rupture fall, / Tho' one small Vent, at first, had sav'd them all'.[98] Likewise, the little world of man ought to fart freely to preserve his health: 'So in the Microcosm of Man, we find, / The like ill Fate attends a FART confin'd; / For Cholic, Vapours, Spleen and Melancholy / Do wreck those who suppress it, for their Folly'.[99] Not only is the thesis reliant on the commonplace analogy between the microcosm and macrocosm, but the imaging of the human body as a universe animated by the free flow of wind is reminiscent of the Æolian principle. Both physical and spiritual well-being are at stake.

   In our discussion of 'Strephon and Chloe' in the previous chapter, we noted the influence of Sir John Harington and his translation of *The School of Salernum*. Harington, in the passage cited, had advised against the 'keeping in a little blast of wind'.[100] Harington goes on to describe the proclamation issued by the Emperor Claudius permitting farting in public in order to prevent illness: '*Claudius* by name, he made a Proclamation, / A *Scape* to be no losse of reputation'.[101] Swift updates the story with reference to James I: 'a Gentleman dying by Suppressing a FART in his Presence, the King had immediately wrote over the Gate in Capital Letters this Inscription, HERE ALL FARTS ARE FREE'.[102] It seems that this proclamation is more necessary in Britain than Holland, where 'a *Fart* is a Freeman in all the Towns' and France in which the ladies think nothing of 'a promiscuous Conversation on a Bog-House'.[103] As well as this allusion to Harington, *The Benefit of Farting Explain'd* cites, complete with page numbers, William Camden's *Remaines Concerning Britain* (see the opening of Chapter 2). The allusion concerns the case of the by now familiar Baldwin le Pettour who 'had his name, and held his land in Suffolke, *Per saltum, sufflum & pettum, sive bumbulum,* for dauncing, poutpuffing, and dooing that before the King of England in Christmasse holy dayes, which the worde *Pet* signifieth in French'.[104] Here, the narrator of *The Benefit of Farting Explain'd* uses the instance in Cambden [*sic*], the great antiquarian, founder of the chair of history at Oxford and headmaster of Westminster school (at which, incidentally, his pupils included Ben Jonson), to demonstrate 'the Ancient Esteem FARTS were in'.[105] All this authority is no substitute for empirical observation and experience, however. Flatulence is 'a great Promoter of Mirth, for I have known one *single* FART, that made an Escape, raise a Laugh of half an Hour; and the Celebrated Author of a Book, called, *Laugh and Be Fat*, proves Laughing to be a very wholsome Exercise'.[106]

Laugh and be Fat, or an Antidote against Melancholy, containing a variety of Comical Intreagues in Town and Country; with pleasant Humours, Frolicks, Fancies, Epigrams, Satyrs and Divertisements. To which is added, Nine Delightful Tales was published in 1700. The compiler of this compendium of comic tales was Ned Ward, hack writer and object of Pope's satirical attacks in *The Dunciad*.[107] At the ending of Gay's 'Trivia', Ward and Charles Gildon are mentioned together as 'mighty Names' (book III, 411).[108] Gay is contrasting his own poetic topography of London with Ward's infamous serialised account of the city, *The London Spy* (1698–1700) of which the publisher (of the first six issues) was John Nutt who, four years later, was to publish *A Tale of a Tub*. Nowadays Ward is usually overlooked. Although Steven Earnshaw has noted that 'few critics have felt able to justify serious discussion of Ward as a writer of literature', he goes on to identify Ward in a tradition of urban, comic prose writers which looks back to Nashe and Dekker and forward to Defoe and Dickens.[109] Of course we need also to supplement this list with Swift's name because, as Earnshaw rightly points out, in *The London Spy*, 'the prevalence of faeces ("sir-reverence") overwhelms everything'.[110] An examination of several episodes from *The London Spy* will support Earnshaw's prioritisation of defecation as well as illustrating the origins of much of the Swiftian scatology we have already extensively examined.

Having newly arrived from the countryside, the narrator is being shown around the capital by an acquaintance. The particularly urban phenomenon of the gong-farmer is encountered early on:

> By and by, came thundering by us a rumbling engine in the dark, which I took for a deadmonger's wagon laden with a stinking corpse (by reason of long keeping), driving post-haste to the next churchyard in order to inter it. But I was soon undeceived by my friend, who told me 'twas a gold-finders' caravan carrying treasure to their landbank by the saltpetre houses. The projectors of this notable design, says my friend, have, at no small expense, discovered the fallacy of an old proverb and can (by your leave, sir) by sound reason and true experience deny shitten luck to be good luck. For, after two or three thousand pounds' disbursement to turn a turd into gunpowder, they found their project would not signify a fart.[111]

Not only does this recall Swift's attentions to the activities of the night-soil man and urban sewerage in such poems as 'City Shower', but the experiments to manufacture explosives echo the efforts of the 'projectors' of Lagado as well as Gulliver's account, given to the Houyhnhnms, of firearms.

Frequently in Swift, as we have seen, it is the toilet or the dressing room which permits a close-up of the female body as it is disrobed, anointed or (more rarely) washed. In the dressing room of the Brobdingnagian Queen, for instance, Gulliver is set astride 'one of [the] nipples' of the waiting women.[112] In *The London Spy* there occurs another scene in a bathroom, but this time the naked body is male. In an extraordinary episode, we hear how a man is placed in a bath which, the masseur (or 'rubber') discovers, contains evidence of its previous female occupant:

> The rubber fishing for the herbs to scour the gentleman's skin, happened to feel something amongst 'em that felt very soft and pappy, and turning his head aside, and smelling to his fingers, found 'twas some unsavory lees which chanced to drop through the bung-hole of that mortal cask which had before been rinsed in the same water.[113]

The gentleman, despite protesting that 'it looks as like a sir-reverence as ever I saw anything in my life', is convinced by his servant that the turd is 'Italian paste, which is accounted the most excellent thing to cleanse and make smooth the skin imagina-ble.'[114] The beau is so taken by this unguent and 'incapable of distinguishing a fair lady's sir-reverence from the excrement of a civet-cat', that he instructs the servant to 'rub me all over with it very well'.[115] The result is that he is extremely pleased and leaves the bath house having generously paid the masseur for his special care. The episode is profoundly Swiftian, not only in the breath-takingly nauseating substance of its story but in the attack on the foppish beau, so eager to sport the latest body lotion that he falls an easy victim to the witty servant's improvisatory quick-thinking. While the episode is deliberately satirical in social terms, undermining the pretensions of the perfumed beau, it also, again reminiscent of *The Alchemist*, illustrates the absurdities of cosmetic affectation, in particular, and scientific endeavour more generally.

Perhaps one of the most amusing sequences of *The London Spy* anticipates *Gulliver's Travels* in its merging of scatology and differ-ences of scale. Two 'lousy subjects of the pickled god Neptune' (that is, sailors), accompanied by a diminutive fiddler, enter a room where they

> happen to espy a hook driven into the mantel-tree, which they immediately converted to a very comical use, by laying violent hands on my little Lord Cowdero, and by the hind slit of his breeches hanging him upon the tenter. Being sorely affrighted at this unexpected elevation, he shot that into his trousers which made the crooked vermin out-stink a polecat. In this condition, pendant like a playhouse machine or a brazen cherub over a church branch, he hung sprawling, begging with humble submis-sion to be set safe upon terra firma, all the time dripping his guts upon the hearth like a roasting woodcock. At last, by wriggling, he broke the string of his breeches, and down came our broiled scraper into his own sauce, upon his feeble instrument, and was a sweet-bit ready to be served up to a weak appetite ... as soon as the angry homunculus had gathered himself up from his own dunghill, he gave the two Tritons such an untunable lesson upon his ill-tuned organ, that the whining of a dog-drawn bitch, or the

winding of a cat-call could not have disobliged our ears with less
grateful harmony. When he had thus given vent to his ungovern-
able indignation he cocked the arm of his humped shoulder upon
his hip, and away rolled the runlet of gall, turning his unsavoury
bung-hole upon the company.[116]

The episode merges together the scientific discourses of exploration, cooking, church and theatre architecture, veterinary
science and music in a climax of flatulent comedy; there is
nothing ignorant about this scatology. The cruelty meted out to
the fiddler takes as its sole justification the amusement of 'the two
Tritons' as well as, obviously, the reader.

If Ward's deft deployment of a range of subjects serves here
and throughout *The London Spy* to explore and map the comic
shitscape which Swift will later inhabit, another later pamphlet
comically acknowledges Swift to be 'the learned Sage' of feces.
*A Full and True Account of the Late Whitehall Hurricane; the Causes
thereof, and the Effects it is liable to produce* (1753) praises Swift
as

> the late celebrated facetious, witty, acute and penetrating Author
> of the *Tale of a Tub*. Who has proved by evident Demonstration,
> deduced from the *Æolian System*, that all Disorders of the Intellects
> take their Origin from Wind; which being generated in the Body,
> either by crude Viands, frothy Liquors, or otherways, endeavours
> to find a Passage downwards but that being denied by some
> Obstruction, it directly ascends, according to its natural Course, to
> the upper Regions, and inflates the Brain; unless, sometimes that it
> happens to make its Way through the denticular Orifice, by Means
> of Eructation.[117]

The author of *Whitehall Hurricane* is clearly on top of Swift's work,
noting how Æolian philosophy is typified by 'Reason, Experience
and common Sense ... In this worthy Person, surprising were the
Effects of Wind, that he imbibed during his Studies; for it enabled
him to pen the most extraordinary Pieces; such as *Meditations*
upon *Broomsticks*, Memoirs of the *Clerk* of the Parish [and so on]
besides assisting him to make such strange and important
Discoveries in his Travels; such as Nations of *Giants* and *Pigmies*,
Flying Islands, and Territories inhabited by *Horses*, that for good

Polity and Manners vied with the most civilized People in *Europe*.'[118] Note how the elements of science fiction are predicated upon 'good Polity and Manners'. Houyhnhnm government is clearly on a par – if not better than – that of 'the most civilized People in *Europe*'. It is at this point that the author of *Whitehall Hurricane* develops Æolian science and Houyhnhnm policy into a devastating critique of English parliamentary conduct. Those protesting their opinions in a variety of learned fora may be full not of sagacity but merely of hot air: 'young Members of P————t, young Students of the Universities and Inns of Court, and young Frequenters of the Coffee-Houses, by too voraciously taking in some raw discourses, have been so blown up thereby, for Want of proper Digestion, that on a sudden, they imagined themselves to be able *Statesmen*, great *Philosophers*, Lawyers, Divines, and exquisite Politicians; till by a proper Alteration of Regimen and Diet, they discovered themselves to have only been efflated with Wind and Vapour'.[119] The lesson is clear. Learning is to be slowly digested not gulped down and vomited up:

> What occasions little Squire *Dapperwit* to prattle so prettily in the House, upon every Subject that falls under Debates, or enables the *Stentorian* Baronet Sir *John Tunbelly*, to make such loud Orations there, and to domineer so arbitrarily over his Brother-Justices at a Quarter-Sessions in the Country? but a small quantity of *Wind*, that puffs up the Intellects of the one, and a large Accumulation of the same Element, that swells every Part of the huge Body of the other, which can find no Vent, but only upwards by *Eructation*, or Locution.[120]

While 'little Squire *Dapperwit*' parodies the inexperienced and impressionable MP (as well as recalling the feeble Dapper from *The Alchemist*), it is hard not to see behind the obese Sir *John Tunbelly* the flatulent aristocrat, Sir John Falstaff, while Silence and Shallow lurk somewhere behind 'his Brother-Justices'. The flatulent corruption of Parliament and Law is reminiscent of 'The Fart Censured in the Parliament House' which we considered in Chapter 4: the greater the claim to power, the more puffed-up the institutions of its exercise, the bigger the eventual explosion.

As in *The Benefit of Farting Explain'd* social custom again figures in *Whitehall Hurricane* in terms of flatulent conduct across the different sexes. Although the Haringtonesque dangers of costiveness are by now a familiar topos, the following paragraph is so eloquently phrased as to make its quotation worthwhile:

[I]t must be evident to the Eyes of every judicious Observer, with what a Redundancy of *Wind*, *Spleen* and *Vapour*, the corpulent Duchess of *Bumble* is filled, which makes her Pevish and her Family, splenetic in the gayest Company, and quite ill-natured to every one beneath her . . . All which is entirely owing to the Want of a proper Evacuation, and Discharge of those Fumes, that she daily imbibes, and which requires something extraordinary to help to dispel. When on the other Hand, the polite and affable Lady *Fizzle*, by a proper Regimen and due Use of *Carminatives*, is entirely free from any of those inward Oppressions; and thereby appears with the greatest Elegancy and Ease in all Companies, and in every Situation in Life.[121]

We have come full circle. The 'Fumes' which Bumble 'daily imbibes' are presumably those stinks which so frighten the miasmatists and which arise from London's corruption: 'a city innocent of sewers and full of cesspit odours [that] wasn't far short of a public lavatory'.[122] While Enlightenment philosophy and epistemology attempt to empower Mankind with the latest systems of knowledge, the new science (as this scatological rhetoric consistently demonstrates) comes out of the cultural and educational advances located at the heart of the city, the same city that is mired in excrement. Finally then, we may assert that in their graphic and disgustingly comic descriptions of the privations and filth of city life, the scatological texts of the period are determined palpably to challenge the blithe and abstract assumptions about human perfectibility championed by the scientific and aesthetic pronouncements of the Enlightenment.

NOTES

1 William King, 'Some Remarks on *A Tale of a Tub*', in Kathleen Williams (ed.), *Swift: The Critical Heritage* (Routledge and Kegan Paul: London, 1970), p. 33.

2 T. S. Eliot, *The Sacred Wood: Essays on Poetry and Criticism* (Methuen: London, 1960), p. 169.

3 Carol Houlihan Flynn, *The Body in Swift and Defoe* (Cambridge University Press: Cambridge, 1990), p. 1.
4 Jens Martin Gurr, 'Worshipping Cloacina in the Eighteenth Century: Functions of Scatology in Swift, Pope, Gay, and Sterne', in Stefan Horlacher, Stefan Glomb, and Lars Heiler (eds), *Taboo and Transgression in British Literature from the Renaissance to the Present* (Palgrave Macmillan: New York, 2010), 117–34, pp. 124 and 130.
5 Gurr, 'Worshipping Cloacina', p. 118.
6 Carole Fabricant, *Swift's Landscape* (Johns Hopkins University Press: Baltimore and London, 1982), p. 24.
7 Ned Ward, *The London Spy*, edited by Paul Hyland (Colleagues Press: East Lansing, MI, 1993), pp. 222–3.
8 Vic Gatrell, *City of Laughter: Sex and Satire in Eighteenth-Century London* (Atlantic Books: London, 2006), p. 6.
9 Emily Cockayne, *Hubbub: Filth, Noise and Stench in England, 1600–1770* (Yale University Press: New Haven and London, 2007), pp. 207–8.
10 15 December 1662. Samuel Pepys, *The Diary of Samuel Pepys*, edited by Robert Latham and William Matthews, 11 vols (G. Bell and Sons: London, 1995), III, 283.
11 Cockayne, *Hubbub*, p. 103.
12 Tobias Smollett, *The Expedition of Humphry Clinker* (Dent: London, 1993), p. 124.
13 Pepys, *Diary*, 26 June 1662, III, 120.
14 Ward, *The London Spy*, p. 39.
15 Cited in Peter Ackroyd, *London: The Biography* (Chatto and Windus: London, 2000), p. 201.
16 Ackroyd, *London*, p. 203.
17 Pepys, *Diary*, 16 October 1665, VI, 268.
18 David Inglis, *A Sociological History of Excretory Experience: Defecatory Manners and Toiletry Technologies* (Edwin Mellen Press: Lampeter, 2000), p. 197.
19 Jonathan Swift [?], *Reason Against Coition: A Discourse Deliver'd to a Private Congregation by the Reverend Stephen M***** ... to which is added, A Proposal for making Religion and the Clergy Useful: With the Author's Observations on the Cause and Cure of the Piles and some useful Directions about the wiping the Posteriors* (H. Hook: London, 1732), p. 54. The Wellcome Library attributes the work to Swift.
20 Cited in Cockayne, *Hubbub*, p. 212.
21 Flynn, *The Body in Swift and Defoe*, p. 221.
22 Smollett, *The Expedition of Humphry Clinker*, p. 89.
23 Cockayne, *Hubbub*, p. 132.
24 Sophie Gee, *Making Waste: Leftovers and the Eighteenth-Century Imagination* (Princeton University Press: Princeton and Oxford, 2010), p. 37.

25 Cited in Cockayne, *Hubbub*, p. 133.
26 Smollett, *The Expedition of Humphry Clinker*, p. 90.
27 Smollett, *The Expedition of Humphry Clinker*, p. 123.
28 Cited in Flynn, *The Body in Swift and Defoe*, pp. 19–20.
29 'A Satyr, In Imitation of the Third of Juvenal', in John Oldham, *The Poems of John Oldham*, edited by Harold F. Brooks and Raman Selden (Clarendon Press: Oxford, 1987), p. 249.
30 Ward, *The London Spy*, pp. 205–6.
31 Jonathan Swift, *A Tale of a Tub and Other Works*, edited by Angus Ross and David Woolley (Oxford University Press: Oxford, 1986), p. 44. Edinburgh in particular suffered from the reputation of a city besmirched with defenestrated sewage. Boswell concedes that 'some time ago [it was] too common a practice in my native city of Edinburgh' while Johnson complained to him: 'I smell you in the dark' (James Boswell, *Life of Johnson*, edited by George Birkbeck Hill, 3 vols (Clarendon Press: Oxford, 1934), I, 119). According to Ned Ward the stench in the capital was so bad that 'I thought the whole city (Edinburgh-like) had been overflowed with an inundation of sir-reverence' (*The London Spy*, p. 29). Edinburgh's reputation seems to have been long-lived. As late as 1848 it was a byword for excremental filth; Elizabeth Gaskell cites the city as one of the most filthy: 'Never was the Old Edinburgh cry of "Gardez l'eau," more necessary than in this street' (*Mary Barton*, edited by Stephen Gill (Penguin: Harmondsworth, 1985), p. 98). Inglis also notes that 'Queen Victoria is believed to have found the Palace of Holyrood unbearable to live in, because of its proximity to Edinburgh's meadows, where the city's detritus was dumped and left to fester' (*A Sociological History of Excretory Experience*, p. 232).
32 Jonathan Swift, *The Prose Works of Jonathan Swift*, edited by Herbert Davis, 14 vols (Blackwell: Oxford, 1955), XII, 220–1.
33 Jonathan Swift, *Gulliver's Travels*, edited by Peter Dixon and John Chalker, introduced by Michael Foot (Penguin: Harmondsworth, 1967), p. 222.
34 John Gay, *John Gay: Poetry and Prose*, edited by Vinton A. Dearing and Charles E. Beckwith, 2 vols (Clarendon Press: Oxford, 1974), I, 134.
35 Ben Jonson, *Poems of Ben Jonson*, edited by George Burke Johnson (Routledge and Kegan Paul: London, 1954), pp. 69–75.
36 Brendan O. Hehir identifies the Fleet as 'the notorious cloaca of eighteenth-century London' ('Meaning of Swift's "City Shower"', *English Literary History*, 27 (1960), 194–207, p. 205).
37 Jonathan Swift, *Journal to Stella*, edited by Harold Williams, 2 vols (Clarendon Press: Oxford, 1963), I, 87. First published 1948.
38 Jonathan Swift, *The Complete Poems*, edited by Pat Rogers (Penguin: Harmondsworth, 1983), p. 114. The 'stinking sprats' are perhaps

borrowed from Ward's *The London Spy* in which the narrator arrives at
Billingsgate 'which stunk of stale sprats, piss and sir-reverence' (quoted
above).

39 David Ward, *Jonathan Swift: An Introductory Essay* (Methuen: London,
   1973), p. 189.

40 Hehir, 'Meaning of Swift's "City Shower"', p. 195.

41 Hehir later in the same essay, however, does make the point that 'In both
   classical and neo-classical literature the overflowing of a river was often
   the portent of civil disorders or destruction' ('Meaning of Swift's "City
   Shower"', p. 202). Gill is even more pessimistic about the image of the
   flood: 'there is no suggestion that the flood washes all away, and that a
   new purified London emerges from the clouds' – a reading entirely
   opposed to my own ('"Filth of All Hues"', p. 336).

42 Andrew McRae, '"On the Famous Voyage": Ben Jonson and Civic Space',
   Early Modern Literary Studies, 3 (1998), 8. 1–31, paragraphs 21 and 31.
   McRae cites Swinburne's contempt for the poem: 'Coprology should be
   left to the Frenchmen . . . It is nothing less than lamentable that so great
   an English writer as Ben Jonson should ever have taken the plunge of a
   Parisian diver into the cesspool' (paragraph 2).

43 Mikhail Bakhtin, *Rabelais and his World*, translated by Hélène Iswolsky
   (Indiana University Press: Bloomington, IL, 1984), p. 224.

44 Bakhtin, *Rabelais*, p. 52.

45 Swift, *Gulliver's Travels*, p. 164.

46 Swift, *Gulliver's Travels*, p. 164.

47 Pepys, *Diary*, 20 October 1660, I, 269.

48 Bakhtin, *Rabelais*, p. 175.

49 Swift, *Gulliver's Travels*, p. 310.

50 Swift, *Gulliver's Travels*, p. 301.

51 Swift, *Gulliver's Travels*, p. 309.

52 Swift, *Gulliver's Travels*, p. 301.

53 Norman O. Brown, *Life Against Death: The Psychoanalytical Meaning of
   History* (Wesleyan University Press: Middletown CT, 1959), p. 191.

54 Ned Ward, *A Complete and Humorous Account of the Remarkable Clubs and
   Societies in the Cities of London and Westminster* (J. Wren: London, 1756),
   p. 31.

55 Ward, *Remarkable Clubs*, p. 32.

56 Ward, *Remarkable Clubs*, p. 34.

57 Brown, *Life Against Death*, p. 203.

58 Swift, *Gulliver's Travels*, pp. 62–3.

59 Swift, *Gulliver's Travels*, p. 64.

60 Swift, *Gulliver's Travels*, p. 64.

61 Swift, *Gulliver's Travels*, p. 64.

62 Swift, *Gulliver's Travels*, p. 64.

63 Swift, *The Complete Poems*, p. 441.

64 Smollett, *The Expedition of Humphry Clinker*, p. 205. Robert Adams Day proposes that Smollett's obsession with scatology is a central feature of his artistic vision (more so than for Pope or even Swift): 'however repellent or trivial we may consider scatology to be, it is not a trivial item in the furniture of Smollett's mind'. Day proposes that it may have had a biographical origin: 'the Italian doctor who attended his last illness found chronic diarrhoea' ('Sex, Scatology, Smollett', in Paul-Gabriel Boucé (ed.), *Sexuality in Eighteenth-Century Britain* (Manchester University Press: Manchester, 1982), 225–243, pp. 235 and 230).

65 In *The Expedition of Humphry Clinker*, when Mr Quin is asked whether the mass of people would be improved by their being socially mixed, 'Yes (said he), as a plate of marmalade would improve a pan of sirreverence' (p. 53). In *The Comedy of Errors* Dromio of Syracuse describes the fat kitchen maid who is attempting to seduce him: 'A very reverend body; ay, such a one as a man may not speak of without he say "sir-reverence"' (III.ii.90).

66 In the 1735 edition Smedley is glossed as 'a very stupid, insolent factious, deformed, conceited parson; a vile pretender to poetry' (Swift, *The Complete Poems*, pp. 933 and 824).

67 Thomas B. Gilmore Jr, 'The Comedy of Swift's Scatological Poems', *PMLA*, 91 (1976), 33–43, p. 41.

68 Swift, *The Complete Poems*, p. 306.

69 Unsurprisingly such a scatological work attracted criticism on the grounds that it was profane. In a letter to Anthony Hammond of 21 May 1705, William Wotton condemns Swift's irreligious attitude: 'His whole VIIIth Section concerning the *Aeolists*, in which he banters inspiration, is such a mixture of impiety and immodesty, that I should have as little regard to you, sir, as this author has had to the public, if I should barely repeat after him what is there ... So great a delight has this unhappy writer to play with what some part or other of mankind have always esteemed as Sacred!' (Swift, *A Tale of a Tub and Other Works*, p. 188).

70 Swift, *A Tale of a Tub and Other Works*, p. 73.

71 Swift, *A Tale of a Tub and Other Works*, p. 72.

72 Swift, *A Tale of a Tub and Other Works*, p. 74. Compare William Hogarth's 1726 engraving of *The Punishment Inflicted on Lemuel Gulliver by Applying a Lilypucian Fire Engine to his Posteriors* in which a disorganised mob of Lilypucians attempt to shove an enormous telescopic enema syringe between Gulliver's bared buttocks. (The illustration is reproduced in Gatrell, *City of Laughter*, p. 179.)

73 Swift, *A Tale of a Tub and Other Works*, pp. 73–4.

74 Swift, *A Tale of a Tub and Other Works*, p. 75.

75 Swift, *A Tale of a Tub and Other Works*, p. 76.

76 Brown, *Life Against Death*. p. 203.
77 Swift, *A Tale of a Tub and Other Works*, p. 53.
78 Swift, *A Tale of a Tub and Other Works*, p. 78.
79 Swift, *A Tale of a Tub and Other Works*, p. 80.
80 Swift, *A Tale of a Tub and Other Works*, p. 95.
81 Nigel Wood, *Swift* (Harvester Press: Brighton, 1986), p. 45. Sophie Gee claims something similar of Evelyn's 'alienated' style, attributing it to the apocalypse of post-Fire London: 'Emptiness, or void, gives rise to a mode of narrating: a surplus of unstable impressions and descriptions without a neat narrative trajectory' (*Making Waste*, p. 25).
82 Swift, *A Tale of a Tub and Other Works*, p. 102.
83 Swift, *A Tale of a Tub and Other Works*, p. 16.
84 Swift, *A Tale of a Tub and Other Works*, p. 10.
85 Swift, *A Tale of a Tub and Other Works*, p. 29.
86 Swift, *A Tale of a Tub and Other Works*, p. 17.
87 Jonathan Swift, *The Benefit of Farting Explain'd*, introduced by Clive Davies (Old Abbey Press: Exeter, 1996). The *Gentlemen's Magazine*, 4 (September 1734) contained a poem by 'Fidelia' which cites Swift and includes reference in the same line to 'The *Broomstick*' and '*Benefit of Fa—ing*' (see Margaret Anne Doody, 'Swift Among the Women', *The Yearbook of English Studies*, 18 (1988), 68–92, p. 78).
88 Gatrell, *City of Laughter*, p. 187. In his essay on scatology of the period, Keith Thomas attributes *The Benefit* uncertainly to 'William Dobbs?' ('Bodily Control and Social Unease: The Fart in Seventeenth-Century England', in Angela McShane and Garthine Walker (eds), *The Extraordinary and the Everyday in Early Modern England: Essays in Celebration of the Work of Bernard Capp* (Palgrave: Houndmills, 2010), 9–30, p. 27).
89 Swift, *The Benefit of Farting Explain'd*, p. 8.
90 Swift, *The Benefit of Farting Explain'd*, p. 8.
91 *Remarks on the Life and Writing of Dr Jonathan Swift*, in Williams (ed.), *Swift: The Critical Heritage*, p. 118.
92 See Swift, *A Tale of a Tub and Other Works*, pp. 32 and 63.
93 Swift, *The Benefit of Farting Explain'd*, p. 9.
94 Swift, *Gulliver's Travels*, pp. 235–6.
95 Swift notes elsewhere that 'physicians discover the state of the whole body by consulting only what comes from *behind*' (Swift, *A Tale of a Tub and Other Works*, p. 70).
96 Swift, *The Benefit of Farting Explain'd*, p. 9.
97 Swift, *The Benefit of Farting Explain'd*, p. 9.
98 Swift, *The Benefit of Farting Explain'd*, pp. 11–12.
99 Swift, *The Benefit of Farting Explain'd*, p. 12.
100 Anon., *The School of Salernum*, p. 79.

101 Anon., *The School of Salernum*, p. 79.

102 Swift, *The Benefit of Farting Explain'd*, p. 10.

103 Swift, *The Benefit of Farting Explain'd*, p. 10.

104 William Camden, *Remaines Concerning Britain*, edited by R. D. Dunn (University of Toronto Press: Toronto and London, 1984), p. 114.

105 Swift, *The Benefit of Farting Explain'd*, p. 10.

106 Swift, *The Benefit of Farting Explain'd*, p. 11.

107 See I, 296; III, 34 and 146 in Alexander Pope, *Alexander Pope: The Oxford Authors*, edited by Pat Rogers (Oxford University Press: Oxford, 1993).

108 Gay, *Poetry and Prose*, I, 172.

109 Steven Earnshaw, *The Pub in Literature: England's Altered State* (Manchester University Press: Manchester, 2000), pp. 110–12.

110 Earnshaw, *The Pub*, p. 116. In terms of simple occurrence, Earnshaw's thesis seems a sound one. The word 'sir-reverence' appears at least eight times – see pp. 29, 39, 69, 70, 169, 223, 229 and 253.

111 Ward, *The London Spy*, pp. 29–30.

112 Swift, *Gulliver's Travels*, p. 158.

113 Ward, *The London Spy*, p. 168.

114 Ward, *The London Spy*, p. 169.

115 Ward, *The London Spy*, p. 169.

116 Ward, *The London Spy*, p. 42.

117 Anon., *A Full and True Account of the Late Whitehall Hurricane; the Causes thereof, and the Effects it is liable to produce* (H. Carpenter: London, 1753), pp. 16–17.

118 Anon., *Whitehall Hurricane*, pp. 17–18. Vic Gatrell attributes the popularity of such leaflets to Swift himself: 'Between the 1720s and 1750s something odd happened in the history of English publication. Bookshops were hit then by a small boom in excretion-obsessed pamphlets and verses; thereafter they mysteriously died out. It was Swift's scatology – in *Gulliver's Travels* (1726) – particularly that activated this taste, though a few of the texts predated *Gulliver* and might even have influenced it' (*City of Laughter*, p. 185).

119 Anon., *Whitehall Hurricane*, pp. 23–4.

120 Anon., *Whitehall Hurricane*, p. 24.

121 Anon., *Whitehall Hurricane*, p. 26.

122 Gatrell, *City of Laughter*, p. 180.

Bibliography

Ackroyd, Peter, *London: The Biography* (Chatto and Windus: London, 2000)

Aden, John M., 'Corinna and the Sterner Muse of Swift', *English Language Notes*, 4 (1966), 23–31

Aers, David, *Chaucer* (Harvester: Brighton, 1986)

Allen, Percy, *Times Literary Supplement*, 1859 (18 September 1937)

Allen, Valerie, *On Farting: Language and Laughter in the Middle Ages* (Palgrave: Houndmills, 2007)

Anon., *Vlysses vpon Aiax* (Thomas Gubbins: London, 1596)

Anon., *The Famelie of Love* (John Helmes: London, 1608)

Anon., *A Full and True Account of the Late Whitehall Hurricane; the Causes thereof, and the Effects it is liable to produce* (H. Carpenter: London, 1753)

Anon., *The School of Salernum*, translated by Sir John Harington, edited by Francis R. Packard and Fielding H. Garrison (Augustus M. Kelley: New York, 1970)

Arderne, John, *Treatises of Fistula in Ano, Hæmorrhoids, and Clysters*, edited by D'Arcy Power, EETS, o.s. 139 (Kegan Paul, Trench, Trübner and Co.: London, 1910)

Bacon, Francis, *Essays*, edited by Michael J. Hawkins (J. M. Dent and Sons: London, 1973)

Bakhtin, Mikhail, *Rabelais and His World*, translated by Hélène Iswolsky (Indiana University Press: Bloomington, 1984)

Banks, Iain, *The Wasp Factory* (Abacus: London, 1990)

Barker, Francis, *The Tremulous Private Body: Essays on Subjection* (Methuen: London and New York, 1984)

Barton, Anne, *The Names of Comedy* (Clarendon Press: Oxford, 1990)

Bastard, Thomas, *Chrestoleros. Seuen bookes of Epigrames written by T B, 'in Vlyssem'* (Iohn Broome: London, 1598)

Beechy, Tiffany, 'Devil Take the Hindmost: Chaucer, John Gay, and the Pecuniary Anus', *The Chaucer Review*, 41 (2006), 71–85

Beidler, Peter G., 'Art and Scatology in The *Miller's Tale'*, *The Chaucer Review*, 12 (1977), 90–102

Birney, Earl, 'Structural Irony within the *Summoner's Tale'*, *Anglia*, 78 (1960), 204–18

Bishop, Louise M., '"Of Goddes pryvetee nor of his wyf": Confusion of Orifices in Chaucer's *Miller's Tale'*, *Texas Studies in Language and Literature*, 44 (2002), 231–46

Blake, William, *William Blake's Writings*, edited by G. E. Bentley, 2 vols (Clarendon Press: Oxford, 1978)

Block, K. S. (ed.), *Ludus Coventriae or The Plaie called Corpus Christi*, EETS, e.s. 120 (Oxford University Press: London, 1922)

Boehrer, Bruce, 'The Privy and Its Double', in Richard Dutton and Jean E. Howard (eds), *A Companion to Shakespeare's Works*, 4 vols (Blackwell: Oxford, 2003), IV, 69–88

Boswell, James, *Life of Johnson*, edited by George Birkbeck Hill, 3 vols (Clarendon Press: Oxford, 1934)

Bourke, John G., *Scatalogic Rites of All Nations* (W. H. Lowdermilk: Washington, DC, 1891)

Bowers, Rick, *Radical Comedy in Early Modern England: Contexts, Cultures, Performances* (Ashgate: Aldershot, 2008)

Braddy, Haldeen, 'Chaucer: Realism or Obscenity?', *Arlington Quarterly*, 2 (1969), 121–38

Briggs, Julia, *This Stage-Play World: English Literature and Its Background, 1580–1625* (Oxford University Press: Oxford, 1983)

Brown, Huntington, *Rabelais in English Literature* (Harvard University Press: Cambridge, MA, 1933)

Brown, John Russell, 'More About Laughing at "M.O.A.I." (A Response to Inge Leimberg)', *Connotations*, 1 (1991), 187–90

Brown, Kerry, Review of *When a Billion Chinese Jump: How China will Save Mankind – or Destroy It* by Jonathan Watts, *Times Higher Education*, 1955 (8 July 2010), 48–9

Brown, Norman O., *Life Against Death: The Psychoanalytic Meaning of History* (Wesleyan University Press: Middletown, CT, 1950)

Browne, Thomas, *Pseudodoxia Epidemica*, edited by Robin Robbins, 2 vols (Clarendon Press: Oxford, 1981)

Burton, Robert, 'A note of Mr Robert Burton; books given to the library by his last will and Testament', 1639 (Bodleian Library, MS Selden Supra 80)

Burton, Robert, *The Anatomy of Melancholy* (William Tegg and Co: London, 1849)

Butterworth, Philip, *Theatre of Fire: Special Effects in Early English and Scottish Theatre* (Society for Theatre Research: London, 1998)

Callaghan, Dympna, '"And all is semblative a woman's part": Body Politics and *Twelfth Night*', *Textual Practice*, 7 (1993), 428–52

Camden, William, *Remaines of a Greater Worke Concerning Britaine* (Simon Waterson: London, 1605)

Camden, William, *Remaines Concerning Britian*, edited by R. D. Dunn (University of Toronto Press: Toronto and London, 1984)

Carroll, William C., *The Metamorphosis of Shakespearean Comedy* (Princeton University Press: Princeton, 1985)

Cauchi, Simon, 'Sir John Harington and Sir John Falstaff', *N & Q*, n.s., 35 (1988), 468–9

Chaucer, Geoffrey, *The Canterbury Tales*, edited by John Matthews Manly (Holt: New York, 1929)

Chaucer, Geoffrey, *The Miller's Tale*, edited by James Winny (Cambridge University Press: Cambridge, 1971)

Chaucer, Geoffrey, *The Riverside Chaucer*, edited by Larry D. Benson (Oxford University Press: Oxford, 1988)

Chernaik, Warren, '"I loath the Rabble": Friendship, Love and Hate in Rochester', in Nicholas Fisher (ed.), *That Second Bottle: Essays on John Wilmot, Earl of Rochester* (Manchester University Press: Manchester and London, 2000), 7–19

Clark, Stephen, '"Something Generous in Meer Lust"?: Rochester and Misogyny', in Edward Burns (ed.), *Reading Rochester* (Liverpool University Press: Liverpool, 1995), 21–41

Clarke, Charles Cowden, *Tales from Chaucer in Prose* (Effingham Wilson: London, 1833)

Clayton, Thomas (ed.), *Cavalier Poets* (Oxford University Press: Oxford, 1978)

Cockayne, Emily, *Hubbub: Filth, Noise and Stench in England* (Yale University Press: New Haven and London, 2007)

Cogan, Thomas, *The Haven of Health* (William Norton: London, 1584)

Cohen, Martin, 'Profits of Doom', *Times Higher Education*, 1958 (29 July 2010), 34–9

Cook, Ann Jennalie, *Making a Match: Courtship in Shakespeare and his Society* (Princeton University Press: Princeton, 1991)

Cook, John, 'Carnival and *The Canterbury Tales*: "Only equals may laugh" (Herzen)', in David Aers (ed.), *Medieval Literature: Criticism, Ideology and History* (St Martin's Press: New York, 1986), 169–91

Cooper, Tarnya (ed.), *Searching for Shakespeare* (National Portrait Gallery: London, 2006)

Copland, Robert, *Jyl of Breyntfords Testament*, edited by Frederick J. Furnivall (Printed for Private Circulation: London, 1871)

Copland, Robert, *Poems*, edited by Mary Carpenter Erler (University of Toronto Press: Toronto, 1993)

Cotgrave, John, *The English Treasury of Wit and Language Collected Out of the Most, and Best of our English Drammatick Poems* (Humphrey Moseley: London, 1655)

Cowley, Abraham, *The Collected Works of Abraham Cowley*, edited by Thomas O. Calhoun, Laurence Heyworth and J. Robert King (University of Delaware Press: Newark, 1993)

Cox, Lee Sheridan, 'The Riddle in *Twelfth Night*', *Shakespeare Quarterly*, 13 (1962), 360

Cox, Rosie, *et al.*, *Dirt: The Filthy Reality of Everyday Life* (Profile Books: London, 2011)

Craig, D. H., *Sir John Harington* (Twayne Publishers: Boston, 1985)

Craig, Hardin, (ed.), *The Coventry Corpus Christi Plays* (Oxford University Press: London, 1957)

Craik, Henry, *The Life of Edward Earl of Clarendon*, 2 vols (Smith, Elder & Co.: London, 1911)

Craik, R. J., *Sir Thomas Urquhart of Cromarty (1611–1660): Adventurer, Polymath, and Translator of Rabelais* (Mellen Research University Press: Lewiston/Lampeter, 1993)

Craik, Roger, 'Sir Thomas Urquhart's *Apollo and the Muses*', *Yale University Library Gazette*, 70 (1996), 135–42

Craik, T. W., *The Comic Tales of Chaucer* (Methuen: London, 1964)

Crook, Keith, *A Preface to Swift* (Longman: London and New York, 1998)

Culler, Jonathan, *Saussure* (Fontana/Collins: London, 1976)

Danson, Lawrence, 'Metonymy and *Coriolanus*', *Philological Quarterly*, 52 (1973), 30–42

Davies, John, *The Scourge of Folly. Consisting of satyricall Epigramms and others in honour of many noble and worthy Persons of our Land Together With a pleasant (though discordant) Descant vpon most English Prouerbes: and others* (Richard Redmer: London, 1611)

Davies, John, *Wits Bedlam, Where is had Whipping-cheer, to cure the Mad* (James Dauies: London, 1617)

Davies, Michael, '"Bawdy in Thoughts, Precise in Words": Decadence, Divinity and Dissent in the Restoration', in Michael St John (ed.), *Romancing Decay: Ideas of Decadence in European Culture* (Ashgate: Aldershot, 1999), 39–63

Day, Cyrus, 'Pills to Purge Melancholy', *Review of English Studies*, 8 (1932), 177–84

Day, John, *The Ile of Gvls* (Iohn Hodgets: London, 1606)

Day, Robert Adams, 'Sex, Scatology, Smollett', in Paul-Gabriel Boucé (ed.), *Sexuality in Eighteenth-Century Britain* (Manchester University Press: Manchester, 1982), 225–43

de Sola Pinto, Vivian, 'John Wilmot, Earl of Rochester', in Boris Ford (ed.), *The Pelican Guide to English Literature*, 7 vols (Penguin: Harmondsworth, 1965), IV, 142–55

Decker [*sic*], Tho [mas] and Iohn Webster, *West-Ward Hoe* (John Hodgets: London, 1607)

Delany, Paul, 'Constantinus Africanus' *De Coitu*: A Translation', *Chaucer Review*, 4 (1970), 55–65

Dentith, Simon, 'Negativity and Affirmation in Rochester's Lyric Poetry', in Edward Burns (ed.), *Reading Rochester* (Liverpool University Press: Liverpool, 1995), 84–97

Donne, John, *John Donne: The Oxford Authors*, edited by John Carey (Oxford University Press: Oxford, 1990)

Doody, Margaret Anne, 'Swift Among the Women', *The Yearbook of English Studies*, 18 (1988), 68–92

Douglas, Mary, *Purity and Danger: An Analysis of the Concept of*

Pollution and Taboo (Routledge: London, 2002)

Dryden, John, *Essays of John Dryden*, edited by W. P. Ker, 2 vols (Clarendon: Oxford, 1900)

Dusinberre, Juliet, 'As *Who* Liked It?', *Shakespeare Survey*, 46 (1994), 9–21

Earnshaw, Steven, *The Pub in Literature: England's Altered State* (Manchester University Press: Manchester, 2000)

Eccles, Mark (ed.), *The Macro Plays*, EETS, 262 (Oxford University Press: London, 1969)

Edmond, Mary, 'It was for Gentle Shakespeare Cut', *Shakespeare Quarterly*, 42 (1991), 339–44

Elias Jr, A. C., 'Laetitia Pilkington on Swift: How Reliable Is She?', in Christopher Fox and Brenda Tooley (eds), *Walking Naboth's Vineyard: New Studies in Swift* (University of Notre Dame Press: Notre Dame, 1995), 127–42

Eliot, George, *Mary Barton*, edited by Stephen Gill (Penguin: Harmondsworth, 1985)

Eliot, T. S., *The Sacred Wood: Essays on Poetry and Criticism* (Methuen: London, 1960)

Eliot, T. S., *Collected Poems, 1909–1962* (Faber: London, 1974)

Engel, William E., 'Was Sir John Harington the English Rabelais?', in Barbara C. Bowen (ed.), *Rabelais in Context* (Summa Publications: Birmingham, Alabama, 1993), 147–56

Erskine-Hill, Howard, 'Rochester and Falstaff', in Nicholas Fisher (ed.), *That Second Bottle: Essays on John Wilmot, Earl of Rochester* (Manchester University Press: Manchester and London, 2000), 35–45

Everett, Barbara, 'The Sense of Nothing', in Jeremy Treglown (ed.), *Spirit of Wit: Reconsiderations of Rochester* (Basil Blackwell: Oxford, 1982), 1–41

Fabricant, Carole, 'Rochester's World of Imperfect Enjoyment', *Journal of English and Germanic Philology*, 73 (1974), 338–50

Fabricant, Carole, *Swift's Landscape* (Johns Hopkins University Press: Baltimore and London, 1982)

Farley-Hills, David (ed.), *Rochester: the Critical Heritage* (Barnes and Noble: New York, 1972)

Farley-Hills, David, *Rochester's Poetry* (Bell and Hyman: London, 1978)

Farrell, Thomas J., 'Privacy and the Boundaries of the Fabliau in
    The *Miller's Tale*', *English Literary History*, 56 (1989), 773–95
Fenton, Roger, *A Treatise of Vsurie* (William Aspley: London, 1611)
Ferry, Anne, *The Art of Naming* (University of Chicago Press:
    Chicago and London, 1988)
Feyens, Jean, *A New and Needful Treatise of Wind Offending Mans
    Body*, translated by William Rowland (Benjamin Billingsley:
    London, 1676)
Florio, John, *Queen Anna's New World of Words* (Edw. Blount and
    William Barret: London, 1611)
Flynn, Carol Houlihan, *The Body in Swift and Defoe* (Cambridge
    University Press: Cambridge, 1990)
Foard [*sic*], John and Tho[mas] Decker [*sic*], *The Sun's Darling: A
    Moral Masque* (Andrew Penneycuicke: London, 1656)
Foucault, Michel, *The Order of Things: The Archaeology of Human
    Sciences* (Tavistock Publications: London, 1970)
Foucault, Michel, *The History of Sexuality*, translated by Robert
    Hurley (Penguin: Harmondsworth, 1981)
Frese, Dolores Warwick, 'The Homoerotic Underside in Chaucer's
    The Miller's Tale and *The Reeve's Tale*', *Michigan Academician*, 10
    (1977), 143–50
Furnivall, F. J., 'Sir John Harington's Shakespeare Quartos', *N & Q*,
    7th series, 9 (1890), 382–3
Galen, *On the Natural Faculties* (Encyclopædia Britannica: Chicago,
    1990)
Garzoni, Tommaso, *The Hospitall of Incvrable Fooles*, translated by
    Edward Blount (Edward Blount: London, 1600)
Gatrell, Vic, *City of Laughter: Sex and Satire in Eighteenth-Century
    London* (Atlantic Books: London, 2006)
Gay, John, *John Gay: Poetry and Prose*, edited by Vinton A. Dearing
    and Charles E. Beckwith, 2 vols (Clarendon Press: Oxford, 1974)
Gee, Sophie, *Making Waste: Leftovers and the Eighteenth-Century
    Imagination* (Princeton University Press: Princeton and Oxford,
    2010)
Georgianna, Linda, 'Lords, Churls, and Friars: The Return to
    Social Order in *The Summoner's Tale*', in Susanna Greer Fein,
    David Raybin and Peter C. Braeger (eds), *Rebels and Rivals: The
    Contestive Spirit in The Canterbury Tales* (Western Michigan

University Press: Kalamazoo, 1991), 149–72

Gill, Pat, '"Filth of All Hues and Odors": Public Parks, City Showers, and Promiscuous Acquaintance in Rochester and Swift', *Genre*, 27 (1994), 333–50

Gilmore Jr, Thomas B., 'The Comedy of Swift's Scatological Poems', *PMLA*, 91 (1976), 33–43

Glendinning, Victoria, *Jonathan Swift* (Hutchinson: London, 1998)

Goldberg, Jonathan, 'Textual Properties', *Shakespeare Quarterly*, 37 (1986), 213–17

Goldberg, Jonathan, *Sodometries: Renaissance Texts, Modern Sexualities* (Stanford University Press: Stanford, 1992)

Goldsworthy, Cephas, *The Satyr: An Account of the Life and Work, Death and Salvation of John Wilmot, Second Earl of Rochester* (Weidenfeld & Nicolson: London, 2001)

Green, William, 'Humours, Characters, and Attributive Names in Shakespeare's Plays', *Names*, 20 (1972), 157–65

Greenblatt, Stephen, 'Towards a Poetics of Culture', in H. Aram Veeser (ed.), *The New Historicism* (Routledge: New York and London, 1989), 1–14

Greene, Donald, 'On Swift's "Scatological" Poems', *Sewanee Review*, 75 (1967), 672–89

Greene, Graham, *Lord Rochester's Monkey* (Penguin: New York, 1974)

Greig, James 'The Investigation of a Medieval Barrel-latrine from Worcester', *Journal of Archaeological Science*, 8 (1981), 265–82

Grose, Francis, *A Classical Dictionary of the Vulgar Tongue* (S. Hooper: London, 1785)

Gurr, Andrew, *The Shakespearian Playing Companies* (Clarendon Press: Oxford, 1996)

Gurr, Jens Martin, 'Worshipping Cloacina in the Eighteenth Century: Functions of Scatology in Swift, Pope, Gay, and Sterne', in Stefan Horlacher, Stefan Glomb, and Lars Helier (eds), *Taboo and Transgression in British Literature from the Renaissance to the Present* (Palgrave Macmillan: New York, 2010), 117–34

Hackel, Heidi Brayman, '"Rowme" of its Own: Printed Drama in Early Libraries', in John D. Cox and David Scott Kastan (eds), *A*

New History of Early English Drama (Columbia University Press: New York, 1997), 113–30

Hammond, Brean S., '"An Allusion to Horace", Jonson's Ghost and the Second Poets' War', in Edward Burns (ed.), *Reading Rochester* (Liverpool University Press: Liverpool, 1995), 166–86

Hammond, Brean, 'Swift's Reading', in Christopher Fox (ed.), *The Cambridge Companion to Jonathan Swift* (Cambridge University Press: Cambridge, 2003), 73–86

Hammond, Paul, 'Rochester's Homoeroticism', in Nicholas Fisher (ed.) *That Second Bottle: Essays on John Wilmot, Earl of Rochester* (Manchester University Press: Manchester and London, 2000), 47–62

Hanks Jr, D. Thomas, '"Goddes Pryvetee" and Chaucer's Miller's Tale', *Christianity and Literature*, 33 (1984), 7–12

Harington, John, *A New Discourse of a Stale Subject, Called the Metamorphosis of Aiax* (Richard Field: London, 1596)

Harington, John, *Letters and Epigrams of Sir John Harington*, edited by Norman Egbert McClure (University of Pennsylvania Press: Philadelphia, 1930)

Harington, John, *The Metamorphosis of Ajax*, edited by Elizabeth Story Donno (Routledge and Kegan Paul: London, 1962)

Harries, Richard, 'Rochester's "death-bed repentance"', in Nicholas Fisher (ed.), *That Second Bottle: Essays on John Wilmot, Earl of Rochester* (Manchester University Press: Manchester and London, 2000), 191–6

Harris, Jonathan Gil, 'This is Not a Pipe: Water Supply, Incontinent Sources, and the Leaky Body Politic', in Richard Burt and John Michael Archer (eds), *Enclosure Acts: Sexuality, Property, and Culture in Early Modern England* (Cornell University Press: Ithaca and London, 1994), 203–28

Hasenfratz, Robert, 'The Science of Flatulence: Possible Sources for the *Summoner's Tale*', *The Chaucer Review*, 30 (1996), 241–61

Hassel Jr, Chris R., 'The Riddle in *Twelfth Night* Simplified', *Shakespeare Quarterly*, 25 (1974), 356

Hayes, Mary, 'Privy Speech: Sacred Silence, Dirty Secrets in the *Summoner's Tale*', *The Chaucer Review*, 40 (2006), 263–88

Hazlitt, William, *Lectures on the English Poets*, in David Farley-Hills (ed.), *Rochester: The Critical Heritage* (Barnes & Noble: New York, 1972)

Healy, Thomas, *New Latitudes: Theory and English Renaissance Literature* (Edward Arnold: London, 1992)

Hearne, Thomas, *Remarks and Collections of Thomas Hearne*, edited by C. E. Doble, 11 vols (Clarendon: Oxford, 1884–1918)

Hehir, Brendan O., 'Meaning of Swift's "City Shower"', *English Literary History*, 27 (1960), 194–207

Herrick, Robert, *The Poetical Works of Robert Herrick*, edited by L. C. Martin (Clarendon Press: Oxford, 1956)

Hill, Christopher, *God's Englishman: Oliver Cromwell and the English Revolution* (Penguin: Harmondsworth, 1972)

Hill, Geoffrey, 'Jonathan Swift: The Poetry of "Reaction"', in Brian Vickers (ed.), *The World of Jonathan Swift* (Basil Blackwell: Oxford, 1968), 195–212

Hobbes, Thomas, *Leviathan*, edited by C. B. Macpherson (Penguin: Harmondsworth, 1968)

Hotson, Leslie, *The First Night of Twelfth Night* (Hart Davis: London, 1954)

Hughes, Geoffrey, *Swearing: A Social History of Foul Language, Oaths and Profanity in English* (Blackwell: Oxford, 1991)

Hughey, R., 'The Harington Manuscript at Arundel Castle and Related Documents', *Library*, 15 (1934–5), 388–444

Hunt, Maurice, 'Malvolio, Viola, and the Question of Instrumentality: Defining Providence in *Twelfth Night*', *Studies in Philology*, 90 (1993), 277–97

Hunter, G. K., *English Drama, 1586–1642* (Clarendon Press: Oxford, 1997)

Hutton, Henry, *Follie's anatomie. Or satyres and satyricall epigrams* (M. Walbanke: London, 1619)

Huxley, Aldous, *Do What You Will: Essays* (Chatto and Windus: London, 1929)

Huxter, Robert, *Reg and Ethel: Reginald Reynolds, His Life and Work and His Marriage to Ethel Mannin* (Sessions Book Trust: York, 1992)

Inglis, David, *A Sociological History of Excretory Experience: Defecatory Manners and Toiletry Technologies* (Edwin Mellen Press: Lampeter, 2000)

Jackson, Stanley W., *Melancholia and Depression: From Hippocratic Times to Modern Times* (Yale University Press: New Haven and London, 1986)

Jakobson, Roman, 'Two Aspects of Language and Two Aspects of Aphoric Disturbances', in *Selected Writings*, 2 vols (Mouton: The Hague, 1971)

Johnson, James William, *A Profane Wit: The Life of John Wilmot, Earl of Rochester* (University of Rochester Press: Rochester, NY, 2004)

Johnson, Ronald W., 'Rhetoric and Drama in Rochester's "Satyr against Reason and Mankind"', *Studies in English Literature*, 15 (1975), 365–73

Jonson, Ben, *The Works of Ben Jonson*, edited by C. H. Herford and Percy and Evelyn Simpson, 11 vols (Oxford University Press: Oxford, 1925–51)

Jonson, Ben, *Poems of Ben Jonson*, edited by George Burke Johnson (Routledge and Kegan Paul: London, 1954)

Jonson, Ben, *Sejanus His Fall*, edited by W. F. Bolton (Ernest Benn: London, 1966)

Jonson, Ben, *The Alchemist*, edited by F. H. Mares (Methuen: London, 1971)

Jordan, Tracey, 'Fairy Tale and Fabliau: Chaucer's *The Miller's Tale*', *Studies in Short Fiction*, 21 (1984), 87–93

Keyes, Laura, 'Hamlet's Fat', in Sidney Homan (ed.), *Shakespeare and the Triple Play: From Study to Stage to Classroom* (Associated University Presses: London and Toronto, 1988), 89–104

King, William, 'Some Remarks on *A Tale of a Tub*', in Kathleen Williams (ed.), *Swift: The Critical Heritage* (Routledge and Kegan Paul: London, 1970)

Kinghorn, Jonathan, 'A Privvie in Perfection: Sir John Harrington's [*sic*] Water Closet', *Bath History*, 1 (1986), 173–88

Kirby, Thomas A., 'Theodore Roosevelt on Chaucer and a Chaucerian', *Modern Language Notes*, 68 (1953), 34–7

Knapp, Peggy, 'Robyn the Miller's Thrifty Work', in Steve Ellis (ed.), *Chaucer: The Canterbury Tales* (Longman: London, 1998), 62–77

Knight, G. Wilson, *The Sovereign Flower* (Methuen and Co.: London, 1958)

Kökeritz, Helge, 'Punning Names in Shakespeare', *Modern Language Notes*, 65 (1950), 240–3

Lamb, Jeremy, *So Idle a Rogue: The Life and Death of Lord Rochester* (Sutton: Stroud, 2005)

Lancashire, Ian, 'Moses, Elijah and the Back Parts of God: Satiric Scatology in Chaucer's *Summoner's Tale*', *Mosaic*, 14 (1981), 17–30

Langland, William, *The Vision of Piers Plowman*, edited by A. V. C. Schmidt (J. M. Dent: London, 1978)

Law, Robert Adger, 'On Certain Proper Names in Shakespeare', *Texas Studies in English*, 30 (1951), 61–5

Lee, Jae Num, *Swift and Scatological Satire* (University of New Mexico Press: Albuquerque, 1971)

Leicester Jr, H. Marshall, 'Newer Currents in Psychoanalytic Criticism, and the Difference "It" Makes: Gender and Desire in The *Miller's Tale*', *English Literary History*, 61 (1994), 473–99

Leimberg, Inge, '"M.O.A.I.": Trying to Share the Joke in *Twelfth Night* 2.5 (A Critical Hypothesis)', *Connotations*, 1 (1991), 78–95

Leimberg, Inge, 'Maria's Theology and Other Questions (An Answer to John Russell Brown)', *Connotations*, 1 (1991), 191–6

Leonard, John, *Naming in Paradise: Milton and the Language of Adam and Eve* (Clarendon Press: Oxford, 1990)

Levin, Harry, *Shakespeare and the Revolution of the Times: Perspectives and Commentaries* (Oxford University Press: Oxford, 1976)

Levitan, Alan, 'The Parody of Pentecost in Chaucer's *Summoner's Tale*', *University of Toronto Quarterly*, 40 (1971), 236–46

Levith, Murray J., 'Juliet's Question and Shakespeare's Names', in Murray J. Levith (ed.), *Renaissance and Modern: Essays in Honor of Edwin M. Moseley* (Skidmore College: New York, 1976), 21–32

Levy, Bernard S., 'Biblical Parody in the *Summoner's Tale*', *Tennessee Studies in Literature*, 11 (1966), 45–60

Lewin, Ralph A., *Merde: Excursions into Scientific, Cultural and Socio-Historical Coprology* (Aurum Press: London, 1999)

Lewis, Cynthia, '"A Fustian Riddle"?: Anagrammatic Names in *Twelfth Night*', *English Language Notes*, 22 (1984–5), 32–7

Lewis, Cynthia, 'Whodunit? Plot, Plotting, and Detection in *Twelfth Night*', in James Schiffer (ed.), *Twelfth Night: New Critical Essays* (Routledge: London, 2011), 258–72

Lochrie, Karma, 'Women's "Pryvetees" and Fabliau Politics in the *Miller's Tale*', *Exemplaria*, 6 (1994), 287–304

Longmate, Norman, *King Cholera: The Biography of a Disease* (H. Hamilton: London, 1966)

Lonsdale, Roger (ed.), *Eighteenth-Century Women Poets: An Oxford Anthology* (Oxford University Press: Oxford and New York, 1989)

Lumiansky, R. M. and David Mills (eds), *The Chester Mystery Cycle*, EETS, s.s. 3 (Oxford University Press: London, 1974)

Lyly, John, *Endymion*, edited by David Bevington (Manchester University Press: Manchester, 1996)

Lyons, Bridget Gellert, *Voices of Melancholy: Studies in Literary Treatments of Melancholy in Renaissance England* (Routledge: London, 1971)

Magan, James H., 'Verbal Excess and Sexual Abstinence: The Legacy of Sir Thomas Urquhart', *Logophile*, 3 (1979), 1–7

Maguire, Laurie, *Shakespeare's Names* (Oxford University Press: Oxford, 2007)

Mahon, Derek, 'Reveller at Life's Feast', *The Guardian*, 4 March 2006

Marlowe, Christopher, *Tamburlaine the Great*, edited by J. S. Cunningham (Manchester University Press: Manchester, 1981)

Marston, John, *The Poems of John Marston*, edited by Arnold Davenport (Liverpool University Press: Liverpool, 1961)

Marvell, Andrew, *The Poems of Andrew Marvell*, edited by Hugh MacDonald (Routledge and Kegan Paul: London, 1952)

Marvell, Andrew, *The Poems and Letters of Andrew Marvell*, edited by H. M. Margoliouth, 2 vols (Clarendon Press: Oxford, 1952)

Matthews, David, 'Infantilizing the Father: Chaucer Translations and Moral Regulation', in *Studies in the Age of Chaucer*, 22 (2000), 93–114

McDowell, Nicholas, 'Urquhart's Rabelais: Translation, Patronage, and Cultural Politics', *English Literary History*, 35 (2005), 273–303

McRae, Andrew, '"On the Famous Voyage": Ben Jonson and Civic Space', *Early Modern Literary Studies*, 3 (1998), 8.1–31

Mennes, John and James Smith, *Musarum Deliciae: or The Muses Recreation* (Henry Herringman: London, 1655)

Middleton, Thomas, *The Collected Works*, edited by Gary Taylor and John Lavagnino (Clarendon Press: Oxford, 2007)

Milton, John, *Complete English Poems, Of Education, Areopagitica*, edited by Gordon Campbell (J. M. Dent and Sons: London, 1990)

Montaigne, Michel de, *The Essayes of Michael Lord of Montaigne*, translated by John Florio (George Routledge and Sons: London, 1891)

Morrison, Susan Signe, *Excrement in the Late Middle Ages: Sacred Filth and Chaucer's Fecopoetics* (Palgrave: Houndmills, 2008)

Mowat, Barbara M., 'The Theater and Literary Culture', in John D. Cox and David Scott Kastan (eds), *A New History of Early English Drama* (Columbia University Press: New York, 1997), 231–48

Nabbes, Thomas, *Microcosmus. A Morall Maske* (Charles Greene: London, 1637)

Narain, Mona, 'Libertine Spaces and the Female Body in the Poetry of Rochester and Ned Ward', *English Literary History*, 72 (2005), 553 76

Nashe, Thomas, *Christs Teares over Ierusalem* (James Roberts: London, 1593)

Nashe, Thomas, *The Works of Thomas Nashe*, edited by Ronald B. McKerrow, 5 vols (A. H. Bullen: London, 1904–10)

Neuss, Paula, '*Double-Entendre* in *The Miller's Tale*', *Essays in Criticism*, 24 (1974), 325–40

Nevinson, J. L., 'Shakespeare's Dress in his Portraits', *Shakespeare Quarterly*, 18 (1967), 101–6

Northall, G. F., *A Warwickshire Word Book*, English Dialect Society, no. 79 (London, 1896)

O'Callaghan, Michelle, 'Performing Politics: The Circulation of the "Parliament Fart"', *Huntingdon Library Quarterly*, 69 (2006), 121–38

Oldham, John, *The Poems of John Oldham*, edited by Harold F. Brooks and Raman Selden (Clarendon Press: Oxford, 1987)

Oliver, Raymond, 'Urquhart's *Rabelais*', *Southern Humanities Review*, 8 (1974), 317–28

Orwell, George, 'Politics vs Literature: An Examination of *Gulliver's Travels*', in Sonia Orwell and Ian Angus (eds), *The Collected Essays, Journalism and Letters of George Orwell*, 4 vols (Penguin: Harmondsworth, 1970) IV, 241–61

Ovid, *The xv. Bookes of P. Ouidius Naso, Entituled Metamorphosis*, translated by Arthur Golding (John Windet and Thomas Judson: London, 1584)

Parker, Patricia, *Literary Fat Ladies* (Methuen: London, 1987)

Parrot, Henry, *Laquei Ridiculosi: or Springes for Woodcocks, Caueat Emptor* (John Busby: London, 1613)

Partridge, Eric, *Shakespeare's Bawdy* (Routledge: London and New York, 1968)

Paster, Gail Kern, *The Body Embarrassed: Drama and the Disciplines of Shame in Early Modern England* (Cornell University Press: Ithaca, NY, 1993)

Patterson, Lee, '"No Man his Reson Herde": Peasant Consciousness, Chaucer's Miller, and the Structure of the *Canterbury Tales*', in Lee Patterson (ed.), *Literary Practice and Social Change in Britain, 1380–1530* (University of California Press: Berkeley, 1990), 113–55

Paxson, James J., 'Theorizing the Mysteries' End in England, the Artificial Demonic, and the Sixteenth-Century Witch-Craze', *Criticism*, 39 (1997), 481–502

Pearson, D'Orsay W., 'Gulled into an "I"-word, or, Much Ado About a Pronoun', *Journal of the Rocky Mountain Medieval and Renaissance Association*, 8 (1987), 119–30

Pendry, E. D., *Elizabethan Prisons and Prison Scenes*, 2 vols (Universität Salzburg: Salzburg, 1974)

Pepys, Samuel, *The Diary of Samuel Pepys*, edited by Robert Latham and William Matthews, 11 vols (G. Bell and Sons: London, 1970–83)

Persels, Jeff and Russell Ganim (eds), *Fecal Matters in Early Modern Literature and Art: Studies in Scatology* (Ashgate: Aldershot, 2004)

Persels, Jeffrey C., '"Straitened in the bowels", or Concerning the Rabelaisian Trope of Defecation', *Etudes Rabelaisiennes*, 31 (1996), 101–12

Petronella, Vincent, 'Anamorphic Naming in Shakespeare's *Twelfth Night*', *Names*, 35 (1987), 139–46

Phillips, Edward, *The New World of English Words* (Nath. Brooke: London, 1658)

Pitcher, John, 'Names in *Cymbeline*', *Essays in Criticism*, 43 (1993), 1–16

Plato, *Cratylus*, translated by N. H. Fowler (Heinemann: London, 1926)

Plutarch, *Plutarch's Lives of the Noble Grecians and Romanes*, translated by Thomas North, 8 vols (Clarendon Press: Oxford, 1928)

Pollak, Ellen, 'Swift among the Feminists', in Peter J. Schakel (ed.), *Critical Approaches to Teaching Swift* (AMS Press: New York, 1992), 65–75

Pope, Alexander, *Alexander Pope: The Oxford Authors*, edited by Pat Rogers (Oxford University Press: Oxford, 1993)

Porter, Peter, 'The Professional Amateur', in Jeremy Treglown (ed.), *Spirit of Wit: Reconsiderations of Rochester* (Basil Blackwell: Oxford, 1982), 58–74

Poulton, Mike, *Chaucer's The Canterbury Tales, Adapted for the Stage* (Nick Hern Books: London, 2005)

Prescott, Anne Lake, *Imagining Rabelais in Renaissance England* (Yale University Press: New York and London, 1998)

Puttenham, George, *The Arte of English Poesie*, edited by Gladys Doidge Willcock and Alice Walker (Cambridge University Press: Cambridge, 1936)

Rabelais, François, *Gargantua and Pantagruel*, edited by J. M. Cohen (Penguin: London, 1955)

Rabelais, François, *Gargantua and Pantagruel*, translated by Sir Thomas Urquhart and Pierre Le Motteux, introduced by Terence Cave (Everyman: London, 1994)

Raylor, Timothy, *Cavaliers, Clubs and Literary Culture: Sir John Mennes, James Smith and the Order of the Fancy* (Delaware University Press: Newark, NJ, 1994)

Reaney, Percy Hide, *The Origin of English Surnames* (Routledge: London, 1967)

Rendle, William, *Old Southwark and Its People* (W. Drewett: London, 1878)

Reynolds, Reginald, *Cleanliness and Godliness* (George Allen and Unwin: London, 1943)

Reynolds, Reginald, *My Life and Crimes* (Jarrolds: London, 1956)

Robinson, Ken, 'The Art of Violence in Rochester's Satire', *Yearbook of English Studies*, 14 (1984), 93–108

Root, Robert Kilburn, *The Poetry of Chaucer: A Guide to its Study and Appreciation* (Peter Smith: Gloucester, MA, 1957)

Roth, Philip, *Sabbath's Theater* (Vintage: London, 1996)

Rudat, Wolfgang E. H., 'The Misdirected Kiss in *The Miller's Tale*', *Journal of Evolutionary Psychology*, 3 (1982), 103–7

Sabine, Ernest L., 'Latrines and Cesspools of Mediaeval London', *Speculum*, 9 (1934), 303–21

Said, Edward W., *The World, the Text and the Critic* (Vintage: London, 1991)

Sanchez, Melissa E., 'Libertinism and Romance in Rochester's Poetry', *Eighteenth-Century Studies*, 38 (2005), 441–59

Schlike, Paul (ed.), *Oxford Reader's Companion to Dickens* (Oxford University Press: Oxford, 1999)

Schlueter, June, 'Martin Droeshout *Redivivus*: Reassessing the Folio Engraving of Shakespeare', *Shakespeare Survey*, 60 (2007), 237–51

Schuckman, Christiaan, 'The Engraver of the First Folio Portrait of William Shakespeare', *Print Quarterly*, 8 (1991), 40–3

Scott-Warren, Jason, *Sir John Harington and the Book as Gift* (Oxford University Press: Oxford, 2001)

Scragg, Leah, '"Her C's, her U's, and her T's: Why That?": A New Reply for Sir Andrew Aguecheek', *Review of English Studies*, n.s., 42 (1991), 1–16

Shakespeare, William, *Twelfe Night*, edited by Horace Howard Furness (J. B. Lippincott Company: Philadelphia, 1901)

Shakespeare, William, *Hamlet*, edited by John Dover Wilson (Cambridge University Press: Cambridge, 1934)

Shakespeare, William, *Hamlet*, edited by Bernard Lott (Longmans: London, 1968)

Shakespeare, William, *As You Like It*, edited by Agnes Latham (Routledge: London, 1975)

Shakespeare, William, *Twelfth Night*, edited by J. M. Lothian and T. W. Craik (Methuen: London, 1975)

Shakespeare, William, *Hamlet*, edited by Harold Jenkins (Routledge: London and New York, 1982)

Shakespeare, William, *Hamlet*, edited by G. R. Hibbard (Clarendon Press: Oxford, 1987)

Shakespeare, William, *As You Like It*, edited by Alan Brissenden (Oxford University Press: Oxford, 1994)

Shakespeare, William, *Twelfth Night*, edited by Roger Warren and Stanley Wells (Oxford University Press: Oxford, 1994)

Shakespeare, William, *The Complete Works*, edited by John Jowett, William Montgomery, Gary Taylor and Stanley Wells (Clarendon Press: Oxford, 2005)

Shakespeare, William, *Twelfth Night*, edited by Keir Elam (Cengage Learning: London, 2008)

Sigerist, Henry E., 'An Elizabethan Poet's Contribution to Public Health: Sir John Harington and the Water Closet', *Bulletin of the History of Medicine*, 13 (1943), 229–43

Sinden, Donald, 'Malvolio in *Twelfth Night*', in Philip Brockbank (ed.), *Players of Shakespeare* (Cambridge University Press: Cambridge, 1985), 41–66

Smith, Peter J., 'MOAI: "What Should That Alphabetical Position Portend?" An Answer to the Metamorphic Malvolio', *Renaissance Quarterly*, 51 (1998), 1199–224

Smith, Peter J. and Greg Walker, 'Play Review: *The Canterbury Tales*', *Cahiers Elisabéthains*, 69 (2006), 53–7

Smollett, Tobias, *The Expedition of Humphry Clinker* (Dent: London, 1993)

Spencer, T. J. B. and Stanley Wells (eds), *A Book of Masques* (Cambridge University Press: Cambridge, 1967)

Stevens, Martin and A. C. Cawley (eds), *The Townley Plays*, EETS, s.s. 13 (Oxford University Press: Oxford, 1994)

Stockton, Will, *Playing Dirty: Sexuality and Waste in Early Modern Comedy* (University of Minnesota Press: Minneapolis and London, 2011)

Stow, John, *A Survey of London*, 2 vols (Clarendon Press: Oxford, 1971)

Swift, Jonathan [?], *Reason Against Coition: A Discourse Deliver'd to a Private Congregation by the Reverend Stephen M***** [...] to which is added, A Proposal for making Religion and the Clergy*

Useful: With the Author's Observations on the Cause and Cure of the Piles and some useful Directions about the wiping the Posteriors (H. Hook: London, 1732)

Swift, Jonathan, *Prose Works of Jonathan Swift,* edited by Herbert Davis, 14 vols (Basil Blackwell: Oxford, 1939–68)

Swift, Jonathan, *The Poems of Jonathan Swift,* edited by Harold Williams, 3 vols (Clarendon Press: Oxford, 1958)

Swift, Jonathan, *Journal to Stella,* edited by Harold Williams, 2 vols (Clarendon Press: Oxford, 1963)

Swift, Jonathan, *Gulliver's Travels,* edited by Peter Dixon and John Chalker, introduced by Michael Foot (Penguin: Harmondsworth, 1967)

Swift, Jonathan, *The Complete Poems,* edited by Pat Rogers (Penguin: Harmondsworth, 1983)

Swift, Jonathan, *A Tale of a Tub and Other Works,* edited by Angus Ross and David Woolley (Oxford University Press: Oxford, 1986)

Swift, Jonathan, *The Benefit of Farting Explain'd,* introduced by Clive Davies (Old Abbey Press: Exeter, 1996)

Szittya, Penn R., 'The Friar as False Apostle: Antifraternal Exegesis and the *Summoner's Tale*', *Studies in Philology,* 71 (1974), 19–46

Taylor, Gary and John Lavagnino (eds), *Thomas Middleton and Early Modern Textual Culture* (Clarendon Press: Oxford, 2007)

Taylor, John, *The Praise of Hemp-seed* (H. Gosson: London, 1620)

Taylor, John, *A common whore with all these graces grac'd, Shee's very honest, beautifull and chaste* (H. Gosson: London, 1635)

Thomas, Keith, 'Bodily Control and Social Unease: The Fart in Seventeenth-Century England', in Angela McShane and Garthine Walker (eds), *The Extraordinary and the Everyday in Early Modern England: Essays in Celebration of the Work of Bernard Capp* (Palgrave: Houndmills, 2010), 9–30

Tilley, M. P., *A Dictionary of the Proverbs in England in the Sixteenth and Seventeenth Centuries* (University of Michigan Press: Ann Arbor, 1950)

Tobin, J. J. M, 'Malvolio and His Capitals', *American Notes and Queries,* 23 (1985), 69–71

Train, John, *Remarkable Names of Real People* (Crown Publications: New York, 1977)

Travis, Peter W., 'Thirteen Ways of Listening to a Fart: Noise in Chaucer's *The Summoner's Tale*', *Exemplaria*, 16 (2004), 323–48

Tripp Jr, Raymond P., 'The Darker Side to Absolon's Dawn Visit', *The Chaucer Review*, 20 (1986), 207–12

Vienken, Heinz J., 'Swift's Library, His Reading, and His Critics', in Christopher Fox and Brenda Tooley (eds), *Walking Naboth's Vineyard: New Studies in Swift* (University of Notre Dame Press: Notre Dame, 1995)

Vieth, David M., 'Rochester and the Restoration: An Introductory Note and Bibliography', *Papers on Language and Literature*, 12 (1976), 260–72

Wagenknecht, Edward, *The Personality of Chaucer* (Norman: University of Oklahoma Press, 1968)

Walker, Greg, 'Rough Girls and Squeamish Boys: The Trouble with Absolon in *The Miller's Tale*', in Elaine Treharne (ed.), *Essays and Studies 2002* (D. S. Brewer: Cambridge, 2002), 61–91

Walker, Jeffrey, 'Anagrams and Acrostics: Puritan Poetic Wit', in Peter White (ed.), *Puritan Poets and Poetics: Seventeenth-Century American Poetry in Theory and Practice* (Pennsylvania State University Press: Pennsylvania and London, 1985), 247–57

Ward, David, *Jonathan Swift: An Introductory Essay* (Methuen: London, 1973)

Ward, Ned, *A Complete and Humorous Account of the Remarkable Clubs and Societies in the Cities of London and Westminster* (J. Wren: London, 1756)

Ward, Ned, *The London Spy*, edited by Paul Hyland (Colleagues Press: East Lansing, MI, 1993)

Weidhorn, Manfred, 'The Rose and Its Name: On Denomination in *Othello, Romeo and Juliet, Julius Caesar*', *Texas Studies in Language and Literature*, 11 (1969–70), 671–86

Whitby, C. L., 'Character Names in the Comedies of Shakespeare', unpublished MA dissertation, University of Birmingham, 1975

Wilcoxon, Reba, 'Pornography, Obscenity, and Rochester's "The Imperfect Enjoyment"', *Studies in English Literature*, 15 (1975), 375–90

Williams, David, 'Radical Therapy in *The Miller's Tale*', *The Chaucer Review*, 15 (1981), 227–35

Williams, Gordon (ed.), *A Dictionary of Sexual Language and*

Imagery in Shakespearean and Stuart Literature, 3 vols (Athlone: London, 1994)

Williams, Gordon (ed.), *A Glossary of Shakespeare's Sexual Language* (Athlone: London, 1997)

Williams, Kathleen (ed.), *Swift: The Critical Heritage* (Routledge and Kegan Paul: London, 1970)

Wilmot, John, *Poems of John Wilmot, Earl of Rochester*, edited by Vivian de Sola Pinto (Routledge and Kegan Paul: London, 1953)

Wilmot, John, *The Letters of John Wilmot, Earl of Rochester*, edited by Jeremy Treglown (Basil Blackwell: Oxford, 1980)

Wilmot, John, *The Works of John Wilmot, Earl of Rochester*, edited by Harold Love (Oxford University Press: Oxford, 1999)

Wood, Nigel, *Swift* (Harvester Press: Brighton, 1986)

Wordsworth, Dorothy, *Journals of Dorothy Wordsworth*, edited by E. de Selincourt, 2 vols (Macmillan: London, 1952)

Wordsworth, William, *The Fourteen-Book Prelude*, edited by W. J. B. Owen (Cornell University Press: Ithaca and London, 1985)

Wright, J., *English Dialect Dictionary*, 6 vols (Oxford University Press: Oxford, 1898–1905)

Wyclif, John, *The English Works Hitherto Unprinted*, edited by F. D. Matthew, EETS, o.s. 74 (Trübner & Co.: London, 1880)

Yeats, W. B., *Yeats's Poems*, edited by A. Norman Jeffares (Macmillan: London, 1989)

Ziff, Larzer, *Puritanism in America: New Culture in a New World* (Viking Press: New York, 1973)

Index